TOWER HAMLETS

91 000 004 583 45 6

KU-017-996

Library Learning Information

To renew this item call:

0115 929 3388

or visit

www.ideastore.co.uk

TOWER HAMLETS

Created and managed by Tower Hamlets Council

When the
Facts Change

WITHDRAWN

ALSO BY TONY JUDT

Thinking the Twentieth Century (with Timothy Snyder)

The Memory Chalet

Ill Fares the Land

Reappraisals: Reflections on the Forgotten Twentieth Century

Postwar: A History of Europe Since 1945

The Politics of Retribution in Europe (edited with Jan Gross and István Deák)

*The Burden of Responsibility: Blum, Camus, Aron,
and the French Twentieth Century*

Language, Nation, and State: Identity Politics in a Multilingual Age
(edited with Denis Lacorne)

A Grand Illusion?: An Essay on Europe

Past Imperfect: French Intellectuals, 1944–1956

Marxism and the French Left: Studies on Labour and Politics in France 1930–1982

Resistance and Revolution in Mediterranean Europe 1939–1948 (editor)

*Socialism in Provence 1871–1914: A Study in
the Origins of the Modern French Left*

La reconstruction du Parti Socialiste 1921–1926

ALSO BY JENNIFER HOMANS

Apollo's Angels: A History of Ballet

When the Facts Change

Essays, 1995–2010

Tony Judt

EDITED AND INTRODUCED BY

Jennifer Homans

125 YEARS

WILLIAM HEINEMANN: LONDON

TOWER HAMLETS
LIBRARIES

91000004583456

Bertrams	03/02/2015
909.82	£25.00
THISWH	TH14000689

1 3 5 7 9 10 8 6 4 2

William Heinemann
20 Vauxhall Bridge Road
London SW1V 2SA

William Heinemann is part of the Penguin Random House group of companies whose
addresses can be found at global.penguinrandomhouse.com.

Penguin
Random House
UK

Copyright © The Estate of Tony Judt 2015
Introduction © Jennifer Homans 2015

'What Is to Be Done?' is published for the first time in this volume.
'Israel Must Unpick Its Ethnic Myth' first appeared in the *Financial Times*.
'Crimes & Misdemeanors' and 'Freedom and Freedonia' first appeared in *The New Republic*.
'A Lobby, Not a Conspiracy', 'Fictions on the Ground', 'Israel Without Clichés' and 'Generations in the
Balance' first appeared in the *New York Times*.
The other selections first appeared in the *New York Review of Books*.

First published by William Heinemann in 2015
(First published in the United States by Penguin Press, Penguin Group (USA) LLC, New York in 2015)

www.randomhouse.co.uk

A CIP catalogue record for this book is available from the British Library.

ISBN 9780434023080

Printed and bound in Great Britain by Clays Ltd, St Ives plc

Book design by Meighan Cavanangh

Penguin Random House is committed to a sustainable future for our business, our readers and our
planet. This book is made from Forest Stewardship Council® certified paper.

MIX
Paper from
responsible sources
FSC® C018179

For Joe

When the facts change, I change my mind. What do you do, sir?

—QUOTATION COMMONLY ATTRIBUTED TO JOHN MAYNARD KEYNES

Other men will make history. . . . All I can say is that on this earth there are pestilences and there are victims—and as far as possible one must refuse to be on the side of the pestilence.

—ALBERT CAMUS, *The Plague*

CONTENTS

Introduction: In Good Faith   *1*

Part One

1989: Our Age

CHAPTER I Downhill All the Way   *13*

CHAPTER II Europe: The Grand Illusion   *30*

CHAPTER III Crimes and Misdemeanors   *47*

CHAPTER IV Why the Cold War Worked   *65*

CHAPTER V Freedom and Freedonia   *85*

Part Two

Israel, the Holocaust, and the Jews

CHAPTER VI The Road to Nowhere   *107*

CHAPTER VII Israel: The Alternative   *115*

CHAPTER VIII A Lobby, Not a Conspiracy   124

CHAPTER IX The "Problem of Evil" in Postwar Europe   129

CHAPTER X Fictions on the Ground   142

CHAPTER XI Israel Must Unpick Its Ethnic Myth   147

CHAPTER XII Israel Without Clichés   151

CHAPTER XIII What Is to Be Done?   156

Part Three

9/11 and the New World Order

CHAPTER XIV On *The Plague*   171

CHAPTER XV Its Own Worst Enemy   183

CHAPTER XVI The Way We Live Now   202

CHAPTER XVII Anti-Americans Abroad   218

CHAPTER XVIII The New World Order   234

CHAPTER XIX Is the UN Doomed?   252

CHAPTER XX What Have We Learned, if Anything?   269

Part Four

The Way We Live Now

CHAPTER XXI The Glory of the Rails   285

CHAPTER XXII Bring Back the Rails!   294

CHAPTER XXIII The Wrecking Ball of Innovation 303

CHAPTER XXIV What Is Living and What Is Dead in

Social Democracy? 319

CHAPTER XXV Generations in the Balance 339

Part Five
———

In the Long Run We Are All Dead

CHAPTER XXVI François Furet (1927–1997) 347

CHAPTER XXVII Amos Elon (1926–2009) 355

CHAPTER XXVIII Leszek Kołakowski (1927–2009) 360

Chronological List of Tony Judt's Published Essays and Criticism 367

Index 375

Introduction:
In Good Faith

by Jennifer Homans

The only way for me to write this introduction is to separate the man from the ideas. Otherwise, I get pulled back into the man, who I loved and was married to from 1993 until his death in 2010, rather than forward into the ideas. As you read these essays, I hope that you, too, will focus on the ideas, because they are good ideas, and they were written in good faith. "In good faith" may have been Tony's favorite phrase and highest standard, and he held himself to it in everything he wrote. What he meant by it, I think, was writing that is free of calculation and maneuver, intellectual or otherwise. A clean, clear, honest account.

This is a book about our age. The arc is down: from the heights of hope and possibility, with the revolutions of 1989, into the confusion, devastation, and loss of 9/11, the Iraq war, the deepening crisis in the Middle East, and—as Tony saw it—the self-defeating decline of the American republic. As the facts changed and events unfolded, Tony found himself turned increasingly and unhappily against the current, fighting with all of his intellectual might to turn the ship of ideas, however slightly, in a different direction. The story ends abruptly, with his untimely death.

This book is also, for me, a very personal book, since "our age" was also "my age" with Tony: the early essays date to the first years of our marriage and the birth of our son Daniel, and follow through our time together in Vienna,

Paris, New York, the birth of Nicholas, and the growing up of our family. Our life together began, not coincidentally, with the fall of Communism in 1989: I was a graduate student at New York University, where Tony taught. In the summer of 1991, I traveled across Central Europe, and when I got back I wanted to know more. I was advised to take an independent study with Tony Judt.

I did, and our romance began, over books and conversations about European politics, war, revolution, justice, art. It wasn't the usual dating arrangement: our second "course meeting" took place in a restaurant over dinner. Tony pushed the books aside, ordered wine, and told me of his time in Prague under Communism, and then in 1989, walking through silent snow-covered squares and streets deep into the night soon after the Velvet Revolution, clearly in awe at the turn of historical fate—and the feelings that were already apparent between us. We watched movies, went to art exhibitions, ate Chinese food, he even cooked (badly). Finally—the key to our courtship—he invited me on a trip to Europe: Paris, Vienna, Budapest, a hair-raising drive over the Simplon Pass in a storm (I drove—he had migraines). We took trains, and I watched him pouring over timetables, clocking departures and arrivals like a kid in a candy store: Zermatt, Brig, Florence, Venice.

It was a great romance, and it was a European romance, part of a larger romance with Europe that defined Tony's life, and his life's work. At times, I think he even thought of himself as European. But he wasn't really. Sure, he spoke French, German, Italian, Hebrew, Czech, some Spanish, but he was never "at home" in any of these places. He was more *Central* European, but not exactly that either—he didn't quite have that history, except by professional engagement and family roots (Russian, Polish, Romanian, and Lithuanian Jews). He was very English, too, by habit and upbringing (he could move effortlessly between his childhood cockney and confident Oxbridge prose), but he wasn't really that either—too Jewish, too Central European. It's not that he was alienated from any of these places, although in some cases he was; it was more that he was attached to bits of all of them, which is why he couldn't let go of any of them.

So perhaps it is not surprising that although we settled in New York from the start, we spent much of our life together planning to live—or living—somewhere else. We were expert packers and often joked that we would write a book together called something like "At Home in Europe: Everything You Need to Know about Schools and Real Estate." By far the best gift I ever gave to Tony was a subscription to Thomas Cooks Railway Timetable.

It was only after 2001 that he really settled. This was partly because of his health: that year he was diagnosed with a serious cancer and underwent major surgery, radiation, and other draining therapies. Partly, too, because of the WTC attack. It became increasingly difficult to travel, and the horror of the event itself, combined with his illness, had a homing effect; he wanted to be here with me and the boys. Whatever the reasons, in the years that followed he slowly became more and more, though never quite, American—ironically at the very moment when he found greatest reasons to be critical of its politics. He acquired citizenship: "Quiz me," he would say to the kids in the weeks before the test, and they would gleefully take him through the paces, no matter that he had taught American politics for years at Oxford. Around 2003 I noticed a shift in his thinking, and in his writing, from "them" to "us": "The Way *We* Live Now."

These were also the years of the Remarque Institute, which Tony founded in 1995 and directed until his death. It was built along the same two axes that preoccupied him in his writing: bringing together Europe and America, history and contemporary politics. At the same time, he was writing *Postwar* (2005), a mammoth undertaking, which tested daily his physical and intellectual strength and discipline, especially as he recovered from cancer. I remember well his exhaustion and determination as he insisted on writing the essays in this volume, too, even as he was (as he put it) "in the coal mines" of a major book about Europe. I worried at how hard he pushed himself, but in retrospect I see that he couldn't help it. As he immersed himself in *Postwar*, he was hearing canaries in the mines of our own time: these essays, which beg us—and especially "us" Americans—to look back on the twentieth century as we make our way in the twenty-first, were one result.

———

SO THIS IS A COLLECTION of essays, but it is also a collection of obsessions. Tony's obsessions. They are all here: Europe and America, Israel and the Middle East, justice, the public sphere, the state, international relations, memory and forgetting, and above all history. His caution, which reappears across these essays, that we were witnessing an "economic age" collapse into an "era of fear"* and entering "a new age of insecurity"† was a sign of just how depressed and worried he was at the direction politics was taking. He expected a lot and was a keen observer. You will find in these essays, I think, both a clear-eyed realist—who believed in facts, events, data—and an idealist who aimed at nothing less than the well-lived life; not just for himself, but for society.

I have presented the essays chronologically as well as thematically because chronology was one of his greatest obsessions. He was, after all, a historian, and he had little patience for postmodern fashions of textual fragmentation or narrative disruption, especially in historical writing. He wasn't really interested in the idea that there is no single truth (wasn't that obvious?), or the deconstruction of this or that text. The real job, he believed, was not to say what *wasn't* but what *was*—to tell a convincing and clearly written story from the available evidence, and to do it with an eye to what is right and just. Chronology was not merely a professional or literary convention, it was a prerequisite—even, when it came to history, a moral responsibility.

A word about facts: I have never met anyone as committed to facts as Tony, something his children learned from the start: it is to Daniel, now nineteen, that we owe the title of this volume, which comes from a (probably apocryphal) quote from Keynes that was one of Tony's favorite mantras: "when the facts change, I change my mind—what do you do, sir?" I learned this early on about Tony, in one of those domestic situations that does so much to illuminate a man. When we were first married we bought a house in Princeton,

———

*Chapter XXIII: "The Wrecking Ball of Innovation."
†Chapter XXIV: "What Is Living and What Is Dead in Social Democracy?"

New Jersey (his idea)—but it was more of a house in theory than in practice. In theory, Tony wanted to live there, but in practice we were living in New York, or traveling to Europe, or on our way somewhere else. Eventually, I wanted to sell the house—it was draining us financially and frankly I had a horror of ever living there. There ensued a long and difficult discussion about what to do with the house, which turned into a debate and finally a silent and angry standoff about the emotional, historical, geographical meaning of houses and home, and why this particular one was or wasn't right for us.

Arguing with Tony was a real challenge because he was a master at the dialectical switchback and could turn any point you made against you. Finally I created a spreadsheet that laid out the facts—a desperate strategic move on my part: finances, commuter train schedules, fares, total hours spent at Penn Station, the works. He studied it carefully and agreed on the spot to sell the house. No regrets, no remorse, no recriminations, no further discussion necessary. He was already on to the next plan. To me, it was an astounding and admirable quality. It gave him a kind of clarity of thinking—he wasn't wedded to his ideas or, as I later discovered, to his prose. When the facts changed—when a better, more convincing argument was made—he really did change his mind and move on.

He had great inner certainty. This was not an existential attribute, it was hard earned: he read, ingested, absorbed, memorized more facts, and knew more "real stuff," as he liked to put it, than anyone I have ever met. For this reason, he didn't like social events or parties: he was shy, in a way, and preferred to stay home and read—he could get more from books, he said, away from the distracting "blah blah" of the "chattering classes." He was almost machinelike in his recall, and he arrived at his positions quickly and decisively, sifting a given problem through his extraordinary store of knowledge and sharply analytic mind. It is not that he trusted himself absolutely—like all of us, he had emotional gaps and moments when reason and good judgment deserted him, but these were mostly in his life, not in his writing. When it came to ideas, he was not a doubter; he had a kind of pure intellectual command and ability to summon ideas and arguments without complication.

He was a great writer because he was always fine-tuning his words, crafts-manlike, to this inner pitch. He had a system for writing, and the essays in this book were all written according to the same method, even those from 2008 to 2010 when he was ill and quadriplegic. First, he read everything he could on a subject, taking copious notes by hand, on lined yellow legal pads. Then came the outline, color-coded A, B, C, D, with detailed subcategories: A1 i, A1 ii, A2 iii, etc. (more legal pads). Then he sat for hours on end, monklike, at the dining room table assigning each line in his notes, each fact, date, point, or idea, to a place in the outline. Next—and this was the killer and the key—he retranscribed *all* of his original notes in the order of the outline. By the time he sat down to write the essay, he had copied, recopied, and memorized most of what he needed to know. Then, door closed, eight-hour days of writing back to back until the piece was done (small breaks for marmite sandwiches and strong espresso). Finally—"polishing."

When he became ill, none of this changed, it just got harder. Someone else had to be the hands, turning the pages of books, assembling materials, search-ing the Web, and typing. As his body failed, he retaught himself how to think and write—the most private of events—with someone else, a tribute to the flexibility of his extraordinary mind. He worked with an assistant, but he had to do most of the work by memory, in his own mind, usually at night, compos-ing, sorting, cataloguing, rewriting his mental notes according to his outline—A, B, C, D—to be typed in the morning by me, our boys, a nurse, or his assistant.

This was not just a method, I think, it was a map of his mind. The logic, the patience, the intense concentration and careful construction of the argument, the soldierly attention to fact and detail, the confidence of his convictions—unlike most writers, he rarely deviated from his original design. The difficulty came when he bumped into things inside himself that he didn't fully see or know: not the "facts on the ground," but the "facts inside"—the things that were just there, like furniture in his mind. The most obvious had to do with being Jewish.

For Tony, being Jewish was a given—the oldest piece of furniture in the place. It was the only identity that he possessed unequivocally. He was not religious, never went to synagogue, never practiced anything at home; he liked to quote Isaac Deutscher (whose books were given to him by his father, Joe, when he was a boy) on the "non-Jewish Jews." If he talked about being Jewish, it was about the past: Friday night dinners as a child with his Yiddish-speaking grandparents in the East End of London; his father's (very Jewish) secular humanism ("I don't believe in race, I believe in humanity") and his mother's determined renunciation—she stood in her living room when the Queen of England appeared on TV and didn't want *her* grandchildren circumcised lest "bad times" come again; or his grandfather Enoch, the proverbial wandering Jew, who always had his bags packed and spent as much of his life as he could on the road.

Another fact: the hat. Some years ago, we were on our way to the bat mitzvah of a close friend's daughter at a synagogue on New York's Upper East Side. We were late and almost there in a taxi traveling uptown, when Tony literally panicked: he had forgotten his hat. Did it really matter, I asked, we were late already and he would miss part of the service if he went back. Couldn't he go without it? No, really he couldn't, and I was taken aback at the heightened and inexplicable anxiety that seemed to overtake him. He went back for the hat, which was a well-appointed but old-fashioned thing I couldn't remember having ever seen before. When he slipped into the synagogue to rejoin me, he was astonished to find that he was the only one: the other guests were all wearing black-tie. He was indignant and a bit offended, but mostly confused—and manifestly out of place. What kind of Jews were these?

Tony had had a bar mitzvah himself ("we did our duty," his father later explained), and as a passionate (later disabused) Zionist in his youth, he spoke good Hebrew and had been a translator in Israel during the 1967 war. When our boys were young we agreed that we would like them to have at least some religious education. My background was Protestant but above all atheist, so we soon dismissed the idea of Sunday school and instead found Itay—a graduate student at the Jewish Theological Seminary, who came to our apartment on Washington Square weekly to teach the boys Hebrew, biblical history, culture. There was—Tony's decision—no bar mitzvah. To my mind, the message was clear: within the limits of their decidedly American upbringing, Tony wanted the boys to know the wheres and whys of the hat. After that, it was up to them. When they later both insisted that, in fact, they did not feel Jewish at all, the conversation quickly turned to the Holocaust. Nicholas didn't miss a beat: I don't have to be Jewish to understand how sad and tragic it was. Tony was surprised at their ambivalence, but not upset; they, after all, did not have his past.

What about the Holocaust? A friend who knew Tony well once commented to me that Tony had never written about the Holocaust, that he had focused his scholarship on the nineteenth and early twentieth centuries, and then jumped to the postwar era. This is true, but—and it is an overwhelming but—the war and its killing fields were central to *Postwar,* and to much of his other work, even if they were not his subject: the epilogue to *Postwar* is entitled "From the House of the Dead."

Soon after the book was published, moreover, I thanked Tony for dedicating it to me but told him that I knew that deep down it was also dedicated to someone else: to Toni. He wept—and he was not a man who wept easily or often. Toni was his namesake and his father's cousin, who had perished at Auschwitz. She was the ghost of the book, and a kind of dark presence in his mind all the time. Was it guilt, maybe? Not exactly survivor guilt—he was born in 1948—but a kind of black hole in his mind, I came to believe, weighty, incomprehensible, like evil or the devil, where this moment in history and this aspect of his Jewishness lay. It was murky and emotional, but what seemed clear to me was that Toni's tragedy was a responsibility in Tony's life, tied in some way to the idea of good faith.

Which brings us to Israel. In a series of articles beginning in 2002, Tony laid out his positions and reached for pragmatic solutions. The essays here give an idea, I hope, of how and why he ventured into these troubled waters. After "Israel: The Alternative" was published in 2003 there were ugly threats and a level of noxious and ad hominem vituperation in the press that sadly demonstrated the impossibility of an open discussion of the subject, at least in America. This and the essays that followed speak for themselves. I can only report that the rage his positions aroused, and the increasingly intractable and racist politics of Israel itself, disturbed him deeply.

After his June 2009 piece on the settlements in the *New York Times*, a colleague wrote to Tony: what is to be done? He wanted to answer, but he was by then ill and coping with the difficult physical complications of his rapidly progressing disease. Nonetheless, he took up the topic with a determined if grim resolve and wrote an energetic and ambitious response—with the help of an assistant, who typed tirelessly for long days, often without a moment to eat or drink, as Tony urgently dictated and revised the text. He called it "What Is to Be Done?" I worked on it with him more, and we discussed it at length; I did not feel it was up to his usual level and told him so. Frustrated by his physical disability, and unable to hone the argument to his satisfaction, he became discouraged and abruptly set it aside.

Reading it again now, the reasons for this are not entirely clear to me. The ideas, if flawed at moments—and only at moments—remain strong. Why did he back away, and am I wrong to publish it now? I can't know what he would do, but I offer it here because I see in the essay—perhaps precisely *because* it is raw—a kind of true intellectual grit. It has Tony's characteristic resistance to dogma, broken eggs, entrenched positions; his willingness to pick up the political thread wherever events wind it (note the return to a two-state solution) and try, with as much imagination as he can muster, to bring history, morality, pragmatism—the facts on the ground—to bear on seemingly unsolvable issues. In an impossible situation, both personal and political, he was aiming for an honest and clear account.

That same year, two of his greatest intellectual supports died: Amos Elon and Leszek Kołakowski. He wrote about each of them, even as he was planning and facing his own death, which he knew was imminent. "In the long run we are all dead," he liked to quip, when he was up to it: Keynes again. Tony did not really have heroes, but he did have shades, dead people he had known or never known except in books who were all around all the time. I got to know them well. Keynes was one of them. Some of the others (there were many) were Isaiah Berlin, Raymond Aron, A.J.P. Taylor, Bernard Williams (a friend, but nonetheless), Alexander Pope, Philip Larkin, Jean Renoir, and Vittorio De Sica. There was also, of course, Karl Marx, and—double of course—the Marx Brothers, who appeared in ritual screenings, along with Orson Welles in *The Third Man*. The two he kept close by him and admired perhaps most of all were Albert Camus, whose photo sat on his desk, and George Orwell, who it always seemed to me anyway, was everywhere. These were some of the shoulders he stood on, and the men he tried to live up to, in good faith.

In his final month, he turned to another pressing subject and started an essay called "The Afterlife." It begins "I have never believed in God," an interesting formulation for a man of the Enlightenment, which is what he really was, since it leaves the question ever so slightly open. The facts, after all, might change when you are dead. In the meantime, he began to build an argument about legacy, memorials, and what we can leave behind, which was the only afterlife he knew anything about. What he could leave behind, of course, were memories, and his writings. He never finished the essay—it breaks off midway in notes and scattered thoughts. One of them says this:

> You cannot write with a view to impact or response. That way you distort the latter and corrode the integrity of the writing itself. In that sense, it is like shooting at the moon—you have to allow that it won't be in the same place by the time the rocket gets there. Better to know why you are sending it up in the first place and worry less about its safe landing. . . .
>
> You cannot anticipate either the context of the motives of readers in unconstrained futures. So all you can do is write what you should, whatever that means. A very different sort of obligation.

Part One

1989: Our Age

CHAPTER I

Downhill All the Way

A mong historians in the English-speaking world there is a discernible "Hobsbawm generation." It consists of men and women who took up the study of the past at some point in the "long nineteen-sixties," between, say, 1959 and 1975, and whose interest in the recent past was irrevocably shaped by Eric Hobsbawm's writings, however much they now dissent from many of his conclusions. In those years he published a quite astonishing body of influential work: *Primitive Rebels*, which first appeared in 1959, introduced young urban students to a world of rural protest in Europe and overseas that has now become much more familiar to us, in large measure thanks to the work of scholars whose imaginations were first fired by Hobsbawm's little book. *Labouring Men, Industry and Empire,* and *Captain Swing* (with George Rude) substantially recast the economic history of Britain and the story of the British labor movement; they brought back to scholarly attention a half-buried tradition of British radical historiography, reinvigorating research into the conditions and experiences of the artisans and workers themselves, but bringing to this engaged concern an unprecedented level of technical sophistication and a rare breadth of knowledge.

If the conclusions and interpretations of these books seem conventional today, that is only because it is difficult now to remember what their subject matter looked like before Hobsbawm made it his own. No amount of revisionist sniping or fashionable amendment can detract from the lasting impact of this body of work.

But Hobsbawm's most enduring imprint on our historical consciousness has come through his great trilogy on the "long nineteenth century," from 1789 to 1914, the first volume of which, *The Age of Revolution, 1789–1848*, appeared in 1962. It is hard to assess the influence of that book precisely because it has become so indelibly part of our sense of the period that all subsequent work either unconsciously incorporates it or else works against it. Its overall scheme, interpreting the era as one of social upheaval dominated by the emergence and rise to influence of the bourgeoisie of northwest Europe, eventually became the "conventional" interpretation, now exposed to steady criticism and revision. It was followed in 1975 by *The Age of Capital, 1848–1875,* a masterly survey of the middle years of the last century that drew on a remarkable range of material and depth of understanding. That book remains, in my view, Hobsbawm's single greatest work, drawing together the many mid-Victorian transformations of the world and framing them in a unified and still forceful historical narrative. In *The Age of Empire, 1875–1914,* which appeared twelve years later, there was an unmistakable elegiac air, as though the leading historian of the last century were somehow sorry to see it come to a close at his hands. The overall impression is of an era of protean change, where a high price was paid for the rapid accumulation of wealth and knowledge; but an era, nonetheless, that was full of promise and of optimistic visions of radiant and improving futures. The nineteenth century, as Hobsbawm reminds us in his latest book, was "my period"; like Marx, he is at his best as a dissector of its hidden patterns, and he left little doubt of his admiration and respect for its astonishing achievements.

It comes, therefore, as a surprise that Eric Hobsbawm should have chosen to add a fourth volume dealing with the "short twentieth century."* As he

---

* Eric Hobsbawm, *The Age of Extremes: A History of the World, 1914–1991* (New York: Pantheon, 1995).

admits in the preface, "I avoided working on the era since 1914 for most of my career." He offers conventional grounds for this aversion: we are too close to the events to be dispassionate (in Hobsbawm's case, born in 1917, he has lived through most of them), a full body of interpretative material is not yet at hand, and it is too soon to tell what it all means.

But it is clear that there is another reason, and one which Hobsbawm himself would certainly not disavow: the twentieth century has ended with the apparent collapse of the political and social ideals and institutions to which he has been committed for most of his life. It is hard not to see in it a dark and gloomy tale of error and disaster. Like the other members of a remarkable generation of British Communist or ex-Communist historians (Christopher Hill, Rodney Hilton, Edward Thompson) Hobsbawm directed his professional attention to the revolutionary and radical past, and not only because the Party line made it virtually impossible to write openly about the near present. For a lifelong Communist who is also a serious scholar, the history of our century presents a number of near insuperable obstacles to interpretation, as his latest work inadvertently demonstrates.

Nonetheless, Hobsbawm has written what is in many ways an extraordinary book. Its argument is explicit and directly reflected in its tripartite structure. The first section, "The Age of Catastrophe," covers the period from the outbreak of World War I to the defeat of Hitler; the second, "The Golden Age," is an account of the remarkable and unprecedented era of economic growth and social transformation that began around 1950 and ended in the midseventies, provoking "The Landslide," as Hobsbawm calls the third and final section of his book, which deals with the history of the last two decades. Each section has a dominant theme, against which are set the details of its history. For the decades following the assassination at Sarajevo, the author depicts a world stumbling for forty years "from one calamity to another," an era of misery and horrors, a time when millions of refugees wandered helplessly across the European subcontinent and when the laws of war, so painstakingly forged over the previous centuries, were abandoned wholesale. (Of 5.5 million Russian prisoners of war in World War II, approximately 3.3 million died, one statistic among many that would have been utterly inconceivable to an earlier generation.)

Of the "Golden Age" following World War II, Hobsbawm notes that it was the moment when, for 80 percent of humankind, the Middle Ages finally ended, a time of dramatic social change and dislocation in Europe no less than in the colonial world over which the European powers now relinquished their control. But the explosive success of postwar Western capitalism, generating economic growth at an unprecedented rate while distributing the benefits of that growth to an ever-increasing number of people, carried within it the seeds of its own corruption and dissolution. It is not for nothing that Eric Hobsbawm has acquired a reputation for sophisticated and subtle Marxist readings of his material.

The expectations and institutions set in motion by the experience of rapid expansion and innovation have bequeathed to us a world with few recognizable landmarks or inherited practices, lacking continuity and solidarity between generations or across occupations. To take but one example, the democratization of knowledge and resources (including weapons) and their concentration in uncontrolled private hands threaten to undermine the very institutions of the capitalist world which brought them about. Without shared practices, common cultures, collective aspirations, ours is a world "which [has] lost its bearings and slid into instability and crisis."

IN SHORT, Eric Hobsbawm's history of the twentieth century is the story of the decline of a civilization, the history of a world which has both brought to full flowering the material and cultural potential of the nineteenth century and betrayed its promise. In wartime certain states have reverted to the use of chemical weapons upon unarmed civilians (their own included, in the case of Iraq); the social and environmental inequities arising from uncontrolled market forces are on the rise, while any collective sense of shared interests and inheritances is shrinking fast. In politics, "the decline of the organized mass parties, class-based, ideological or both, [has] eliminated the major social engine for turning men and women into politically active citizens." In cultural matters everything is now "post-" something:

> postindustrial, postimperial, postmodern, poststructuralist, post-Marxist, post-Gutenberg, or whatever. Like funerals, these prefixes [take] official recognition of death without implying any consensus or indeed certainty about the nature of life after death.

There is a Jeremiah-like air of impending doom about much of Hobsbawm's account.

However, this does not detract from its strengths. Like everything else Hobsbawm has written, "the age of extremes" is described and analyzed in simple, clean prose, utterly free of jargon, pomposity, and pretension. Important points are made in brief, striking, often witty phrases: the political impact of World War I is captured in the observation that "no old government was left standing between the borders of France and the Sea of Japan"; we are reminded of Hitler's low estimation of democracies—"The only democracy he took seriously was the British, which he rightly regarded as not entirely democratic." Hobsbawm's own rather low opinion of the New Left of the sixties is made explicit:

> At the very moment when hopeful young leftists were quoting Mao Tse-tung's strategy for the triumph of revolution by mobilizing the countless rural millions against the encircled urban strongholds of the status quo, those millions were abandoning their villages and moving into the cities themselves.[1]

The reference to the peasant millions is a reminder that though unashamedly Eurocentric, Eric Hobsbawm has a unique range.[2] His sympathetic and firsthand knowledge of Latin America in particular enriches his account of the worldwide impact of the Depression, just as his comparison of Poland's Solidarity with the Brazilian Workers' Party, both of them nationwide popular labor movements that developed during the eighties in opposition to the politics of a repressive regime, is suggestive and original. To be sure, his omnivorous reading is directed toward the South rather than the East, with unfortunate results to be discussed below; but he has apparently kept up his close acquaintance with the literature on Peruvian radicals and Neapolitan bandits (and with the men themselves), which he uses to telling effect in his discussion of social and economic transformations in backward societies. And he can with equal ease introduce evidence from the 1982 *Food and Food Production Encyclopedia* (an article on "Formed, Fabricated and Restructured Meat Products") to make a point about consumerism.

THIS BOOK IS ALSO A reminder that Eric Hobsbawm is by training and inclination an economic historian, and an analytical one at that. He is at his best when discussing the Depression, or the nature and consequences of the postwar "boom," and mostly avoids military or political narrative. His descriptions of the economic absurdities of the Soviet world ("an energy-producing colony of more advanced industrial economies—i.e., in practice largely its own Western satellites") or of Socialist economics as a "rather archaic industrial system based on iron and smoke" are distinctly superior to his political surveys of those same societies.

In a similar way he is more at ease when treating Fascism as a product of the world economic crisis than in his rather brief discussion of its political sources. His account of the dramatic collapse of Communist regimes in 1989 verges on the economically determinist; this is not to deny that debt crises and economic mismanagement were important factors in the downfall of Communism—far from it; but in discussing them Hobsbawm is clearly on familiar territory, where he prefers to remain. However, this gives considerable strength to his account of Western developments since the turning point of 1974. He gives a clear and convincing analysis of the long-term dilemmas of the international economy. Equally lucid is his description of the crisis of national welfare economics that arose when national leaders sought to avert the

political costs of economic downturn by taxing a shrinking working population to subsidize the victims of their policies.

DESPITE THIS EMPHASIS on long-term economic trends and broad secular
patterns (a feature of all Hobsbawm's writing), *The Age of Extremes* is also his
most personal book; indeed the mood oscillates between a rather formal interpretative perspective and a close, almost private, commentary. He says that he
has studied the twentieth century by "watching and listening," and we believe
him.[3] The inflation after World War I is caught in the image of his Austrian
grandfather cashing in his matured insurance policy and finding himself with
just enough money for a drink at his favorite café, while Hobsbawm's own
aesthetic distaste at the urban blight of the sixties is contrasted with childhood
memories of "the great architectural monuments of the liberal bourgeoisie" of
Vienna. When he writes that he believes the fall of colonial empires did not
seem imminent in 1939, this is based on personal recollection; he and others in
a school for young Communists from Britain and the colonies did not expect
it at the time.

For evidence of social change in Palermo, unemployment in São Paulo, or
the risks of introducing capitalism in China he can draw on conversations
with Sicilian bandits, Brazilian labor organizers, and Chinese Communist bu-
reaucrats (it is not for nothing that in his entry in *Who's Who* he gives as his
recreation "travel"). As a fellow of King's College, Cambridge, he knew Alan
Turing, the ill-fated inventor of the computer, while his Communist connections allow him to draw on the private testimony of the (Communist) mayor of
Bologna concerning the favorable conditions for an emerging agro-industrial
economy in the Emilia-Romagna region.[4]

There is also a disarming directness and honesty about Hobsbawm's account of his personal experience of the century.[5] He includes himself among
the "attentive and unquestioning multitudes" who listened to Castro rambling
for hours on end; he reminds us that the "left tradition" has preferred not to
acknowledge the support that Fascism, once in power, could count on from

formerly Socialist and Communist workers; and he recounts the innocent shock of a (London-based) British Communist organizer at discovering the comparative affluence of Coventry workers: "Do you realize that up there the comrades have *cars*?"

He himself was sometimes wrong and says so, and on more than one occasion he expresses his admiration for professional journalists who saw things that he, the Marxist scholar, missed. The prophecy forty years ago, by a China correspondent for the *Times* of London, that by the twenty-first century Communism would have disappeared everywhere except China, where it would have been transformed into the national ideology, shocked Hobsbawm at the time, as he admits; but today it sounds distinctly plausible. Toward the end of the book, musing on the dilemmas of our own time, he concedes that Marx, too, was wrong: mankind does *not* always "set itself only such problems as it can solve."

IF THE VIRTUES OF THIS book derive from its engaged and personal quality, so do its defects—or rather its defect, for there is really only one, though it takes many forms. Because this is a story of Hobsbawm's own lifetime—a lifetime devoted since youth, as he recently reminded us on BBC radio, to a single cause—he is understandably inclined to see the main outlines and conflicts of the era much as he saw them when they were unfolding. In particular, the categories right/left, Fascist/Communist, progressive and reactionary seem to be very firmly set, and pretty much as they first presented themselves to Hobsbawm in the thirties. Thus he readily acknowledges the tragic errors of Communist strategy, or the curiously similar public aesthetic preferences of Fascist and Communist leaders, and even the sheer awfulness of Communism as a system. But it does not for a moment occur to him to reconsider the conventional polarities of the time and treat Fascism and Communism as more than just occasional and paradoxical allies.

This seems to me a missed opportunity. For Hobsbawm, the Spanish Civil War and the alliances and allegiances it helped shape remain "the only political cause which, even in retrospect, appears as pure and appealing as it did in 1936." But for just that reason the Spanish Civil War, and more generally the circumstantial divisions of the thirties, are now an obstacle to a radical rethinking of the illusions to which they gave rise.

Thus Hobsbawm not only does not discuss the use to which the Spanish conflict was put by Stalin, who settled local and international scores under the guise of supporting an anti-Fascist war; he also neglects to consider the way in which the whole experience of "anti-Fascist unity" helped forge a new image for international Communism following the military, economic, and strategic disasters of its first two decades. If we are to understand the twentieth century, this radical refashioning of Communism (which was repeated in a minor key after 1943) needs to be appreciated. Instead the pattern of Communist thought and practice is described here much as it was understood and presented at the time, even down to the language and categories used, so that the phenomenon of Bolshevism is accorded no critical analytical attention except on its own restricted terms.

HOBSBAWM IS THUS QUITE EXPLICIT in treating the Bolshevik revolution and the subsequent Communist regime as "a programme for transforming backward countries into advanced ones," a line of reasoning that was once widespread among "revisionists" and other sympathetic critics of the Left in their attempts to explain the way Lenin's revolution had become Stalin's autocracy. But he does not consider whether it was not also and above all the first and greatest of the "third world" coups d'état that he describes so well elsewhere, in which revolutionary modernizers capture the capital city and forcibly seize power in an archaic society. The distinction may seem minor, but it is crucial. By excluding the Bolshevik revolution from the category of mere "coups" and by insisting throughout that it was a revolution made possible by the "masses," Hobsbawm preserves the sui generis quality of the Communist experience, and thereby cleaves to an interpretation of our century which seems increasingly inadequate now that that experience is behind us.

In a similar way, Hobsbawm's treatment of Fascism misses the chance to consider the extent to which Hitler's war amounted, de facto, to a major European revolution, transforming Central and Eastern Europe and preparing the way for the "Socialist" regimes of the postwar years which built upon the radical change Hitler had brought about—notably the destruction of the intelligentsia and urban middle class of the region, first through the murder of the Jews and then as a result of the postwar expulsion of Germans from the liberated Slav lands. Because he is concerned to play down any "revolutionary" qualities in Fascism, Hobsbawm's treatment of World War II is thus uncharacteristically conventional, neglecting the irony inherent in the process whereby Hitler prepared the way for Stalin. This, too, seems to me a consequence of continuing to see the world the way it seemed at the time, when both ideologically and militarily Fascism and Communism were in total conflict, and Stalin represented the "left wing" of the victorious forces of the Enlightenment.

THE RESULTS OF THIS APPROACH are most obvious, however, in Hobsbawm's treatment of Eastern Europe—or rather his nontreatment of it; "real Socialism" in the lands between Germany and Russia merits just six pages in a book nearly six hundred pages long, with the infamous show trials of the fifties accorded less than a paragraph. In his mildly revisionist account of the origins of the cold war Hobsbawm suggests that it was only after the Americans had pressured Communists out of office in France and Italy (in May 1947), and threatened intervention if the 1948 election in Italy went the "wrong" way, that "the USSR followed suit by eliminating the non-Communists from their multi-party 'people's democracies' which were henceforth reclassified as 'dictatorships of the proletariat.'" Until then, in his words, "where Moscow controlled its client regimes and communist movements, these were specifically committed to *not* building states on the model of the USSR, but mixed economies under multi-party parliamentary democracies . . ."

The precise allocation of responsibility for the cold war may be a subject for debate, but the timing and purpose of the Communist strategy *within* Eastern Europe is surely unambiguous. Whatever Stalin and his followers had in mind in 1945 for the "friendly" regimes of the region, it was certainly not "multi-party democracies" in any intelligible sense of the word. The construction of "geographically-contiguous replica regimes" (as the political scientist Kenneth Jowitt put it) was under way well before the Italian elections of April 1948. The most obvious instances are Romania (where Andrei Vyshinsky arrived in February 1945 to dictate who could and who could not join the "coalition" government) and Bulgaria (where Nikola Petkov, leader of the Agrarian Party, was arrested in June 1947 and executed three months later following a disgraceful show trial).

In Czechoslovakia and Hungary the situation was more confused, at least until 1947, although in the Hungarian case Communist intimidation of the popular Smallholder Party forced its representatives to withdraw from the Parliament in 1946. Even in Czechoslovakia, where the local Communists had strong popular support and had obtained 38 percent of the votes cast in the 1946 elections, their electoral backing was falling away sharply during 1947. In response the Communists used their influence in the police and in the interior ministry to slander and discredit their opponents (notably the Slovak Democratic and Czech National Socialist parties) and, in February 1948—two months before the Italian elections of that year—they took power in a political coup.[6]

In Poland there were no illusions about a "multi-party democracy." In the postwar cabinet of 1945 fourteen of the twenty-two members had been in the Communists' Committee of National Liberation (the "Lublin" Committee) designated in July 1944 by the Soviet forces to administer liberated Poland. The results of a referendum of July 1946, following a violent campaign in which the government harassed and intimidated non-Communist activists, were cynically rigged, as were the January 1947 general elections: Peasant Party spokesmen were kept off the radio and their supporters arrested by the thousands; their electoral lists were disqualified and accusations of espionage were made in Parliament and elsewhere to discredit their leadership. Even so, the ballot boxes had to be stuffed to prevent a Communist defeat. The result provoked international protest, to no avail. In October 1947 Stanislaw Mikolaj-czyk, the Peasant Party chief, fled abroad in fear for his life. Here as elsewhere these tactics had resulted by early 1949 in what was effectively a one-party state, with non-Communist parties licensed only as allies or obedient vassals, their leaders in exile, in prison, or dead. To suggest that this process was insti-tuted only as a direct consequence of American intervention in the domestic affairs of its Western partners, and not until then, is simply wrong.

THAT SO METICULOUS A HISTORIAN as Eric Hobsbawm should make such an odd mistake cannot, as he might say, be an accident. The difficulty seems to be that, like Marx, he is not much interested in these little nations. To refer to the years 1950–1974 as a "Golden Age" cannot help but sound ironic to someone from, say, Prague. And it takes a degree of uncharacteristic insou-ciance to write thus: "What happened to Warsaw in 1944 was the penalty of premature city risings: they have only one shot in their magazine, though a big one." As a proposition about urban revolt it is of course broadly true, but as an account of what happened in Poland when the Red Army waited for the Nazis to destroy the Polish Resistance before crossing the Vistula it is histori-cally disingenuous, to say the least.

But like another famous British historian of the Left, Hobsbawm seems to find something mildly annoying about "the lands between."[7] How else shall we account for his justification of the Bolshevik model as the only alternative in 1917 to "the disintegration which was the fate of the other archaic and de-feated empires, namely Austria-Hungary and Turkey. Unlike these, the Bol-shevik Revolution preserved most of the multinational territorial unity of the old Tsarist state at least for another seventy-four years." That this is no casual remark is made clear later in his book when he describes the disintegration of the USSR as leaving an "international void between Trieste and Vladivostok" for the first time since the mid-eighteenth century.

For residents of that "void," the history of the twentieth century looks rather different. But then they are perforce "nationalists," and nationalism (like religion) is a rather neglected subject in this book. Even from a purely analytical point of view this seems a mistake; whatever one thinks of national sentiment (and Hobsbawm accords it very little sympathy, here as in his other works), its place in the history of our time surely merits more than dismissive remarks about the "collective egoism" of Slovenes, Croats, Czechs, and their ilk. National self-determination may be a silly and "emotional" reaction to problems which it cannot address, as Hobsbawm puts it; but to say this is to risk missing something fundamental about our times. Without a fuller understanding of faiths of all sorts—secular and religious alike—the historian of the twentieth century is placed under a serious and self-imposed handicap.[8]

THE PROBLEM OF FAITH BRINGS us back to the thirties, and Hobsbawm's own relationship to his material. While he labors under no illusions about the former Soviet Union, he is reluctant to concede that it had no redeeming features (including that of maintaining or imposing stability upon the map of Europe). He thus insists that it had at least the virtue of bequeathing the idea of economic planning to the West, thereby ironically saving capitalism by simultaneously threatening its existence and furnishing it with the means for its survival. But it was not *Gosplan* that lay behind the enthusiasm for planning among young radicals of the thirties and that culminated in the mixed economies of postwar Western Europe.[9] What Hobsbawm neglects to note is that many of the postwar planners got their ideas not from Moscow but from Rome (or, in the French case, Vichy): it was often Fascist, not Communist planning which appealed to the technocrats who took over in the forties. Admiration for Soviet Five Year Plans, on the other hand, was most widespread among intellectuals—the Fabians, André Gide, and others, including left-wing students of Hobsbawm's own generation. Here, too, the history of our times falls too easily victim to private memory.

The desire to find at least some residual meaning in the whole Communist experience seems, finally, to lie behind a rather flat quality to Hobsbawm's account of the Stalinist terror. In his summary of the case for breakneck industrialization he draws upon the analogy with a war economy:

> As in a war economy . . . targets for production can, and indeed often must, be set without considering cost and cost-effectiveness, the test being whether they can be met and when. As in all such life-or-death efforts, the most effective method of fulfilling targets and meeting deadlines is giving urgent orders which produce all-out rushes.

To which one might reply that there wasn't a war on and anyway the "life" at stake was that of the Bolshevik regime, while the "death" was that of millions of human beings. On the subject of these human losses Hobsbawm rightly says that there can be "no justification"; but one longs for a fuller and more historically and humanly sensitive description of the whole tragedy. Here, by contrast, is Hobsbawm's own trenchant comment on optimistic and well-meaning nineteenth-century apologies for the New Poor Law of 1834:

> I daresay the Poor Law reformers honestly believed that paupers were morally improved by the separation of wives and husbands in the workhouse; . . . So far as the victims of these views were concerned, the results were as bad as—perhaps worse than—if they had been achieved by deliberate cruelty: inhuman, impersonal, callous degradation of the spirit of men and women and the destruction of their dignity. Perhaps this was historically inevitable and even necessary. But the victim suffered—suffering is not a privilege of well-informed persons. And any historian who cannot appreciate this is not worth reading.[10]

The fact that the Soviet Union purported to stand for a good cause, indeed the only worthwhile cause, is what mitigated its crimes for many in Hobsbawm's generation. Others might say it just made them worse.[11] In any case, the end of Communism was a source of much happiness for many millions of people, even if that happiness has been diluted by the difficulties that followed, and it rather calls into question Eric Hobsbawm's conclusion that "the old century has not ended well." One is tempted, after all, to ask, "For whom?" The somber, almost apocalyptic tone of the final section of the book obscures the fact that the eighties were also a decade of liberation for many, and not only in Eastern Europe. It is certainly true, as Hobsbawm says on more than one occasion, that no one any longer seems to have any solutions to offer to the world's problems, that we are tapping our way through a global fog, that we live in a world where "the past . . . has lost its role, in which the old maps and charts which guided human beings . . . no longer represent the landscape through which we move." But it is not self-evident that confident large-scale solutions of the sort we have lost were ever such a good thing—on balance they did a lot more harm than good.

IN 1968 I WAS A member of an attentive and admiring student audience whom Eric Hobsbawm was addressing on the theme, as I recall, of the limits of student radicalism. I remember very well his conclusion, since it ran so counter to the mood of the hour. Sometimes, he reminded us, the point is not to change the world but to interpret it. But in order to interpret the world one has also to have a certain empathy with the ways in which it has changed. His latest book is a challenging, often brilliant, and always cool and intelligent account of the world we have now inherited. If it is not up to his very best work it should be recalled just how demanding a standard he has set.

But there are one or two crucial changes that have taken place in the world—the death of Communism, for instance, or the related loss of faith in history and the therapeutic functions of the state about which the author is not always well pleased. That is a pity, since it shapes and sometimes misshapes his account in ways that may lessen its impact upon those who most need to read and learn from it. And I missed, in his version of the twentieth century, the ruthlessly questioning eye which has made him so indispensable a guide to the nineteenth. In a striking *apologia pro vita sua*, Eric Hobsbawm reminds us that historians are "the professional remembrancers of what their fellow-citizens wish to forget." It is a demanding and unforgiving injunction.

This essay first appeared in *The New York Review of Books* in May 1995 as a review of *The Age of Extremes: A History of the World, 1914–1991* by Eric Hobsbawm.

NOTES TO CHAPTER I

[1] For all that he was a hero to many radical students in the sixties, Eric Hobsbawm never conceded anything to the leftist fashions of the day. In his words, "Nobody with even minimal experience of the limitations of real life, i.e., no genuine adult, could have drafted the confident but patently absurd slogans of the Parisian May days of 1968 or the Italian 'hot autumn' of 1969." In this he is mildly reminiscent of Albert Soboul, the great French (Communist) historian of the sansculottes. Many young French *gauchistes*, admirers of his work, assumed before encountering him that Professor Souboul must share the sartorial informality and egalitarian social style of his professional subjects. No one ever made that mistake twice.

[2] Any history of the world in our century is of necessity a history in large measure of the things Europeans (and North Americans) did to themselves and to others, and of how non-Europeans reacted to them and were (usually adversely) affected. That, after all, is what is wrong with the twentieth century, seen from a "third world" perspective, and to criticize Hobsbawm, as some reviewers have done, for understanding this and writing accordingly, seems to me incoherent.

[3] Given the advantages of such firsthand sources, and in view of the large body of available material, it does seem a pity that Hobsbawm has not drawn more on the recorded memories and experiences of other voyagers through the century.

[4] Asked by one of Europe's largest firms whether Bologna would like to be chosen as the site for a major factory, the mayor politely declined the opportunity. As he explained to Hobsbawm, the mixed economy of his region was doing nicely, and did not need to introduce into its midst the industrial problems of major cities like Milan or Turin.

[5] Though with no reference to his own professional trajectory, where he paid a significant price for his political affiliation, at least in the early years.

[6] In the memoirs of former Hungarian and Czech Communists as well as their opponents it is

clear that from the moment the Germans were ousted the local Communists intended to defeat and discredit their domestic political enemies: by falsifying ballots, by political and legal intimidation, by the exploitation of their Soviet protection. That they could also count on a real, albeit rapidly diminishing, fund of popular support should not obscure this. See, e.g., Eugen Loebl, *My Mind on Trial* (New York: Harcourt Brace Jovanovich, 1976); Béla Szász, *Volunteers for the Gallows: Anatomy of a Show-Trial* (New York: Norton, 1971); Josephine Langer, *Une Saison à Bratislava* (Paris: Seuil, 1979); Stephen Kertesz, *Between Russia and the West: Hungary and the Illusions of Peacemaking 1945–1947* (South Bend, IN: University of Notre Dame Press, 1986). The Czech National Socialists had no relation to the German variety, except to the extent that both could indirectly trace their origins to ethnic divisions within the labor movement in late-nineteenth-century Bohemia.

[7] Writing in 1941, G. D. H. Cole thought that indefensible sovereign states in Eastern Europe had no future and that it would be better if a victorious postwar Soviet Union simply absorbed Poland, Hungary, and the Balkans. G. D. H. Cole, *Europe, Russia and the Future*, quoted in Serban Voinea, "Satéllisation et libération," *Revue socialiste* (March 1957), p. 226.

[8] Among secular faiths should be included the ideological myths that have moved intellectuals in our century, without which many of the worst features of the "descent into barbarism" cannot be properly explained. On these Hobsbawm has curiously little to say.

[9] Nor were these as universally "planned" as Hobsbawm sometimes implies. There were many variations on the planning theme after 1945, ranging from nationalization without planning (in Great Britain) to selective planning with some nationalization (France) to coordinated economic strategy with neither formal planning nor nationalization (West Germany). Although he gives Maynard Keynes due credit for having undermined the plausibility of noninterventionary laissez-faire economic theory, the relationship between Keynesian economics, wartime social planning, and postwar economic practice is not much discussed in this book.

[10] E. J. Hobsbawm, "History and the 'Dark Satanic Mills,'" in *Labouring Men: Studies in the History of Labour* (New York: Basic Books, 1964), p. 118. The same cool interpretive distance is maintained in Hobsbawm's treatment of Fascist terror, too, and contrasts with his powerful image of our century as a time of crime and folly. What seems to be missing is more firsthand description, to offset the distancing impact of large-scale analyses.

[11] Contrast the reflections of the Polish writer Alexander Wat: "The loss of freedom, tyranny, abuse, hunger would all have been easier to bear if not for the compulsion to call them freedom, justice, the good of the people." Alexander Wat, *My Century: The Odyssey of a Polish Intellectual* (Berkeley: University of California Press, 1990), p. 173.

CHAPTER II

Europe: The Grand Illusion

I.

The European community was founded nearly forty years ago, with the stated object of promoting the "ever-closer" union of its members. It is a remarkable accomplishment, albeit not quite so remarkable as its advocates suggest. There are few who oppose its objectives in principle, and the practical benefits it affords its members, such as unrestricted trade, are obvious. That, after all, is why nearly everyone wants to join it. It is now engaging in negotiations among its member states to construct a single European currency and mechanisms for common decision taking and collective action, while simultaneously holding out to the countries of former Communist Europe the promise of membership in years to come.

The likelihood that the European Union can fulfill its own promises of ever-closer union, while remaining open to new members on the same terms, is slim indeed. In the first place, the unique historical circumstances of the years between 1945 and 1989 cannot be reproduced. Indeed, the disruptive effect of the events of 1989 has been at least as great in the West as in the East. The essence of the Franco-German condominium around which postwar Western Europe was built lay in a mutually convenient arrangement: the Germans would have the economic means and the French would retain the political initiative. In the early postwar years, of course, the Germans had not yet acquired their present wealth and French predominance was real. But from the mid-fifties this was no longer true; thereafter France's hegemony in West European affairs rested upon a nuclear weapon that the country could not use, an army that it could not deploy within the continent itself, and an international political standing derived largely from the self-interested magnanimity of the three victorious powers at the end of the war.

THIS CURIOUS INTERLUDE IS NOW at an end. One economic fact may illustrate the point. In 1990 a chart of French economic influence shows it to be limited to the "Europe of Nine"—that is to say, the original six (Germany, France, Italy, and the Benelux countries)—plus Britain, Eire, and Denmark. With these countries, France was a major importer and exporter of goods and services. But Germany, in contrast, already encompassed within its range of economic influence not only the present "Europe of Fifteen" but also most of the rest of the continent to the south and east. The significance of this is clear. France has become a regional power, confined to Europe's western edge. Germany, even before unification, was once again the great power of Europe.

The impact of 1989 has also posed new difficulties for the Germans. For just as weakness and declining international power arouse difficult memories for France, so in Germany does an apparent excess of power. German politicians from Adenauer to Helmut Kohl have made a point of playing down German strength, deferring to French political initiatives and emphasizing their own wish for nothing more than a stable Germany in a prosperous Europe; they have thus fallen victim to their own rhetoric, bequeathing to post-1989 Europe a muscle-bound state with no sense of national purpose.

As a consequence, Germany's national agenda today is a little too full. In addition to the economic and political problem of absorbing the eastern *Länder,* Germans must deal with the paradox of pre-unification *Ostpolitik*: that many German politicians, especially on the Left, were well pleased with things the way they were and would have been quite content to see the Wall remain a little longer. Germans have also to reckon with embarrassments about their own capacities—now that they can and manifestly do lead Europe, where should they take it? And of what Europe are they the natural leaders—the West-leaning "Europe" forged by the French, or that traditional Europe of German interests, where Germany sits not on the eastern edge but squarely in the middle?

A Germany at the heart of Europe carries echoes and reminders that many people, Germans perhaps most of all, have sought since 1949 to set aside. But the image of a Germany resolutely turned away from troubling Eastern memories, clinging fervently to its postwar Western allies, as though they alone stood between the nation and its demons, is not very convincing.

EUROPE'S BASIC ECONOMIC CIRCUMSTANCES have also changed. For a generation following the announcement of the European Coal and Steel Community in 1950, Western Europe experienced an unprecedented combination of high growth and near-full employment. From this was born the belief, reflected in a series of optimistic economic forecasts from the OECD, that the cycle of crises that had marked the European economy for the previous half century had been broken for good. The great oil crisis of 1974 should have put an end to such illusions. In 1950 Western Europe depended upon oil for only 8.5 percent of its energy needs; most of the rest was still provided by coal, Europe's indigenous and cheap fossil fuel. By 1970 oil accounted for 60 percent of European energy consumption. The quadruple increase in oil prices thus put an end to a quarter of a century of cheap energy, sharply and definitively raising the cost of manufacture, transport, and daily living. In the Federal Republic of Germany GNP actually fell by 0.5 percent in 1974 and again, by 1.6 percent, in 1975, unprecedented blips in the postwar *Wirtschaftswunder* that were confirmed in 1981 and 1982, when the West German economy declined again, by 0.2 percent and 1 percent, respectively. In Italy GNP fell (by 3.7 percent) in 1976, for the first time since the end of the war. Neither the German nor any other Western European economy has ever been the same again.

The effect of this on the European Community (later Union) itself was severe. An important feature of the community had been its capacity to serve with equal success the varied needs of its member countries, needs deriving from interwar experiences and memories that differed quite markedly. The Belgians (like the British) feared unemployment more than anything else; the French sought above all to avoid the Malthusian stagnation of earlier decades; Germans lived in terror of an unstable, inflated currency. After 1974 the stalled economy of Europe threatened them all with increasing unemployment, slow growth, and sharply rising prices. There has thus been an unanticipated return to earlier woes. Far from being able to offer the advantages of its economic miracle to an ever-expanding community of beneficiaries, "Europe" can no longer even be sure of being able to provide them to itself. The events of 1989 brought this problem into the open, but the source of the Union's inability to address it can be found fifteen years earlier.

The memory of unemployment between the wars varies from country to country. It was never a great scourge in France, averaging just 3.3 percent per annum throughout the 1930s. But in Britain, where 7.5 percent of the labor force was already unemployed during the 1920s, the annual average of 11.5 percent in the thirties was something that politicians and economists of every stripe swore should never happen again. In Belgium and Germany, where the unemployment rate was nearly 9 percent, similar sentiments prevailed. It was thus one of the glories of the postwar West European economy that it maintained close to full employment through much of the 1950s and 1960s. In the 1960s the annual average unemployment rate in Western Europe was just 1.6 percent. In the following decade it rose to an annual average of 4.2 percent. By the late 1980s it had doubled again, with annual average rates of unemployment in the EC at 9.2 percent; by 1993 the figure stood at 11 percent.

Within these depressing figures one could see patterns that were more truly disturbing. In 1993 registered unemployment among men and women under twenty-five exceeded 20 percent in six EU countries (Spain, Eire, France, Italy, Belgium, and Greece). The long-term unemployed accounted for more than one-third the total of those without work in those six nations as well as the UK, the Netherlands, and the former West Germany. The redistributive impact of the inflation of the 1980s worsens the effect of these figures, widening the gap between people in work and the unemployed. What is more, upturns in the economy no longer have the effect, as they did during the boom years after 1950, of absorbing surplus labor and pulling up the worse-off. Who now remembers the fantasies of the 1960s, when it was blithely believed that production problems had been solved, and all that remained was to redistribute the benefits?

The combination of rapid urban growth and subsequent economic stagnation has brought to Western Europe not only a renewed threat of economic insecurity, something unknown to most Europeans since the late 1940s, but also greater social disruption and physical risk than at any time since the early Industrial Revolution. In Western Europe today one can now see desolate satellite towns, rotting suburbs, and hopeless city ghettos. Even the great capital cities—London, Paris, Rome—are neither as clean, as safe, nor as hopeful as they were just thirty years ago. They and dozens of provincial cities from Lyon to Lübeck are developing an urban underclass. If this has not had more explosive social and political consequences, the credit lies with the systems of social welfare with which Western Europeans furnished themselves after 1945.

THE CRISIS OF the welfare state is thus the third reason why the European Union cannot expect to project its achievements and promise into the indefinite future. The Western European population is aging. Ever since the mid-sixties the general trend has been for fewer children per family, to the point that in some countries, notably Italy and Spain, the population is not even maintaining itself. In Spain the birth rate per thousand in 1993 was just 1.1, a historic low. Europeans must now support a large and growing population of older people on the backs of fewer and fewer younger people, many of whom are not employed. A generous system of social services designed for flourishing economies where a large number of employed young people supported the social needs of a relatively small population of the old and sick is now under serious pressure.

In Northern and Western Europe the population aged sixty-five and over has grown by between 12 percent and 17 percent (depending on the country) since the mid-1960s. Moreover, even those under sixty-five can no longer be counted automatically on the "productive" side of the national equation: in West Germany the percentage of men aged sixty to sixty-four who were in paid employment fell from 72 to 44 in the two decades after 1960; in the Netherlands the figures were 81 and 58, respectively. At the moment the underemployed elderly are merely an expensive burden. But once the baby boomers begin to retire (around 2010), the presence of a huge, frustrated, bored, unproductive, and ultimately unhealthy population of old people could become a major social crisis.

It is clear to most European politicians that the costs of maintaining the welfare state in its postwar form cannot be carried indefinitely. The difficulty lies in knowing whom to displease first—the shrinking number of contributors or the growing number of involuntary beneficiaries. Both parties can vote. So far a combination of habit and good intentions has favored retaining as many social benefits as possible. But during the past few years another factor in the "welfare" debate has threatened to distort national political judgment out of all proportion to its size. This is the so-called "immigrant question."

AS A RESULT OF IMMIGRATION from former colonies and from its Mediterranean fringe, attracted by job prospects in an economy sucking in labor to fuel its rapid growth, Western Europe by the early 1960s had an excess of immigrants over emigrants for the first time this century. By 1973 the high point of the "foreign presence" in Western Europe, the EEC nations together with Austria, Switzerland, Norway, and Sweden had some 7.5 million foreign workers, of whom nearly 5 million were in France and Germany, comprising about 10 percent of the labor force in both countries. Despite a sharp fall-off in numbers since then, because governments have restricted immigration for both economic and political reasons, the "immigrant" presence has remained significant. According to data from 1990, about 6.1 percent of the German population, 6.4 percent of the French population, 4.3 percent of the Dutch population, and 3.3 percent of the British population are foreigners. These figures do not include naturalized immigrants, or locally born children of foreigners, though in some countries—notably Germany—these continue to be counted as foreigners and lack full citizens' rights.

In recent years these immigrants and their children have become the target of resentment and fear on the part of the "native" population, sentiments fanned and exploited by extremist and mainstream politicians alike. Just how far this process has now gone may be seen in France. In May 1989, 28 percent of Jacques Chirac's Gaullist supporters pronounced themselves "globally in agreement" with the ideas about immigrants expressed in the program of Jean-Marie Le Pen's National Front. In 1991 the figure was 50 percent. And if the Communist and Socialist voters were less sympathetic, that was only because a significant number of them had already switched their allegiance to Le Pen: in the presidential elections of 1995, he won 30 percent of the votes of the employed working class, the Socialist candidate Lionel Jospin obtaining just 21 percent.

Thus by the end of the 1980s a large minority of mainstream voters in France saw nothing disreputable about expressing agreement with policies that twenty years before would have been regarded as unacceptably close to Fascism (among the proposals in Le Pen's November 1991 list of "Fifty measures to be taken on immigration" was one to withdraw previously granted naturalizations, an act of retroactive injustice last practiced in France under the government of Philippe Pétain). In Austria Jörg Haider's far-right Freedom Party got 22 percent of the vote in the December 1995 national elections. In Germany, too, increasing restrictions on "guest workers" and other would-be immigrants have been imposed "in their own interest."

The politics of immigration will not soon subside, because cross-continental and intercontinental migrations are once again a feature of European society, and local fears and prejudices will ensure that they continue to be seen as disruptive and politically exploitable. Prejudice in earlier decades against Polish or Italian or Portuguese immigrants was eventually muted as their children, distinguished by neither religion nor language nor color, blended into the social landscape. These advantages of cultural and physical invisibility are not available to their successors from Turkey, Africa, India, or the Antilles. There is very little tradition in Europe of effective assimilation— or, alternatively, "multiculturalism"—when it comes to truly foreign communities. Immigrants and their children will join the ranks of the "losers" in the competition for Western Europe's reduced resources.

Hitherto, the "losers" in Europe's postwar history have been sustained by complicated, expensive systems of regional aid that the European Union put in place within and between countries. These amount to a form of institutionalized relief—constantly correcting for market deformations that have concentrated wealth and opportunity in the rich northwestern core without doing much to alter the causes of the disparity. Southern Europe, the peripheries (Eire, Portugal, Greece), the economic underclass, and the "immigrants" thus constitute a community of the disadvantaged for whom the EU is the only source of relief on the one hand—for without succor from Brussels much of Western Europe, from depressed mining communities to unprofitable peasant villages, would be in even worse trouble than it is—and envy and resentment on the other. For where there are losers there are also winners.

To see "Europe" at work for the winners one has only to spend a few days in the triangle made up by the towns of Saarbrücken (Germany), Metz (France), and Luxembourg. Here prosperous citizens of three countries travel freely across all-but-vanished frontiers. People, employment, commodities, and entertainment move easily back and forth among languages and states, seemingly unconscious of the historic tensions and enmities that marked this very region in the quite recent past. Local children continue to grow up in

France, Germany, or Luxembourg, and learn their histories according to national instructional rites, but what they learn no longer corresponds very well with what they see. All in all, that is to the good. The natural logic of the union of the Saarland with Lorraine has been achieved, not under the auspices of the German high command or of a French army of occupation, but following the benign designs of the European Commission. *C'est magnifique, mais ce n'est pas l'Europe*. Or, to be fair, it is indeed "Europe," but from a very distinctive angle. For of what does *this* Europe consist, geographically speaking? What are its capitals, and where are its institutions? The Commission and its civil service sit in Brussels. The Parliament and its committees meet in Strasbourg and Luxembourg. The European Court is in The Hague. Crucial decisions regarding further unification are taken at Maastricht, while an agreement to pool frontier regulations and police aliens was signed in the Luxembourg town of Schengen. All six towns, within easy reach of one another, lie athwart the line running from the North Sea to the Alps that formed the centerpiece and primary communications route of the ninth-century Carolingian monarchy. Here, one might say, lies the heart (and, some would add, the soul) of today's European Union. But the instinctive, atavistic (and politically calculated) location of these modern capitals of "Europe" should serve as a cautionary reminder that what is true about today's Europe may not be very new, and what is proclaimed as new perhaps not wholly true.

THERE IS ANOTHER CURIOUS FEATURE of Europe today. Its winners, those people and places which have done well in the Union and associate their prosperity with an emphatically European identity, are best described by reference not to nation-states but to regions. The great success stories of contemporary Europe are Baden-Württemberg, in southwestern Germany; the Rhône-Alpes region of France; Lombardy; and Catalonia. Three of these "super-regions" (none of which contains the national capital of its country) are grouped around Switzerland, as though wishing they could somehow clamber out of the constraints of their association with poorer regions of Italy,

Germany, and France and become, by proximity and affinity, prosperous little Alpine republics themselves. Their disproportionate prosperity and economic power is striking. The Rhône-Alpes region, together with Greater Paris, accounts for about a third of French gross domestic product. Catalonia, in 1993, was responsible for 19 percent of Spain's GDP, 23 percent of Spanish exports, and one-quarter of all foreign investment; its per capita income was some 20 percent higher than the average for Spain as a whole.

The wealthy regions of Western Europe have discovered a strong interest in associating with one another, directly or through the institutions of Europe. And in the nature of things, it is an interest that puts them ever more at odds with the older nation-state of which they are still constituent parts. This is not a new source of disagreement. In Italy the resentment of northerners at sharing the country with a "parasitic" south is a theme as old as the state itself. Flemish national separatism in Belgium, which flourished under the Nazis and for that very reason was somewhat quiescent after the war, has benefited in recent years from the economic decline of industrial Wallonia; we Flemings, the argument now runs, claim not just linguistic equality and separate administration but our own (non-Belgian) identity—and state.

The common claim of separatists, in Spain, Italy, and Belgium, but also in Slovenia and the Czech lands before the "velvet divorce," is this: "we"—the hard-working, tax-paying, better-educated, linguistically and/or culturally distinct northerners—are "European"; while "they"—the rural, backward, lazy, subsidized (Mediterranean) "south"—are less so. The logical imperative of a "European" identity that distinguishes itself from undesirable neighbors with whom it shares a state is to seek an alternative center of authority, choosing "Brussels" over Rome or Madrid. The appeal of "European Union" under these circumstances is that of cosmopolitan modern development against old-fashioned, restrictive, and "artificial" national constraints.

This in turn may account for the special attraction of "Europe" to the younger intelligentsia in these lands. The Soviet Union once appealed to many Western intellectuals as a promising combination of philosophical ambition and administrative power, and "Europe" has some of the same allure. For its admirers, the "Union" is the latest heir to the enlightened despotism of the eighteenth century. For what is "Brussels," after all, if not a renewed attempt to achieve the ideal of efficient, universal administration, shorn of particularism and driven by reason and the rule of law, which the reforming monarchs—Catherine the Great, Frederick the Great, Maria Theresa, and Joseph II—strove to install in their ramshackle lands? It is the very rationality of the European Union ideal that commends it to an educated professional class which, in east and west alike, sees in "Brussels" an escape from hidebound practices and provincial backwardness—much as eighteenth-century lawyers, traders, and writers appealed to modernizing royals over the heads of reactionary parliaments and diets.

But there is a price to be paid for all this. If "Europe" stands for the winners, who shall speak for the losers—the "south," the poor, the linguistically, educationally, or culturally disadvantaged, underprivileged, or despised Europeans who don't live in golden triangles along vanished frontiers? The risk is that what remains to *these* Europeans is "the nation," or, more precisely, nationalism; not the national separatism of Catalans or the regional self-advancement of Lombards but the preservation of the nineteenth-century state as a bulwark against change. For this reason, and because an ever-closer bonding of the nations of Europe is in practice unlikely, it is perhaps imprudent to insist upon it. In arguing for a more modest assessment of Euro-prospects I don't wish to suggest that there is something *inherently* superior about national institutions over supranational ones. But we should recognize the reality of nations and states, and note the risk that, when neglected, they become an electoral resource of nationalists.

II.

Should the European Union take in the countries of Eastern Europe? In the former East Germany an optimistic belief that economic prosperity would bring the divided country together and wash away unhappy memories—an attempt, in short, to reproduce the "economic miracle" of the Federal Republic and its attendant benefits—has foundered not so much on the presence of those memories as upon the absence of any economic transformation comparable to that which West Germany enjoyed in the early fifties. The same difficulty would apply to any attempt to absorb into the Union the lands to its east.

In economic terms alone such an expansion would make for onerous and unpopular burdens. In the 1992 EU budget, only four countries were net contributors: Germany, Great Britain, France, and the Netherlands (in descending order of per capita contribution). The beneficiaries, in the same order per capita, were Luxembourg, Eire, Greece, Belgium, Portugal, Denmark, Spain, and Italy. True, the subsequent newcomers—Sweden, Finland, and Austria—are all potential contributors, but their economies are small and their share will not amount to much. Conversely *all* conceivable future members of the Union (Switzerland apart) fall unambiguously into the category of beneficiaries. It has been estimated (in a 1994 study by the Bertelsmann Foundation) that the four "Visegrad Group" countries—Poland, the Czech Republic, Slovakia, and Hungary—alone would cost the European Union DM20 billion per year in direct payments. Clearly, it would cost the Union a lot of money—more than it can presently afford—to bring in such future members *on the same terms as present ones.*

For reasons I have suggested, the European Union cannot realistically promise even its existing members a future as secure and as prosperous as its past. Subterfuges like "inner core," "fast track," "variable geometry," or "Partnership for Peace" are all devices to postpone or avoid the impossible choice of either saying no to newcomers or else expanding the Union on equal terms. For the foreseeable future it would be an expensive act of charity, economically speaking, for the EU to absorb the countries to its east on any acceptable terms. But would it not, perhaps, be in Western Europe's self-interest to make the sacrifice notwithstanding (always supposing it can afford to do so)?

Let us set aside the issue of cultural affinity—whether, that is, Western Europe is lacking a vital part of itself if it is in any way separated from Central or Eastern Europe. The perceived self-interest of Western Europe today lies in securing itself against demographic and economic threats to its east and south. As for threats of a more conventional sort, it is an unspoken assumption of all European defense planners that Russia remains the only significant military threat to the rest of Europe. That the major states of Western and Central Europe have the same interest they have always had in maintaining "buffer states" to separate them from Russia is clear. But whether these perform their geo-strategic role better in or out of a formal Union remains an open question.

IN ANY CASE, West European debate is now focused upon the workings of the European Union itself. Should collective European undertakings be decided by unanimous agreement (as now) or by majority voting? And in the latter case, how should majorities be construed, and how binding are their decisions to be? Helmut Kohl, the late François Mitterrand, and their political advisers favored the introduction of a system of majority voting, to eliminate the risk of deadlock that would arise from any attempt to meet the needs and demands of so many member states. The British, supported by some of the smaller member states, favor retention of the veto (the same veto wielded by Charles de Gaulle to keep the British out in January 1963!) precisely to prevent decisions being taken against their interests—and indeed, to prevent the taking of too many decisions of any sort at all. It is not by chance that these conflicts have come to the fore. In the "Europe of Fifteen" it is going to be near impossible to find strong majorities, much less unanimity, for decisions requiring hard choices.

This will be especially true in defense and foreign policy, matters in which Europe has hitherto been inactive. The option of military quiescence is no longer open to Europe; the United States cannot be counted on to involve itself in European affairs whenever its services are required. The European Union has utterly failed to bring its members together for any common policy or action in military or foreign affairs. And what has proven difficult for fifteen members would be out of the question for a larger number still. Where the

European Union and its forebears once resembled the UN—taking unanimous decisions on areas of common interest and agreeing to disagree, or just not make a decision, on difficult or divisive topics—it will now begin to look like the League of Nations, with members simply opting out of decisions from which they dissent. The moral and political damage that can be done when a single member forces unanimous indecision upon the whole—*vide* the Greek refusal to recognize Macedonia, or Italy's insistence that Slovenia be excluded from consideration for EU membership until long-standing but trivial legal disputes between the two countries had been addressed—would be nothing compared to a refusal by Britain or France, for example, to accept the foreign policy of a majority composed of Germany and her smaller supporters.

WHAT, THEN, of Western Europe's general interest in stability, in guaranteeing countries like Hungary or Slovakia against their own internal demons? This is in fact the strongest argument Central Europeans can offer in support of their candidacy for admission to the EU—protect us against ourselves, against the domestic consequences of a failed "post-Communist transition"—and it is particularly persuasive for their neighbors immediately to the west, notably Germany. But it is a purely prudential argument, which is why the EU has tried to meet it with the offer of partial membership, interim affiliation, and so on, and it raises a hypothetical future problem at a time when the West is preoccupied with real and immediate difficulties. Even if concerns about Eastern European stability succeed in prizing open the European door, these will only do so at the cost of a significant dilution of the meaning and practices of union. And the protective arm of "Europe" will surely not extend beyond the old Habsburg center (the Czech Republic, Hungary, Slovakia, Slovenia, and Poland), making of it a sort of depressed Euro suburb beyond which "Byzantine" Europe (from Latvia to Bulgaria) will be left to fend for itself, too close to Russia and Russian interests for it to be prudent for the West to make an aggressive show of absorption and engagement.

Meanwhile, Europe will be dominated by Germany. Since 1990 a united

Germany has been seeking partners for its strategy of expansion into Central Europe. If it can act in concert with fellow members of a European "fast track," Bonn will not seem quite so obviously to be striding out ahead. Thus investments in Eastern Europe made by German firms using Austrian subsidiaries or "fronts," for example, raise fewer local hackles than those coming directly from the Federal Republic. Just as West German foreign policy before 1989 might be characterized as a triple balancing act, neither favoring nor displeasing the United States, Moscow, or Paris, so post-unification German policy is seeking to follow the logic of Germany's power, and its historical place in Central and Eastern Europe, without frightening its West European allies or arousing Germans' own fears of revived national ambition.

The difficulty, as some German writers have noted, is that Germany cannot help destabilizing Europe, its own best intentions notwithstanding. The Europe that Adenauer and his contemporaries helped to make, and that in turn allowed the Federal Republic to forge its post-Hitler identity, is now in question, the postwar settlement having come to a close. The more dramatic historical analogies are misleading—a de facto alliance of Germany with Austria inside the EU is not the *Anschluss* of 1938, and a revival of German expansionism, much less militarism, is not likely, at least for the foreseeable future. But it remains true, as it has since 1871, that a powerful Germany in the middle of Europe, with interests of its own, is an unsettling presence for its neighbors.

YET A EUROPE DOMINATED by Germany, in striking contrast to the past, may be characterized above all by its unwillingness to intervene actively in international affairs. Whether this will always be so is another matter—the legacy of Nazism cannot continue to weigh upon the German public conscience indefinitely, and there must come a point when German politicians and their electors will be less inhibited about behaving like any other power: sending soldiers abroad, using force or the threat of force to achieve national goals, and so forth. But in the meantime the chief difficulty posed to its members by a German-dominated Europe is a sort of inertia, forcing the European community to restrict its collective international interventions to uncontentious issues of an environmental or humanitarian nature.

This is the first lesson of the Yugoslav tragedy, illustrating as it does the weakness of European initiatives, the compulsion to avoid engagement, and the absence of any agreed collective strategic interest beyond maintaining the status quo. The war in Yugoslavia since 1991 is also a timely reminder that Germans are not the only people for whom German hegemony in Europe is unwelcome. One of the strongest points in Serbian propaganda, first against Slovenian and Croatian independence and then against external "interference" in Bosnia, has been its claim that Germany and Austria are seeking to restore a "German-Catholic" *Mitteleuropa* and that the whole enterprise of dismantling Yugoslavia is a sort of Teutono-Habsburg plot. Fear of giving hostages to this argument prevented Europe's most powerful state from intervening actively in the war until four years had passed, and even then the decision to send a small German military contingent—confined to strictly noncombat duties—was only taken against much opposition from intellectual and political circles in Germany.

This is not to say that the behavior of France or Great Britain has been exemplary. But the French and the British have been constrained to do *something*, however inadequate and even perfidious—hence the dispatch of a small "Rapid Reaction Force" to Sarajevo in 1995, after it became embarrassingly clear just how ineffectual the UN presence there had become.* But just because this force was a Franco-British one, and not operating under any sort of "European" aegis, it confirmed another lesson taught by events in the Balkans, that the "European" edifice is fundamentally hollow, selfishly obsessed with fiscal rectitude and commercial advantage. Just as there is no effective

---

*It did not go unremarked in Bosnia, however, that the main objective of this force was to protect other foreign troops (French and British especially) operating under UN authority.

international community, so there is, for these purposes, no European one either. There are merely powers, great and not so great; and for the moment at least, a German-led Europe is not among them.

How France and Britain will use the limited international initiative this gives them will depend on what lesson, if any, their governments choose to learn from the humiliations of their Bosnian adventure. But forty years after the Anglo-French disgrace at Suez they are about to rediscover the charms, and burdens, of relative diplomatic autonomy. The United States is no longer looking over their shoulder, and "Europe" is no longer a credible bolt hole. The years 1945–1989 are coming to seem more and more like a parenthesis. As we move further away from World War II the reasons why it was so important to build something different will seem less pressing. That is why we must remind ourselves not just that real gains have been made, but that the European community which helped to make them was a means, not an end.

For if we look to European Union as a catchall solution, chanting "Europe" like a mantra, and waving the banner of "Europe" in the face of recalcitrant "nationalist" heretics, we may wake up one day to find that far from solving the problems of our continent, the myth of "Europe" has become an impediment to recognizing them. We shall discover that it has become little more than the politically correct way to paper over local difficulties, as though the mere invocation of the promise of a united Europe could substitute for solving problems and crises in the present. To be sure, there is a certain self-fulfilling advantage in speaking of Europe as though it already existed in some stronger, collective sense. But there are some things it cannot do, some problems it does not address. "Europe" is more than a geographical notion but less than an answer.

This essay first appeared in *The New York Review of Books* in July 1996.

CHAPTER III

Crimes and Misdemeanors

We are at a watershed in the history (and the historiography) of Europe. Fifty years after World War II, some long-standing assumptions about good and evil in that war and its aftermath are being shaken. Nearly a decade after the fall of Communism, the conventional Western understanding of Lenin's place in the history of this century is undergoing serious revision. The end of the European empires and the resurrection of Eastern Europe have dated most general histories of the old continent beyond recovery. The time is ripe for a new perspective, for a genuinely fresh account of how Europe came to its present condition.

A glance at Norman Davies's ambitious new history of the continent, from its geological origins through 1992, seems to promise precisely such a book.* It has certainly been welcomed warmly in its country of origin. Widely praised for its scope, its form, and its verve, *Europe: A History* was a best-seller in Great Britain, where it was also selected as "Book of the Year" by a variety of historians, journalists, and editors. And it is certainly a significant accomplishment to cover 3,000 years of European history in just under 1,400 pages, and to do so in consistently readable prose. Davies's book displays evidence of wide reading and a real enthusiasm for its subject. As a historian of Poland, he promises

---

*Norman Davies, *Europe: A History* (New York: Oxford University Press, 1996).

greater attention to Europe's eastern half and advertises his book as unique among surveys of its kind in precisely this respect. Another distinctive feature of the book is the 300 "capsules" scattered through the text, averaging a page each: these present a brisk, idiosyncratic and easily digestible account of a person, a place, an idea, or an event; and some of them, such as the ones on "Musike" and "St. Gotthard," are entertaining and informative. And there are numerous appendices with the usual array of charts, genealogies, and maps.

Yet *Europe: A History* does not fulfill its author's grand ambition. It is not a good work of history at all; and it must not become a work of reference for readers seeking to understand the European past. This is not owing to its minor defects, though these are many: Davies has a cute, self-advertising style that begins to grate; he can be shamelessly self-promoting (even encouraging a comparison of himself to Gibbon); he seems to know little about the history of art or ideas (he is better on music), and even less about economic development; and, despite a long introduction in which he pours scorn on virtually all previous histories and historians for their distorted perspectives, he lacks any guiding vision of his own. There are other minor annoyances: his chapter and capsule titles are often linguistically and referentially obscure, intended more to show off the author's own erudition than to enlighten his readers, while the capsules themselves (which take up a quarter of the text) get in the way of the narrative, to which they are often only loosely related; all of the political maps of Europe are pointlessly turned by 90 degrees, such that Portugal appears at the top and Warsaw is always at the very epicenter (the ideology behind the cartography emerges pretty quickly); and the book has an inadequate index and badly organized notes.

Of course, most ambitious general histories have these or comparable flaws. The important delinquencies of Davies's book are much more serious. It falls short of the requirements of a responsible synoptic history; and, in a more serious respect, it is a truly unsavory book.

For a start, Davies can't get his facts straight. I don't mean that he gets a few dates and names wrong. I mean that his book is littered with embarrassing and egregious errors of the sort that his own teachers would once have called "schoolboy howlers." In Davies's book, Henry VIII of England and Francis I of France hold a famous meeting on the wrong date, at a time when one of them wasn't even king; the reigns of all but one of the British Tudors are misdated; the Dutch Revolt breaks out on various dates, one of them correct (a misfortune that also befalls the Crimean War three centuries later); and Pascal is described as an "inmate" in Port Royal. In the nineteenth century, among other curiosities, the Second Empire in France begins four years early, the Tolpuddle martyrs in Britain move to another part of the country, and the Franco-Russian Dual Alliance of 1894 changes its name and its date.

As for the twentieth century, which takes up a fifth of the book: the Fascist regimes in Italy and Spain begin on the wrong dates, and in Spain, poor Largo Caballero, the well-meaning Spanish Socialist, becomes the head of the Communist Party; Franz von Papen gets the support of the Nazi deputies in the Reichstag (he didn't) and General von Schleicher becomes a member of the Reichstag (he wasn't); the Germans occupy the Vichy Zone in 1943, a year late; the number of wartime collaborators punished in France and Belgium at the Liberation and after is exaggerated by many thousands; Maurice Schumann changes the spelling of his name, becomes the brother of the hitherto unrelated Robert Schuman (twenty-five years his senior, and whose own name and "Plan" are misspelled in the index), and they are jointly miscredited with founding an important postwar French political party; the Nuclear Non-Proliferation Treaty is moved from 1968 to 1963, while Spain and Portugal join the European Community three years early; the British Empire in Africa is said to begin its demise with Nigerian independence in 1951, whereas the first independent state was Ghana in 1957, with Nigeria breaking away only three years later; François Mauriac's famous bon mot about liking Germany so much that he preferred two of them is assigned to an unnamed French minister; and the Berlin Wall falls nearly a week late.

These are just some of the mistakes that I spotted on a first reading, and they do not include misinterpretations of texts or events. Others will doubtless have similar misgivings for the periods about which they know more—though many general readers no better versed in classical history than myself will surely share my surprise at finding the precocious Hannibal crossing the Alps a full century before he intended. Davies has even included (on page 865) a childish "deliberate mistake," which would seem a little less foolish were it not overwhelmed by all its undeliberate fellows. The cumulative effect of all these errors is utterly to destroy the reader's confidence in *Europe: A History*.

Then there is the problem of Davies's lack of a sense of proportion. His legitimate frustration at Western ignorance of Eastern Europe is restated ad nauseam, but he himself largely ignores the complicated social and economic context of Eastern Europe's historical backwardness and consequent political weakness. The misfortunes of Europe's eastern half are copiously and lachrymosely displayed, but they are rarely explained. (Though blame is generously assigned, usually elsewhere.) The index, such as it is, reflects this unbalanced, compensatory approach: there are eleven entries for Pilsudski, who thus outranks Charlemagne, Bismarck, and most of Europe's other leaders, and three entries for the Polish nationalist demagogue Roman Dmowski, but there are only two for Metternich, one for Freud, and none for the three-time French Socialist premier Léon Blum.

There is distortion, too, in Davies's language, notably in his unstinting abuse of terms such as "genocide." The French Revolution is described as an occasion for "genocide franco-francais," an era in which the enemies of the counterrevolutionary Chouans, whose "moral integrity" is a matter of some concern to the author, "did not hesitate to employ genocidal measures." A century and a half later, Nazi policy toward the Poles is classed as similarly "genocidal." This is silly. Instances of the mass murder of counterrevolutionaries in eighteenth-century France normally affected dozens or hundreds of victims or, in one notorious case, about 2,000. Robespierre and his colleagues were not proto-Pol Pots, plotting to kill half the French nation. Similarly, the Nazis, as Davies acknowledges, set out to eliminate the educated elite of occupied Poland, not to round up, to imprison, and to kill every living Pole. By invoking "genocide" so loosely, Davies fails to discriminate between true attempts at mass extermination (of Armenians, of Jews) in modern times, and equally

murderous attacks, but on a significantly smaller scale and with quite different purposes, on various communities and nations—Albigensians, Hugue-
nots, Jews, Irish, Poles, and others—over the past centuries. He seems confused
about these distinctions, and he will confuse his readers as well.

In one respect, however, Davies goes beyond simply confusing his categories. He has a weakness for inappropriate comparisons and equivalences—he
calls them "juxtapositions"—a number of which have to do with the Jews in
general and the Holocaust in particular. Actually, Jews receive quite a lot of
attention in *Europe: A History,* albeit in odd ways. The capsule called "Bata-
via," for example, ends for no obvious reason with a reminder that the leading
historian of the Dutch Republic, Simon Schama, is a "British scholar of Dutch-
Jewish parentage." When this was queried in an American review of his book,
Davies responded tetchily that it was no different from reminding people that
he, Davies, is a Lancastrian, a remark that can at best be described as disingenuous.

In a paragraph on modern art Kandinsky is described as a Russian exile,
and Picasso is described as a Catalan exile, but Marc Chagall is described as a
"Jewish exile." (From where?) In a passage on the birth of Christianity, we are
authoritatively informed that "notwithstanding the doctrine of forgiveness, it
is the hardest thing in the world for Christians and Jews to see themselves as
partners in the same tradition. Only the most Christian of Christians can contemplate calling the Jews 'our elder brethren.'" But then, as Davies tells us
hundreds of pages later in a paragraph on Jewish emancipation, "modern concern with the roots of anti-Semitism sometimes overlooks the severity of the
Jews' own laws of segregation." This is strikingly misleading: after their
emancipation, even believing Jews dropped most of these communal requirements. Here, as elsewhere on such matters, Davies is distinctly more Catholic
than the pope.

His "juxtapositions" go further still. In a capsule purportedly devoted to
the "Noyades," the deliberate sinking at Nantes of boats filled with Vendeen
rebels and their supporters, Davies first implies an exaggerated number of

victims ("by the thousand," he writes, when the actual figure was between 2,000 and 2,500) and then moves swiftly to his main purpose. A mere ten lines are given over to the tragic events at Nantes in 1793 (Davies gets the year wrong), and they are followed by one and a half pages on a "juxtaposition" with gas chambers and crematoria. The ostensible point is that each generation invents the technology that it needs to commit mass murder. But the real emphasis is elsewhere. Davies's tone is well captured in the following excerpt: "A view might be entertained that the Nazi gas chambers reflected a 'humanitarian approach,' akin to that of well-regulated abattoirs. If the inmates had to die, it was better that they die quickly rather than in protracted agony or from cold and starvation. In practice, there is ample evidence that the operation of the Nazi death camps was accompanied by gratuitous bestiality." What are we supposed to infer from this? "A view might be entertained" that, in an appropriately nongratuitous form, bestiality has its place? A conscientious historian might usefully entertain the view that the killing of Vendeen rebels was an act of terroristic revenge in a civil war. But what light does it cast on the planned extermination of people whose crime was their very existence?

And this capsule is not an aberration. In a later piece, "BATT-101," purportedly devoted to the "ordinary men" in the German police battalions who massacred Jews on the Eastern Front, nearly two-thirds of the text is given over to "juxtaposing" these commonplace mass murderers with a summary of the "crimes" committed by Jewish ghetto policemen and by Jews working for the Communists after the war in the Polish U.B. (Security Office), who in Davies's words engaged in "torture, sadistic beatings and murder." Davies is much less movingly evocative in his description of the German killings of Jews. The scale, the context, and the gravity of these crimes are utterly unrelated—as Polish scholars have recently demonstrated, Davies overstates the Jewish presence in the U.B.—but somehow Davies manages to bind them together, with no discussion of the Polish context or of Polish behavior before, during, or after the war. This is his conclusion: "In this light, it is difficult to justify the widespread practice whereby the murderers, the victims, and the bystanders of wartime Poland are each neatly identified with specific ethnic groups." (Translation:

Germans were not just murderers, but also victims of Jews; and Jews were not just victims, but also murderers and persecutors of Germans and Poles.) Just what the reader is supposed to make of this account is unclear and more than a little disturbing.

Those familiar with Davies's earlier writings will not be surprised to encounter these "juxtapositions" or equivalences. In *God's Playground,* his two-volume history of Poland that appeared in 1982, Davies assured his readers that "Polish hostility towards the Jews was complemented by Jewish hostility towards the Poles." He advised that for students of wartime Poland "to ask why the Poles did little to help the Jews is rather like asking why the Jews did nothing to assist the Poles." In a later article in the journal *Polin,* seeking to demonstrate that Polish-Jewish hostility and fear before World War II was a two-way street—in a country where Jews were just 10 percent of the population!—Davies wrote affectingly of Polish "apprehension" in Eastern Galician towns as the "Betar movement marched its young people around the town square to chants of 'We will conquer Palestine' and 'We're not afraid of Arabs.'" (His descriptions of attacks on Jews in interwar Poland are less gripping.)

Indeed, a significant part of Davies's career as a historian has been devoted to revealing such equivalences, as in his comparison of the characteristics of Jewish and Polish nationalism, something he once described as "a fruitful line of enquiry." The fruits of that line of enquiry seem to have been sufficient to encourage him to extend it in his latest book to bizarre equivalences between Nazi extermination battalions and the corrupt ventures of small-time ghetto criminals assigned a spurious intracommunal authority on the eve of their programmed extinction.

Recognizing the rather controversial nature of his "juxtapositions," not to mention their insensitive phrasing and their obsession with the persecution of Jews, Davies covers himself in footnote ninety-nine on page 1,168. He invokes an authority for his view that there is nothing wrong in comparing and contrasting the Holocaust with other events. His authority is Isaiah Berlin. Those who refuse such historical comparisons and insist upon the "uniqueness" of the Holocaust have, he says, quoting Berlin, "a political motive." No mean backing, if you can get it. The problem is that Davies never got it. In the text from which Davies is quoting—it is on pages 18 and 19 of *The Unresolved Past: A Debate in German History,* edited by Ralf Dahrendorf and published in London in 1990—Berlin says the opposite of what Davies claims that he said.

In the relevant passage, Berlin is very clearly questioning the "political motives" of precisely those who insist upon certain sorts of implausible historical comparisons. Here are his words:

> Obviously, it's sensible to say, if uniqueness of a phenomenon, particularly of a horrifying phenomenon, is examined, we mustn't rush to the conclusion that it's unique in human history before we have compared it to other phenomena which in some ways may resemble it. That is what is being applied to the Holocaust. But think of unique events like the French Revolution. Nobody went about saying, is the French Revolution really unique, does it really resemble the "Glorious Revolution," Cromwell and the Puritans, something which happened in Athens in 405, the Roman Principate, and if so, what political conclusions should be drawn? Even with the Russian Revolution, which some of its makers thought analogous to the French Revolution, you don't come across writings either for or against, trying to emphasize its uniqueness or non-uniqueness, its similarity or dissimilarity to what went on before. Therefore, there must be a good deal more to the question of uniqueness the "placing in context" of this event than a mere historical assessment of an objective kind. It had a conspicuously political motive.

Only a massively egregious misreading could allow Davies to turn what is a devastating criticism of his own approach into a shield against his critics. I am happy to assume that this error arises merely from his inability to read a text with scholarly care. Still, Berlin is right. This is a politically motivated book. Buyer, beware.

Some of the failings of *Europe: A History* can be attributed to the distinctive personality of its author—"historian, populist and self-styled iconoclast," in the words of one American journalist covering his promotional appearances. (American journalists and interviewers have been quicker than their British counterparts to remark upon Davies's less endearing foibles.) Norman Davies has a history of inattention to accuracy, despite his patronizing criticism of poor Thomas Carlyle in the book's introduction. ("It is important," he observes, against Carlyle's historical writing, "to check and to verify.") A sympathetic reviewer of Davies's first book on the Polish-Soviet War of 1919–1920 wrote in 1973 that "it is hard not to express surprise that this young scholar should include so much inaccurate information," and his two-volume general history of Poland was variously described by otherwise favorable commentators as being "rather bored with detail" (Antony Polonsky) and containing "many faulty transcriptions from Polish and factual errors" (L. R. Lewitter). At the time of Davies's much publicized dispute with Stanford over that institution's refusal to offer him a chair, the university's provost felt constrained to make public some comments from academic referees who described Davies as showing "an inclination to sacrifice exactitude to a well-turned phrase" and wrote of his "occasionally erratic judgments and generalizations" and "the many factual errors which seem to be due to haste."

Davies's desire to shock probably accounts for many of the other irritating features of his new book. In addition to his self-confessed desire to be Gibbon, there is a capsule devoted to the history of Oxford University Press, whose greatest achievements are listed as including *Burton's Anatomy of Melancholy, The Book of Common Prayer, Blackstone's Commentaries, Alice in Wonderland*, and . . . *God's Playground* by Norman Davies! But there is also an undercurrent of resentment that lapses occasionally into paranoia. Davies's book is sadly disfigured by hints of various scores in need of settlement. After condemning Stanford and other leading North American universities for their inadequate efforts to teach European history, Davies castigates one historian in Cambridge, England, for his failure to appreciate the importance of Hungary in the European past: "all this means is that the Magyars did not reach Cambridge." The Oxford medievalist Maurice Keen is ridiculed for the Western orientation of the *Pelican History of Medieval Europe* that he wrote in 1969.

The Oxford faculty of modern history is pilloried for its long-standing emphasis upon medieval (Western) texts, and we are told that in Britain "the English
majority are apt to perceive all cultural gradients sloping steadily downhill
from the Himalayan peaks of Oxford. . . ." By the end of this, and much
more in a similar vein, one is put irresistibly in mind of *The Wind in the
Willows,* with Mr. Toad barreling boastfully along the open road and singing
to himself:

> The Clever Men at Oxford Know all that there is to be knowed But they
> none of them know one half as much As intelligent Mr Toad.

Mr. Toad's unself-conscious immodesty is nicely captured in Davies's assertion that only East European specialists such as himself truly understand
European history as a whole. In an essay published in the *New Statesman* and
characteristically titled "How I Conquered Europe," he asserts that "if an all-
European history was to be written, it could only be written by one of us."
"One of us": this is the point at which Davies's own suspicion of "them" merges
with the propensity of many (but by no means all) East Europeans and their
historians to see around them cabals, plots, and other devices intended to keep
"their" part of Europe out of the story of Western civilization. In Davies's resentful words: "Generally speaking, Western Civilisation is not taken to extend to the whole of Europe (although it may be applied to distant parts of the
globe far beyond Europe)."

Far from making a valid point here, Davies is actually doing it to death.
There has long been a need to recast Western understanding of the European
past and present—to treat of the whole continent and not just its more fortunate western regions. But by insisting on the "really vicious quality" of "nearly
all" accounts of Western civilization, by blaming "the western imagination"
for inventing, say, "the Slav Soul," by echoing the debilitating East European
inclination to blame local misfortune upon outside malevolence, and by turning his history of Europe into a propaganda exercise on behalf of eastern ap-

plicants to the E.U., Davies goes way beyond the bounds of the historian's vocation.

The same applies to Davies's remarks on Jewish themes. He insists that he is not anti-Semitic and we must take him at his word. He claims that it is simply impossible to write fairly about "Eastern Europe" without raising hackles; and it is undoubtedly true that much of the modern history of Eastern Europe is so problematically intertwined with the history of the Jews that all sorts of sensibilities are on the line every time certain subjects are raised. Still, this does not sufficiently account for Davies's own reaction to criticism. As he once told an American journalist, "things I write about East Europe don't suit various people, especially in America." And which people in America might those people be? His response to Stanford's rejection was to inform its provost that any scholar dealing with East Europe or Poland was "bound to alarm a number of vested interests, among them those of international Zionism or communism."

Well, that is pretty clear. In *God's Playground,* indeed, the reader is told that "it has always lain in the interests of the Zionist movement . . . to paint Polish life in the most unfavourable colours." In *Europe: A History,* we learn that Marek Edelman (a survivor of the Warsaw Ghetto revolt who has chosen to remain in Poland) is "pilloried" for "opposing the dominant Zionist viewpoint" on the Holocaust. (This is not the first time that the unfortunate Edelman has been pressed into involuntary service as an ally of Davies's, sometimes at the price of a subtle shift in the meaning of his own words.)

It seems reasonable to infer, then, that Davies is simply anti-Zionist. Anti-Zionism, of course, is quite distinct from anti-Semitism—though in the context of post–1948 East European usage, with which Davies is proudly familiar, such a distinction has often been shorn of its difference. It is most unfortunate, therefore, that the section on the Holocaust in *Europe: A History* refers readers to footnotes in which the so-called "revisionists" are given equal space with legitimate scholars. In a book intended for the general reader, this is astonishing.

In one of these footnotes, one source for Davies's criticism of the "Holo-caust industry" turns out to be *They Dare to Speak Out* by Paul Findley, an overheated and quite unrelated diatribe against the role of the "Israel lobby" in American politics written by an ex-congressman with a grudge.

Meanwhile, in an interview with the *Daily Telegraph* in London last De-cember, Davies was asked to account for the distinctly unfavorable review of his book by Theodore Rabb in *The New York Times Book Review,* which stood in marked contrast to its glutinously fawning reception in Britain. He offered various explanations, none of them about a professional historian's concern for accuracy, balance, and so forth. Instead, he asserted that "Rabb is putting out a few signals to his comrades-in-arms that there is a Jewish issue in the Europe book—although of course he won't say it." This is especially curious, given that Davies's treatment of this subject was accorded just two sentences in the review. The ever-vigilant Davies thus accounts for the entirety of Rabb's criti-cism on this flimsy basis: And who are those "comrades-in-arms?" Elders, perhaps?

In fact, Davies is neither anti-Semitic, nor anti-Zionist, nor even pro-East European. He is merely pro-Polish. This is the key to the man, to the book, to the controversy. As he joked with an admiring audience in Chicago, *Europe: A History* was an attempt "to write another history of Poland in disguise." It is surely no accident that the only ruler since Charlemagne to get the capsule treatment in Davies's new book is a Pole. The book's obsessions and resent-ments and emphases are Polish: "East Europe" is, in this sense, a facade. Thus Tomáš Masaryk, the creator of Czechoslovakia, gets no entries in the index, and the formerly Polish provincial city of Lvov not only has more index entries than Manchester, Milan, and Marseille combined, but also more than Buda-pest, Bratislava, Bucharest, and Belgrade put together.

Davies's Polonophilia accounts for the sour tone and the historical inade-quacy of his description of the Enlightened Monarchies (they partitioned the lamented Polish-Lithuanian Republic), the Jews (they abandoned Poland) and the West since 1939 (it, too, abandoned Poland); and for the distorted, prejudiced version of Russian history from Peter I to Gorbachev as it is here presented. A capsule on "Pogroms" is inserted in this book solely for the purpose of excusing Poles from responsibility for a murderous riot in Lemberg (Lvov) in 1918. And Poland is given most of the credit for ending the cold war, to which end the international history and arms treaties of the 1980s are grotesquely mishandled. The self-pitying ressentiment of the "long-suffering author," as Davies has taken to describing himself, is perhaps a reflection of Poland's own sometime self-image as the sorely victimized "Christ of nations."

Davies's treatment of Russia and the Soviet Union is the most mischievous of all, and should alone disqualify the book as serious history. It is presented here as a counterpoint to what Davies darkly labels the "Allied Scheme of History." The latter, which has apparently dominated all Western scholarship since 1941, has a "demonological fascination" with Germany, is indulgent of Russia, is obsessed with the Atlantic community, and is uncaring and ignorant of Europe's eastern half. Once again, Davies goes so far over the top as to hit the wrong target altogether. To be sure, Yalta (or its aftermath) was a deal done over the heads of helpless victims (though a historian should tell the reader why this happened and what alternatives were available to Western policymakers at the time); and scholars and writers in the United States and Britain have sometimes been ignorant of the crimes and the complexities of the recent past in the lands east of Vienna. But the notion that Stalin's crimes are unknown or undiscussed is ridiculous. And how does Davies propose to redress the balance by claiming that "half a century after that war [World War II] was fought, the majority of episodes which contradict the Allied myth continue to be minimized or discounted?"

Davies has two lessons to teach. The first is that Russian history since the seventeenth century is one long, aggressive enterprise directed, mostly, at Poles. The Russian czars made deals with Prussia and Austria to destroy the Polish-Lithuanian Republic (1772–1795); they seized Polish land and they exiled Polish martyrs. They were responsible for the emergence of radical Zionism among Lithuanian Jews ("Littwaks"), who then came to Poland and upset the comity of Poles and Jews, with Poles being unfairly blamed for the subsequent upsurge in local anti-Semitism. The czars' Soviet successors made a deal with Germany once again (in 1939) to destroy Poland, after which Russians exiled Poles, massacred Polish officers (in Katyn), and yet again sent in disruptive Jews, this time as Communist policemen, causing renewed and understandable offense to Poles with unfortunate postwar local results (for the Jews). And nobody in the West knows or cares.

The second lesson seems to be that, as a consequence of our failure to see Russia straight, we have been unfair to Germany and to other enemies of Russia. Hence our obsession with the Holocaust, which was perpetrated by Germans, and our ignorance of Polish suffering, which came at least as much at Russian hands as at German hands and lasted for half a century. Davies even comes close to defending the actions of "Slovaks, Croats and Baltic nations" in the Second World War: they "were thought [sic!] to have rejected the friends of the West or to have collaborated with the enemy." The Allied bombing of Dresden in February 1945 gets its own capsule, naturally; but with a special twist. The bombing is presented as a response to a Soviet request for air support, and the German victims are described as "hundreds of thousands of refugees displaced by the Soviet advance." Thus the raid on Dresden becomes a form of Allied complicity in a Soviet-sponsored criminal undertaking. Predictably, perhaps, there is a footnote that refers to David Irving.

A capsule on the Carpathian city of Czernowitz is the occasion for Davies to bemoan Soviet responsibility for the reduction of "rich layers of local Jewish, Romanian, Polish and Ruthenian life . . . [to] a drab provincial backwater of Ukraine." There is no mention of the rather prominent role of the Nazis in expediting that reduction by destroying the single largest element in the communal mix. Finally, and with a thoroughly irresponsible insouciance, Davies inserts in his main text the suggestion by James Bacque that the United States, by means of studied neglect and worse, deliberately allowed German prisoners of war to die in very large numbers after 1945. Only those readers who find their way to footnote four on page 1,170 will learn that this thesis has been "vehemently contested" by credible historians. Actually, it has been thoroughly discredited, and its author with it. Maybe Davies doesn't know that.

Léon Blum once called the French Communists a "foreign national party." Norman Davies is a foreign national historian. He has "gone native," and has taken upon himself the prejudices characteristic of some of his adopted compatriots. His case is not unique. Keith Hitchins, the American author of the recently published *Oxford History of Romania,* is another such historian, and his book, too, is largely vitiated by being written from within the assumptions of a certain popular version of the local national story.

Such total identification with one's subject is surely not a necessary condition of close, empathetic scholarship. The late Richard Cobb, the Oxford-based historian of the French Revolution, understood very well that his immersion in France constituted, as he put it in one of his books, a "Second Identity"—and for scholarly purposes he always reverted to his first one. Moreover, Cobb worked steadily against the flow of contemporary French prejudices; his life's work was a standing refutation of the dominant national revolutionary myth of modern France. The late A. J. P. Taylor, another great British iconoclastic historian, and one whom Davies admires, constitutes a similar counterexample to Davies's own misunderstanding of historical method. Taylor, too, made a career of shocking his fellow scholars and rubbing conventional opinion the wrong way. But he was meticulous with the facts; and he wrote against the grain of his own prejudices. Taylor cordially disliked Germany, but his most controversial book, *The Origins of the Second World War,* is a brilliantly misconceived attempt to relieve Hitler of responsibility for World War II. The idea that one might produce better history by setting oneself in opposition to national clichés and national consolations seems never to have occurred to Norman Davies, for all his easy shots at the "Allied Scheme."

Why, then, was this book received with such acclaim in Britain? (It took some time for the more considered responses to come in.) To be sure, British academic reviewers noted some of its shortcomings, but almost without exception they concluded that, notwithstanding its "indulgence towards ... wartime Axis collaborators" (Michael Burleigh), its "embarrassing number of errors" (Adam Roberts), the "callous impression" left by its juxtapositions (Neal Ascherson), its "gobbets of journalistic erudition" (Felipe Fernandez-Armesto), and its "self-indulgence" (Timothy Blanning and Raymond Carr), it is a great work of history. Few reviewers questioned the claims that Davies advances on his own behalf or the use that he makes of his sources.

One answer might be that British book reviewing, once so acerbic and unforgiving, has had its teeth drawn by the recently inaugurated system of centralized academic appraisal, whereby points (and money) are given to universities according to the achievements of their faculty as assessed by outsiders. Until this year Norman Davies was a senior professor at London University, and the habit of being nice to powerful colleagues in the hope that they will return the favor when it comes time for peer review may have permeated, however unconsciously, the mental dispositions of his reviewers. Whether or not this is so, it cannot explain why Professor Blanning of Cambridge University should have felt constrained in the *TLS* (under the heading "Gibbon Goes East") to restrict his comments on Davies's insensitive 'juxtapositions" to the disturbing remark that "great will be the offence taken in certain quarters at certain passages." This is a disgraceful dodge. Either Davies's passages are offensive, in which case Blanning should say so and draw the appropriate conclusions; or they are not offensive, in which case we must conclude that our ethical and scholarly sensibilities in such matters are bounded by ethnic or religious allegiances. This is a glib multiculturalist excuse for an abdication of critical responsibility, and one does not expect to come across it in such quarters.

Another explanation might be sought in the remarkable publicity campaign conducted on behalf of this book. The urge to console themselves for Britain's shrunken international status may account for a *London Times* editorial promoting Davies's book with the headline "A Great New Work by a Great British Scholar," or for Noel Malcolm's hymn of praise in the *London Sunday Telegraph* to the "vitality of our historical writing ... surely the most extraordinary unsung glory of contemporary British cultural life." Still, journalists in London were rounded up not just to praise Davies, but also to cast into the outer darkness all competitors. One reviewer, in London's *Daily Telegraph*, sneered at recent histories of Europe by John Merriman and John Roberts as "'meaner beauties of the night' when set against the moon that is Professor Davies." Another reviewer, in *History Today*, dismissed Davies's errors as "inattention to detail," while condemning for its mistakes of fact a work by the French historian Marc Ferro, concluding sniffily of the latter: "In areas where the reader is unsure of the facts in advance, it is impossible to trust the author." Two weights, two measures.

In the *London Review of Books*, Neal Ascherson, whom Davies elsewhere calls a "fellow spirit" (that is, another besieged admirer of Eastern Europe), invoked the Stanford affair while pompously advising British readers that they were "entitled to know something of the background" to any American criticism of Norman Davies. And a London columnist named Anne Applebaum used her own review as an occasion to attack the "spouters of clichés" who seek to silence Davies for questioning the "Allied Scheme of History"— that "Scheme" which "makes anyone like Norman Davies, who has devoted his career to those nasty East Europeans, seem somewhat suspect." Applebaum has actually reviewed Davies's book three times, and with each review her aggression toward the "enemies" of Davies seems to grow fiercer. There is even an ominous threat: If the spouters of clichés win this round as well, *Europe: A History* may be the last book "as enjoyable as this" to appear in the U.S. (Like Davies, she blames Oxford University Press for the book's mistakes. She even manages the distinctly unpleasant suggestion that they are really all the consequence of the Press's decision to have the book copyedited in India. American readers can get a flavor of Applebaum's innuendoes in the May issue of *The New Criterion*.)

It is a melancholy reflection on the culture as a whole that it is so desperate to find a "flagship" historian, a "great British scholar," that it should have fallen over itself to overlook his factual, methodological, and interpretative failings; to forgive him his unfortunate locutions; and to take at face value

Davies's own account of the qualities of his book. For *Europe: A History* is not just full of error, disproportion, prejudice, resentment, and boastfulness. It is also strikingly conventional. Finally this is just another old-fashioned kings-and-wars history of Europe, with an unusually large number of Polish examples. If you want something original, you should look elsewhere. And if you want a conventional history of Europe, there are better ones out there (including the work of the much-maligned John Roberts, whose *History of Europe* is about to be published here by Viking). They are not marred by academic squabbles and geopolitical grudges, and they get the facts right, too.

This review of *Europe: A History* by Norman Davies first appeared in the *New Republic* in September 1997.

CHAPTER IV

Why the Cold War Worked

I.

Postwar London, where I grew up, was a world fueled by coal and driven by steam, where market vendors still used horses, where motor cars were uncommon and supermarkets (and much of what they sell) unknown. In its social geography, its climate and environment, its class relations and political alignments, its industrial trades, and its habits of social deference, London in 1950 would have been immediately recognizable to an observer from half a century before. Even the great "Socialist" projects of the postwar Labour governments were really the late flowering of the reforming ideas of Edwardian-era Liberals. Much had changed, of course; in Britain as in the rest of Europe war and economic decline had changed the physical and moral landscape. Yet for just that reason the distant past seemed closer and more familiar than ever. In important ways, mid-twentieth-century London was still a late-nineteenth-century city. Even so, the cold war had long since begun.

It is helpful to understand just how different the world was fifty years ago if we are to appreciate a point on which John Gaddis lays much emphasis in his excellent book.* The cold war lasted a very long time—forty-three years,

---

* John Lewis Gaddis, *We Now Know: Rethinking Cold War History* (New York: Oxford University Press, 1997).

from the collapse of postwar negotiations with the USSR in 1947 to the unification of Germany in 1990. That is considerably longer than the interminable wars of the French Revolution and Napoleon, longer than the infamous Thirty Years' War of the seventeenth century, and just one year short of the span of time separating, say, the death of Thomas Jefferson from the birth of Lenin.

In 1951, at the height of the Korean War, Europe was governed by men from a very different age: the British prime minister, Winston Churchill, and the German chancellor, Konrad Adenauer, had both been born shortly after the first unification of Germany under Bismarck's Prussia (in 1874 and 1876, respectively); and Bismarck was still the dominant figure on the international diplomatic scene when they first took cognizance of public affairs. Even their "younger" contemporaries, like the Italian Christian Democratic leader Alcide de Gasperi or Josef Stalin himself, had come to maturity a decade before the outbreak of the First World War, and their views on politics and especially on international relations had been forged by the configurations and conflicts of an earlier time. Before we too readily conflate the cold war with the dilemmas of the post-atomic age, we should keep in mind that the men who first fought it could not help but see the world through a very different lens.

HIS SENSITIVITY TO THIS CONSIDERATION is one of the many qualities of Gaddis's book, which is not so much a history of the cold war as a series of essays, in loosely chronological order, on the major themes and crises that marked it—the division of Europe, the German question, conflicts in Asia, the paradoxes of nuclear strategy, and so forth. Gaddis writes clearly, takes a commonsense and mostly unpolemical approach to highly contested and volatile debates, and has an impressive knowledge of the English-language secondary literature on a daunting range of topics. He has already written four full-length studies of the cold war era, all drawing on his expertise in the history of U.S. foreign policy.[1] But in this book he has tried to bring together the copious body of material that has been discovered since in the Soviet and East European archives, as well as revelations from recently released U.S.

sources, and to weave them all into a general interpretation covering the present state of our knowledge.

Hence the perhaps unfortunate title of the book. Correctly inflected, with the emphasis on "now," it suggests that Gaddis is summarizing the present state of our knowledge of the history of the last fifty years, on the understanding that things may look different when we learn more. But readers, like some reviewers, may be tempted to read it as an assertion of confident finality: we now know what happened and why. That would be a pity, for Gaddis is entirely aware of the danger of overestimating the knowledge and understanding to be gained from newly opened archives, however promising they may appear. An "archive," after all, whether it contains the minutes of Communist Party discussions, the intercepted transmissions of foreign governments, reports from spies, or even a police list of informers and "collaborators," is not a fount of truth. The motives and goals of those creating the documents, the limits of their own knowledge, the incorporation of gossip or flattery into a report for someone senior, the distortions of ideology or prejudice have all to be taken into account.

Even if we could somehow be assured of both the truth and the significance of a given source, no document can ever surface that will finally settle a major historical controversy—the archives of eighteenth-century France, for example, have been open for many generations now without putting an end to acrimonious historiographical debates over the origins and meaning of the French Revolution. In the case of the cold war we do not even know for certain what documentary materials we still lack (from both sides), though the inaccessibility of the archives of the president of the Russian Federation certainly means that historians remain unable to describe Soviet-era decisions or decision-taking at the highest level.[2] For all these reasons caution is required. The selective and politically motivated release of archives and personal files in former Communist countries has done much harm; the publication (especially in France) of popular histories that ransack newly accessible Soviet and East European archives to "reveal" past traitors has brought some discredit upon the whole enterprise.[3]

GADDIS IS CAUTIOUS. He makes full use of the work done by scholars who
have used the Russian Center for the Conservation and Study of Records for
Modern History and of the *Bulletin of the Cold War International History Project*, the periodical in which much of the newly researched material is discussed. But he uses this material mostly for illustrative purposes, and only
rarely—as in the case of Kim Il Sung's correspondence with Stalin in 1950—
to stake a firm interpretive claim: he concludes that Stalin was at first reluctant to back Kim's aggressive designs, and only agreed to support him once it
was clear that the initiative and responsibility would rest with the Chinese.

Like the specialists whose work he uses, he recognizes that however interesting the new materials, they are not telling us things about which we were
utterly ignorant. Thanks to the selective documentation published by the Yugoslavs during their quarrel with Stalin, for example, or material released
during brief moments of "reform Communism" in Poland (in 1956) and
Czechoslovakia (in 1968), the internal history of decisions and conflicts within
the Soviet bloc has never been a complete blank.

Indeed, in the light of the new information now being published and debated, it is striking how much we already "knew." When we take account of
the memoirs of participants from all sides, partial primary documentation,
perceptive firsthand observation, and discriminating historical analysis, the
history of the cold war has been available to us all along. In the words of two
scholars who have made copious use of the new primary documentation, it
now seems clear that "Western 'Cold War' historiography of Soviet domination of [Eastern Europe] was fundamentally on target."[4] The failure of some
Western politicians (and scholars) to grasp the nature of the cold war, especially in its early days, derived less from a shortage of documentation than
from a failure of imagination. In George Kennan's words, "Our national leaders in Washington had no idea at all, and would probably have been incapable
of imagining, what a Soviet occupation, supported by the Russian secret police
of Beria's time, meant for the peoples who were subjected to it."[5]

THE USE TO WHICH new materials can be put to deepen our understanding of a particular moment in cold war history is nicely illustrated by the recent co-publication, under the auspices of the Fondazione Giangiacomo Feltrinelli and the Russian Center for the Conservation of Records, of the complete minutes of the three conferences of the Cominform, 1947–1949, together with a full scholarly apparatus of introductions and annotations.* The Cominform was established by the Soviet Union in 1947 ostensibly to serve as a clearinghouse for the exchange of information (and instructions) between Moscow and the Communist parties of Eastern and Central Europe as well as those of Italy and France.

At its first, September 1947, meeting at Sklarska Poreba, in Poland, Andrei Zhdanov laid out the line that the West and the Soviet Union were to be seen as two irreconcilable "camps," the view that was to serve as the doctrinal basis for Soviet foreign policy until Stalin's death. At the Cominform's second meeting, in Bucharest in June 1948, the Soviet-Yugoslav conflict was brought into the open and the "Titoist" heresy was defined and condemned; the "struggle against Titoism" would then be used to shape and justify the persecutions and show trials of the following years. Its last meeting, in Hungary in November 1949, served only to confirm the now rigid domestic and internal lines of Communist policy. Thereafter the activities of the Cominform were confined to the publication of a newsletter and it was finally abandoned in 1956, overtaken by the changes of the Khrushchev era.

The Cominform is important because its founding and the proceedings of its conferences, especially the first, are a vital clue to the motives and timing of the apparent Communist shift during 1947 to confrontation with the Western powers. We have always been quite well informed about it. Both of the Yugoslav delegates to the first conference, Milovan Djilas and Edvard Kardelj, have

---

* Giuliano Procacci, ed., *The Cominform: Minutes of the Three Conferences, 1947/1948/1949* (Milan: Fondazione Giangiacomo Feltrinelli, 1994).

published their memoirs. One of the two Italian delegates, Eugenio Reale, later left the Italian Communist Party and wrote a book describing his experiences at the founding Cominform meeting. The Yugoslav government published selections of its own correspondence with Stalin and other documents dating from the preparation of the second conference in order to defend itself against Stalin's charges. The Cominform published its own bowdlerized account of its proceedings. What more can we hope to learn from the complete minutes?[6]

The records of the Cominform, together with the preparatory materials discovered in Russian archives, permit us to see things somewhat differently in three respects, and they are not insignificant. In the first place, and this confirms something that emerges from Norman Naimark's recent study of the Soviet occupation of eastern Germany, Stalin was by no means clear in his own mind over how to proceed in his zone of European influence.[7] His underlying strategy was never in question—to gain full and permanent Communist control of every state in the region. But the tactical options remained open. As late as June 1946, in a conversation with Tito, Stalin said he was firmly opposed to a resurrection in any form of the old, centralized Comintern which had exercised rigid control and issued detailed instructions to all Communist parties from Moscow and had been shut down in 1943. But the proposal of the Marshall Plan in 1947, and the unresolved division of Germany, led Stalin, in any case chronically predisposed to perceive a Western threat even when none existed, to seek tighter doctrinal and administrative control over all the Communist parties of Central Europe, especially those like the Czechs who were still under the illusion that they might pursue a distinctive "road" to Socialism. The various drafts of Zhdanov's Cominform speech, as they were prepared during the summer of 1947, reveal a progressive clarification, a hardening of the line.

Second, the relative disarray of international Communism in the immediate postwar years is now clearer than it once was. The tactics of the Italian and French Communists, seeking to capitalize on their Resistance aura and obtain power through parliamentary means, had failed by May 1947, when they, like the Belgian Communists, left their coalition governments. At the Cominform meeting in Poland they were duly attacked by the Russians and the Yugoslavs for their lack of revolutionary fervor, for their erstwhile commitment to a non-revolutionary path to power, and for their failure to anticipate the "changed circumstances" that led Stalin, via Zhdanov, to denounce the path of "peaceful coexistence." It was long supposed, and Eugenio Reale in particular insisted on this point, that criticism of the French and Italians for their "right-wing deviationism" was a Soviet ploy to shift onto the hapless Western Communist parties the blame for the failure of Moscow's own previous tactic of "cooperation" with the former allies in Western Europe.

But it now seems possible, from a letter by Zhdanov to the French Communist leader Maurice Thorez, dated June 2, 1947, a copy of which was sent to other Communist chiefs (one was recently discovered in the Party archives in Prague), that Moscow was at times as much in the dark about the tactics of the French CP as anyone else: "Many think that the French Communists coordinated their activities [with Moscow]. You know this is not true. Your steps were a total surprise to us." The Cominform, then, really was established to put an end to the comparative tactical anarchy that had seeped into the Communist camp during and after the war. In this it was a complete success. Suitably chagrined, even the Italians cleaved assiduously to the Moscow line thenceforth, at some cost to their own domestic political credibility. As late as April 1963, long after the dismantling of the Cominform and shortly before his death, Palmiro Togliatti, the historic leader of the Partito Communista Italiano (PCI), wrote to Antonin Novotny, Dubček's predecessor as general secretary of the Czech Communist Party, begging him to postpone the forthcoming public "rehabilitation" of Rudolf Slánsky and the other victims of the December 1952 Prague trial. Such an announcement, he wrote (implicitly acknowledging the PCI's complicity in defending the show trials of the early fifties), "would unleash a furious campaign against us, bringing to the fore all the most idiotic and provocative anti-Communist themes [*i temi più stupidi e provocatori dell'anticommunismo*] and hurting us in the forthcoming elections."[8]

Thirdly, and in contrast with interpretations based on the memory of participants who had no firsthand knowledge of Soviet intentions, we now know that the Cominform was not brought into being for the purpose of trying to pull the Yugoslavs into line, even though it acquired that function in due course. To be sure, Tito was a nagging problem for Stalin and had been since 1945. The Yugoslav efforts to acquire parts of Austrian Carinthia and the Istrian city of Trieste were an embarrassment to Stalin in his dealings with the Western allies, and an impediment to the domestic progress of the Italian Communists especially. Tito's initial support for the Greek Communists was similarly embarrassing, since Greece fell unambiguously into the Western "sphere." Yugoslav ambitions to create and lead a Balkan Federation incorporating Albania and Bulgaria ran afoul of Stalin's preference for maintaining his own direct control over each country in his sphere of influence. And the unabashedly revolutionary domestic policies of the Yugoslav Party—which held power without the constraint of alliances with "friendly" parties and was thus far more radical and ruthless than other East European Communists— risked putting in the shade the Soviet model. In matters of revolution Tito was becoming more Catholic than the Soviet pope.

IN SPITE OF THIS, the Cominform was not set in place as a device to bring the Yugoslavs to order. The attack on the French and Italians at the Sklarska Poreba meeting in 1947 was led by the Yugoslav delegates with self-righteous fervor and not a little arrogance—which helps account for the enthusiasm with which those same French and Italian Communists welcomed the Yugoslavs' later fall from favor, and for the stridently anti-Titoist ardor of the French and Italian Communist leadership in years to come.[9] But the Yugoslavs were not just following Soviet orders in a devious, Machiavellian scheme, as later commentators supposed. Zhdanov's own drafts for his critique of the Western Communists were no less hostile than those of his Balkan comrades, and the Yugoslavs, for their part, clearly believed everything they said. Certainly it was part of Stalin's technique to mobilize one set of deviants against another, only to deal with the first group later on, a method he had perfected in the intraparty struggles of the 1920s. But although the "leftist" heresy of Titoism was duly condemned the following year, there appears to be no evidence that this was planned in 1947.

The newly exploited sources for the history of the Cominform, then, will not change the broad picture dramatically. But they allow us to amend our understanding in small matters, and the accumulation of such amendments enables us to construct a more accurate and finely meshed picture. How does the overall story now look? To begin with, the cold war always existed in Stalin's head and in one version of the Soviet world picture. Nothing Western statesmen did or didn't do would have altered that. But beyond his determination to control a significant zone of Europe, Stalin had no ambitious master plan—indeed, he was markedly averse to taking risks. In Molotov's words, "our ideology stands for offensive operations when possible, and if not, we wait."[10] It probably follows from this that the policy of "containment" adopted in 1947 might well have worked earlier than it did, had it been attempted. But whenever it was applied, it did not "begin" the cold war.

ONE REASON FOR THIS IS that the "Sovietization" of Eastern Europe and the eastern zone of Germany, while it was not part of a fully worked-out scheme, was probably inevitable under the circumstances. As Norman Naimark wisely remarks, "Soviet officers bolshevized the zone not because there was a plan to do so, but because that was the only way they knew to organize society."[11] Much the same applies to the treatment meted out to other countries of Eastern Europe. Nothing short of the expulsion of the Red Army troops could have prevented this outcome, and no Western leader seriously considered an attempt to expel them. And once tight Soviet control had been established, Western policymakers had little choice but to suppose that it would be applied further west, if opportunity permitted, and to plan accordingly. It now seems unlikely that Stalin would have seriously contemplated moving further west. But in Gaddis's words, "It would be the height of arrogance for historians to condemn those who made history for not having availed themselves of histories yet to be written. Nightmares always seem real at the time—even if, in the clear light of dawn, a little ridiculous."

Once the battle lines were clearly drawn, in Europe at least, there seem to have been very few "missed opportunities" for erasing them. The most famous of these, Stalin's suggestion of March 1952 for an agreement to disengage in Germany, can now be seen for what its critics at the time took it to be: a readiness to sacrifice East Germany, certainly, but only in exchange for a united but "neutral" Germany under effective Soviet domination. The centrality of the future of a divided Germany, and more generally of Europe, in the shaping of the cold war is also very clear. Conflicts in Korea, Malaya, Cuba, Vietnam, or Angola, bloody as they were, remained peripheral to the main contest in Europe, at least until the series of crises and confrontations over Berlin (1948–1949, 1953, 1958–1961) was brought to an end with the building in August 1961 of the Berlin Wall—when both Great Powers, whatever they said in public, heaved a private sigh of relief.

It is perhaps odd, in retrospect, that the wartime Allies should have gone to such enormous trouble and nearly come to blows in order to protect the interests of client states in the land of their former enemy. But it is a characteristic of cold wars (ours was not the first) that they concentrate contention on symbols—and the unresolved status of Germany was the symbol of the unfinished postwar settlement. For this reason the rulers of West and East Germany alike were able for many years to exercise a leverage over Great Power politics utterly disproportionate to their own strength or importance.

II.

There was no room for maneuver in Europe; each side depended on an arsenal (the Soviets on conventional ground forces, NATO on airborne atomic weapons) in which it was vastly superior to its foe. In view of this stalemate, movement and misunderstanding were likely to take place elsewhere. The recent evidence available shows that Harry Truman and other Western leaders were wrong to suppose that the North Korean attack on the South was intended by Stalin either to divert both the attention and the military forces of the Western powers or as a prelude to an attack in Europe—but they did believe this, and their reaction, to strengthen NATO and propose the rearmament of West Germany, was rational and prudent in the circumstances.

Unfortunately, the propensity to treat events elsewhere as indicators or replicas of the situation in Europe, rather than as processes at work in the non-European world, characterized much U.S. policy in the coming decades, from John Foster Dulles's "bungling" in the Middle East, as Gaddis puts it, to the disaster of Vietnam. But this tendency derived from the understanding that whatever happened elsewhere in the world, the cold war was about Europe; it was in Europe that it must be prevented from heating up, and only in Europe could it be ended. As we now know, this was very much the way things looked from the Kremlin, too. Stalin supported Kim Il Sung's aggression with reluctance, and he and his successors expressed grave reservations about the impetuousness of Mao Tse-tung. But in the end they condoned risks in Korea, Vietnam, and elsewhere that they would never have approved in Germany or the Balkans.

ACCESS TO THE ARCHIVES closes off a number of avenues of interpretation that remained stubbornly open until after the fall of the Soviet Union. "Revisionism," the wishful search for evidence that the United States bore primary responsibility for the origin and pursuit of the cold war, is now a dead duck. Certainly the West, especially Western Europe, gained much from the division of Europe and the world into spheres of influence, but this was far from clear in 1947. In any case it was not the Americans but the British, Foreign Secretary Ernest Bevin in particular, who first came to the conclusion that it might be just as well if postwar efforts to resolve the German question were put on ice. American negotiators, in the Rooseveltian tradition, took rather longer to disengage from the search for agreement with the Russians. An alternative revisionist strategy was to suggest that the cold war, and its related hot conflicts, were the outcome of social and political processes set in motion long before. It might seem as though someone was responsible for starting something, but in practice blame could not be assigned to one side or the other. In Bruce Cumings's words, "Who started the Korean War? This question should not be asked."[12] But except in the trivial sense that all immediate causes have long-term determinants, this position is no longer tenable. With the benefit of somewhat better information we can, now, assign responsibility mostly to the USSR for, among other events, the breakdown of German negotiations in 1947, the outbreak of the Korean War, various confrontations over Berlin.

The revisionist search for evidence of Western guilt was sometimes associated with a cultivated distaste in scholarly circles for the notion that "intelligence" mattered in the making of history, that spies seriously affected the course of events. In view of the intelligence community's miserable record (on both sides) when it came to predicting outcomes, this is an understandable prejudice, but it turns out to be mistaken. Spies were quite important in the cold war, the early years especially, and not only in the famous theft of atomic secrets. The French foreign ministry, like the British ruling class, leaked exuberantly for many years and provided Moscow's Paris embassy, as well as the Soviet agents in Berlin, with a steady stream of inside information. The Soviet intelligence network was distinctly superior to that of the West—as well it might be, since it had been in place in some countries since the late twenties. Its weakness lay in the inability of the Moscow leadership to hear, or understand, what its agents were trying to tell it—a long-standing problem in the USSR, which in its most egregious instance led Stalin in the spring of 1941 to reject all warnings that Hitler was about to attack. As Dean Acheson once noted in another context, "We were fortunate in our opponent."[13]

Conversely, many of those Western analysts of the cold war who did understand the role of intelligence, and more generally of *Realpolitik*, in the international affairs of the age did not always grasp that if the Soviet Union behaved like a great power in its pursuit of its interests, it was nonetheless not just another empire; it was a Communist empire. One of the most interesting revelations of the new source material, and Gaddis pays it due attention, is the place of ideology in the thinking of Soviet leaders. On this there were for a long time three competing schools of thought. The first held that Soviet policymakers should be regarded as behaving and thinking roughly like Americans: playing off domestic interest groups, calculating economic or military advantage, and pursuing goals convergent, albeit competitive, with those of their Western opponents. The public language they used when pursuing these goals was neither here nor there.

The second school insisted that Soviet policymakers were the heirs of the Tsars: their first concern was the geopolitical interests of Russia. Their ideological language should be treated as a contingent and secondary feature and need not be taken too much into account when dealing with them. A third group argued that the Soviet Union was a Communist state, and that the terms in which its leaders described the world were also the terms in which they understood it; therefore their ideological presuppositions were the most important thing to know about them.

THE FIRST SCHOOL DOMINATED U.S. "Sovietology" for many years but is now defunct, along with the political system it so miserably failed to understand. The second school, whose most sophisticated spokesman was George Kennan, clearly had a case. Even if we knew little of Communism we could still make reasonably good sense of Soviet foreign policy in the years between 1939 and 1990 by reference to "conventional" diplomatic criteria alone, given an informed appreciation of Russian history. Moreover, no one who ever had any dealings with the last generation of Communist "apparatchiks" in Eastern Europe would ever suppose that these were men driven by higher ideals or the search for doctrinal consistency for its own sake. Nonetheless, it now seems clear that ideology did play a role in the thinking of Soviet leaders in the cold war era, from Stalin to Gorbachev. Like Truman, Eisenhower, or Kennedy, their understanding of the world was shaped by their presuppositions about it. In the Soviet case those presuppositions were basically Marxist, which by the time of Stalin's death denoted little more than crude economic determinism spiced with the expectation of ultimate victory on the international battle-ground of class.

What that meant in practice, for example, was that when Andrei Zhdanov learned of the Truman Doctrine he referred to it in his report for the first Cominform meeting as growing evidence of an Anglo-American rift, because of the U.S. "expulsion of Britain from its sphere of influence in the Mediter-ranean and the Near East." Truman himself was described in an internal 1946 Kremlin memo exclusively in terms of the economic interests ("circles of American monopoly capital") he purportedly represented. Berlin-based intel-ligence officials consistently analyzed the behavior and discussions of Western leaders (about which they were otherwise well informed) as deriving from the "economic tensions" among them, and so on.

Again and again the behavior of the West was thus reduced to hypotheti-cal motives and interests that were exclusively economic. It doesn't ultimately matter whether everyone, from Molotov to the lowliest intelligence operative or party functionary, "really" believed what they said; the point is that every-thing they said, to one another as well as to the outside world, was couched in this wooden, twilight language. Even Gorbachev—or perhaps above all Gorbachev, who was a product of three generations of "Marxist" political pedagogy—thought and often spoke thus, which is why he was genuinely taken aback at the outcome of his own actions.

JOHN GADDIS RIGHTLY CRITICIZES WESTERN "realists" for failing to understand that men are motivated by what they think and believe and not just by objective or measurable interests. But he goes a little further. The cold war's move out of its European birthplace, through Asia and on into the most unlikely places—Mozambique, Ethiopia, Somalia, Angola, and especially Cuba—was what he calls, referring to Khrushchev and Brezhnev, "a pattern of geriatric over-exertion." In their old age, he thinks, these men were rediscover-ing in exotic locales the revolutionary romance of their Russian youth—no longer aging Communist apparatchiks, they were once again revolutionary Bolsheviks—albeit working through intermediaries. This seems perhaps over-imaginative, and anyway redundant. Why can we not agree that the history of the Soviet Union (and thus of the cold war) makes no sense unless we take seriously the ideological outlook of its leaders, while at the same time conceding with Molotov that they were in the business of advancing their political interests whenever and wherever the chance arose? Of course they invoked the case for revolution when justifying interventions abroad—and in Khrushchev's case he was truly moved to enthusiasm by the Cubans, as we know from his memoirs. But interest, belief, and emotion are not inherently incompatible sources of human behavior.

The emphasis upon the "geriatric" delusions of the Soviet leadership brings us back to my starting point. From the perspective of the United States—and until recently most writings on the history of the cold war have perforce been written from the point of view of the United States in particular—the cold war began in 1947 with the collapse of the wartime Allied coalition. As John Lukacs has noted, there was a dramatic and unprecedented policy shift in Washington over a period of about eighteen months in the years 1946–1947, and American state policy and public opinion have not been the same since.[14] Gaddis, however, wants us to understand the cold war from a different perspective, as an organic outgrowth of the Second World War itself—and particularly of Stalin's desire to absorb the new territory occupied by his armies—rather than a sort of unfortunate international traffic accident that befell the world in that war's aftermath. But why not go a little further? From the point of view of contemporaries, after all, Europe in 1945 was not just a prelude to some unknown future; it was also the heir to a real and well-remembered past.

From the perspective of a European statesman looking at the years 1900–1945—and most senior leaders were in a position to do so from personal recollection and involvement—Europe (and therefore the world) faced four related dilemmas: how to restore the international balance upset by the rise of a Prussian-dominated Germany after 1871; how to bring Russia back into the concert of nations in some stable way, following the distortions produced by the Russian Revolution and its international aftermath; how to rescue the international economy from the disastrous collapse of the interwar years and somehow recapture the growth and stability of the pre-1914 era; and how to compensate for the anticipated decline of Great Britain as an economic and political factor in international affairs.

Between 1944 and 1947 a variety of possible solutions to these problems was debated, and all of them presumed a degree of continuity with the past. The French would have gone a long way to get a Russian alliance, on the model of that of 1894, but France no longer had anything to offer the Russians in return.[15] Many West Germans, Adenauer in particular, were not at all averse to abandoning the Prussian east—which as Catholic Rhinelanders they in any case cordially disliked and feared—in exchange for closer ties to the historically familiar lands to their west. The French Socialist leader Léon Blum (born in 1872) shared Winston Churchill's forward-looking enthusiasm for a Western European community to compensate for the drastically weakened condition of the region's separate nation-states. And Stalin, echoing the imperatives of a long Great Russian history as well as the lessons of the recent past, saw a chance to take advantage of German weakness (much as his predecessors had exploited that of eighteenth-century Poland) in order to secure the USSR's imperial hinterland in the west.

WHAT MADE THESE FAMILIAR STRATEGIES difficult to pursue in the circumstances of 1945 was, first, the existence of independent states in the space separating Russia from Germany; second the distinctive character of the Russo-Soviet regime itself; and thirdly the absence of sufficient countervailing power to Germany's west. Before World War I none of these impediments had existed. In 1914 the Baltic states, Poland, Czechoslovakia, Hungary, Yugoslavia, and much of Romania lay within the borders of German, Austrian, Turkish, or Russian empires. The independence of these countries established at Versailles in 1919 could not be sustained—as Hitler had demonstrated and

Stalin was now confirming—without the very sort of will and power that the Western Europeans failed to exercise in 1938 and did not have in 1945. But the fact that they had now known independence made Russian occupation particularly repugnant. Meanwhile, the nature of the Communist regime made its imperial ambition much more threatening to a war-weakened Western Europe than the Tsarist designs on Central or Southeastern Europe in days past. And Britain's economic exhaustion, combined with the disappearance of France as a factor in international politics, gave the leaders of these countries no option but to persuade the United States to take their place.

In these circumstances the cold war represented not a problem but a solution, which is one reason why it lasted so long. By bringing America into Europe to provide security against further change, the West Europeans assured themselves of the stability and protection required for the reconstruction of their half of the continent. Ironically, the United States thus behaved much as Tsarist Russia had for two decades following Napoleon's defeat in 1815, i.e., as a sort of continental policeman whose presence guaranteed that there would be no further disruption of the status quo by an unruly revolutionary power. The Soviet Union meanwhile was left to get on with the dictatorial governance of its half of the continent, with a promise of noninterference in return for its abstention from further adventures—an arrangement that was actually quite satisfactory to Stalin and his heirs.[16] This was hardly an outcome calculated to please the millions of Poles and others thereby incarcerated under "Socialist" rule; but since they had not been regarded by most Allied policymakers as part of the problem, it is hardly surprising that they did not figure prominently in the solution, either.

Seen thus, the cold war can take its place in the *longue durée* of European and international history. Complications arose for two reasons. First, alignments and divisions in Europe became intertwined with the politics of national independence movements and of decolonization in Asia, Africa, Latin America, and the Middle East, with seriously misleading consequences for all parties involved. From 1956 to 1974 there grew up a curious commerce: Western Europe and the United States exported nineteenth-century liberal ideas and institutions to the developing world, holding the capitalist West up as a model for emulation and urging the adoption of its customs and practices; they received in exchange revolutionary myths and prototypes calculated to challenge their own bland (and relative) prosperity. The Soviet Union engaged in a similar trade. It, too, exported a nineteenth-century ideology—Marxist Socialism—and received in return the rather spurious fealty of fresh would-be revolutionaries, whose activities cast a brief, retroactive glow of credibility upon the faded Bolshevik heritage.

The second complication was the presence of nuclear weapons. For a long time these added confusion, and thus risk, to the making of policy. The Soviet Union was nearly always far behind in the arms race (though the well-oiled techniques of Prince Potemkin's heirs kept this fact hidden from the United States for many years); but this inferiority only inclined its leaders to strike compensatory aggressive poses. U.S. policymakers, meanwhile, took many years (and spent inordinate sums of money) to learn what Truman appears to have grasped instinctively from the start—that nuclear weapons were strikingly unhelpful as instruments of statecraft. In contrast to spears, they really were only good for sitting on. Nonetheless, as a deterrent device a nuclear arsenal had its uses—but only if both you and your opponent could be convinced that it might, ultimately, be deployed. For this reason the cold war for many years sustained a prospect of terror out of all proportion to the issues at stake—or the intentions of most of the participants.

Because of these two new elements, the cold war seemed to change its nature and become something radically different from anything that had gone before. And when it ended, with the collapse of one adversary, there were therefore some who supposed that we had entered a new era in human history. Since 1990 we can see that this was not altogether the case. The world has certainly changed utterly since 1950: the horses are gone and so has the coal, together with the social dispositions and forms of work that they symbolized. The great reforming projects are gone, too, at least for the time being. But now that we won the cold war we can see better than we could before that some of the dilemmas it addressed (or screened from view) are still with us. Recent history suggests that the solution will be as elusive as ever.

This essay, a review of *We Now Know: Rethinking Cold War History* by John Lewis Gaddis and *The Cominform: Minutes of the Three Conferences 1947/1948/1949*, edited by Giuliano Procacci, first appeared in *The New York Review of Books* in October 1997.

Notes to Chapter IV

[1] *The United States and the Origins of the Cold War, 1941–1947* (New York: Columbia University Press, 1972); *The Long Peace: Inquiries into the History of the Cold War* (New York: Oxford University Press, 1987); *Strategies of Containment: A Critical Appraisal of Postwar American National Security Policy* (New York: Oxford University Press, 1982); *The United States and the End of the Cold War: Implications, Reconsiderations, Provocations* (New York: Oxford University Press, 1992).

[2] See the discussion in Norman Naimark and Leonid Gibianskii, eds., *The Establishment of Communist Regimes in Eastern Europe, 1944–1949* (Boulder, CO: Westview, 1997), Introduction, pp. 1–17.

[3] See, e.g., the publications of Thierry Wolton: *Le Grand Recrutement* (Paris: Grasset, 1993) and *La France sous influence* (Paris: Grasset, 1997). A recent book by Karel Bartosek, *Les Aveux des Archives: Prague-Paris-Prague 1948–1968* (Paris: Seuil, 1996), created a stir by claiming that Czech archives reveal Artur London to have remained in the service of the Czech authorities long after his release from prison and the publication of his acclaimed autobiographical account of the show trials, *L'Aveu* (The Confession). Bartosek made copious use of hitherto secret archives, but the evidence he accumulated is suggestive and circumstantial rather than conclusive.

[4] Naimark and Gibianskii, *The Establishment of Communist Regimes,* Introduction, pp. 9–10. See, e.g., Hugh Seton-Watson, *The East European Revolution* (London: Methuen, 1950), Adam B. Ulam, *Titoism and the Cominform* (Cambridge, MA: Harvard University Press, 1952), and Vojtech Mastny, *Russia's Road to Cold War* (New York: Columbia University Press, 1979).

[5] George Kennan, "The View from Russia," in Thomas T. Hammond, ed., *Witnesses to the Origins of the Cold War* (Seattle: University of Washington Press, 1982), p. 29.

[6] Milovan Djilas, *Rise and Fall* (New York: Harcourt Brace Jovanovich, 1985); Edvard Kardelj, *Reminiscences: The Struggle for Recognition and Independence: The New Yugoslavia, 1944–1957*

(London: Blond and Briggs, 1982); Eugenio Reale, *Nascita del Cominform* (Milan: Mondadori, 1958), translated into French as *Avec Jacques Duclos au banc des accusés à la Réunion Constitutive du Kominform à Sklarska Poreba (22–27 septembre 1947)* (Paris: Plon, 1958).

[7] Norman Naimark, *The Russians in Germany: A History of the Soviet Zone of Occupation, 1945–1949* (Cambridge, MA: Harvard University Press, 1995).

[8] See Bartosek, *Les Aveux des Archives*, p. 372, Appendix 28. For Zhdanov's letter to Thorez, see Vladislav Zubok and Constantine Pleshakov, *Inside the Kremlin's Cold War* (Cambridge, MA: Harvard University Press, 1996), p. 129.

[9] Having been forced to grovel at Sklarska Poreba and apologize for the French Communists' failure to learn from the heroic Yugoslav example, Jacques Duclos (who led the French delegation on both occasions) took his revenge at Bucharest the following year. "It is evident," he remarked, "that the leaders of the Yugoslav Communist Party deny the Leninist principle of the need for criticism and self-criticism." It was perfectly normal, he insisted, that the Information Bureau should examine the situation in the Yugoslav Party: "The leaders of that Party ought to have been the first to agree to this, especially since, at the previous conference of the Information Bureau, they did not fail to make use of their right to criticise other Parties." To which, according to the minutes, Andrei Zhdanov interjected "Even to excess"—a delicious dash of Stalinist humbug (see *The Comintern: Minutes of the Three Conferences*, p. 557).

[10] Vyacheslav Molotov, *Molotov Remembers: Inside Kremlin Politics; Conversations with Felix Chuev,* Albert Resis, ed. (Lanham, MD: Ivan R. Dee, 1993), p. 29, quoted by Gaddis, *We Now Know*, p. 31.

[11] Naimark, *The Russians in Germany*, p. 467. For the same general point in a different context see Jan T. Gross, *Revolution from Abroad: The Soviet Conquest of Poland's Western Ukraine and Western Belorussia* (Princeton, NJ: Princeton University Press, 1988).

[12] Bruce Cumings, *The Origins of the Korean War: The Roaring of the Cataract, 1947–1950* (Princeton, NJ: Princeton University Press, 1990), p. 621, quoted in Gaddis, *We Now Know*, p. 71. Cumings is unusual in drawing heavily on foreign-language primary sources. Most revisionist scholars were experts in U.S. foreign policy, used few if any non-U.S. sources, and tended to project onto the rest of the world the prejudices of U.S. domestic politics (real and academic).

[13] Dean Acheson, *Present at the Creation: My Years in the State Department* (New York: Norton, 1969), p. 646. Acheson was discussing the way in which Soviet bullying of Adenauer in 1952 helped secure West German support for American goals.

[14] *George F. Kennan and the Origins of Containment, 1944–1946* (Columbia, MO: University of Missouri Press, 1997), introduction by John Lukacs, p. 7.

[15] On the occasion of his visit to Moscow in December 1944, seeking a Russian alliance as security against the revival of Germany, Charles de Gaulle is reported to have explained to his entourage that ideology need be no impediment to the pursuit of timeless French interests: "I deal with Stalin as François I dealt with Suleiman—with this difference, that in sixteenth-century France there was no Muslim party." See Wolton, *La France sous influence*, p. 57.

[16] Stalin's post-1947 rejection of "peaceful coexistence"—echoing to the phrase an identical policy switch in 1927—can thus be understood as not so much a prelude to foreign adventure as a signal of coming domestic repression. And so it proved.

CHAPTER V

Freedom and Freedonia

I.

Eastern Europe is a complex place. From Shakespeare ("And what should I do in Illyria?") to Neville Chamberlain, Western commentators have found it remote, obscure, and troubling. Until recently, few have made the effort to visit it, to learn its languages, or to fathom its lands, its past, or its cultures. Until 1918, its distinctive parts were mostly invisible to outsiders and inaudible in international affairs, unless conjoined in diplomatic conversations under the heading of the "Eastern Question." In between the two world wars, the vulnerable little states between Germany and the Soviet Union were just one more unstable element in an unstable world. And after Hitler's defeat, the whole region became a part of the Soviet realm: as late as the 1980s, undergraduates reading politics at Oxford could study Eastern Europe only under the rubric "Soviet and East European Politics," and even then only in the context of a primary concentration upon the USSR itself.

As a result, not only is Eastern Europe complex, but Eastern Europeans have a complex about it. You cannot understand us, they chastise Western audiences. Your Western scholars have ignored us, and your Western leaders, when they have deigned to take us into account, have abandoned us. (Yalta, Munich, Sarajevo . . .) And, adding geographical insult to historical injury, you have the nerve to classify us as "Eastern" Europe when it is you who dwell on the periphery and we who are (or were, until you threw us to the wolves) Central Europe. We speak and read your languages, your poetry, your plays and novels. What do you know of ours?

Warsaw, say the Poles, is the "heart of Europe." Prague, observe the Czechs, lies west of Vienna and Stockholm and is a better showpiece for High European Baroque than any city of Italy or France. Budapest, affirm the Hungarians, has at least as good a claim as Vienna to be the capital of a recovered Central Europe (rather a better claim, actually). And Bucharest, Zagreb, Sarajevo, and Belgrade have all been variously proposed in recent years as intrinsically and quintessentially "European" cities, precisely because they stand guard at the frontier where European civilization encounters (and rebuffs) the barbarians to the east or south.

We know what it means to be European, they all insist, because our Europeanness has for so long been under threat. We have sacrificed and suffered so that Europe, your Europe, might live and thrive. Why aren't you listening? Why don't you see? Eastern Europeans have thrown down the gauntlet; and in recent years it has been picked up by a new generation of Western scholars and Western journalists. One reason for the increased interest, of course, has been the remarkable developments in the region, from the Prague Spring through Solidarity, Charter 77, and the revolutions of 1989 to the Third Balkan Wars. The contemporary history of the region is simply too dramatic to ignore. But there is another factor, and it is that a sea change has occurred in scholarly tastes.

We used to study states, nations, classes. But for some time now, following a shift in fashion within the disciplines of anthropology and history especially, we study not the thing itself but the way it is represented—by the protagonists and by those who study them. Owing in large measure to the influence of the anthropologist Benedict Anderson, we investigate not nationalism but "imagined communities." And since the publication in 1983 of a seminal collection of essays edited by Eric Hobsbawm and Terence Ranger, it is not tradition but "the invention of tradition" that preoccupies historians of modern popular culture and political spectacle.

Eastern (or "Central") Europe is a ready-made, heaven-sent playground for such notions. After all, the states of Eastern Europe either did not exist until recently, or else had to be reconstructed in the modern era following their obliteration by greater powers in earlier times. From a Western perspective (though not necessarily in the eyes of the locals), Czechs, Slovaks, Croats, and Bosnians—to cite only the best known—are all invented nations. Poland, Serbia, Ukraine, the Baltic states, even Greece, whatever the real or imagined glories of their distant past, have all been constituted and reconstituted out of lands and peoples whose history was once submerged in someone else's story. Eastern Europe, in short, has been both present and absent, real and unreal, depending on your perspective and your location.

Neither Anderson nor Hobsbawm and Ranger paid much attention to the region, but their approaches (or at least the titles of their books) have inspired a growing literature charting the ways in which the West has "imagined," "invented," or (borrowing from postmodern styles in literary criticism) "(mis) represented" its Eastern Other. At its best—say, in Larry Wolff's *Inventing Eastern Europe,* which appeared in 1994—the result has been an illuminating contribution to Western intellectual history, a fine excursion into uncharted waters that helps to map the ways in which Western European writers have frozen into place a certain topography of civilization, and thereby condemned Eastern Europe to a moral as well as a spatial marginality in the Western story.

But the constructionist approach has its hazards. Between "invention," "imagination," "representation," and the invocation of "Otherness," the story of the West's failure to see Eastern Europe as it was and as it is runs the risk of sinking under the weight of overtheorized scholarly suspicion. Add "Orientalism" to the mix—the charge that Western writers have deployed patronizing, distancing devices to romanticize Eastern or Southeastern Europe, the better to control it—and the region gets lost all over again, this time in a marshland of well-intentioned compensatory subtlety.

II.

Vesna Goldsworthy's book is an instructive illustration of this lamentable outcome.* She has certainly chosen a glorious topic. From Byron to Malcolm Bradbury, British writers especially have set poems, moral tales, travel narratives, adventure stories, gothic mysteries, romantic comedies, and comic operas in Europe's eastern marches. As H. H. Munro ("Saki") put it, the region was "familiarly outlandish"—sufficiently distant and unspoiled to serve as a setting for romantic fantasies and epic dreams, recognizable enough to be juxtaposed with the civilized universe that it uncomfortably abuts.

First came the Greece of Byron and Shelley; and then the obscure half-Germanic, half-Oriental Transylvania of Bram Stoker's *Dracula* (1897), and the less topographically precise but recognizably middle-European statelets of Anthony Hope's *The Prisoner of Zenda* (1894) and *Sophy of Kravonia* (1906). John Buchan's *The Thirty-Nine Steps* (1915) and the Balkan stories of Saki were followed by Graham Greene's *Stamboul Train* (1932), Agatha Christie's *Murder on the Orient Express* (1934), Rebecca West's *Black Lamb and Grey Falcon* (1941), and, a generation later, Olivia Manning's *Balkan Trilogy* (1960–65).

In between came Joseph Sheridan Le Fanu's *Carmilla* (1871), set in Styria; Bernard Shaw's *Arms and the Man* (1894), set in Bulgaria; Edith Durham's *The Burden of the Balkans* (1905) and *High Albania* (1909); Dorothea Gerard's *The Red-Hot Crown* (1909), set in Serbia; Lawrence Durrell's *Esprit de Corps* (1957), set in Yugoslavia; and many more obscure works.

There is a rich literary vein to be mined here, and Goldsworthy has a nice critical eye when working directly with the texts. Thus she notes the importance of trains, the way in which so many novels and travelogues in this genre begin with a farewell to the West at some border town or station, or depend for their plot upon Western (usually English) travelers being caught up in an

---

*Vesna Goldsworthy, *Inventing Ruritania: The Imperialism of the Imagination* (New Haven: Yale University Press, 1998).

intrigue while enclosed in a railway car: a "tinned Occident" moving through the Balkans, she calls it.

She also captures the curious ambivalence of the English in these tales. They may find the European East (usually the Balkans) bizarre and unruly, but they end up feeling almost at home there. The ex-centric "Ruritanians" and the eccentric Englishmen somehow find common ground. English men or women ascend "Ruritanian" thrones by accident and end up falling half in love with a prince, a princess, or even the simple countryfolk with whom they have become embroiled. Indeed, in a number of these tales, from *The Prisoner of Zenda* to Evelyn Waugh's *Unconditional Surrender,* they are more than a little ambivalent about returning home to England. Goldsworthy suggests that this is because they can display among the natives a natural superiority of character and integrity, whereas at home they would be anonymous and indistinguishable from the suburban mass. She has a point.

Yet the Byronic model for much of her subject matter is also an important clue. In Greece, in Transylvania, in "Ruritania," the English adventurer can put the world to rights, and can exercise a power of moral and political initiative denied him (and certainly her) at home. And there is also another, often forgotten aspect of English letters, from William Cobbett through William Morris to George Orwell: a sustained romantic nostalgia for the lost world of rural England, for simpler, untroubled times. This longing for "Ruritania"— and in some of these novels there is even, as Goldsworthy notes, a preserved Ruritania within Ruritania, a mountain fastness where good, loyal peasants remain immune to the cynicism and double-dealing of court and city— suggests that a lot of the literature of adventure that she describes is even more about England than she realizes.

So what, then, is wrong with this book? It is, for a start, methodologically tendentious. Everything is imagined, represented, constructed, Orientalized. This would be merely annoying, if the literary creations or the travelers' observations were juxtaposed with local experience, so as to draw the contrast between them and to point up the ways in which English writers collectively forged an enduring and distorted image of another part of the world. But in

Goldsworthy's socially constructed universe, there is no reality check. Reality dissolves into culture. When words such as "real," "documentary," or "objective" appear in Goldsworthy's book, they are almost always accompanied by inverted commas, becoming, as it were, ontologically challenged. Thus we read about the "real" Balkans, "objective" descriptions, and "documentary" writing. Even the Balkans themselves are armored with scare quotes—"the Balkans"—to warn the reader against any attempt to measure narrative accounts or literary images against some concrete setting or place.

This mixture of constructionism and irony protects Goldsworthy against any charge that she has herself misread Balkan or East European reality. Sometimes the Balkans exist, as when she notes that Dracula or Zenda are myths about Central Europe and should not be confused with places farther south; but mostly they are only inventions. And the fact that in its verbal and adjectival forms ("balkanize," "balkanized") the term carries pejorative connotations leads Goldsworthy to protect almost the whole of the eponymous peninsula from any association with it. The Balkans, in short, are not "Balkan." We are dealing only with images, strategies, prejudices, representations, fantasies. There is no there there.

But it is not just the Archimedean point of an actual place that is missing from this story of its misappropriation by foreign texts. Goldsworthy is herself curiously absent from her own account. To be sure, she evinces frustration, even hints of anger, at what she calls the exploitation (no scare quotes this time) of the region for English literary advantage. But we are never told whether English writers purloined and abused an existing resource or invented it ex nihilo. Is Bram Stoker's account of Transylvania accurate? Is Anthony Hope's Zenda faithful to the facts? Of course not, Goldsworthy seems to suggest. It is a stupid and inappropriate question. And yet, when E. M. Forster stays in Bucharest in 1930 as a guest of the British Legation, he is described as having had an "encounter with the 'real' Balkans. . . ." Presumably truer to life than Dracula's castle, but no less unreal for that.

A properly postmodern conclusion should thus apply: there is no "Central Europe," no "Balkans." There is just fiction—which at least pretends to be nothing else, but nonetheless creates images that people take for fact—or "reality," which is a spectrum of illusions best treated as fiction. Yet this would undermine Goldsworthy's very theme. For surely the book is about the way in which English writers took over and made over a distinct and material part of the known world. Reality has to intrude. And so she offers a concession: "There could be as many Balkan 'truths' as there are tellers, and instead of truth we can more usefully talk about the changing perceptions of truthfulness." But this is not very helpful. It explains why we should not try to measure Rebecca West against Lawrence Durrell, or either of them against any "neutral" description; but it does not explain why we should not measure Rebecca West against the places she wrote about. And it certainly does not tell us what Goldsworthy herself thinks.

Fortunately, we have a clue in her book's subtitle: "The Imperialism of the Imagination." As she remarks, "this book seeks to explore the way in which one of the world's most powerful nations exploited the resources of the Balkans to supply its literary and entertainment industries." According to Goldsworthy, the world today sees the Balkans through English eyes because "faced with the economic power of the Western industries of the imagination, indigenous Balkan produce had as much chance of competing as the cotton industry in India when its markets were flooded with British manufactures." And things have not changed: "The power of British-created Balkan 'brand-names' continues to scar thinking about the Balkans as surely as British irrigation programmes have salinated the fertile lands of the Punjab."

There is much, much more in this vein, where Cultural Studies meets Late Marxism in an unhappy marriage of convenience. Poor Lawrence Durrell is condemned for writing about the Balkans "in a deliberately 'repro' format . . . with possible financial gain so firmly in his mind," thereby revealing a "recognition of the profitability of the type of imaginative colonisation through which the literary 'Balkans' [*sic*] continued to be ruthlessly exploited." Goldsworthy even ventures a neo-Leninist interpretation, though she is careful to keep a pusillanimous distance from the resulting crassness of her formulation.

In assuaging the demands of the popular imagination, the imperialism perpetrated by the entertainment industry plays a role analogous to that played by the more familiar forms of economic imperialism. Indeed a Marxist critic could argue that it provides a substitute "opium of the masses," based on the subordination of other peoples, thereby delaying the class struggle.

Whoever that benighted Marxist critic might be, he or she would at least have noted that Bernard Shaw's jokes at the expense of his Bulgarians in *Arms and the Man* are about class, not ethnicity; the same is true of the sneering asides about the denizens of a Balkan ballroom in David Footman's *Pemberton*. A Balkan setting can disguise a distinctly intra-British prejudice or quip.

The problem is not just that when Cultural Studies dilutes Marxism, everyone loses. It is also that Goldsworthy utterly lacks any sense of humor, any feeling for the ridiculous. She is so certain that her English writers are patronizing their Balkan characters and settings, laughing at their "Eastern" foibles, that she misses her best material. If the Hollywood production of *The Prisoner of Zenda* (1937) represents the acme of ruthless capitalist exploitation, what are we to make of *Duck Soup* (1933)?

The other Marxes receive no mention in this book, but their film is by far the best-known "exploitation" of Balkan stereotypes in Western popular culture, now that the cinematic Dracula has been cut loose from his trans-Danubian roots. To be sure, *Duck Soup* plays off the literary and cinematic stereotype to merciless effect; but the result is a magnificent inversion. When we laugh at Freedonia, we are not sneering at Serbia or Romania; we are sharing a joke at the expense of the movie industry's own clichés. The same quality of internal reference is also present in Durrell's parody of earlier Balkan intrigues, though you would never know it from Goldsworthy. As for Malcolm Bradbury's *Rates of Exchange* (1983), itself dependent on internal reference to earlier works such as Greene's *The Third Man,* its tale of a hapless English lecturer in late-Communist Bucharest is not just funny, it is painfully accurate.

If *Inventing Ruritania* fails to appreciate the strain of parody, pastiche, slap-stick, and self-mockery present in much English writing set in "the Balkans," it is not just because its author has a tin ear. It is also because accuracy and parody alike seem to cause her considerable discomfort. She does not like En-glish (or West European) criticism of Greece's discreditable behavior during the Balkan crises ("patronising . . . [a] symbolic 'Balkanization' of the Hel-lenes"), and she attributes it to prejudice and a colonial cast of mind. Golds-worthy does acknowledge that the turbulent history of Serbian and Bulgarian politics in the earlier years of this century is fairly—and rather benignly—reflected in some of the novels that she discusses (the chief difference being that in Ruritania the endings are happier and there is less cruelty), but she passes over the implications of this verisimilitude as quickly as possible.

The truth is that Goldsworthy evinces a high degree of ressentiment to-ward her material. Foreigners, quite simply, are not welcome and should leave the region alone: "Of outsiders' views on Balkan problems we are, most of us, tired," she writes, quoting with italicized approval a remark of Edith Durham in *High Albania*. When outsiders ignore the Balkans, they are scorning and demeaning the region. When they appropriate it for literary purposes, they are abusing and exploiting it.

And if foreigners take the trouble to learn about the region and even to intervene sympathetically, that will not do either. In recent years, Goldswor-thy writes, "the degree to which the area has presented a blank canvas upon which Europe's political unconscious plays out its taboos and hidden anxieties has become apparent once again." Her book concludes with a tirade against "media-based industries of conscience" that need to manufacture, "in order to meet an insatiable appetite for involvement [*sic*] . . . countless new 'Others' both at home and abroad." The "Other" in question, one is driven to conclude, is the Serbs. Together with her manifest sympathy for the Serbophile Rebecca West, the only English writer to get a truly soft ride in this book, this suggests a parochial and partisan perspective that Goldsworthy was unable altogether to repress.

III.

It is a relief to move from the Balkans to Central Europe. That is not always the case: Central European history, with all its grievances and obsessions, can match anything the Balkans have to offer. Hitler came from Central Europe, after all, and his paranoid obsession with the German-Slav conflict is rooted in a distinctively Austro-Bohemian past. (Goldsworthy rightly takes Robert Kaplan to task for suggesting, in *Balkan Ghosts,* a Balkan dimension to this Central European element in Hitler's background.) And nothing in the Balkans can match the Poles or the Czechs at their glummest, caught between grim, skeptical irony and sorrowful, self-pitying bathos. Inventing Bohemia, or a compensatory history of unknown Central Europe, would be a lugubrious book indeed.

But Derek Sayer's *The Coasts of Bohemia* is nothing of the kind.* It is an ambitious, elegantly written, and sympathetic account of the art, the literature, and the politics of the Czech people. Concentrating on the history of the Czech Lands, but above all on Bohemia and especially Prague, from the National Awakening in the nineteenth century through the decades of Communist decline, Sayer saunters gracefully and with sure footing back and forth across centuries of Czech religion, mythology, and history, displaying enthusiasm and engagement but immune to the usual self-serving national illusions. He hardly ever gives in to the temptation to overcompensate for centuries of foreign persecution or neglect. Perhaps the worst thing to be said of Sayer's book is that it is inebriated by the abundance of its material, and so the author occasionally resorts to lists of names and works of art, resulting in pages of cascading examples that can at times become encyclopedic, and even a bit confusing.

What little defensiveness Sayer betrays on behalf of his material comes at the beginning of his book, when he reminds his reader of the injustices to

---

*Derek Sayer, *The Coasts of Bohemia: A Czech History* (Princeton: Princeton University Press, 1998).

which the Czech past has been subject. Bohemia is not in Eastern Europe, he insists. It is not even particularly "bohemian." Left to its own devices, it would have been, and occasionally it was, just like the West, and a part of it, too. As it is, "we" take account of it only when its crises intersect with mainstream history: in 1620, at the Battle of White Mountain (when the Protestant Bohemian Estates were destroyed by the armies of the Counter-Reformation at the start of the Thirty Years' War); in 1938; in 1968; in 1989. Otherwise it disappears from Western consciousness.

Worse, in Sayer's view, Bohemia has been denied its rightful place not just in its own history but in ours. How many cultivated Westerners know about Czech achievements in linguistics, or in modern art? Sayer complains that "it is acceptable for the Museum of Modern Art in New York to stage what it calls a 'comprehensive' retrospective show on 'Dada, Surrealism and Their Heritage,' whose extensive catalogue contains not one reference to Prague or the Czechoslovak Surrealist Group in its text, its very detailed chronology, or its bibliography." He is right; and because he doesn't make a meal of it, his point is well taken. Before the redrawing of Europe's maps after 1948, Czech avant-garde artists such as Karel Teige were indeed better known and understood in the West—though even before the Munich capitulation Alfons Mucha, the great national painter of Bohemian epic narratives and the illustrator of Czechoslovak postage stamps, was better known (and still is) as Alphonse Mucha, the fin-de-siecle Paris-based designer of art-deco posters.

Once Sayer hits his stride, and has drawn the obligatory contrast between the depth and range of modern Czech art and thought and the parochial ignorance of British prime ministers, and made the requisite bows toward Czech cosmopolitanism stifled in its flower by war, occupation, and foreign ignorance, his book is a delight. It is based almost without exception on Czech-language sources: encyclopedias, memoirs, antiquarian notices, biographies, exhibition and museum catalogues, travel guides, and much else, including an older generation of Czech historical scholarship, which might itself be thought a form of compensatory scholarship in its own right. But the uses to which Sayer puts these sources are, with one exception, exemplary.

The exception is Sayer's depiction of the Hungarian repression of Slovak schools and the Slovak language in the years before World War I. In his account, he draws exclusively on Czech data and sources. But the story looks rather different from Hungary. And anyway, as Sayer is the first to concede in other contexts, it is not at all clear what is meant by the "Slovak" language, or "Slovak" peasants, in the decades before 1914. One could with equal justice write of Slavonic-tongued Hungarian peasants. A lot depends on who is reporting what data, and why.

Sayer has a tireless eye and ear for detail and illustration, and the volume of local riches that he describes and classifies in his passage from the Bohemian National Awakening through the early 1960s is remarkable not so much for the quality of the material—Sayer makes no overreaching claims for the more obscure composers, painters, and poets whom he assiduously lists—as for its range. If nations are indeed constructed or imagined into being, then the birth of "Czechness" is a fine instance of the protean scale on which the enterprise can be undertaken, from billboards to book illustration, from picture galleries to sports clubs, from public parks to political theater.

The Czech case—for this is, after all, a story that could be told of other places—is interesting for a number of reasons. There almost certainly was a Czech sense of identity—of Czechness—as early as the Hussite reformation, a century before Luther and much earlier than in most other parts of Europe. Long after Jan Hus was burned for heresy, in 1415, Prague and Bohemia remained a stronghold of literary and religious dissent, which was crushed in 1620 when the country's ruling class was punitively expropriated, exiled, or killed by the forces of Empire and the Catholic Church, to be replaced by a new elite of German-speaking Imperial camp followers and agents. For over two hundred years, the Czech language, and what remained of a distinctive Czech identity, was driven into the countryside, where it survived, barely, but only in spoken form.

In the mid-Victorian era, Bohemia and Moravia (the Czech Lands) still consisted of a German-speaking aristocracy and urban bourgeoisie surrounded by isolated and mostly illiterate Slav-language-speaking peasants. By

1910, however, thanks to huge efforts by the advocates and artisans of the National Awakening, and abetted by a rapid industrialization that sucked Czech-speaking villagers into the towns at an unprecedented rate, Prague and most other large towns were overwhelmingly Czech speaking (though German was still the language of the cultivated). By the time independence from Austria was declared, in 1918, the Czechs had reinvented themselves as a nation, defined by a language that only they could speak and by the cultural identity that was being forged within it.

Sayer has much to say about all this—about language and identity, about self-serving national myths (and historical forgeries that helped create and sustain them), and about the uses of identity and identification in nation building and state building. He has no illusions about even the most admired and sanctified of his protagonists, Tomáš Masaryk. *The Czech Question,* an influential pedagogic text by Czechoslovakia's first president, opportunistically exploited religious prejudice and national mythology in order to claim a politically expedient lineage for Czech national identity; and Sayer says so. Of Alfons Mucha's *Slovanska epopej* (*Slav Epic,* completed in 1928), a monumental series of pictorial depictions of the Czech story from medieval myths to the present, he writes: "On one level his indiscriminate plundering [of religious motifs] testifies to just how secularized religion had by then become. But it equally witnesses the ascension of the national and the ethnic into the realm of the sacred."

Notably impressive is the way Sayer handles the most sensitive issue of all, and one which is, once again, a distinctively Czech variation on a common Eastern European theme. Despite the fact that, by prevailing regional standards, interwar Czechoslovakia was a liberal, constitutional, and egalitarian society, it was far from perfect. After 1918, Czechs represented just half the total population ruled from Prague—the rest consisting of Slovaks, Germans, Jews, Hungarians, and sub-Carpathian Ruthenes (from what is now part of western Ukraine). As Sayer points out, writing of the emphasis well before independence upon Czechness in everything from artistic subjects to street names, "this newly nationalized social space was, of course, a set of cultural representations institutionally imposed upon a demographic reality which was still, as a matter of fact, multiethnic."

But the national mythology, the monuments, the museums, the school curricula, and much else spoke above all of Czechness, of the Czech national revival of the previous century, the glories of Czech poetry, music, language, and so on. In Sayer's words, again, discussing the nationalist and anti-German political uses to which nineteenth-century cultural history was put after 1918, "the National Museum, the art gallery in the Sternberk palace, the Bohemian Royal Society, and the rest of these institutions were not the early manifestations of a Czech national rebirth. Many of them were hijacked for that project later, and their foundation retrospectively appropriated for nationalist genealogies."

The image presented after independence, to the country and to the world at large, was thus rather parochial—and, to the extent that it was advertised as liberal and cosmopolitan, misleading. Ruthenes and Hungarians were ignored. Slovaks, who were still mostly peasants with elementary education at best, were scorned. Jews were not subject to discrimination, but they faced a steady undercurrent of anti-Semitic resentment, for being German speakers and for being Jews. The Germans themselves, now a majority only in the "Sudeten" regions of northern and southern Bohemia and Moravia, were historically resented and politically slighted. When, in the aftermath of Munich, the country fell apart, with Hungary and Poland each grabbing a small corner, the Slovaks declaring independence, and Germany claiming the rest, only the Czechs (and the Jews, who had come to identify with the Republic and anyway had no alternatives) were sorry.

Sayer cannot resist a hint of nostalgia for the First Czechoslovak Republic. It was, like Weimar Germany, a place in which increasingly ugly politics and innovative art flourished side by side; but he is quick to acknowledge that there had been an undercurrent of national populism, inherited from the National Awakening, which always boded ill. During World War II, the Czech Lands did not suffer overmuch. Sayer reminds us that of the 360,000 Czech and Slovak victims of Hitler, 260,000 were Jews, a point carefully underemphasized in postwar commemoration.

And once Hitler had all but rid the land of one minority, the Czechs in 1945 set about finishing the job by expelling the remaining German and Hungarian population by force. As a result, the reconstituted postwar Czechoslovak state was virtually homogenous, consisting of Czechs and Slovaks alone. Thanks to Hitler, the nineteenth-century nationalist claim that land and people were one and were Czech (or, grudgingly, Slovak) had come true. "What was left was a denuded landscape, shorn of its ethnic and social complexities and ripe for the imposition of a unitary national script."

It was in these circumstances that the Communists came to power in February 1948. Sayer cuts right into a controversial thicket here, and he makes clear his view that Czech Communism, far from being an alien Russian imposition, had roots deep in the political and cultural soil of the place. In support of this, he adduces not just the well-known election results of 1946, when the local Communists did better in a free and open vote in the Czech Lands (Slovaks were more reticent) than anywhere else in Europe. He also points to the Communists' successful and copious appropriation of prevailing pre-war Czech motifs in popular art, music, history, pedagogy, and folklore.

Sayer reminds his readers that much of the moral and material prologue to Communism was performed by President Edvard Beneš and the legislation that he promulgated and supported between May 1945 and February 1948: expropriating owners, expelling minorities, nationalizing businesses, and punishing political opponents by imprisonment or exclusion from public life. And he rightly concludes that if the Czech Communists were able to impose so repressive, uniform, relentless, and resentful a regime, which was harsh and bleak even by Communism's own standards, some part of the responsibility must lie with their national-liberal and even Socialist predecessors, whose emphasis on "us" against "them," Czechs against outsiders, the people against rapacious rulers and other privileged minorities, made their task so much easier.

This provincial element in Czech national sentiment, before and during the

Communist era, is well captured in the popular nineteenth-century phrase *Male ale nase*—(it may be small, but it's ours)—applied to everything from domestic landscapes to sporting achievements. Sayer records this, and notes, too, the protean range of the Czech phrase *U nas,* meaning everything from "our place," as in "come to dinner at our place tonight," to "our fatherland," with the "our" implicitly excluding those who are not of the native soil. He should have added that this linguistic propensity to slide effortlessly from cozy domesticity into ethnocentric exclusivism in one phrase is present in many other European languages, including Hungarian, the other Slav languages, German (*Bei Uns*) and French (*Chez nous*). English and Italian, by contrast, lack this facility, the easy and chilling conflation of hearth, home, homeland, homogeneity, and Heimat.

IV.

Anyone interested in Czechoslovakia and the modern Czech Republic should read this book; it is sad that there is no equivalent for any other country in the region. Despite his self-confessed enthusiasm for a place and a theme that represented for him a new scholarly departure, Sayer has avoided the usual pitfalls—a patronizing Western distance, or the temptation to "go native" and be more national and defensive than the locals themselves; and he has engaged some of the thorniest and most disputed issues in the modern Czech past. He seems even to share Milan Kundera's distaste for the Czech (and Eastern European) assimilation of culture and people, in which the writer, the artist, and the intellectual are highly esteemed, but are expected in return to respond and be responsible to the community: that "national circle of intimacy" in which, as Kundera has written, "everything and everyone (critics, historians, compatriots as well as foreigners) hooks the art onto the great national family portrait photo and will not let it get away."

This is an important if disquieting reminder of another aspect of Central Europe, the Balkans, and the rest of Eastern Europe. The insecurity of national identity—in a part of the world where states, nations, and peoples have been made and unmade with unnerving frequency—inevitably leads not just to a pressure on local artists and scholars to be "national," or at least loyal, but also to what one might call the Ancient Mariner syndrome: the propensity to grip the outsider by the shoulder and insist on telling and retelling the tragic national story, lest it be lost or forgotten. It is not for nothing that the Czech national anthem is *Kde domuv muj?*, or "Where is my homeland?"

The role of the Western audience in this drama is mostly to listen respectfully. Still, there are things that only an outsider can say, and they are no less pertinent for being said from the outside. To begin with, the history of Western Europe's dealings with Eastern Europe is only imperfectly captured in the metaphor of "colonialism," however generously conceived. Locally based historians of countries that have fallen victim to foreign predators have understandably been disposed to see their past as one in which "they" did it to "us"; and since 1989 the claim has been heard once again, this time to account for the depredations of Communism.

To be sure, Hitler and Stalin were responsible for their crimes; but the extent to which the active engagement of any other power, such as Britain, France, Italy, or the United States, can be held accountable for the fate of many of the peoples of Central and Eastern Europe is much less clear. And even Hitler and Stalin were made more or less welcome, and received more or less local encouragement, in different parts of Eastern Europe at different times. It is true that the Eastern European states have lacked the sort of international autonomy that goes with size and wealth; but it is also true that they have been more than just passive victims of the marauding intentions of others.

One reason for this is precisely the fact of national independence. As František Palacký, the "Father of the Czech Nation," famously expressed it in April 1848: "Imagine the Austrian Empire fragmented into a multitude of greater and lesser republics. What a nice basis for universal Russian monarchy." We cannot reconstitute Habsburgia—though I would go so far as to say that the breakup of the Austro-Hungarian Empire in 1918 was perhaps the worst thing that could have happened to almost all of its lands and citizens.

Yet it is the experience of national independence, and the resulting zero-sum conflicts with other self-described nations within borders and across them, that have contributed more than anything to the tragedy of modern Central and Southeastern European history. Membership in the European Union may help make good, in Central Europe at least, some of the grim history of the region since 1918; but a clear-eyed understanding of that same history will help, too.

Which brings us back to the Balkans. It is a sad irony that Tito's success in keeping Yugoslavia out of Stalin's grasp after 1948 contributed indirectly to the present morass by deluding his country's own intelligentsia—and their foreign admirers—into forgetting their own past. The intellectuals of Belgrade and Zagreb told themselves and their readers fond tales of historical conflicts resolved, of national and social divisions overcome, of successful experiments in workers' control, and so on. Similar fables were being spun, of course, in Soviet-controlled Eastern Europe, but there nobody believed them. That is the difference. Vesna Goldsworthy's post-Marxist lucubrations on the theme of colonial appropriation would provoke dismissive hilarity in Warsaw or Budapest today; but the shell-shocked victims of Yugoslavia's collapse have yet to come to terms with their own damaged condition.

When they do, they may come to reflect that the problem in the lands between Austria and Istanbul for many long years has been not too much foreign interest and foreign involvement but too little. I was in Zagreb with a group of liberal Croatian intellectuals when the Dayton Accords were signed. "There," one of them said, "the Americans have finally got what they want." "What do you mean?" I asked. "Don't you see?" replied my friend. "The United States has managed to get a military foothold in the Balkans. It's what they've been waiting for. They'll never leave now." "But you told me," I replied, "that the problem was that the West didn't care enough about the region." "That's true," he said, "they don't." The idea that the United States, or any other Western power, should have the remotest intention of "getting a foothold" in the Balkans had never crossed my mind. I had supposed that the real problem was utter and callous Western indifference. For a Croatian intellectual, however, or a Serbian intellectual, the Balkans have been uppermost in English and American and Western thoughts for more than a century. Or they should have been. Or both. How else can you explain anything?

The gap between the dispassionate reflections of *The Coasts of Bohemia* and the resentful denials of *Inventing Ruritania* is thus indicative of more than just their authors' disparate methods and concerns. It illustrates the speed with which the Czechs' own discussion of Czech history is catching up with the history itself; and the same is true of Hungary and Poland. In Serbia and Croatia, meanwhile, as in Romania and even Greece, much of that history, when presented to a local audience, is subject to taboo or to scholarly self-censorship. There delusion abounds.

In truth, most Westerners knew little and cared less about the former Yugoslavia, and for this Yugoslav intellectuals must bear some of the responsibility. Between resentment at outsiders for interfering or supporting what are seen locally as partisan positions, and the fading illusions of the Belgrade-based Praxis school of Marxism, many Yugoslav writers, scholars, and artists could not think straight about their own country, and so they missed the chance to explain it to the world. This is one of the reasons why Yugoslav Communist apparatchiks-turned-nationalists have been able to sell themselves to the international community as domestic leaders and international interlocutors.

After all, no Western leader in the decades before 1989 was seriously deluded into thinking he could "work" with petty Communist dictators. And thanks in some measure to the earlier efforts of men such as Adam Michnik and Vaclav Havel, no American or Western European diplomat would have asserted that Czechoslovakia's Gustav Husak was a man "with whom one could do business," or that the erstwhile First Secretaries of the Communist Parties of Bulgaria or even Poland were "statesmen." Yet that is precisely how Franjo Tudjman and Slobodan Milosevic have been variously described by Richard Holbrooke and Bill Clinton.

This state of affairs has led the Western allies and the United Nations from one Balkan fiasco to another, and it cannot reasonably be attributed to post-colonial or para-Ruritanian illusions. Tudjman of Croatia looks and sometimes acts like the dictator of a latter-day Freedonia; but far from being snubbed or mocked, he is taken—and is thus encouraged to take himself—altogether seriously. A little more knowledge of the ghastlier episodes of the recent Balkan past might make the leaders of the West pause in their choice of words and friends. It would certainly equip them better to intervene more effectively.

For the Balkan past is ghastly. And some unpleasing images just are true. Vesna Goldsworthy writes dismissively of what she calls the "new orientalising move" of the 1990s: "that the Balkans are not truly 'European' in so far as wars of 'Balkan' brutality are unthinkable elsewhere in Europe at the end of the twentieth century." But the fact is that such wars are unthinkable in most of the rest of Europe. This is not because the rest of the subcontinent is a superior place, though it has certainly been a more fortunate one. It is because the history of the second half of our century has ordained things thus.

Let's face it. The truly brutal European wars of our century have been confined to Eastern and Southeastern Europe. Nothing in modern American, British, French, Italian, or even Spanish experience can match the traumatic dislocation, the murderous violence, and the sheer sustained sadism of the civil wars in and between Balkan states before 1914, between 1941 and 1948, or since 1991. Only the German war of extermination carried out in Poland, the Baltic lands, and Ukraine is comparable, and it has long since become our modern parable of absolute evil. To pretend that the history of Eastern or Southeastern Europe would look like that of Western Europe if only Western observers didn't "orientalize" the region is a grievous error. There are reasons for the sheer awfulness of Balkan conflicts, of course; but awful they are. There is nothing imagined, invented, represented, constructed, appropriated, or orientalized about such a claim. It is a fact.

This essay, a review of *Inventing Ruritania: The Imperialism of the Imagination* by Vesna Goldsworthy and *The Coasts of Bohemia: A Czech History* by Derek Sayer, first appeared in the *New Republic* in September 1998.

Part Two

Israel, the Holocaust, and the Jews

CHAPTER VI

The Road to Nowhere

In 1958, at the height of the Algerian crisis, with Arabs bombing French cafés in Algiers, Paris tacitly condoning the use of torture by the occupying French army, and paratroop colonels demanding a free hand to end terror, the French philosopher Raymond Aron published a small book, *L'Algérie et la République*.[1] Cutting through the emotive and historical claims of both sides, Aron explained in his characteristically cool prose why the French had to quit Algeria. France lacked both the will and the means either to impose French rule on the Arabs or to give Arabs an equal place in France. If the French stayed the situation would only deteriorate and they would inevitably leave at some later date—but under worse conditions and with a more embittered legacy. The damage that France was doing to Algerians was surpassed by the harm the Republic was bringing upon itself. However impossible the choice appeared, it was nonetheless very simple: France must go.

Many years later Aron was asked why he never engaged the heated questions of the time: torture, terrorism, the French policy of state-sponsored political assassination, Arab national claims, and the colonial heritage of the French. Everyone, he replied, was talking about these things; why add my voice? The point was no longer to analyze the origins of the tragedy, nor assign blame for it. The point was to do what had to be done.

In the cacophony of commentary and accusation swirling around the calamity in the Middle East, Aron's icy clarity is sorely missed. For the solution to the Israel-Palestine conflict is also in plain sight. Israel exists. The Palestinians and other Arabs will eventually accept this; many already do. Palestinians can be neither expunged from "Greater Israel" nor integrated into it: if they *were* expelled into Jordan, the latter would explode, with disastrous consequences for Israel. Palestinians need a real state of their own and they will have one. The two states will be delineated in accordance with the map drawn up at the Taba negotiations in January 2001, according to which the 1967 borders will be modified, but nearly all of the occupied territories will come under Palestinian rule. The Israeli settlements in the occupied territories are thus foredoomed, and most of them will be dismantled, as many Israelis privately acknowledge.

There will be no Arab right of return; and it is time to abandon the anachronistic Jewish one. Jerusalem is already largely divided along ethnic lines and will, eventually, be the capital of both states. Since these states will have a common interest in stability and shared security concerns, they will learn in time to cooperate. Community-based organizations like Hamas, offered the chance to transform themselves from terrorist networks into political parties, will take this path. There are numerous precedents.

IF THIS IS THE FUTURE of the region, then why is it proving so tragically hard to get there? Four years after Aron's essay, De Gaulle extricated his countrymen from Algeria with relative ease. Following fifty years of vicious repression and exploitation, white South Africans handed over power to a black majority who replaced them without violence or revenge. Is the Middle East so different? From the Palestinian point of view, the colonial analogy fits and foreign precedent might apply. Israelis, however, insist otherwise.

Most Israelis are still trapped in the story of their own uniqueness. For some, this lies in the primordial presence of an ancient Jewish state on the territory of modern Israel. For others it rests in a God-given title to the lands of Judea and Samaria. Many still invoke the Holocaust and the claim that it authorizes Jews to make upon the international community. Even those who reject all such special pleading point to geography in defense of their distinction. We are so vulnerable, they say, so surrounded by enemies, that we cannot take any risks or afford a single mistake. The French could withdraw across the Mediterranean; South Africa is a very large country. We have nowhere to go. Finally, behind every Israeli refusal to face the inevitability of hard choices stands the implicit guarantee of the United States.

The problem for the rest of the world is that since 1967 Israel has changed in ways that render its traditional self-description absurd. It is now a regional colonial power, by some accounts the world's fourth-largest military establishment. Israel is a state, with all the trappings and capacities of a state. By comparison the Palestinians are weak indeed. While the failings of the Palestinian leadership have been abysmal and the crimes of Palestinian terrorists extremely bloody, the fact is that Israel has the military and political initiative. Responsibility for moving beyond the present impasse thus falls primarily (though as we shall see not exclusively) on Israel.

But Israelis themselves are blind to this. In their own eyes they are still a small victim-community, defending themselves with restraint and reluctance against overwhelming odds. Their astonishingly incompetent political leadership has squandered thirty years since the hubris-inducing victory of June 1967. In that time Israelis have built illegal compounds in the occupied territories and grown a carapace of cynicism: toward the Palestinians, whom they regard with contempt, and toward a United States whose erstwhile benevolent disengagement they have manipulated shamelessly.

Israel poses no lasting threat to Syria or to the Hezbollah in Lebanon, the military wing of Hamas or any other extremist organization. On the contrary, these have long thrived on its predictable reaction to their attacks. But the present government of Israel *has* come close to destroying the Palestinian Authority. After the events of the last month Palestinian politicians foolish enough to take Israelis at their word will be castigated as quislings, and dispatched accordingly. The state of Israel has largely deprived itself of credible Palestinian interlocutors.

This is the distinctive achievement of Ariel Sharon, Israel's dark id. Notorious among soldiers for his strategic incompetence—his tactical success with bold tank advances was never matched by any grasp of the bigger picture—Sharon has proven as bad as so many of us feared. He has repeated (or in the case of the expulsion of Arafat, tried to repeat) all the mistakes of his 1982 occupation of Lebanon, down to the very rhetoric. Sharon's obsession with Yasser Arafat brings to mind Victor Hugo's Inspector Javert, his life and career insanely given over to the destruction of Jean Valjean at the price of all measure and reason, including his own (the literary comparison flatters Sharon and Arafat alike).

Meanwhile he has single-handedly raised Arafat's international stature to its highest point in years. If he ever gets rid of Arafat, and the bombers keep coming, as they will, what will Sharon do then? And what will he do when young Arabs from Israel itself, inflamed by Israel's treatment of their cousins in occupied Jenin and Ramallah, volunteer for suicide missions? Will he send the tanks into the Galilee? Put up electric fences around the Arab districts of Haifa?

SHARON AND THE ISRAELI POLITICAL establishment—not to mention the country's liberal intelligentsia who, Pilate-like, have washed their hands of responsibility—are chiefly to blame for the present crisis, but they are not alone. Precisely because the Israelis assume that they have a blank check from Washington, the United States is willy-nilly a party to this mess. All serious efforts in the past thirty years to find peace in the Middle East, from Henry Kissinger to Bill Clinton, have begun with American urging and intervention. Why, then, did the Bush administration step aside for so long, provoking international ire and jeopardizing its future influence?

Why did the American president continue to confine himself in late March and early April to the disingenuous suggestion that "Arafat should do more" to rein in suicide bombers, while the leader of the Palestinian Authority sat imprisoned in three rooms, a single cell phone at his disposal? Why, during the buildup to the present crisis, did a man of the sophistication and intelligence of Colin Powell docilely accept Sharon's cynical demand for an arbitrary period of "absolute calm" (saving sporadic Israeli assassinations) before any political discussions could begin? Why has the United States stood by while, as the *New York Times* put it on April 9, "more than 200 Palestinians have been killed and more than 1,500 wounded since Israeli tanks and helicopter gunships rolled into the West Bank on March 29"? Why, in short, has the United States voluntarily attached itself to a leash marked "terrorism" with which Sharon can jerk it to and fro at will?

The answer, sadly, is September 11. Until then, even Bush was mindful of the need to warn Israelis against "targeted assassinations," as he did last August. But since September 11 the very words "terrorism" and "terrorist" have silenced rational foreign policy debate. Ariel Sharon had only to declare Yasser Arafat the head "of a terrorist network" for Washington to fall sheepishly in line behind any military action he takes. We are mesmerized by the new rhetoric of this "war on terror": any politician who can convincingly label his domestic or foreign critics as "terrorists" is guaranteed at least the ear of the American government, and usually something more.

"Terrorist" risks becoming the mantra of our time, like "Communist," "capitalist," "bourgeois," and others before it. Like them, it closes off all further discussion. The word has its own history: Hitler and Stalin typically described their opponents as "terrorists." Terrorists really exist, of course, just as there are real bourgeois and genuine Communists; terror against civilians is the weapon of choice of the weak. But the problem is that "terrorist," like "rogue state," is a protean rhetorical device which can boomerang: Jewish terrorists were among the founders of the state of Israel and it may not be long before the United Nations passes a resolution defining Israel as a rogue state.

The first stage of any solution in the Middle East, then, is for the United States to abandon its self-defeating rhetorical obsession with a war on terrorism, which has put U.S. foreign policy into Ariel Sharon's back pocket, and start behaving like the great power it is. Instead of being blackmailed into silence by the Israeli prime minister, Washington must require of him and any

Palestinian representatives who have survived his attentions that they begin talking. Two years ago, even one year ago, it might have been reasonable to demand of the Palestinian Authority that all bombings halt before such talks begin. But thanks to Ariel Sharon, no Palestinian open to negotiations is in a position to meet such a demand. So it must be talks and a peace agreement with or without bombings.

The Israelis, of course, will ask how they can speak to men who have condoned suicide bombings of Israeli civilians. Palestinians will retort that they have nothing to say to those who claim to want a permanent peace but have built thirty new colonial settlements in the past year alone. Both sides have good grounds for mistrust. But there is no alternative; they must both be made to talk.[2] And then they will have to start forgetting.

THERE IS MUCH TO FORGET. Palestinians remember the mass expulsions of 1948, land expropriations, economic exploitation, the colonization of the West Bank, political assassinations, and a hundred petty daily humiliations. Israelis remember the war of 1948, the Arab refusal to recognize their state before 1967 and since, reiterated threats to drive the Jews into the sea, and the terrifying, random civilian massacres of the past year.

But Middle Eastern memories are neither unique nor even distinctive in their scale. For two decades the Irish Republican Army regularly shot to death Protestant civilians on their doorsteps, in front of their children. Protestant gunmen responded in kind. The violence continues, though much reduced. This has not stopped moderate Protestants from talking publicly to their Sinn Fein counterparts; Gerry Adams and Martin McGinnis are now accepted as legitimate political leaders. Elsewhere, less than six years after the 1944 massacre at the village of Oradour, where the SS burned alive seven hundred French men, women, and children, France and Germany came together to form the core of a new European project.

In the final convulsions of World War II, hundreds of thousands of Poles and Ukrainians were killed or expelled from their respective territories by neighboring Ukrainians and Poles, in a frenzy of intercommunal violence unmatched by anything ever seen in the Middle East; at their present rate it would take Jews and Arabs many decades to reach comparable death tolls. Yet today Poles and Ukrainians, for all their tragic memories, live not only at peace but in growing collaboration and cooperation along a tranquil border.

It can be done. In the Middle East today each side dwells within hermetically sealed memories and national narratives in which the other side's pain is invisible and inaudible. But so did the Algerians and the French, the French and the Germans, the Ukrainians and the Poles, and, especially, Protestants and Catholics in Ulster. There is no magic moment when the walls come down, but the sequence of events is clear: first comes the political solution, typically imposed from outside and above, often when mutual resentment is at its peak. Only then can the forgetting begin.

The present moment, with Ariel Sharon about to set in motion a long cycle of death and decay across the region, may be the eleventh hour, as the American president has belatedly acknowledged. It surely is for Israel. Long before the Arabs get their land and their state, Israel will have decayed from within. The fear of seeming to show solidarity with Sharon, which already inhibits many from visiting Israel, will rapidly extend to the international community at large, making of Israel a pariah state. Bad as he is for the Palestinians, they will survive Sharon. The prospects for Israel are less sure. For the rest of the world the Middle East crisis represents an enhanced risk of international war, and a likely guarantee that America's war on terror, however described, will fail.[3]

Well-meaning observers of the contemporary Middle East sometimes place their faith in the enlightened self-interest of the warring parties. Palestinians, they suggest, would be so much better off accepting Israeli hegemony in return for material prosperity and personal security that sooner or later they will surely abandon their demands for full independence. To the extent that there is a strategic calculation behind Sharon's tanks, this is it: sufficiently cowed, the Arabs will see how much they have to lose by fighting and agree to a peaceful life on Israel's terms.

This is perhaps the most dangerous of all colonial illusions. There is little doubt that most Algerian Arabs would have been better off under French rule than under the repressive indigenous regimes that replaced it. The same is true for the citizens of many of the postcolonial states once ruled from London. But the measure of the well-lived life is not readily taken by calculations of income, longevity, or even safety. As Aron observed, "It is a denial of the experience of our century to suppose that men will sacrifice their passions for their interests." That is why, in their treatment of their Arab subjects, the Israelis are on the road to nowhere. There is no alternative to peace negotiations and a final settlement. And if not now, when?

This essay first appeared in *The New York Review of Books* in May 2002.

Notes to Chapter VI

[1] Paris: Plon, 1958. See also his *La Tragédie algérienne* (Paris: Plon, 1957).

[2] One real impediment is that Ariel Sharon is on record as opposing any final peace settlement remotely acceptable to anyone outside Israel. He cannot negotiate in good faith. The Israelis need to find someone who can.

[3] American commentators and officials are quick to deny any link between anti-Americanism and the Israel-Palestine conflict. But to just about everyone else in the world the relationship is grimly obvious.

CHAPTER VII

Israel: The Alternative

The Middle East peace process is finished. It did not die: it was killed. Mahmoud Abbas was undermined by the president of the Palestinian Authority and humiliated by the prime minister of Israel. His successor awaits a similar fate. Israel continues to mock its American patron, building illegal settlements in cynical disregard of the "road map." The president of the United States of America has been reduced to a ventriloquist's dummy, pitifully reciting the Israeli cabinet line: "It's all Arafat's fault." Israelis themselves grimly await the next bomber. Palestinian Arabs, corralled into shrinking Bantustans, subsist on E.U. handouts. On the corpse-strewn landscape of the Fertile Crescent, Ariel Sharon, Yasser Arafat, and a handful of terrorists can all claim victory, and they do. Have we reached the end of the road? What is to be done?

At the dawn of the twentieth century, in the twilight of the continental empires, Europe's subject peoples dreamed of forming "nation-states," territorial homelands where Poles, Czechs, Serbs, Armenians, and others might live free, masters of their own fate. When the Habsburg and Romanov empires collapsed after World War I, their leaders seized the opportunity. A flurry of new states emerged; and the first thing they did was set about privileging their national, "ethnic" majority—defined by language, or religion, or antiquity, or all three—at the expense of inconvenient local minorities, who were consigned to second-class status: permanently resident strangers in their own home.

But one nationalist movement, Zionism, was frustrated in its ambitions. The dream of an appropriately sited Jewish national home in the middle of the defunct Turkish Empire had to wait upon the retreat of imperial Britain: a process that took three more decades and a second world war. And thus it was only in 1948 that a Jewish nation-state was established in formerly Ottoman Palestine. But the founders of the Jewish state had been influenced by the same concepts and categories as their fin-de-siècle contemporaries back in Warsaw, or Odessa, or Bucharest; not surprisingly, Israel's ethno-religious self-definition, and its discrimination against internal "foreigners," has always had more in common with, say, the practices of post-Habsburg Romania than either party might care to acknowledge.

The problem with Israel, in short, is not—as is sometimes suggested—that it is a European "enclave" in the Arab world; but rather that it arrived too late. It has imported a characteristically late-nineteenth-century separatist project into a world that has moved on, a world of individual rights, open frontiers, and international law. The very idea of a "Jewish state"—a state in which Jews and the Jewish religion have exclusive privileges from which non-Jewish citizens are forever excluded—is rooted in another time and place. Israel, in short, is an anachronism.

IN ONE VITAL ATTRIBUTE, however, Israel is quite different from previous insecure, defensive microstates born of imperial collapse: it is a democracy. Hence its present dilemma. Thanks to its occupation of the lands conquered in 1967, Israel today faces three unattractive choices. It can dismantle the Jewish settlements in the territories, return to the 1967 state borders within which Jews constitute a clear majority, and thus remain both a Jewish state and a democracy, albeit one with a constitutionally anomalous community of second-class Arab citizens.

Alternatively, Israel can continue to occupy "Samaria," "Judea," and Gaza, whose Arab population—added to that of present-day Israel—will become the demographic majority within five to eight years: in which case Israel will be either a Jewish state (with an ever-larger majority of unenfranchised non-Jews) or it will be a democracy. But logically it cannot be both.

Or else Israel can keep control of the Occupied Territories but get rid of the overwhelming majority of the Arab population: either by forcible expulsion or else by starving them of land and livelihood, leaving them no option but to go into exile. In this way Israel could indeed remain both Jewish and at least formally democratic: but at the cost of becoming the first modern democracy to conduct full-scale ethnic cleansing as a state project, something which would condemn Israel forever to the status of an outlaw state, an international pariah.

Anyone who supposes that this third option is unthinkable above all for a Jewish state has not been watching the steady accretion of settlements and land seizures in the West Bank over the past quarter century, or listening to generals and politicians on the Israeli right, some of them currently in government. The middle ground of Israeli politics today is occupied by the Likud. Its major component is the late Menachem Begin's Herut Party. Herut is the successor to Vladimir Jabotinsky's interwar Revisionist Zionists, whose uncompromising indifference to legal and territorial niceties once attracted from left-leaning Zionists the epithet "Fascist." When one hears Israel's deputy prime minister, Ehud Olmert, proudly insist that his country has not excluded the option of assassinating the elected president of the Palestinian Authority, it is clear that the label fits better than ever. Political murder is what Fascists do.

THE SITUATION OF ISRAEL IS not desperate, but it may be close to hopeless. Suicide bombers will never bring down the Israeli state, and the Palestinians have no other weapons. There are indeed Arab radicals who will not rest until every Jew is pushed into the Mediterranean, but they represent no strategic threat to Israel, and the Israeli military knows it. What sensible Israelis fear much more than Hamas or the al-Aqsa Brigade is the steady emergence of an Arab majority in "Greater Israel," and above all the erosion of the political culture and civic morale of their society. As the prominent Labor politician Avraham Burg recently wrote, "After two thousand years of struggle for survival, the reality of Israel is a colonial state, run by a corrupt clique which scorns and mocks law and civic morality."[1] Unless something changes, Israel in half a decade will be neither Jewish nor democratic.

This is where the United States enters the picture. Israel's behavior has been a disaster for American foreign policy. With American support, Jerusalem has consistently and blatantly flouted UN resolutions requiring it to withdraw from land seized and occupied in war. Israel is the only Middle Eastern state known to possess genuine and lethal weapons of mass destruction. By turning a blind eye, the United States has effectively scuttled its own increasingly frantic efforts to prevent such weapons from falling into the hands of other small and potentially belligerent states. Washington's unconditional support for Israel even in spite of (silent) misgivings is the main reason why most of the rest of the world no longer credits our good faith.

It is now tacitly conceded by those in a position to know that America's reasons for going to war in Iraq were not necessarily those advertised at the time.[2] For many in the current U.S. administration, a major strategic consideration was the need to destabilize and then reconfigure the Middle East in a manner thought favorable to Israel. This story continues. We are now making belligerent noises toward Syria because Israeli intelligence has assured us that Iraqi weapons have been moved there—a claim for which there is no corroborating evidence from any other source. Syria backs Hezbollah and the Islamic Jihad: sworn foes of Israel, to be sure, but hardly a significant international threat. However, Damascus has hitherto been providing the United States with critical data on al-Qaeda. Like Iran, another long-standing target of Israeli wrath whom we are actively alienating, Syria is more use to the United States as a friend than an enemy. Which war are we fighting?

On September 16, 2003, the United States vetoed a UN Security Council resolution asking Israel to desist from its threat to deport Yasser Arafat. Even American officials themselves recognize, off the record, that the resolution was reasonable and prudent, and that the increasingly wild pronouncements of Israel's present leadership, by restoring Arafat's standing in the Arab world, are a major impediment to peace. But the United States blocked the resolution all the same, further undermining our credibility as an honest broker in the region. America's friends and allies around the world are no longer surprised at such actions, but they are saddened and disappointed all the same.

Israeli politicians have been actively contributing to their own difficulties for many years; why do we continue to aid and abet them in their mistakes? The United States has tentatively sought in the past to pressure Israel by threatening to withhold from its annual aid package some of the money that goes to subsidizing West Bank settlers. But the last time this was attempted, during the Clinton administration, Jerusalem got around it by taking the money as "security expenditure." Washington went along with the subterfuge, and of $10 billion of American aid over four years, between 1993 and 1997, less than $775 million was kept back. The settlement program went ahead unimpeded. Now we don't even try to stop it.

This reluctance to speak or act does no one any favors. It has also corroded American domestic debate. Rather than think straight about the Middle East, American politicians and pundits slander our European allies when they dissent, speak glibly and irresponsibly of resurgent anti-Semitism when Israel is criticized, and censoriously rebuke any public figure at home who tries to break from the consensus.

BUT THE CRISIS IN THE Middle East won't go away. President Bush will probably be conspicuous by his absence from the fray for the coming year, having said just enough about the "road map" in June to placate Tony Blair. But sooner or later an American statesman is going to have to tell the truth to an Israeli prime minister and find a way to make him listen. Israeli liberals and moderate Palestinians have for two decades been thanklessly insisting that the only hope was for Israel to dismantle nearly all the settlements and return to the 1967 borders, in exchange for real Arab recognition of those frontiers and a stable, terrorist-free Palestinian state underwritten (and constrained) by

Western and international agencies. This is still the conventional consensus, and it was once a just and possible solution.

But I suspect that we are already too late for that. There are too many settlements, too many Jewish settlers, and too many Palestinians, and they all live together, albeit separated by barbed wire and pass laws. Whatever the "road map" says, the real map is the one on the ground, and that, as Israelis say, reflects facts. It may be that over a quarter of a million heavily armed and subsidized Jewish settlers would leave Arab Palestine voluntarily; but no one I know believes it will happen. Many of those settlers will die—and kill—rather than move. The last Israeli politician to shoot Jews in pursuit of state policy was David Ben-Gurion, who forcibly disarmed Begin's illegal Irgun militia in 1948 and integrated it into the new Israel Defense Forces. Ariel Sharon is not Ben-Gurion.[3]

The time has come to think the unthinkable. The two-state solution—the core of the Oslo process and the present "road map"—is probably already doomed. With every passing year we are postponing an inevitable, harder choice that only the far right and far left have so far acknowledged, each for its own reasons. The true alternative facing the Middle East in coming years will be between an ethnically cleansed Greater Israel and a single, integrated, binational state of Jews and Arabs, Israelis and Palestinians. That is indeed how the hard-liners in Sharon's cabinet see the choice; and that is why they anticipate the removal of the Arabs as the ineluctable condition for the survival of a Jewish state.

But what if there were no place in the world today for a "Jewish state"? What if the binational solution were not just increasingly likely, but actually a desirable outcome? It is not such a very odd thought. Most of the readers of this essay live in pluralist states which have long since become multiethnic and multicultural. "Christian Europe," *pace* M. Valéry Giscard d'Estaing, is a dead letter; Western civilization today is a patchwork of colors and religions and languages, of Christians, Jews, Muslims, Arabs, Indians, and many others—as any visitor to London or Paris or Geneva will know.[4]

Israel itself is a multicultural society in all but name; yet it remains distinctive among democratic states in its resort to ethno-religious criteria with which to denominate and rank its citizens. It is an oddity among modern nations not—as its more paranoid supporters assert—because it is a *Jewish* state and no one wants the Jews to have a state; but because it is a Jewish *state* in which one community—Jews—is set above others, in an age when that sort of state has no place.

FOR MANY YEARS, Israel had a special meaning for the Jewish people. After 1948 it took in hundreds of thousands of helpless survivors who had nowhere else to go; without Israel their condition would have been desperate in the extreme. Israel needed Jews, and Jews needed Israel. The circumstances of its birth have thus bound Israel's identity inextricably to the *Shoah*, the German project to exterminate the Jews of Europe. As a result, all criticism of Israel is drawn ineluctably back to the memory of that project, something that Israel's American apologists are shamefully quick to exploit. To find fault with the Jewish state is to think ill of Jews; even to imagine an alternative configuration in the Middle East is to indulge the moral equivalent of genocide.

In the years after World War II, those many millions of Jews who did not live in Israel were often reassured by its very existence—whether they thought of it as an insurance policy against renascent anti-Semitism or simply a reminder to the world that Jews could and would fight back. Before there was a Jewish state, Jewish minorities in Christian societies would peer anxiously over their shoulders and keep a low profile; since 1948, they could walk tall. But in recent years, the situation has tragically reversed.

Today, non-Israeli Jews feel themselves once again exposed to criticism and vulnerable to attack for things they didn't do. But this time it is a Jewish state, not a Christian one, which is holding them hostage for its own actions. Diaspora Jews cannot influence Israeli policies, but they are implicitly identified with them, not least by Israel's own insistent claims upon their allegiance. The behavior of a self-described Jewish state affects the way everyone else looks at

Jews. The increased incidence of attacks on Jews in Europe and elsewhere is primarily attributable to misdirected efforts, often by young Muslims, to get back at Israel. The depressing truth is that Israel's current behavior is not just bad for America, though it surely is. It is not even just bad for Israel itself, as many Israelis silently acknowledge. The depressing truth is that Israel today is bad for the Jews.

In a world where nations and peoples increasingly intermingle and inter-marry at will; where cultural and national impediments to communication have all but collapsed; where more and more of us have multiple elective iden-tities and would feel falsely constrained if we had to answer to just one of them; in such a world Israel is truly an anachronism. And not just an anach-ronism but a dysfunctional one. In today's "clash of cultures" between open, pluralist democracies and belligerently intolerant, faith-driven ethno-states, Israel actually risks falling into the wrong camp.

To convert Israel from a Jewish state to a binational one would not be easy, though not quite as impossible as it sounds: the process has already begun de facto. But it would cause far less disruption to most Jews and Arabs than its religious and nationalist foes will claim. In any case, no one I know of has a better idea: anyone who genuinely supposes that the controversial electronic fence now being built will resolve matters has missed the last fifty years of history. The "fence"—actually an armored zone of ditches, fences, sensors, dirt roads (for tracking footprints), and a wall up to twenty-eight feet tall in places—occupies, divides, and steals Arab farmland; it will destroy villages, livelihoods, and whatever remains of Arab-Jewish community. It costs ap-proximately $1 million per mile and will bring nothing but humiliation and discomfort to both sides. Like the Berlin Wall, it confirms the moral and in-stitutional bankruptcy of the regime it is intended to protect.

A binational state in the Middle East would require a brave and relent-lessly engaged American leadership. The security of Jews and Arabs alike would need to be guaranteed by international force—though a legitimately constituted binational state would find it much easier policing militants of all kinds inside its borders than when they are free to infiltrate them from outside and can appeal to an angry, excluded constituency on both sides of the border.[5] A binational state in the Middle East would require the emergence, among Jews and Arabs alike, of a new political class. The very idea is an unpromising mix of realism and utopia, hardly an auspicious place to begin. But the alternatives are far, far worse.

This essay first appeared in *The New York Review of Books* in October 2003.

Notes to Chapter VII

[1] See Burg's essay, "*La révolution sioniste est morte*," *Le Monde*, September 11, 2003. A former head of the Jewish Agency, the writer was speaker of the Knesset, Israel's parliament, between 1999 and 2003 and is currently a Labor Party member of the Knesset. His essay first appeared in the Israeli daily *Yediot Aharonot*; it has been widely republished, notably in the *Forward* (August 29, 2003) and the London *Guardian* (September 15, 2003).

[2] See the interview with Deputy Secretary of Defense Paul Wolfowitz in the July 2003 issue of *Vanity Fair*.

[3] In 1979, following the peace agreement with Anwar Sadat, Prime Minister Begin and Defense Minister Sharon did indeed instruct the army to close down Jewish settlements in the territory belonging to Egypt. The angry resistance of some of the settlers was overcome with force, though no one was killed. But then the army was facing three thousand extremists, not a quarter of a million, and the land in question was the Sinai Desert, not "biblical Samaria and Judea."

[4] Albanians in Italy, Arabs and black Africans in France, Asians in England all continue to encounter hostility. A minority of voters in France or Belgium or even Denmark and Norway, support political parties whose hostility to "immigration" is sometimes their only platform. But compared with thirty years ago, Europe is a multicolored patchwork of equal citizens, and that, without question, is the shape of its future.

[5] As Burg notes, Israel's current policies are the terrorists' best recruiting tool: "We are indifferent to the fate of Palestinian children, hungry and humiliated; so why are we surprised when they blow us up in our restaurants? Even if we killed 1,000 terrorists a day it would change nothing." See Burg, "*La révolution sioniste est morte*."

CHAPTER VIII

A Lobby, Not a Conspiracy

In its March 23, 2006, issue the *London Review of Books,* a respected British journal, published an essay titled "The Israel Lobby." The authors are two distinguished American academics (Stephen Walt of Harvard and John Mearsheimer of the University of Chicago) who posted a longer (eighty-three-page) version of their text on the Web site of Harvard's Kennedy School.

As they must have anticipated, the essay has run into a firestorm of vituperation and refutation. Critics have charged that their scholarship is shoddy and that their claims are, in the words of the columnist Christopher Hitchens, "slightly but unmistakably smelly." The smell in question, of course, is that of anti-Semitism.

This somewhat hysterical response is regrettable. In spite of its provocative title, the essay draws on a wide variety of standard sources and is mostly uncontentious. But it makes two distinct and important claims. The first is that uncritical support for Israel across the decades has not served America's best interests. This is an assertion that can be debated on its merits. The authors' second claim is more controversial: American foreign policy choices, they write, have for years been distorted by one domestic pressure group, the "Israel Lobby."

Some would prefer, when explaining American actions overseas, to point a finger at the domestic "energy lobby." Others might blame the influence of Wilsonian idealism, or imperial practices left over from the cold war. But that a powerful Israel lobby exists could hardly be denied by anyone who knows how Washington works. Its core is the American Israel Public Affairs Committee, its penumbra a variety of national Jewish organizations.

Does the Israel lobby affect our foreign policy choices? Of course—that is one of its goals. And it has been rather successful: Israel is the largest recipient of American foreign aid, and American responses to Israeli behavior have been overwhelmingly uncritical or supportive.

But does pressure to support Israel distort American decisions? That's a matter of judgment. Prominent Israeli leaders and their American supporters pressed very hard for the invasion of Iraq; but the United States would probably be in Iraq today even if there had been no Israel lobby. Is Israel, in Mearsheimer-Walt's words, "a liability in the war on terror and the broader effort to deal with rogue states?" I think it is; but that too is an issue for legitimate debate.

The essay and the issues it raises for American foreign policy have been prominently dissected and discussed overseas. In America, however, it's been another story: virtual silence in the mainstream media. Why? There are several plausible explanations. One is that a relatively obscure academic paper is of little concern to general-interest readers. Another is that claims about disproportionate Jewish public influence are hardly original—and debate over them inevitably attracts interest from the political extremes. And then there is the view that Washington is anyway awash in "lobbies" of this sort, pressuring policymakers and distorting their choices.

Each of these considerations might reasonably account for the mainstream press's initial indifference to the Mearsheimer-Walt essay. But they don't convincingly explain the continued silence even after the article aroused stormy debate in the academy, within the Jewish community, among the opinion magazines and Web sites, and in the rest of the world. I think there is another element in play: fear. Fear of being thought to legitimize talk of a "Jewish conspiracy"; fear of being thought anti-Israel; and thus, in the end, fear of licensing the expression of anti-Semitism.

The end result—a failure to consider a major issue in public policy—is a great pity. So what, you may ask, if Europeans debate this subject with such enthusiasm? Isn't Europe a hotbed of anti-Zionists (read anti-Semites) who will always relish the chance to attack Israel and her American friend? But it was David Aaronovitch, a *Times of London* columnist who, in the course of criticizing Mearsheimer and Walt, nonetheless conceded that "I sympathize with their desire for redress, since there has been a cock-eyed failure in the U.S. to understand the plight of the Palestinians."

And it was the German writer Christoph Bertram, a long-standing friend of America in a country where every public figure takes extraordinary care to tread carefully in such matters, who wrote in *Die Zeit* that "it is rare to find scholars with the desire and the courage to break taboos."

How are we to explain the fact that it is in Israel itself that the uncomfortable issues raised by Professors Mearsheimer and Walt have been most thoroughly aired? It was an Israeli columnist in the liberal daily *Haaretz* who described the American foreign policy advisers Richard Perle and Douglas Feith as "walking a fine line between their loyalty to American governments . . . and Israeli interests." It was Israel's impeccably conservative *Jerusalem Post* that described Paul Wolfowitz, the deputy secretary of defense, as "devoutly pro-Israel." Are we to accuse Israelis, too, of "anti-Zionism"?

The damage that is done by America's fear of anti-Semitism when discussing Israel is threefold. It is bad for Jews: anti-Semitism is real enough (I know something about it, growing up Jewish in 1950s Britain), but for just that reason it should not be confused with political criticisms of Israel or its American supporters. It is bad for Israel: by guaranteeing it unconditional support, Americans encourage Israel to act heedless of consequences. The Israeli journalist Tom Segev described the Mearsheimer-Walt essay as "arrogant" but also acknowledged ruefully: "They are right. Had the United States saved Israel from itself, life today would be better . . . the Israel Lobby in the United States harms Israel's true interests."

But above all, self-censorship is bad for the United States itself. Americans are denying themselves participation in a fast-moving international conversation. Daniel Levy (a former Israeli peace negotiator) wrote in *Haaretz* that the Mearsheimer-Walt essay should be a wake-up call, a reminder of the damage the Israel lobby is doing to both nations. But I would go further. I think this essay, by two "realist" political scientists with no interest whatsoever in the Palestinians, is a straw in the wind.

Looking back, we shall see the Iraq war and its catastrophic consequences as not the beginning of a new democratic age in the Middle East but rather as the end of an era that began in the wake of the 1967 war, a period during which American alignment with Israel was shaped by two imperatives: cold-war strategic calculations and a newfound domestic sensitivity to the memory of the Holocaust and the debt owed to its victims and survivors.

For the terms of strategic debate are shifting. East Asia grows daily in importance. Meanwhile our clumsy failure to recast the Middle East—and its enduring implications for our standing there—has come into sharp focus. American influence in that part of the world now rests almost exclusively on our power to make war: which means in the end that it is no influence at all. Above all, perhaps, the Holocaust is passing beyond living memory. In the eyes of a watching world, the fact that an Israeli soldier's great-grandmother died in Treblinka will not excuse his own misbehavior.

Thus it will not be self-evident to future generations of Americans why the imperial might and international reputation of the United States are so closely aligned with one small, controversial Mediterranean client state. It is already not at all self-evident to Europeans, Latin Americans, Africans, or Asians. Why, they ask, has America chosen to lose touch with the rest of the international community on this issue? Americans may not like the implications of this question. But it is pressing. It bears directly on our international standing

and influence; and it has nothing to do with anti-Semitism. We cannot ignore it.

This response to the publication of "The Israel Lobby" by John
Mearsheimer and Stephen Walt in the *London Review of Books*
first appeared in *The New York Times* in April 2006.

CHAPTER IX

The "Problem of Evil" in Postwar Europe

The first work by Hannah Arendt that I read, at the age of sixteen, was *Eichmann in Jerusalem: A Report on the Banality of Evil.* It remains, for me, the emblematic Arendt text. It is not her most philosophical book. It is not always right; and it is decidedly *not* her most popular piece of writing. I did not even like the book myself when I first read it—I was an ardent young Socialist-Zionist and Arendt's conclusions profoundly disturbed me. But in the years since then I have come to understand that *Eichmann in Jerusalem* represents Hannah Arendt at her best: attacking head-on a painful topic; dissenting from official wisdom; provoking argument not just among her critics but also and especially among her friends; and above all, *disturbing the easy peace of received opinion.* It is in memory of Arendt the "disturber of the peace" that I want to offer a few thoughts on a subject which, more than any other, preoccupied her political writings.

In 1945, in one of her first essays following the end of the war in Europe, Hannah Arendt wrote that "the problem of evil will be the fundamental question of postwar intellectual life in Europe—as death became the fundamental problem after the last war."[1] In one sense she was, of course, absolutely correct. After World War I Europeans were traumatized by the memory of death: above all, death on the battlefield, on a scale hitherto unimaginable.

The poetry, fiction, cinema, and art of interwar Europe were suffused with images of violence and death, usually critical but sometimes nostalgic (as in the writings of Ernst Jünger or Pierre Drieu La Rochelle). And of course the armed violence of World War I leached into civilian life in interwar Europe in many forms: paramilitary squads, political murders, coups d'état, civil wars, and revolutions.

After World War II, however, the worship of violence largely disappeared from European life. During this war, violence was directed not just against soldiers but above all against civilians (a large share of the deaths during World War II occurred not in battle but under the aegis of occupation, ethnic cleansing, and genocide). And the utter exhaustion of all European nations—winners and losers alike—left few illusions about the glory of fighting or the honor of death. What *did* remain, of course, was a widespread familiarity with brutality and crime on an unprecedented scale. The question of how human beings could do this to each other—and above all the question of how and why one European people (Germans) could set out to exterminate another (Jews)—were, for an alert observer like Arendt, self-evidently going to be the obsessive questions facing the continent. That is what she meant by "the problem of evil."

In one sense, then, Arendt was of course correct. But as so often, it took other people longer to grasp her point. It is true that in the aftermath of Hitler's defeat and the Nuremberg trials, lawyers and legislators devoted much attention to the issue of "crimes against humanity" and the definition of a new crime—"genocide"—that until then had not even had a name. But while the courts were defining the monstrous crimes that had just been committed in Europe, Europeans themselves were doing their best to forget them. And in that sense at least, Arendt was wrong, at least for a while.

FAR FROM REFLECTING UPON THE problem of evil in the years that followed the end of World War II, most Europeans turned their heads resolutely away from it. Today we find this difficult to understand, but the fact is that the *Shoah*—the attempted genocide of the Jews of Europe—was for many years by no means the fundamental question of postwar intellectual life in Europe (or the United States). Indeed, most people—intellectuals and others— ignored it as much as they could. Why?

In Eastern Europe there were four reasons. In the first place, the worst wartime crimes against the Jews were committed there; and although those crimes were sponsored by Germans, there was no shortage of willing collaborators among the local occupied nations: Poles, Ukrainians, Latvians, Croats, and others. There was a powerful incentive in many places to forget what had happened, to draw a veil over the worst horrors.[2] Second, many non-Jewish East Europeans were themselves victims of atrocities (at the hands of Germans, Russians, and others) and when *they* remembered the war they did not typically think of the agony of their Jewish neighbors but of their own suffering and losses.

Thirdly, most of Central and Eastern Europe came under Soviet control by 1948. The official Soviet account of World War II was of an anti-Fascist war—or, within the Soviet Union, a "Great Patriotic War." For Moscow, Hitler was above all a Fascist and a nationalist. His racism was much less important. The millions of dead Jews from the Soviet territories were counted in Soviet losses, of course, but their Jewishness was played down or even ignored, in history books and public commemorations. And finally, after a few years of Communist rule, the memory of *German* occupation was replaced by that of *Soviet* oppression. The extermination of the Jews was pushed even deeper into the background.

In Western Europe, even though circumstances were quite different, there was a parallel forgetting. The wartime occupation—in France, Belgium, Holland, Norway, and, after 1943, Italy—was a humiliating experience and postwar governments preferred to forget collaboration and other indignities and emphasize instead the heroic resistance movements, national uprisings, liberations, and martyrs. For many years after 1945 even those who knew better— like Charles de Gaulle—deliberately contributed to a national mythology of heroic suffering and courageous mass resistance. In postwar West Germany, too, the initial national mood was one of self-pity at Germans' own suffering.

And with the onset of the cold war and a change of enemies, it became inopportune to emphasize the past crimes of present allies. So no one—not Germans, not Austrians, not French or Dutch or Belgians or Italians—wanted to recall the suffering of the Jews or the distinctive evil that had brought it about.

That is why, to take a famous example, when Primo Levi took his Auschwitz memoir *Se questo è un uomo* to the major Italian publisher Einaudi in 1946 it was rejected out of hand. At that time, and for some years to come, it was Bergen-Belsen and Dachau, not Auschwitz, which stood for the horror of Nazism; the emphasis on *political* deportees rather than racial ones conformed better to reassuring postwar accounts of wartime national resistance. Levi's book was eventually published, but in just 2,500 copies by a small local press. Hardly anyone bought it; many copies of the book were remaindered in a warehouse in Florence and destroyed in the great flood there in 1966.

I can confirm the lack of interest in the *Shoah* in those years from my own experience, growing up in England—a victorious country that had never been occupied and thus had no complex about wartime crimes. But even in England the subject was never much discussed—in school or in the media. As late as 1966, when I began to study modern history at Cambridge University, I was taught French history—including the history of Vichy France—with almost no reference to Jews or anti-Semitism. No one was writing about the subject. Yes, we studied the Nazi occupation of France, the collaborators at Vichy, and French Fascism. But nothing we read, in English or French, engaged the problem of France's role in the Final Solution.

And even though I am Jewish and members of my own family had been killed in the death camps, I did not think it strange back then that the subject passed unmentioned. The silence seemed quite normal. How does one explain, in retrospect, this willingness to accept the unacceptable? Why does the abnormal come to seem so normal that we don't even notice it? Probably for the depressingly simple reason that Tolstoy provides in *Anna Karenina*: "There are no conditions of life to which a man cannot get accustomed, especially if he sees them accepted by everyone around him."

Everything started to change after the sixties, for many reasons: the passage of time, the curiosity of a new generation, and perhaps, too, a slackening of international tension.[3] West Germany above all, the nation primarily responsible for the horrors of Hitler's war, was transformed in the course of a generation into a people uniquely conscious of the enormity of its crimes and the scale of its accountability. By the 1980s the story of the destruction of the Jews of Europe was becoming increasingly familiar in books, in cinema, and on television. Since the 1990s and the end of the division of Europe, official apologies, national commemoration sites, memorials, and museums have become commonplace; even in post-Communist Eastern Europe the suffering of the Jews has begun to take its place in official memory.

Today, the *Shoah* is a universal reference. The history of the Final Solution, or Nazism, or World War II is a required course in high school curriculums everywhere. Indeed, there are schools in the United States and even Britain where such a course may be the only topic in modern European history that a child ever studies. There are now countless records and retellings and studies of the wartime extermination of the Jews of Europe: local monographs, philosophical essays, sociological and psychological investigations, memoirs, fictions, feature films, archives of interviews, and much else. Hannah Arendt's prophecy would seem to have come true: the history of the problem of evil has become a fundamental theme of European intellectual life.

So NOW EVERYTHING IS ALL RIGHT? Now that we have looked into the dark past, called it by its name, and sworn that it must never again be repeated? I am not so sure. Let me suggest five difficulties that arise from our contemporary preoccupation with the *Shoah*, with what every schoolchild now calls "the Holocaust." The first difficulty concerns the dilemma of incompatible memories. *Western* European attention to the memory of the Final Solution is now universal (though for understandable reasons less developed in Spain and Portugal). But the "eastern" nations that have joined "Europe" since

1989 retain a very different memory of World War II and its lessons, for the reasons I have suggested.

Indeed, with the disappearance of the Soviet Union and the resulting freedom to study and discuss the crimes and failures of Communism, greater attention has been paid to the ordeal of Europe's eastern half, at the hands of Germans and Soviets alike. In this context, the Western European and American emphasis upon Auschwitz and Jewish victims sometimes provokes an irritated reaction. In Poland and Romania, for example, I have been asked— by educated and cosmopolitan listeners—why Western intellectuals are so particularly sensitive to the mass murder of Jews. What of the millions of non-Jewish victims of Nazism and Stalinism? Why is the *Shoah* so very distinctive? There is an answer to that question; but it is not self-evident to everyone east of the Oder-Neisse line. We in the United States or Western Europe may not like that but we should remember it. On such matters Europe is very far from united.

A second difficulty concerns historical accuracy and the risks of overcompensation. For many years, Western Europeans preferred not to think about the wartime sufferings of the Jews. Now we are encouraged to think about those sufferings all the time. For the first decades after 1945 the gas chambers were confined to the margin of our understanding of Hitler's war. Today they sit at the very center: for today's students, World War II is about the Holocaust. In *moral* terms that is as it should be: the central ethical issue of World War II *is* "Auschwitz." But for historians this is misleading. For the sad truth is that during World War II itself, many people did not know about the fate of the Jews and if they did know they did not much care. There were only two groups for whom World War II was above all a project to destroy the Jews: the Nazis and the Jews themselves. For practically everyone else the war had quite different meanings: they had troubles of their own.

And so, if we teach the history of World War II above all—and sometimes uniquely—through the prism of the Holocaust, we may not always be teaching good history. It is hard for us to accept that the Holocaust occupies a more

important role in our own lives than it did in the wartime experience of occupied lands. But if we wish to grasp the true significance of evil—what Hannah Arendt intended by calling it "banal"—then we must remember that
what is truly awful about the destruction of the Jews is not that it mattered so
much but that it mattered so little.

My third problem concerns the concept of "evil" itself. Modern secular society has long been uncomfortable with the idea of "evil." We prefer more ra-
tionalistic and legal definitions of good and bad, right and wrong, crime and
punishment. But in recent years the word has crept slowly back into moral and
even political discourse.[4] However, now that the concept of "evil" has reen-
tered our public language we don't know what to do with it. We have become
confused.

On the one hand the Nazi extermination of the Jews is presented as a sin-
gular crime, an evil never matched before or since, an example and a warning:
"Nie Wieder! Never again!" But on the other hand we invoke that same
("unique") evil today for many different and far from unique purposes. In
recent years politicians, historians, and journalists have used the term "evil" to
describe mass murder and genocidal outcomes everywhere: from Cambodia
to Rwanda, from Turkey to Serbia, from Bosnia to Chechnya, from the Congo
to Sudan. Hitler himself is frequently conjured up to denote the "evil" nature
and intentions of modern dictators: we are told there are "Hitlers" everywhere,
from North Korea to Iraq, from Syria to Iran. And we are all familiar with
President George W. Bush's "axis of evil," a self-serving abuse of the term
which has contributed greatly to the cynicism it now elicits.

Moreover, if Hitler, Auschwitz, and the genocide of the Jews incarnated
a unique evil, why are we constantly warned that they and their like could
happen anywhere, or are about to happen again? Every time someone smears
anti-Semitic graffiti on a synagogue wall in France we are warned that "the
unique evil" is with us once more, that it is 1938 all over again. We are losing
the capacity to distinguish between the normal sins and follies of mankind—
stupidity, prejudice, opportunism, demagogy, and fanaticism—and genuine

evil. We have lost sight of what it was about twentieth-century political religions of the extreme left and extreme right that was so seductive, so commonplace, so modern, and thus so truly *diabolical*. After all, if we see evil everywhere, how can we be expected to recognize the real thing? Sixty years ago Hannah Arendt feared that we would not know how to speak of evil and that we would therefore never grasp its significance. Today we speak of "evil" all the time—but with the same result, that we have diluted its meaning.

MY FOURTH CONCERN BEARS ON the risk we run when we invest all our emotional and moral energies into just one problem, however serious. The costs of this sort of tunnel vision are on tragic display today in Washington's obsession with the evils of terrorism, its "Global War on Terror." The question is not whether terrorism exists: of course it exists. Nor is it a question of whether terrorism and terrorists should be fought: of course they should be fought. The question is what other evils we shall neglect—or create—by focusing exclusively upon a single enemy and using it to justify a hundred lesser crimes of our own.

The same point applies to our contemporary fascination with the problem of anti-Semitism and our insistence upon its unique importance. Anti-Semitism, like terrorism, is an old problem. And as with terrorism, so with anti-Semitism: even a minor outbreak reminds us of the consequences in the past of not taking it seriously enough. But anti-Semitism, like terrorism, is *not* the only evil in the world and must *not* be an excuse to ignore other crimes and other suffering. The danger of abstracting "terrorism" or anti-Semitism from their contexts—of setting them upon a pedestal as the greatest threat to Western civilization, or democracy, or "our way of life," and targeting their exponents for an indefinite war—is that we shall overlook the many other challenges of the age.

On this, too, Hannah Arendt had something to say. Having written the most influential book on totalitarianism she was well aware of the threat that it posed to open societies. But in the era of the cold war, "totalitarianism," like terrorism or anti-Semitism today, was in danger of becoming an obsessive pre-occupation for thinkers and politicians in the West, to the exclusion of every-thing else. And against this, Arendt issued a warning which is still relevant today:

> The greatest danger of recognizing totalitarianism as the curse of the cen-tury would be an obsession with it to the extent of becoming blind to the numerous small and not so small evils with which the road to hell is paved.[5]

My final worry concerns the relationship between the memory of the Euro-pean Holocaust and the state of Israel. Ever since its birth in 1948, the state of Israel has negotiated a complex relationship to the *Shoah*. On the one hand the near extermination of Europe's Jews summarized the case for Zionism. Jews could not survive and flourish in non-Jewish lands, their integration and as-similation into European nations and cultures was a tragic delusion, and they must have a state of their own. On the other hand, the widespread Israeli view that the Jews of Europe conspired in their own downfall, that they went, as it was said, "like lambs to the slaughter," meant that Israel's initial identity was built upon rejecting the Jewish past and treating the Jewish catastrophe as evidence of weakness: a weakness that it was Israel's destiny to overcome by breeding a new sort of Jew.[6]

But in recent years the relationship between Israel and the Holocaust has changed. Today, when Israel is exposed to international criticism for its mis-treatment of Palestinians and its occupation of territory conquered in 1967, its defenders prefer to *emphasize* the memory of the Holocaust. If you criti-cize Israel too forcefully, they warn, you will awaken the demons of anti-Semitism; indeed, they suggest, robust criticism of Israel doesn't just arouse anti-Semitism. It is anti-Semitism. And with anti-Semitism the route for-ward—or back—is open: to 1938, to *Kristallnacht*, and from there to Treblinka and Auschwitz. If you want to know where it leads, they say, you have only to visit Yad Vashem in Jerusalem, the Holocaust Museum in Washington, or any number of memorials and museums across Europe.

I understand the emotions behind such claims. But the claims themselves are extraordinarily dangerous. When people chide me and others for criticizing Israel too forcefully, lest we rouse the ghosts of prejudice, I tell them that they have the problem exactly the wrong way around. It is just such a taboo that may itself stimulate anti-Semitism. For some years now I have visited colleges and high schools in the United States and elsewhere, lecturing on postwar European history and the memory of the *Shoah*. I also teach these topics in my university. And I can report on my findings.

Students today do not need to be reminded of the genocide of the Jews, the historical consequences of anti-Semitism, or the problem of evil. They know all about these—in ways their parents never did. And that is as it should be. But I have been struck lately by the frequency with which new questions are surfacing: "Why do we focus so on the Holocaust?" "Why is it illegal [in certain countries] to deny the Holocaust but not other genocides?" "Is the threat of anti-Semitism not exaggerated?" And, increasingly, "Doesn't Israel use the Holocaust as an excuse?" I do not recall hearing those questions in the past.

My fear is that two things have happened. By emphasizing the historical uniqueness of the Holocaust while at the same time invoking it constantly with reference to contemporary affairs, we have confused young people. And by shouting "anti-Semitism" every time someone attacks Israel or defends the Palestinians, we are breeding cynics. For the truth is that Israel today is not in existential danger. And Jews today here in the West face no threats or prejudices remotely comparable to those of the past—or comparable to contemporary prejudices against *other* minorities.

Imagine the following exercise: Would you feel safe, accepted, welcome today as a Muslim or an "illegal immigrant" in the United States? As a "Paki" in parts of England? A Moroccan in Holland? A *beur* in France? A black in Switzerland? An "alien" in Denmark? A Romanian in Italy? A Gypsy *anywhere* in Europe? Or would you not feel safer, more integrated, more accepted as a Jew? I think we all know the answer. In many of these countries—Holland, France, the United States, not to mention Germany—the local Jewish minority is prominently represented in business, the media, and the arts. In none of them are Jews stigmatized, threatened, or excluded.

IF THERE IS A THREAT that should concern Jews—and everyone else—it comes from a different direction. We have attached the memory of the Holocaust so firmly to the defense of a single country—Israel—that we are in danger of provincializing its moral significance. Yes, the problem of evil in the last century, to invoke Arendt once again, took the form of a German attempt to exterminate Jews. But it is not just about Germans and it is not just about Jews. It is not even just about Europe, though it happened there. The problem of evil—of totalitarian evil, or genocidal evil—is a universal problem. But if it is manipulated to local advantage, what will then happen (what is, I believe, already happening) is that those who stand at some distance from the memory of the European crime—because they are not Europeans, or because they are too young to remember why it matters—will not understand how that memory relates to them and they will stop listening when we try to explain.

In short, the Holocaust may lose its universal resonance. We must hope that this will not be the case and we need to find a way to preserve the core lesson that the *Shoah* really can teach: the ease with which people—a whole people—can be defamed, dehumanized, and destroyed. But we shall get nowhere unless we recognize that this lesson could indeed be questioned, or forgotten: the trouble with lessons, as the Gryphon observed, is that they really do lessen from day to day. If you do not believe me, go beyond the developed West and ask what lessons Auschwitz teaches. The responses are not very reassuring.

THERE IS NO EASY ANSWER to this problem. What seems obvious to West Europeans today is still opaque to many East Europeans, just as it was to West Europeans themselves forty years ago. Moral admonitions from Auschwitz that loom huge on the memory screen of Europeans are quite invisible to Asians or Africans. And, perhaps above all, what seems self-evident to people of my generation is going to make diminishing sense to our children and grandchildren. Can we preserve a European past that is now fading from memory into history? Are we not doomed to lose it, if only in part?

Maybe all our museums and memorials and obligatory school trips today are not a sign that we are ready to *remember* but an indication that we feel we have done our penance and can now begin to let go and *forget*, leaving the stones to remember for us. I don't know: the last time I visited Berlin's Memorial to the Murdered Jews of Europe, bored schoolchildren on an obligatory outing were playing hide-and-seek among the stones. What I *do* know is that if history is to do its proper job, preserving forever the evidence of past crimes and everything else, it is best left alone. When we ransack the past for political profit—selecting the bits that can serve our purposes and recruiting history to teach opportunistic moral lessons—we get bad morality *and* bad history.

Meanwhile, we should all of us perhaps take care when we speak of the problem of evil. For there is more than one sort of banality. There is the notorious banality of which Arendt spoke—the unsettling, normal, neighborly, everyday evil in humans. But there is another banality: the banality of overuse—the flattening, desensitizing effect of seeing or saying or thinking the same thing too many times until we have numbed our audience and rendered them immune to the evil we are describing. And that is the banality—or "banalization"—that we face today.

After 1945 our parents' generation set aside the problem of evil because— for them—it contained too *much* meaning. The generation that will follow us is in danger of setting the problem aside because it now contains too *little* meaning. How can we prevent this? How, in other words, can we ensure that the problem of evil *remains* the fundamental question for intellectual life, and not just in Europe? I don't know the answer, but I am pretty sure that it is the right question. It is the question Hannah Arendt asked sixty years ago, and I believe she would still ask it today.

This essay first appeared in *The New York Review of Books* in February 2008. It was adapted from a lecture delivered in Bremen, Germany, on November 30, 2007, on the occasion of the award to Tony Judt of the 2007 Hannah Arendt Prize.

NOTES TO CHAPTER IX

[1] "Nightmare and Flight," *Partisan Review*, vol. 12, no. 2 (1945), reprinted in *Essays in Understanding, 1930–1954*, Jerome Kohn, ed. (New York: Harcourt Brace, 1994), pp. 133–135.

[2] For a harrowing instance, see Jan Gross, *Neighbors: The Destruction of the Jewish Community in Jedwabne, Poland* (Princeton, NJ: Princeton University Press, 2001).

[3] For a fuller discussion of this shift in mood, see the epilogue ("From the House of the Dead") in my *Postwar: A History of Europe Since 1945* (New York: Penguin, 2005).

[4] To be sure, Catholic thinkers have not shared this reluctance to engage with the dilemma of evil: see, for example, Leszek Kołakowski's essays "The Devil in History" and "Leibniz and Job: The Metaphysics of Evil and the Experience of Evil," both recently republished with other essays by Kołakowski in *My Correct Views on Everything* (South Bend, IN: St. Augustine's Press, 2005; discussed in *The New York Review*, September 21, 2006). But in the metaphysical confrontation memorably portrayed by Thomas Mann, we moderns have typically opted for Settembrini over Naphta.

[5] *Essays in Understanding*, pp. 271–272.

[6] See Idith Zertal, *Israel's Holocaust and the Politics of Nationhood*, Chaya Galai, trans. (New York: Cambridge University Press, 2005), especially Chapter 1, "The Sacrificed and the Sanctified."

CHAPTER X

Fictions on the Ground

I am old enough to remember when Israeli kibbutzim looked like settlements ("a small village or collection of houses" or "the act of peopling or
colonizing a new country," *Oxford English Dictionary*).

In the early 1960s, I spent time on Kibbutz Hakuk, a small community
founded by the Palmah unit of the Haganah, the pre-state Jewish militia.
Begun in 1945, Hakuk was just eighteen years old when I first saw it, and was
still raw at the edges. The few dozen families living there had built themselves
a dining hall, farm sheds, homes, and a "baby house" where the children were
cared for during the workday. But where the residential buildings ended there
was nothing but rock-covered hillsides and half-cleared fields.

The community's members still dressed in blue work shirts, khaki shorts,
and triangular hats, consciously cultivating a pioneering image and ethos already at odds with the hectic urban atmosphere of Tel Aviv. Ours, they seemed
to say to bright-eyed visitors and volunteers, is the real Israel; come and help us
clear the boulders and grow bananas—and tell your friends in Europe and
America to do likewise.

Hakuk is still there. But today it relies on a plastics factory and the tourists
who flock to the nearby Sea of Galilee. The original farm, built around a fort,
has been turned into a tourist attraction. To speak of this kibbutz as a settlement would be bizarre.

However, Israel needs "settlements." They are intrinsic to the image it has long sought to convey to overseas admirers and fund-raisers: a struggling little country securing its rightful place in a hostile environment by the hard moral work of land clearance, irrigation, agrarian self-sufficiency, industrious productivity, legitimate self-defense, and the building of Jewish communities. But this neocollectivist frontier narrative rings false in modern, high-tech Israel. And so the settler myth has been transposed somewhere else—to the Palestinian lands seized in war in 1967 and occupied illegally ever since.

It is thus not by chance that the international press is encouraged to speak and write of Jewish "settlers" and "settlements" in the West Bank. But this image is profoundly misleading. The largest of these controversial communities in geographic terms is Maale Adumim. It has a population in excess of 35,000, demographically comparable to Montclair, New Jersey, or Winchester, England. What is most striking, however, about Maale Adumim is its territorial extent. This "settlement" comprises more than thirty square miles—making it one and a half times the size of Manhattan and nearly half as big as the borough and city of Manchester, England. Some "settlement."

There are about 120 official Israeli settlements in the occupied territories of the West Bank. In addition, there are "unofficial" settlements whose number is estimated variously from 80 to 100. Under international law, there is no difference between these two categories; both are contraventions of Article 47 of the Fourth Geneva Convention, which explicitly prohibits the annexation of land consequent to the use of force, a principle restated in Article 2(4) of the United Nations Charter.

Thus the distinction so often made in Israeli pronouncements between "authorized" and "unauthorized" settlements is specious—all are illegal, whether or not they have been officially approved and whether or not their expansion has been "frozen" or continues apace. (It is a matter of note that Israel's new foreign minister, Avigdor Lieberman, belongs to the West Bank settlement of Nokdim, established in 1982 and illegally expanded since.)

The blatant cynicism of the present Israeli government should not blind us to the responsibility of its more respectable-looking predecessors. The settler population has grown consistently at a rate of 5 percent annually over the past two decades, three times the rate of increase of the Israeli population as a whole. Together with the Jewish population of East Jerusalem (itself illegally annexed to Israel), the settlers today number more than half a million people: just over 10 percent of the Jewish population of so-called Greater Israel. This is one reason why settlers count for so much in Israeli elections, where proportional representation gives undue political leverage to even the smallest constituency.

But the settlers are no mere marginal interest group. To appreciate their significance, spread as they are over a dispersed archipelago of urban installations protected from Arab intrusion by 600 checkpoints and barriers, consider the following: taken together, East Jerusalem, the West Bank, and the Golan Heights constitute a homogenous demographic bloc nearly the size of the District of Columbia. It exceeds the population of Tel Aviv itself by almost one-third. Some "settlement."

If Israel is drunk on settlements, the United States has long been its enabler. Were Israel not the leading beneficiary of American foreign aid—averaging $2.8 billion a year from 2003 to 2007, and scheduled to reach $3.1 billion by 2013—houses in West Bank settlements would not be so cheap: often less than half the price of equivalent homes in Israel proper.

Many of the people who move to these houses don't even think of themselves as settlers. Newly arrived from Russia and elsewhere, they simply take up the offer of subsidized accommodation, move into the occupied areas, and become—like peasants in southern Italy freshly supplied with roads and electricity—the grateful clients of their political patrons. Like American settlers heading west, Israeli colonists in the West Bank are the beneficiaries of their very own Homestead Act, and they will be equally difficult to uproot.

Despite all the diplomatic talk of disbanding the settlements as a condition for peace, no one seriously believes that these communities—with their half a million residents, their urban installations, their privileged access to fertile land and water—will ever be removed. The Israeli authorities, whether left, right, or center, have no intention of removing them, and neither Palestinians nor informed Americans harbor illusions on this score.

To be sure, it suits almost everyone to pretend otherwise—to point to the 2003 "road map" and speak of a final accord based on the 1967 frontiers. But such feigned obliviousness is the small change of political hypocrisy, the lubricant of diplomatic exchange that facilitates communication and compromise.

There are occasions, however, when political hypocrisy is its own nemesis, and this is one of them. Because the settlements will never go, and yet almost everyone likes to pretend otherwise, we have resolutely ignored the implications of what Israelis have long been proud to call "the facts on the ground."

Benjamin Netanyahu, Israel's prime minister, knows this better than most. On June 14 he gave a much-anticipated speech in which he artfully blew smoke in the eyes of his American interlocutors. While offering to acknowledge the hypothetical existence of an eventual Palestinian state—on the explicit understanding that it exercise no control over its airspace and have no means of defending itself against aggression—he reiterated the only Israeli position that really matters: we won't build illegal settlements but we reserve the right to expand "legal" ones according to their natural rate of growth. (It is not by chance that he chose to deliver this speech at Bar-Ilan University, the heartland of rabbinical intransigence where Yigal Amir learned to hate Prime Minister Yitzhak Rabin before heading off to assassinate him in 1995.) The reassurances Mr. Netanyahu offered the settlers and their political constituency were as well received as ever, despite being couched in honeyed clichés directed at nervous American listeners. And the American news media, predictably, took the bait—uniformly emphasizing Mr. Netanyahu's "support" for a Palestinian state and playing down everything else.

However, the real question now is whether President Obama will respond in a similar vein. He surely wants to. Nothing could better please the American president and his advisers than to be able to assert that, in the wake of his Cairo speech, even Mr. Netanyahu had shifted ground and was open to compromise. Thus Washington avoids a confrontation, for now, with its closest ally. But the uncomfortable reality is that the prime minister restated the unvarnished truth: His government has no intention of recognizing international law or opinion with respect to Israel's land-grab in "Judea and Samaria."

Thus President Obama faces a choice. He can play along with the Israelis, pretending to believe their promises of good intentions and the significance of the distinctions they offer him. Such a pretense would buy him time and favor with Congress. But the Israelis would be playing him for a fool, and he would be seen as one in the Mideast and beyond.

Alternatively, the president could break with two decades of American compliance, acknowledge publicly that the emperor is indeed naked, dismiss Mr. Netanyahu for the cynic he is, and remind Israelis that *all* their settlements are hostage to American goodwill. He could also remind Israelis that the illegal communities have nothing to do with Israel's defense, much less its founding ideals of agrarian self-sufficiency and Jewish autonomy. They are nothing but a colonial takeover that the United States has no business subsidizing.

But if I am right, and there is no realistic prospect of removing Israel's settlements, then for the American government to agree that the mere nonexpansion of "authorized" settlements is a genuine step toward peace would be the worst possible outcome of the present diplomatic dance. No one else in the world believes this fairy tale; why should we? Israel's political elite would breathe an unmerited sigh of relief, having once again pulled the wool over the eyes of its paymaster. The United States would be humiliated in the eyes of its friends, not to speak of its foes. If America cannot stand up for its own interests in the region, at least let it not be played yet again for a patsy.

This essay first appeared in *The New York Times* in June 2009.

CHAPTER XI

Israel Must Unpick Its Ethnic Myth

What exactly is "Zionism"? Its core claim was always that Jews represent a common and single people; that their millennia-long dispersion and suffering has done nothing to diminish their distinctive, collective attributes; and that the only way they can live freely as Jews—in the same way that, say, Swedes live freely as Swedes—is to dwell in a Jewish state.

Thus religion ceased in Zionist eyes to be the primary measure of Jewish identity. In the course of the late-nineteenth century, as more and more young Jews were legally or culturally emancipated from the world of the ghetto or the shtetl, Zionism began to look to an influential minority like the only alternative to persecution, assimilation, or cultural dilution. Paradoxically then, as religious separatism and practice began to retreat, a secular version of it was actively promoted.

I can certainly confirm, from personal experience, that antireligious sentiment—often of an intensity that I found discomforting—was widespread in left-leaning Israeli circles of the 1960s. Religion, I was informed, was for the *haredim* and the "crazies" of Jerusalem's Mea Sharim quarter. "We" are modern and rational and "Western," it was explained to me by my Zionist teachers. But what they did not say was that the Israel they wished me to join was therefore grounded, and could only be grounded, in an ethnically rigid view of Jews and Jewishness.

The story went like this. Jews, until the destruction of the Second Temple (in the first century), had been farmers in what is now Israel/Palestine. They had then been forced yet again into exile by the Romans and wandered the earth: homeless, rootless, and outcast. Now at last "they" were "returning" and would once again farm the soil of their ancestors.

It is this narrative that the historian Shlomo Sand seeks to deconstruct in his controversial book *The Invention of the Jewish People* [available from the AET Book Club]. His contribution, critics assert, is at best redundant. For the last century, specialists have been perfectly familiar with the sources he cites and the arguments he makes. From a purely scholarly perspective, I have no quarrel with this. Even I, dependent for the most part on secondhand information about the earlier millennia of Jewish history, can see that Professor Sand—for example in his emphasis upon the conversions and ethnic mixing that characterize the Jews in earlier times—is telling us nothing we do not already know.

The question is, who are "we"? Certainly in the United States, the overwhelming majority of Jews (and perhaps non-Jews) have absolutely no acquaintance with the story Professor Sand tells. They will never have heard of most of his protagonists, but they are all too approvingly familiar with the caricatured version of Jewish history that he is seeking to discredit. If Professor Sand's popularizing work does nothing more than provoke reflection and further reading among such a constituency, it will have been worthwhile.

But there is more to it than that. While there were other justifications for the state of Israel, and still are—it was not by chance that David Ben-Gurion sought, planned, and choreographed the trial of Adolf Eichmann—it is clear that Professor Sand has undermined the conventional case for a Jewish state. Once we agree, in short, that Israel's uniquely "Jewish" quality is an imagined or elective affinity, how are we to proceed?

Professor Sand is himself an Israeli and the idea that his country has no "raison d'etre" would be abhorrent to him. Rightly so. States exist or they do not. Egypt or Slovakia are not justified in international law by virtue of some theory of deep "Egyptianness" or "Slovakness." Such states are recognized as international actors, with rights and status, simply by virtue of their existence and their capacity to maintain and protect themselves.

So Israel's survival does not rest on the credibility of the story it tells about its ethnic origins. If we accept this, we can begin to understand that the country's insistence upon its exclusive claim upon Jewish identity is a significant handicap. In the first place, such an insistence reduces all non-Jewish Israeli citizens and residents to second-class status. This would be true even if the distinction were purely formal. But of course it is not: being a Muslim or a Christian—or even a Jew who does not meet the increasingly rigid specification for "Jewishness" in today's Israel—carries a price.

Implicit in Professor Sand's book is the conclusion that Israel would do better to identify itself and learn to think of itself as Israel. The perverse insistence upon identifying a universal Jewishness with one small piece of territory is dysfunctional in many ways. It is the single most important factor accounting for the failure to solve the Israel-Palestine imbroglio. It is bad for Israel and, I would suggest, bad for Jews elsewhere who are identified with its actions.

So what is to be done? Professor Sand certainly does not tell us—and in his defense we should acknowledge that the problem may be intractable. I suspect that he favors a one-state solution: if only because it is the logical upshot of his arguments. I, too, would favor such an outcome—if I were not so sure that both sides would oppose it vigorously and with force. A two-state solution might still be the best compromise, even though it would leave Israel intact in its ethno-delusions. But it is hard to be optimistic about the prospects for such a resolution, in the light of the developments of the past two years.

My own inclination, then, would be to focus elsewhere. If the Jews of Europe and North America took their distance from Israel (as many have begun to do), the assertion that Israel was "their" state would take on an absurd air. Over time, even Washington might come to see the futility of attaching American foreign policy to the delusions of one small Middle Eastern state. This, I believe, is the best thing that could possibly happen to Israel itself. It would be obliged to acknowledge its limits. It would have to make other friends, preferably among its neighbors.

We could thus hope, in time, to establish a natural distinction between people who happen to be Jews but are citizens of other countries and people who are Israeli citizens and happen to be Jews. This could prove very helpful. There are many precedents: the Greek, Armenian, Ukrainian, and Irish diasporas have all played an unhealthy role in perpetuating ethnic exclusivism and nationalist prejudice in the countries of their forebears. The civil war in Northern Ireland came to an end in part because an American president instructed the Irish emigrant community in the United States to stop sending arms and cash to the Provisional IRA. If American Jews stopped associating their fate with Israel and used their charitable checks for better purposes, something similar might happen in the Middle East.

This essay first appeared in the *Financial Times* in December 2009.

CHAPTER XII

Israel Without Clichés

The Israeli raid on the Free Gaza flotilla has generated an outpouring of clichés from the usual suspects. It is almost impossible to discuss the Middle East without resorting to tired accusations and ritual defenses: perhaps a little house cleaning is in order.

NO. 1: ISRAEL IS BEING/SHOULD BE DELEGITIMIZED

Israel is a state like any other, long established and internationally recognized. The bad behavior of its governments does not "delegitimize" it, any more than the bad behavior of the rulers of North Korea, Sudan—or, indeed, the United States—"delegitimizes" them. When Israel breaks international law, it should be pressed to desist; but it is precisely because it is a state under international law that we have that leverage.

Some critics of Israel are motivated by a wish that it did not exist—that it would just somehow go away. But this is the politics of the ostrich: Flemish nationalists feel the same way about Belgium, Basque separatists about Spain. Israel is not going away, nor should it. As for the official Israeli public relations campaign to discredit any criticism as an exercise in "delegitimization," it is uniquely self-defeating. Every time Jerusalem responds this way, it highlights its own isolation.

NO. 2: ISRAEL IS/IS NOT A DEMOCRACY

Perhaps the most common defense of Israel outside the country is that it is "the only democracy in the Middle East." This is largely true: the country has an independent judiciary and free elections, though it also discriminates against non-Jews in ways that distinguish it from most other democracies today. The expression of strong dissent from official policy is increasingly discouraged.

But the point is irrelevant. "Democracy" is no guarantee of good behavior: most countries today are formally democratic—remember Eastern Europe's "popular democracies." Israel belies the comfortable American cliché that "democracies don't make war." It is a democracy dominated and often governed by former professional soldiers: this alone distinguishes it from other advanced countries. And we should not forget that Gaza is another "democracy" in the Middle East: it was precisely because Hamas won free elections there in 2005 that both the Palestinian Authority and Israel reacted with such vehemence.

NO. 3: ISRAEL IS/IS NOT TO BLAME

Israel is not responsible for the fact that many of its near neighbors long denied its right to exist. The sense of siege should not be underestimated when we try to understand the delusional quality of many Israeli pronouncements.

Unsurprisingly, the state has acquired pathological habits. Of these, the most damaging is its habitual resort to force. Because this worked for so long—the easy victories of the country's early years are ingrained in folk memory—Israel finds it difficult to conceive of other ways to respond. And the failure of the negotiations of 2000 at Camp David reinforced the belief that "there is no one to talk to."

But there is. As American officials privately acknowledge, sooner or later Israel (or someone) will have to talk to Hamas. From French Algeria through South Africa to the Provisional IRA, the story repeats itself: the dominant power denies the legitimacy of the "terrorists," thereby strengthening their hand; then it secretly negotiates with them; finally, it concedes power, independence, or a place at the table. Israel will negotiate with Hamas: the only question is why not now.

NO. 4: THE PALESTINIANS ARE/ARE NOT TO BLAME

Abba Eban, the former Israeli foreign minister, claimed that Arabs never miss an opportunity to miss an opportunity. He was not wholly wrong. The "negationist" stance of Palestinian resistance movements from 1948 through the early 1980s did them little good. And Hamas, firmly in that tradition though far more genuinely popular than its predecessors, will have to acknowledge Israel's right to exist.

But since 1967 it has been Israel that has missed most opportunities: a forty-year occupation (against the advice of its own elder statesmen); three catastrophic invasions of Lebanon; an invasion and blockade of Gaza in the teeth of world opinion; and now a botched attack on civilians in international waters. Palestinians would be hard put to match such cumulative blunders.

Terrorism is the weapon of the weak—bombing civilian targets was not invented by Arabs (nor by the Jews who engaged in it before 1948). Morally indefensible, it has characterized resistance movements of all colors for at least a century. Israelis are right to insist that any talks or settlements will depend upon Hamas's foreswearing it.

But Palestinians face the same conundrum as every other oppressed people: all they have with which to oppose an established state with a monopoly of power is rejection and protest. If they pre-concede every Israeli demand—abjurance of violence, acceptance of Israel, acknowledgment of all their losses—what do they bring to the negotiating table? Israel has the initiative: it should exercise it.

NO. 5: THE ISRAEL LOBBY IS/IS NOT TO BLAME

There is an Israel lobby in Washington and it does a very good job—that's what lobbies are for. Those who claim that the Israel lobby is unfairly painted as "too influential" (with the subtext of excessive Jewish influence behind the scenes) have a point: the gun lobby, the oil lobby, and the banking lobby have all done far more damage to the health of this country.

But the Israel lobby is disproportionately influential. Why else do an overwhelming majority of congressmen roll over for every pro-Israel motion? No more than a handful show consistent interest in the subject. It is one thing to denounce the excessive leverage of a lobby, quite another to accuse Jews of "running the country." We must not censor ourselves lest people conflate the two. In Arthur Koestler's words, "This fear of finding oneself in bad company is not an expression of political purity; it is an expression of a lack of self-confidence."

NO. 6: CRITICISM OF ISRAEL IS/IS NOT
LINKED TO ANTI-SEMITISM

Anti-Semitism is hatred of Jews, and Israel is a Jewish state, so of course some criticism of it is malevolently motivated. There have been occasions in the recent past (notably in the Soviet Union and its satellites) when "anti-Zionism" was a convenient surrogate for official anti-Semitism. Understandably, many Jews and Israelis have not forgotten this.

But criticism of Israel, increasingly from non-Israeli Jews, is not predominantly motivated by anti-Semitism. The same is true of contemporary anti-Zionism: Zionism itself has moved a long way from the ideology of its "founding fathers"—today it presses territorial claims, religious exclusivity, and political extremism. One can acknowledge Israel's right to exist and still be an anti-Zionist (or "post-Zionist"). Indeed, given the emphasis in Zionism on the need for the Jews to establish a "normal state" for themselves, today's insistence on Israel's right to act in "abnormal" ways because it is a Jewish state suggests that Zionism has failed.

We should beware the excessive invocation of "anti-Semitism." A younger generation in the United States, not to mention worldwide, is growing skeptical. "If criticism of the Israeli blockade of Gaza is potentially 'anti-Semitic,' why take seriously other instances of the prejudice?" they ask, and "What if the Holocaust has become just another excuse for Israeli bad behavior?" The risks that Jews run by encouraging this conflation should not be dismissed.

Along with the oil sheikdoms, Israel is now America's greatest strategic liability in the Middle East and Central Asia. Thanks to Israel, we are in serious danger of "losing" Turkey: a Muslim democracy, offended at its treatment by the European Union, that is the pivotal actor in Near-Eastern and Central Asian affairs. Without Turkey, the United States will achieve few of its regional objectives—whether in Iran, Afghanistan, or the Arab world. The time has come to cut through the clichés surrounding it, treat Israel like a "normal" state, and sever the umbilical cord.

This essay first appeared in *The New York Times* in June 2010.

CHAPTER XIII

What Is to Be Done?

Six years ago, in *The New York Review of Books*, I published an essay on Israel entitled "Israel: The Alternative." In it I argued that the "peace process" and the two-state solution it was intended to achieve were dead. If Israel continued on its present course it would face unappetizing options: either Israel would remain Jewish but cease to be a democracy or else it could become a genuinely multiethnic democracy but would in that case cease to be "Jewish." A third outcome, whereby Israel forcibly removed a majority of its Arabs (or made it intolerable for them to remain) would indeed ensure the survival of a Jewish democracy, but at a grotesque and ultimately self-destructive price. In these circumstances, some sort of binational or federal arrangement seemed the best available option, however unlikely.

Understandably, this essay provoked considerable dissent. Among the more reasonable responses were those from Israelis and Palestinians who recognized the depressing credibility of my assessment, but could not stomach its conclusion. There *must* be a two-state solution, they insisted. Nothing else would work. Whatever the impediments—Israeli settlers, Palestinian bombers, etc.—reasonable voices on both sides must continue to press for the only mutually acceptable resolution. Like Churchill's definition of democracy, a two-state solution in the Middle East is the worst possible answer except for all the others.

Since October 2003 the situation has continued to worsen. Israel has fought two "successful" wars, against Hezbollah and Hamas; it has continued to expand its settlements in the Occupied Territories and parcel up Palestinian territory; it has relinquished control of Gaza; and despite all of this it is farther away from peace and security than ever. In 2006 the Palestinians held one of the freest elections ever recorded in the Arab Middle East: the winner was Hamas, a movement defined by the United States and Europe as "terrorist" and boycotted accordingly. The authority and legitimacy of the PLO, the defeated Palestinian coalition with whom the West continues to deal, has steadily collapsed. The ugly paradox of a Jewish state ruling ever-greater numbers of repressed and resentful Arabs grows daily more explicit. Ever more people talk of a "two-state solution"; fewer and fewer people believe in it. What is to be done?

Let us begin with two insuperable realities. Israel exists, and its critics will not be taken seriously if they fail to acknowledge as much. The overwhelming majority of Palestinians want a real state of their own. This, too, is a simple statement of reality, and should be taken no less into account. Neither side at this point wants to live with the other in a single state, and no one can make them do so. Such a "single-state solution," whether federal or binational or anything else, would only work if each side trusted the other's good faith. But in that case it would not be necessary: we would long since have reached final negotiations for a genuine two-state outcome.

The problem of trust—or its absence—lies at the heart of the Israel/Palestine conundrum. Far from "building trust" as intended, the peace process has contributed actively to its destruction. In Israel, the outcome is disastrous. The country is governed by a coalition whose "moderate" core comprises parties once on the far right of the Israeli political spectrum. The opposition is led by Tzipi Livni, who came out of Likud, the successor party to Menachem Begin's Herut, itself heir to Vladimir Jabotinsky's inter-war Revisionists—the unapologetic nationalist Right of the old Zionist movement. The Left, and much of the center, of Israeli politics has disappeared.

The Israel of Benjamin Netanyahu is certainly less hypocritical than that of the old Labour governments. Unlike most of its predecessors reaching back to 1967, it does not even pretend to seek reconciliation with the Arabs over which it rules. Just last month the Israeli Knesset voted 47–34 to pass the preliminary reading of a private member's bill proposed by Zevulun Orlev of the Jewish Home Party, calling for up to one year's imprisonment for anyone questioning the existence of Israel as a Jewish state. Meanwhile housing minister Ariel Atias (of the ultra-religious Shas Party) warned on July 2, 2009, against the "intermixing" of Arab and Jewish populations in the Galilee: the separation of the populations, he declared, was "a national responsibility."

Meanwhile, Palestinians, however much they wish for a state of their own, grow more skeptical of its likelihood. It cannot be a good sign that Dr. Sari Nusseibeh, president of Al-Quds University and a longtime supporter of the two-state solution, is now writing in favor of binationalism. The failure of the peace process set in motion at Madrid and Oslo has discredited the late Yasser Arafat and his successors. Occupation is its own nemesis: it radicalizes the occupied. The PLO and its representatives are now regarded by many younger Palestinians as collaborators who have benefited from their humiliating dealings with the occupier even as their people suffer. Each time Palestinian Authority president Mahmoud Abbas meets an Israeli prime minister or American president and comes away empty-handed he loses a little more credibility, and Hamas, the "resistance," gains admirers and votes. As in Vichy France (the analogy I have heard cited most frequently) the collaborating authorities will be ill placed to negotiate liberation and lead a free people. But if Abbas is on his way to becoming the Pétain of the Palestinians, who will be their De Gaulle?

Mistrust, no less than illegal settlements or national aspirations, is a fact on the ground and any peace process which averts its eyes from such realities is doomed. The more foreigners talk up the "Oslo peace process" or the "road map," the less seriously we shall be taken by those who matter. It is precisely *because* U.S. administrations now speak freely of a Palestinian state, and even Mr. Netanyahu favors it under ultrarestrictive conditions, that the idea is losing Palestinian favor. Palestinians, like Israelis, are skeptical of any more "staged" negotiations or withdrawal. Sympathetic Western supporters, then, are rapidly falling behind the curve. As Mr. Netanyahu observed, on June 23, 2009, "Settlement debate is a waste of time."[1] He is right. The recent G8 foreign ministers' statement, calling on all parties "to fulfill their obligations under the road map" and "re-enter direct negotiations on all standing issues consistent with the road map, the relevant UNSC resolutions and the Madrid principles . . ." is a representative instance of dysfunctional international noise. If U.S. envoy George Mitchell seriously hopes, as he claims, for "meaningful and productive" peace negotiations to begin soon, he had better have something very different in mind.

So LET US BEGIN INSTEAD with what matters. Land—the central issue for so long in this tragic confrontation—may be the least helpful way to think about a solution. The idea that Palestinians would take a chunk of the Western Negev desert against 9 percent of the fertile West Bank land now occupied by Israel is simply silly, yet it has been seriously mooted. As for a more significant exchange of land on either side of the "security fence": if Israel under Mr. Sharon could not even bring itself to leave a few hundred houses and a handful of swimming pools intact for the Gazan Arabs following its withdrawal thence, why should anyone suppose that the Israel of Mr. Netanyahu will find in its heart the political will or prudential generosity to leave the Palestinians anything worth having in the far more contentious territories of "Judea and Samaria"? Whatever can be achieved by way of a territorial settlement will come only once some sort of trust and mutual goodwill have been established by other means.

What of "security"? Israeli civilians are genuinely worried at the prospect of an armed Palestinian entity within a few dozen miles of their major cities. The Israeli military plays to this fear, even though it suffers few sleepless nights on this account: if there is a genuinely existential threat to Israel's existence, it certainly does not come from a handful of Qassam rockets, even if these were accurately aimed. Israel's problem is not getting rid of the rocket launchers, but rather resolving the political conditions which ensure their infinite replacement. A properly constituted Palestinian state, with all the rights and responsibilities that go along with statehood, would be a far better insurance against rogue rocket firings. Israel's legitimate security concerns are thus best addressed by the creation—sooner rather than later—of a Palestinian state with all the trappings of state power, motivated to get along with its powerful neighbor and repress unstable domestic extremists.

Mutatis mutandis, Palestinians have legitimate security concerns, too. They need early and full statehood in order to be protected against the Israeli propensity to trample over international law, engage in targeted assassinations, and treat Arabs as permanent and legitimate objects of preemptive warfare. Here, too, early statehood would have prophylactic benefits for both parties. Israelis no longer fear Jordanians or Egyptians the way they did within living memory. I can well recall an Israel in which Egyptians in particular were believed to have an unalterable and universal propensity to hate Jews and seek their destruction. If you believe that of people, then only their serial humiliation and defeat can give you a sentiment of security. Paradoxically, then, Israelis will only feel secure when they have a properly established, militarily competent Palestinian state on their frontiers.

What of Jerusalem, the city which both states would wish to treat as their capital? The Israeli annexation of East Jerusalem poses real dilemmas. To be sure, the unilateral unification and colonization of this city is not irreversible, any more than the division of Berlin proved insurmountable. A significant number of Israelis regard the contemporary politics of Jerusalem—a hothouse of religious and nationalist extremism—with some distaste; they would not be sorry to see the discomfiture of the coalition of ideological settlers and religious fanatics who dominate the debate. In the same way, many secular Palestinians would settle for far less than sovereign power over their part of the city, so long as they could be assured that Israeli ultras were not in a position to hold hostage their daily lives and political rights.

But Jerusalem clearly cannot be resolved by the interested parties alone, any more than Berlin was reunited purely as an exercise of German free will. To be sure, 2,500 years of Jewish mythology and folk memory says that Jerusalem is "our" city. But then 2,500 years of mythology and folk memory says lots of things in lots of places, much of it inapplicable to modern political circumstance. Jews do not have a monopoly on old memories and ancient aspirations; like other peoples trailing similar burdens of history and loss, they may have to compromise. The best, in this as other domains, can be the enemy of the good. If there is a role for Barack Obama, George Mitchell, the G8, the UNSC, and other outsiders in this complex story, it will come in their insistence upon the internationalization of Jerusalem as an open city, whoever administers municipal affairs on the ground. If Jews and Muslims (or Christians for that matter) insist on sole control over "their" city, they will never have peace.

But more important—far more important—than land or security or even Jerusalem, is the issue of "recognition." It was the Palestinians' (and other Arabs') longtime refusal to "recognize" the reality of Israel (a refusal still incorporated in the very charter of Hamas) which helps explain Israelis' inability to imagine a modus vivendi with their Arab neighbors and fellow citizens, and is invoked to justify it. Conversely, it is the continuing Israeli denial of the crime committed against the Palestinian Arabs, and their subsequent suffering, which convinces so many Palestinians that the Jews are just not serious when they speak of peace and reconciliation.[2]

The Palestinians of course claim to want more than just recognition of their past sufferings. They also want acknowledgment of their right to return to lands and properties seized from them in the course of Israeli state making. International commentators tend to focus upon the legal and demographic implications of this demand, echoing exaggerated Israeli fears that were such an acknowledgment to be made, hundreds of thousands of Arabs would forthwith demand a "right of return" to Israel. This is not only an implausible prospect in itself—how many Palestinian Arabs truly wish to leave the United States, Europe, Kuwait, or Lebanon in order to live in Mr. Netanyahu's Jewish state?—but it misses the larger point. Recognition of a "right of return" in principle matters above all for the explicit acknowledgment that a great harm had been done to Palestinians and a redress of some sort was owed.

We Jews of all people should understand this. No amount of monetary compensation could ever begin to make up for what the Nazis did. Nor do more than a handful of European Jews or their descendants wish to return to their lands and homes and shops and factories in Poland, or anywhere else (though Polish nationalists have long played up just such a prospect, much as Israeli spokesmen profess to foresee returning hordes of litigious Palestinians). What Jews after World War II sought, and what they have successfully achieved, was acknowledgment and recognition of their sufferings and of the crimes of their persecutors. The Palestinians seek nothing less. What is at issue is not land or money or even bricks and mortar. It is memory; and above all it is history. Just as Israel's legitimacy rests in no small measure upon the implication and recognition of Jewish losses and suffering, so the Palestinian cause and the Palestinian case derive their political energy and moral meaning from Palestinians' losses and suffering. Until and unless this is understood and acknowledged, there will be no end to conflict.

It is easy to become caught up in the apparent uniqueness of the Israel/Palestine dilemma. Jerusalem is unique, Jewish history—culminating in the Holocaust—claims a special place for itself in Western memory, and the Fertile Crescent has long figured at the heart of international religious and political conflict. And it is true that, like all territorial struggles, this one has certain unique features. But it may be helpful to stand back and recall that in most respects this is not at all a unique crisis, but one that shares many features with comparable cases in other times and places. A glance at some of these may suggest ways to break the impasse.

In the first place, we should remind ourselves that multicultural, multireligious, multilingual states are not as unimaginable nor as perennially unstable as we sometimes suppose. Switzerland, Belgium, India, all work more or less well in the face of ostensibly incompatible interests and communities. Yugoslavia—an apparent countercase—actually operated rather smoothly until it was deliberately and cynically fractured by the leader of one of its national components. Quebec, a profoundly divided province whose French-speaking majority resentfully sought independence to secure itself against the "hegemony" of English speakers within and without its frontiers, is now at peace with itself.

It is true that the most enduring solution to overlapping ethnicities and their mutual antagonisms has been separation and even population "exchanges." But these have always followed in the wake of war and wholesale death and destruction—in Asia Minor, for example, or Eastern Europe: a prelude we could hardly wish upon our contemporaries anywhere. So Israelis and Palestinians must work with what they have got. What is striking to the outsider, however, is how much their circumstances really do have in common with those of other peoples facing similar challenges.

Thus from Algeria to Northern Ireland, it is always "moderates" who get squeezed out. To be sure, they gain the respect of other moderates at home and abroad, but in part for just that reason they lose local influence and relevance. It is almost always the erstwhile "extremists" and "terrorists" who negotiate final outcomes and end up in power. This has already happened in Israel and will surely be the case for the Palestinians with Hamas in the driver's seat before long. It is not by chance that the European colonial powers and their successors were constrained to hand over power to men and women they had once imprisoned for "terrorism," from Kenya to Indonesia; from Algeria to South Africa.

Mention of South Africa is a reminder that in the absence of a Mandela the Palestinians are at a severe disadvantage. De Klerk and his fellow Afrikaners had come to realize the unsustainability of apartheid—in this respect they were far ahead of most but not all Israelis—but they were fortunate indeed in facing a political prisoner of extraordinary talents with whom they could negotiate and whom his fellow blacks respected. As Israelis gleefully remind them, the Palestinians have no such person. But even if there were a Palestinian Mandela, he would be unable to establish a Truth and Reconciliation Commission to overcome communal mistrust and fear. Most Israelis are not yet frightened enough to see the need for reconciliation, and thus are under no constraint to acknowledge other peoples' truth. Not enough Israelis have understood that the project of a Greater Israel is doomed. Sadly, then, we must concede that white South Africans were both more sophisticated and less hidebound in their self-understanding. *Their* foundation myth, of a put-upon, hard-working, hard-fighting *volk* surrounded by lazy, second-rate indigenous peoples in need of restriction and direction, crumbled in the face of world antipathy. The Israelis can look forward to something comparable in years to come if things do not change.

Northern Ireland, however, offers better prospects, as George Mitchell is well placed to understand. Moderate politicians there, Protestant and Catholic alike, worked for decades to find a basis for compromise. All they got for their efforts was humiliation and an ever-shrinking share of the vote. It was the extremists, the provisional IRA and Ian Paisley's Democratic Unionists, who emerged as the victors, the interlocutors of Bill Clinton and Tony Blair, and the leaders of an increasingly peaceful and stabilized Ulster. For nearly thirty years these men and their thugs brutalized the North, exhorting their supporters to kill and maim in the name of territorial exclusivism and fear of the other. Until they were brought into the "peace process" nothing was possible. Today, Gerry Adams, Martin McGinnis, and Ian Paisley cooperate in the government of Ulster. They are the new face, however implausible, of a peaceful Northern Ireland at last released from the headlines.

The Troubles in Ulster vastly outrank the Middle East in duration (they date from the late seventeenth century); scale (far more people were killed in Ulster just in the course of the most recent Troubles than have died from suicide bombing or other terrorist murders in Israel since its inception); or complexity. If they could be resolved, the Middle East is not hopeless. Israel (and its international friends) should open negotiations with Hamas directly. This is hardly an original thought: in March 2009 a bipartisan group of influential Americans, including Paul Volker and former Republican senators Chuck Hegel and Nancy Kassebaum, encouraged President Obama to do just this. But if we don't bring Hamas in and give them reason to work productively with serious negotiators—or worse, if the Israelis succeed in assassinating all the movement's leaders—we shall not be left with moderate Palestinians. We shall have jihadis. In this sense Hamas is not our worst fear, but our last hope.

The Ulster analogy is a reminder of another challenge facing the Middle

East. As anyone who has written critically of either Israel or the Palestinians knows well, the most extreme and unreasoning responses come not from the Middle East itself, but from the diaspora. This too should not surprise us. Whether in Croatia or Armenia, Greece or Poland, it is the diasporic communities spread across the world who take the hardest line on sensitive national issues. The Armenians of Armenia itself are perfectly aware of the genocide suffered by their forebears at the hands of the Turks during World War I. But it is the Armenian diaspora which takes the lead in castigating the Turks in international *fori;* in Armenia itself the business of living and trading with their Turkish neighbors has far higher priority.

Similarly, the Croatian diaspora took a far harder line in the course of the recent Yugoslav civil wars than did most of the residents of Croatia itself, all too happy to compromise for the sake of a return to normalcy and Europe. The long-standing and bitter division of Cyprus would have been overcome long since were it not for the malevolence of the intervening outside parties and the extreme stance of far-flung diasporas financing internecine division. And so it is with Palestinians—but above all with Jews. Were it not for American Jewish lobbying and financial support, the ultras of the Israeli settler movement would never have been able to secure their current political leverage and influence. Until and unless the extreme ideologues of the organized diaspora (and their friends in high political circles) are marginalized, effective foreign pressure upon Israel will not be forthcoming. It was President Clinton's willingness to ignore the Provisional IRA's cheerleaders and financiers here in the United States which isolated Sinn Fein and showed Gerry Adams that he had no choice but to compromise. One likes to hope that George Mitchell understands the implications of the precedent.

To summarize: further pursuit of the old "peace process" and "road map" is futile. No one who matters believes in it anymore. By leaving the difficult issues to the end, we have destroyed the faith of all parties in the likelihood of success. The important goal now is to convince Israelis and Palestinians alike that there is no option but to pursue a different path; that this path has some prospect of immediate and enduring benefits; and that the costs of refusing to proceed thus are unacceptable. Only engaged outsiders—above all the United States and the European Union—can achieve this, and they cannot expect to do so if they continue to mouth platitudes or acquiesce in the platitudes of others, or if they continue to listen to the prejudices of the organized diasporas.

The "extremists" should be brought into the conversation forthwith, and compromised moderates gently removed to the edges lest the process be discredited by their presence. Ostensibly "impossible" issues—Jerusalem, security, recognition of Israel, acknowledgment of Palestinian rights of return and past losses should all be given priority. Potentially interminable territorial settlements should be either postponed or handed to secondary officials for discussion. It should be established from the outset that the inevitable difficulty of reaching detailed territorial arrangements will not be allowed to postpone agreement. Both the United States and the European Union should find it within themselves to exercise leverage, pressure, and muscle. The Israelis have long claimed that Arabs only respond to a show of force. The same is true of Israel.

Politics, as we know, is the art of the possible. I don't know whether a settlement of some sort in the Middle East is still possible. But if it is not, then neither Palestinians nor Israelis have much of a future, though as of now only the Palestinians understand this. But it ought not to be beyond the intelligence of even the most hidebound local politicians to see the benefits of imaginative compromise, especially if they can blame it on irresistible foreign pressure. The Arab states today are open to compromise in ways unimaginable a generation back. An Israeli state led by even moderately intelligent statesmen faces unprecedentedly interesting possibilities if only it knows how to seize them. Israel could quite easily stabilize its regional relationships not only by constructing alliances with friendly Arab states but mostly and above all with Turkey and even Russia.

Against such a prospect, the risks that Israel would run by living alongside even a volatile Palestinian state are utterly negligible. But there is no reason to suppose that a properly constituted Palestinian state would be any more volatile than, say, Israel itself. And unlike Israel it would never have a nuclear weapon, or even one of the world's most powerful armies, and would thus not be open to the temptation which one hears in certain Israeli quarters, to invoke the "Samson complex" and bring down the whole world around its ears rather than risk compromising its own interests.

But the present opportunities will not last long and once enough Palestinians draw the logical conclusion from Israel's settlement policy and its intransigence toward them, and give up on a state of their own, Israel will be lost. It will be forced back on the choice I outlined at the outset, and—unless it goes for the least likely option, a binational state—it will be doomed to pariah status indefinitely. Time is not on anyone's side in this business. And we would be well advised to recall that there is no law of nature which says that sooner or later a solution will somehow just "emerge." The consequences of letting things fester, as we have done for too long, or leaving them in the hands of the incompetent mediocrities currently running both Israel and the Palestinian Authority, would be catastrophic. Thanks to the "Jewish State's" abusive treatment of the Palestinians, the Israel/Palestine imbroglio is the chief proximate cause of the resurgence of anti-Semitism worldwide. It is the single most effective recruiting agent for radical Islamist movements. It makes nonsense of U.S. and European foreign policy in one of the world's most sensitive and unstable regions. Something different has to be done.

This essay was written in the summer of 2009 and was never completed or submitted for publication. It appears here for the first time, in its draft form.

Notes to Chapter XIII

[1] *Haaretz,* July 2, 2009, T. S. Eliot.

[2] As though to illustrate contemporary Israel's moral autism, in May 2009 the ministerial committee for legislation of the Knesset approved a bill making it illegal for Israeli Jews and Palestinian citizens of Israel to commemorate the Naqba, the Palestinian catastrophe of 1948.

Part Three

9/11 and the New World Order

CHAPTER XIV

On *The Plague*

Penguin Books has just published a new translation by Robin Buss of *La Peste*, by Albert Camus, and the text that follows is my introduction, written some months ago. Many readers will be familiar with its fable of the coming of the plague to the North African city of Oran in 194–, and the diverse ways in which the inhabitants respond to its devastating impact on their lives. Today, *The Plague* takes on fresh significance and a moving immediacy.

Camus's insistence on placing individual moral responsibility at the heart of all public choices cuts sharply across the comfortable habits of our own age. His definition of heroism—ordinary people doing extraordinary things out of simple decency—rings truer than we might once have acknowledged. His depiction of instant ex cathedra judgments—"My brethren, you have deserved it"—will be grimly familiar to us all.

Camus's unwavering grasp of the difference between good and evil, despite his compassion for the doubters and the compromised, for the motives and mistakes of imperfect humanity, casts unflattering light upon the relativizers and trimmers of our own day. And his controversial use of a biological epidemic to illustrate the dilemmas of moral contagion succeeds in ways the writer could not have imagined. Here in New York, in November 2001, we are better placed than we could ever have wished to feel the lash of the novel's premonitory final sentence.

The Plague is Albert Camus's most successful novel. It was published in 1947, when Camus was thirty-three, and was an immediate triumph. Within a year it had been translated into nine languages, with many more to come. It has never been out of print and was established as a classic of world literature even before its author's untimely death in a car accident in January 1960. More ambitious than *L'Étranger*, the first novel that made his reputation, and more accessible than his later writings, *The Plague* is the book by which Camus is known to millions of readers. He might have found this odd—*The Rebel*, published four years later, was his personal favorite among his books.

The Plague was a long time in the writing, like much of Camus's best work. He started gathering material for it in January 1941, when he arrived in Oran, the Algerian coastal city where the story is set. He continued working on the manuscript in Le Chambon-sur-Lignon, a mountain village in central France where he went to recuperate from one of his periodic bouts of tuberculosis in the summer of 1942. But Camus was soon swept into the Resistance and it was not until the liberation of France that he was able to return his attention to the book. By then, however, the obscure Algerian novelist had become a national figure: a hero of the intellectual Resistance, editor of *Combat* (a daily paper born in clandestinity and hugely influential in the postwar years), and an icon to a new generation of French men and women hungry for ideas and idols.

Camus seemed to fit the role to perfection. Handsome and charming, a charismatic advocate of radical social and political change, he held unparalleled sway over millions of his countrymen. In the words of Raymond Aron, readers of Camus's editorials had "formed the habit of getting their daily thought from him." There were other intellectuals in postwar Paris who were destined to play major roles in years to come: Aron himself, Simone de Beauvoir, and of course Jean-Paul Sartre. But Camus was different. Born in Algeria in 1913, he was younger than his Left Bank friends, most of whom were already forty years old when the war ended. He was more "exotic," coming as he did from distant Algiers rather than from the hothouse milieu of Parisian schools and colleges; and there was something special about him. One contemporary observer caught it well: "I was struck by his face, so human and sensitive. There is in this man such an obvious integrity that it imposes respect almost immediately; quite simply, he is not like other men."[1]

Camus's public standing guaranteed his book's success. But its timing had something to do with it, too. By the time the book appeared the French were beginning to forget the discomforts and compromises of four years of German occupation. Marshal Philippe Pétain, the head of state who initiated and incarnated the policy of collaboration with the victorious Nazis, had been tried and imprisoned. Other collaborating politicians had been executed or else banished from public life. The myth of a glorious national resistance was carefully cultivated by politicians of all colors, from Charles de Gaulle to the Communists; uncomfortable private memories were soothingly overlaid with the airbrushed official version in which France had been liberated from its oppressors by the joint efforts of domestic resisters and Free French troops led from London by De Gaulle.

In this context, Albert Camus's allegory of the wartime occupation of France reopened a painful chapter in the recent French past, but in an indirect and ostensibly apolitical key. It thus avoided raising partisan hackles, except at the extremes of left and right, and took up sensitive topics without provoking a refusal to listen. Had the novel appeared in 1945 the angry, partisan mood of revenge would have drowned its moderate reflections on justice and responsibility. Had it been delayed until the 1950s its subject matter would probably have been overtaken by new alignments born of the cold war.

WHETHER *THE PLAGUE* SHOULD BE READ, as it surely was read, as a simple allegory of France's wartime trauma is a subject to which I shall return. What is beyond doubt is that it was an intensely personal book. Camus put something of himself—his emotions, his memories, and his sense of place— into all his published work; that is one of the ways in which he stood apart from other intellectuals of his generation, and it accounts for his universal and lasting appeal. But even by his standards *The Plague* is strikingly introspective and revealing. Oran, the setting for the novel, was a city he knew well and cordially disliked, in contrast to his much-loved home town of Algiers. He found it boring and materialistic and his memories of it were further shaped by the fact that his tuberculosis took a turn for the worse during his stay there. As a result he was forbidden to swim—one of his greatest pleasures—and was constrained to sit around for weeks on end in the stifling, oppressive heat that provides the backdrop to the story.

This involuntary deprivation of everything that Camus most loved about his Algerian birthplace—the sand, the sea, physical exercise, and the Mediterranean sense of ease and liberty that Camus always contrasted with the gloom and gray of the north—was compounded when he was sent to the French countryside to convalesce. The Massif Central of France is tranquil and bracing, and the remote village where Camus arrived in August 1942 might be thought the ideal setting for a writer. But twelve weeks later, in November 1942, the Allies landed in North Africa. The Germans responded by occupying the whole of southern France (hitherto governed from the spa town of Vichy by Pétain's puppet government) and Algeria was cut off from the continent. Camus was thenceforth separated not just from his homeland but also from his mother and his wife, and would not see them again until the Germans had been defeated.[2]

Illness, exile, and separation were thus present in Camus's life as in his novel, and his reflections upon them form a vital counterpoint to the allegory. Because of his acute firsthand experience, Camus's descriptions of the plague and of the pain of loneliness are exceptionally vivid and heartfelt. It is indicative of his own depth of feeling that the narrator remarks early in the story that "the first thing that the plague brought to our fellow citizens was exile," and that "being separated from a loved one . . . [was] the greatest agony of that long period of exile."

This in turn provides, for Camus and the reader alike, a link to his earlier novel: for disease, separation, and exile are conditions that come upon us unexpectedly and unbidden. They are an illustration of what Camus meant by the "absurdity" of the human condition and the seemingly chance nature of human undertakings. It is not by accident that one of his main characters, Grand, for no apparent reason, reports a conversation overheard in a tobacco shop concerning "a young company employee who had killed an Arab on a beach." This, of course, is an allusion to Meurseault's seminal act of random violence in *L'Étranger*, and in Camus's mind it is connected to the ravages of pestilence in *The Plague* by more than just their common Algerian setting.

BUT CAMUS DID MORE THAN INSERT into his story vignettes and emotions drawn from his writings and his personal situation. He put himself very directly into the characters of the novel, using three of them in particular to represent and illuminate his distinctive moral perspective. Rambert, the young journalist cut off from his wife in Paris, is initially desperate to escape the quarantine city. His obsession with his personal suffering makes him indifferent to the larger tragedy, from which he feels quite detached—he is not, after all, a citizen of Oran, but was caught there by the vagaries of chance. It is on the very eve of his getaway that he realizes how, despite himself, he has become part of the community and shares its fate; ignoring the risk and in the face of his earlier, selfish needs, he remains in Oran and joins the "health teams." From a purely private resistance against misfortune he has graduated to the solidarity of a collective resistance against the common scourge.

Camus's identification with Dr. Rieux echoes his shifting mood in these years. Rieux is a man who, faced with suffering and a common crisis, does what he must and becomes a leader and an example not out of heroic courage or careful reasoning but rather from a sort of necessary optimism. By the late 1940s Camus was exhausted and depressed at the burden of expectations placed on him as a public intellectual: as he confided to his notebooks, "everyone wants the man who is still searching to have reached his conclusions." From the "existentialist" philosopher (a tag that Camus always disliked) people awaited a polished worldview; but Camus had none to offer.[3] As he expressed it through Rieux, he was "weary of the world in which he lived"; all he could offer with any certainty was "some feeling for his fellow men and [he was] determined for his part to reject any injustice and any compromise."

Dr. Rieux does the right thing just because he sees clearly what needs doing. In a third character, Tarrou, Camus invested a more developed exposition of his moral thinking. Tarrou, like Camus, is in his midthirties; he left home, by his own account, in disgust at his father's advocacy of the death penalty—a subject of intense concern to Camus and on which he wrote widely in the postwar years.[4] Tarrou has reflected painfully upon his past life and commitments, and his confession to Rieux is at the heart of the novel's moral message: "I thought I was struggling against the plague. I learned that I had indirectly supported the deaths of thousands of men, that I had even caused their deaths by approving the actions and principles that inevitably led to them."

This passage can be read as Camus's own rueful reflections upon his passage through the Communist Party in Algeria during the 1930s. But Tarrou's conclusions go beyond the admission of political error: "We are all in the plague. . . . All I know is that one must do one's best not to be a plague victim. . . . And this is why I have decided to reject everything that, directly or indirectly, makes people die or justifies others in making them die." This is the authentic voice of Albert Camus, and it sketches out the position he would take toward ideological dogma, political or judicial murder, and all forms of ethical irresponsibility for the rest of his life—a stance that would later cost him dearly in friends and even influence in the polarized world of the Parisian intelligentsia.

TARROU/CAMUS'S APOLOGIA for his refusals and his commitments returns us to the status of *The Plague*. It is a novel that succeeds at various levels as any great novel must, but it is above all and unmistakably a moral tale. Camus was much taken with *Moby-Dick* and, like Melville, he was not embarrassed to endow his story with symbols and metaphors. But Melville had the luxury of moving freely back and forth from the narrative of a whale hunt to a fable of human obsession; between Camus's Oran and the dilemma of human choice there lay the reality of life in Vichy France between 1940 and 1944. Readers of *The Plague*, today as in 1947, are therefore not wrong to approach it as an allegory of the occupation years.

In part this is because Camus makes clear that this is a story about "us." Most of the story is told in the third person. But strategically dispersed through the text is the occasional "we," and the "we" in question—at least for Camus's primary audience—is the French in 1947. The "calamity" that has befallen the citizens of fictionalized Oran is the one that came upon France in 1940, with the military defeat, the abandonment of the Republic, and the establishment of the regime of Vichy under German tutelage. Camus's account of the coming of the rats echoed a widespread view of the divided condition of France itself in 1940: "It was as though the very soil on which our houses were built was purging itself of an excess of bile, that it was letting boils and abscesses rise to the surface which up to then had been devouring it inside." Many in France, at first, shared Father Paneloux's initial reaction: "My brethren, you have deserved it."

For a long time people don't realize what is happening and life seems to go on—"in appearance, nothing had changed." "The city was inhabited by people asleep on their feet." Later, when the plague has passed, amnesia sets in—"they denied that we [*sic*] had been that benumbed people." All this and much more—the black market, the failure of administrators to call things by their name and assume the moral leadership of the nation—so well described the recent French past that Camus's intentions could hardly be misread.

Nevertheless, most of Camus's targets resist easy labels, and the allegory runs quite against the grain of the polarized moral rhetoric in use after the war. Cottard, who accepts the plague as too strong to combat and who thinks the "health teams" are a waste of time, is clearly someone who "collaborates" in the fate of the city. He thrives in the new situation and has everything to lose from a return to the "old ways." But he is sympathetically drawn, and

Tarrou and the others continue to see him and even discuss with him their actions. All they ask, in Tarrou's words, is that he "try not to spread the plague knowingly."

At the end Cottard is brutally beaten by the newly liberated citizenry—a reminder of the violent punishments meted out at the Liberation to presumed collaborators, often by men and women whose enthusiasm for violent revenge helped them and others forget their own wartime compromises. Camus's insight into the anger and resentment born of genuine suffering and guilty memory introduces a nuance of empathy that was rare among his contemporaries, and it lifts his story clear of the conventions of the time.

The same insights (and integrity—Camus was writing from personal experience) shape his representation of the resisters themselves. It is not by chance that Grand, the mousy, downtrodden, unaspiring clerk, is presented as the embodiment of the real, unheroic resistance. For Camus, as for Rieux, resistance was not about heroism at all—or, if it was, then it was the heroism of goodness. "It may seem a ridiculous idea, but the only way to fight the plague is with decency." Joining the "health teams" was not in itself an act of great significance—rather, "not doing it would have been incredible at the time." This point is made over and over again in the novel, as though Camus were worried lest it be missed: "When you see the suffering it brings," Rieux remarks at one point, "you have to be mad, blind or a coward to resign yourself to the plague."

Camus, like the narrator, refuses to "become an overeloquent eulogist of a determination and heroism to which he attaches only a moderate degree of importance." This has to be understood in context. There was of course tremendous courage and sacrifice in the French Resistance; many men and women died for the cause. But Camus was uncomfortable with the smug myth of heroism that had grown up in postwar France, and he abhorred the tone of moral superiority with which self-styled former Resisters (including some of his famous fellow intellectuals) looked down upon those who did nothing. In Camus's view it was inertia, or ignorance, which accounted for people's failure to act. The Cottards of the world were the exception; most people are better than you think—as Tarrou puts it, "You just need to give them the opportunity."[5]

IN CONSEQUENCE, some of Camus's intellectual contemporaries did not particularly care for *The Plague*. They expected a more "engaged" sort of writing from him and they found the book's ambiguities and the tone of disabused tolerance and moderation politically incorrect. Simone de Beauvoir especially disapproved strongly of Camus's use of a natural pestilence as a substitute for (she thought) Fascism—it relieves men of their political responsibilities, she insisted, and runs away from history and real political problems. In 1955 the literary critic Roland Barthes reached a similarly negative conclusion, accusing Camus of offering readers an "antihistorical ethic." Even today this criticism sometimes surfaces among academic students of Camus: he lets Fascism and Vichy off the hook, they charge, by deploying the metaphor of a "nonideological and nonhuman plague."

Such commentaries are doubly revealing. In the first place they show just how much Camus's apparently straightforward story was open to misunderstanding. The allegory may have been tied to Vichy France, but the "plague" transcends political labels. It was not "Fascism" that Camus was aiming at— an easy target, after all, especially in 1947—but dogma, compliance, and cowardice in all their intersecting public forms. Tarrou, certainly, is no Fascist; but he insists that in earlier days, when he complied with doctrines that authorized the suffering of others for higher goals, he too was a carrier of the plague even as he fought it.

Second, the charge that Camus was too ambiguous in his judgments, too unpolitical in his metaphors, illuminates not his weaknesses but his strengths. This is something that we are perhaps better placed to understand now than were *The Plague*'s first readers. Thanks to Primo Levi and Václav Havel we have become familiar with the "gray zone." We understand better that in con-

ditions of extremity there are rarely to be found comfortingly simple categories of good and evil, guilty and innocent. We know more about the choices
and compromises faced by men and women in hard times, and we are no
longer so quick to judge those who accommodate themselves to impossible
situations. Men may do the right thing from a mixture of motives and may
with equal ease do terrible deeds with the best of intentions—or no intentions
at all.

It does not follow from this that the plagues that humankind brings down
upon itself are "natural" or unavoidable. But assigning responsibility for
them—and thus preventing them in the future—may not be an easy matter.
And with Hannah Arendt we have been introduced to a further complication: the notion of the "banality of evil" (a formulation that Camus himself
would probably have taken care to avoid), the idea that unspeakable crimes
can be committed by very unremarkable men with clear consciences.[6]

These are now commonplaces of moral and historical debate. But Albert
Camus came to them first, in his own words, with an originality of perspective and intuition that eluded almost all his contemporaries. That is what they
found so disconcerting in his writing. Camus was a moralist who unhesitatingly distinguished good from evil but abstained from condemning human
frailty. He was a student of the "absurd" who refused to give in to necessity.[7]
He was a public man of action who insisted that all truly important questions
came down to individual acts of kindness and goodness. And, like Tarrou, he
was a believer in absolute truths who accepted the limits of the possible: "Other
men will make history. . . . All I can say is that on this earth there are pestilences and there are victims—and as far as possible one must refuse to be on
the side of the pestilence."

Thus *The Plague* teaches no lessons. Camus was a *moraliste* but he was no
moralizer. He claimed to have taken great care to try to avoid writing a "tract,"
and to the extent that his novel offers little comfort to political polemicists of
any school he can be said to have succeeded. But for that very reason it has not
merely outlived its origins as an allegory of occupied France but has tran-

scended its era. Looking back on the grim record of the twentieth century we can see more clearly now that Albert Camus had identified the central moral dilemmas of the age. Like Hannah Arendt, he saw that "the problem of evil will be the fundamental question of postwar intellectual life in Europe—as death became the fundamental problem after the last war."[8]

Fifty years after its first appearance, in an age of posttotalitarian satisfaction with our condition and prospects, when intellectuals pronounce the End of History and politicians proffer globalization as a universal palliative, the closing sentence of Camus's great novel rings truer than ever, a firebell in the night of complacency and forgetting:

> The plague bacillus never dies or vanishes entirely, . . . it can remain dormant for dozens of years in furniture or clothing, . . . it waits patiently in bedrooms, cellars, trunks, handkerchiefs, and old papers, and . . . perhaps the day will come when for the instruction or misfortune of mankind, the plague will rouse its rats and send them to die in some well-contented city.

This essay first appeared in *The New York Review of Books* in November 2001.

Notes to Chapter XIV

[1] Julien Green, *Journal*, February 20, 1948, quoted in Olivier Todd, *Albert Camus: Une Vie* (Paris: Gallimard, 1996), pp. 419–420.

[2] The literary editor Jean Paulhan, meeting Camus in Paris in January 1943, noted how he "suffered" from his inability to return to Algiers, to "his wife and his climate." Jean Paulhan to Raymond Guérin, January 6, 1943, in Paulhan, *Choix de lettres, 1937–1945* (Paris: Gallimard, 1992), p. 298.

[3] "I am not a philosopher and I never claimed to be one." In "Entretien sur la révolte," *Gazette des lettres*, February 15, 1952.

[4] In his posthumous autobiographical novel *Le Premier homme*, Camus writes of his own father coming home after watching a public execution and vomiting.

[5] It is worth noting here that it was in Le Chambon-sur-Lignon, the very same mountain village where Camus was convalescing in 1942–1943, that the local Protestant community united behind their pastor to save the lives of a large number of Jews who took refuge among the remote, inaccessible farms and hamlets. This uncommon act of collective courage, sadly rare in those years, offers a historical counterpoint to Camus's narrative of moral choice—and a confirmation of his intuitions about human decency. See Philip P. Hallie, *Lest Innocent Blood Be Shed: The Story of the Village of Le Chambon and How Goodness Happened There* (New York: Harper and Row, 1979).

[6] See Hannah Arendt, *Eichmann in Jerusalem: A Report on the Banality of Evil* (New York: Viking, 1963). The point is well illustrated in Christopher Browning's study of mass murder on the Eastern Front in World War II: *Ordinary Men: Reserve Police Battalion 101 and the Final Solution in Poland* (New York: Aaron Asher Books, 1992).

[7] In an early (1938) review of Jean-Paul Sartre's *La Nausée*, written long before they met, Camus observed: "The mistake of a certain sort of writing is to believe that because life is wretched it is tragic. . . . To announce the absurdity of existence cannot be an objective, merely a starting point." See *Alger républicain*, October 20, 1938.

[8] Hannah Arendt, "Nightmare and Flight," *Partisan Review*, vol. 12, no. 2 (1945), reprinted in *Essays in Understanding*, Jerome Kohn, ed. (New York: Harcourt Brace, 1994), p. 133.

CHAPTER XV

Its Own Worst Enemy

I.

America's current status as a hegemonic, unrivaled, unchallengeable "hyperpower," the subject of Joseph Nye's book, is exemplified in its military establishment.* Before September 11, before President Bush proposed a 14 percent ($48 billion) increase in defense spending this year, the United States was already in a league of its own. It has bases, ships, planes, and soldiers all around the globe. Washington spends more on its armed forces than any nation in history: the U.S. defense budget will soon outdistance the annual defense expenditures of the next nine states *combined*. True, the member states of the E.U. between them have more soldiers than the United States, and collectively their defense spending totaled nearly 70 percent that of Washington's pre-2002 outlays; but the results in technology and hardware are simply not comparable. The United States can intervene or make war almost anywhere in the world. No one else even comes close.

But the "America" that much of the world carries in its head is not defined by throw weights, smart bombs, or even GIs. It is more subtle and dif-

---

*Joseph S. Nye Jr., *The Paradox of American Power: Why the World's Only Superpower Can't Go It Alone* (New York: Oxford University Press, 2002).

fuse than that. In some places it is a fading memory of liberation. In others it is a promise of freedom, opportunity, and plenty: a political metaphor and a private fantasy. Elsewhere, or in the same places at other times, America has been identified with local repression. In short, America is everywhere. Americans—just 5 percent of the world's population—generate 30 percent of the world's gross product, consume nearly 30 percent of global oil production, and are responsible for almost as high a share of the world's output of greenhouse gases. Our world is divided in many ways: rich/poor; North/South; Western/non-Western. But more and more, the division that counts is the one separating America from everyone else.

The anti-Americanism now preoccupying commentators should thus come as no surprise. The United States, by virtue of its unique standing, is exposed to the world's critical gaze in everything it does or fails to do. Some of the antipathy the United States arouses is a function of what it is: long before America rose to global dominion foreign visitors were criticizing its brash self-assurance, the narcissistic confidence of Americans in the superiority of American values and practices, and their rootless inattentiveness to history and tradition—their own and other people's. The charge sheet has grown since the United States took the world stage, but it has not changed much. This "cultural" anti-Americanism is shared by Europeans, Latin Americans, and Asians, secular and religious alike. It is not about antipathy to the West, or freedom, or the Enlightenment, or any other abstraction exemplified by the United States. It is about America.[1]

RESENTED FOR WHAT IT IS, America also stokes antipathy by what it does. Here things have recently changed for the worse. The United States is often a delinquent international citizen. It is reluctant to join international initiatives or agreements, whether on climate warming, biological warfare, criminal justice, or women's rights; the United States is one of only two states (the other being Somalia) that have failed to ratify the 1989 Convention on Children's Rights. The present U.S. administration has "unsigned" the Rome Treaty establishing an International Criminal Court and has declared itself no longer bound by the Vienna Convention on Law of Treaties, which sets out the obligations of states to abide by treaties they have yet to ratify. The American attitude toward the United Nations and its agencies is cool, to say the least. Earlier this year the U.S. ambassador for human rights called for the early dismissal of the ad hoc tribunals for Rwanda and former Yugoslavia—even though these are integral to any serious war on international terror and the United States itself spent millions of dollars to bribe Belgrade into handing Slobodan Milošević over to the Hague tribunal.

To many outsiders this inconsistent approach to international organizations and agreements, some of which Washington helped to establish, belies America's claim to share international interests and seek multilateral partners for its goals. The same is true of American economic practices. The United States is both advocate and exemplar of globalization—free-market capitalism untrammeled by frontiers, special interests, restrictive practices, protectionism, or state interference. But at home Washington applies steel tariffs, farm supports, and de facto government subsidies (notably for the defense industries) for domestic political gain. The European Union does this, too, of course—the notorious Common Agricultural Policy consumes 45 percent of the Brussels budget and is at least as damaging in blocking the produce of African farmers as any U.S. farm bill. But the cost to America's image is far greater: the United States is intimately identified with the very international norms it is transgressing.

To foreign critics, these contradictions in American behavior suggest hypocrisy—perhaps the most familiar of the accusations leveled at the United States. They are all the more galling because, hypocritical or not, America is indispensable. Without American participation, most international agreements are dead letters. American leadership seems to be required even in cases—such as Bosnia between 1992 and 1995—where the British and their fellow Europeans had the means to resolve the crisis unaided. The United States is cruelly unsuited to play the world's policeman—Washington's attention span is famously short, even in chronically troubled regions like Kashmir, the Balkans, the Middle East, or Korea—but it seems to have no choice. Meanwhile everyone else, but the Europeans especially, resent the United States when it fails to lead, but also when it leads too assertively.

The predictable backlash has been a new tone in American policy, an arrogant impatience with foreign opinion of any kind. The cold war is over, runs the unilateralist creed of the Bush administration and its supporters, and the dust has now cleared. We know who we are, and we know what we want. Foreign policy is about national interests. National interests are served by the exercise of power. Power is about arms and the will to use them, and we have both. In the words of the columnist Charles Krauthammer, in June 2001, "The new unilateralism seeks to strengthen American power and unashamedly deploy it on behalf of self-defined global ends."[2]

IN THE IMMEDIATE AFTERMATH of September 11 the Bush administration's unilateralist rhetoric was muted, to ease the search for allies in the coming war on terror. Overseas commentators, abashed by the carnage, earnestly returned the compliment—"We are all Americans now," pronounced *Le Monde*, while NATO invoked Article V of its charter for the first time, committing all its members to solidarity with a United States under attack. But the honeymoon was short-lived. Most American allies firmly supported the war on Afghanistan, whatever their private misgivings. But in January 2002, when President Bush alluded in his State of the Union speech to an "axis of evil" (North Korea, Iran, Iraq), the breach was reopened.

What caused offense in that speech was less its substance than its form. Most of America's allies doubt the wisdom of alienating Iran from the Western nations, and some of them question Washington's way of handling Saddam Hussein. But these are not new disagreements. However, just four months after the administration declared itself keen to build alliances and collaborate closely with its friends in the struggle against a common enemy, Bush's account of America's global struggle against the forces of darkness didn't even mention America's allies. This raised hackles.[3]

The American response was to feign surprise—"So what unilateral action have we taken that has them all so shocked?" asked Colin Powell on February 17. But the Europeans had not misread the signs from Washington. Powell notwithstanding, the realist (some might say cynical) consensus in the administration was that since America's allies are irrelevant to its military calculations and have no political choice but to tag along, nothing is gained by consulting them in advance or taking their sensitivities into consideration. In its crudest form this conclusion was well summarized, once again, by Charles Krauthammer:

> Our sophisticated European cousins are aghast. The French led the way, denouncing American *simplisme*. They deem it a breach of manners to call evil by its name. They prefer accommodating to it. They have lots of practice, famously accommodating Nazi Germany in 1940. . . . We are in a war of self-defense. It is also a war for Western civilization. If the Europeans refuse to see themselves as part of this struggle, fine. If they wish to abdicate, fine. We will let them hold our coats, but not tie our hands.[4]

It is typical of the ugly mood in parts of Washington today that Krauthammer omits to mention not only that France lost 100,000 men in six weeks of fighting against the Germans in 1940, but also that the United States maintained full diplomatic relations with the evil Nazis for a further eighteen months, until Hitler declared war on America in December 1941.

Krauthammer, of course, is just a columnist. But the new tone of American foreign policy today is dryly summarized by Powell himself—for many foreigners the lone voice of multilateral moderation in Bush's administration. Speaking in Rome, after the recent Bush-Putin meeting and the subsequent establishment of a NATO–Russia Council, he insisted that U.S. foreign policy remains as "multilateralist" as ever. Our task, he explained, is to try to persuade our friends that our policies are right. But if that fails, "then we will take the position we believe is correct and I hope the Europeans are left with a better understanding of the way in which we want to do business."[5]

It is this condescending indifference to outside opinion that grates on foreign ears and that has so disappointed America's allies after the raised expectations of September 2001. Together with Bush's recently pronounced strategic doctrine of "unilaterally determined preemptive self-defense" and the alarming prospect of new earth-penetrating nuclear weapons for possible use in Iraq— an unprecedented break with America's historical reluctance to countenance first-strike weapons of this sort—it paints once more the picture of an American leadership deaf to criticism or advice.[6] It is a leadership that all too often seems contemptuous and bellicose, and, in the words of *El País*, fuels "public alarm" by its obsessions and self-serving warnings of imminent Armageddon.

JOSEPH NYE IS DEAN of the Kennedy School at Harvard and was a senior defense and intelligence official under President Clinton. His book-length essay on American foreign policy was written before the attacks of September 11 and hastily updated for publication, but it could not be more timely. Nye is not a Wilsonian idealist, bemoaning American reluctance to join the international community in a search for a better world—in 1990 he published *Bound to Lead*, in which he correctly predicted the coming American hegemony.[7] He is not embarrassed by the reality of American supremacy.

Nevertheless, he has written a strong critique of unilateralism in American foreign policy—the widespread disposition to "go it alone," paying a minimum of attention to the wishes of others. He is also implicitly skeptical of "realism," the approach to international relations that disparages a priori concern with rights, transnational laws, or moral objectives and confines diplomacy to the advance of American interests by all appropriate means. But this is not a book about international relations theory.[8] Nye's objection to unilateralism, or realism in the sense used here, is not that they are conceptually insecure; his point is that they just don't work.

In Nye's view, international relations today resemble a particularly intricate game of three-dimensional chess. On one level there is hard military power, a terrain where the United States reigns uncontested. On the second level there is economic power and influence: in this field the European Union already challenges the United States in trade, the regulation of monopolies, and the setting of industrial standards, and outdistances America in telecommunications, environmental policy, and much else. And there are other players besides.

At the third level Nye places the multifarious and proliferating nongovernmental activities shaping our world: currency flows, migration, transnational corporations, NGOs, international agencies, cultural exchanges, the electronic media, the Internet, and terrorism. Nonstate actors communicate and operate across this terrain virtually unconstrained by government interference; and the power of any one state, the United States included, is readily frustrated and neutralized.

The trouble with the people in charge of shaping and describing U.S. policy today, according to Nye, is that they are only playing at the first level, their vision restricted to American military firepower. In his words, "Those who recommend a hegemonic American foreign policy based on such traditional descriptions of American power are relying on woefully inadequate analysis." Before September 11, Americans in Nye's view were willfully deaf to the world around them. They blithely ignored even those, like the former senators Gary Hart and Warren Rudman, who warned them in 1999 of a coming catastrophe: "Americans will likely die on American soil, possibly in large numbers."[9] September 11 ought to have been a clear call for a fresh perspective, but America's present leadership appears not to be listening.

IF THE UNITED STATES is to win its war on terror, if it is to succeed in its assertion of world leadership, it is going to need the help and understanding of others, particularly in dealing with poor Arab and Muslim states and others resentful at their own backwardness. This is perfectly obvious. International police actions and the regulation and oversight of intercontinental movements of currency, goods, and people require international cooperation.[10] "Failed states," in whose detritus terrorists flourish, need to be rebuilt—the United States is culpably uninterested in this task and no longer much good at it, in depressing contrast to its performance after 1945. America does the bombing, but the complicated and dangerous work of reconstruction is left to others.

The European Union (including its candidate members) currently contributes ten times more peacekeeping troops worldwide than the United States, and in Kosovo, Bosnia, Albania, Sierra Leone, and elsewhere the Europeans have taken more military casualties than the United States. Fifty-five percent of the world's development aid and two-thirds of all grants-in-aid to the poor and vulnerable nations of the globe come from the European Union. As a share of GNP, U.S. foreign aid is barely one-third the European average. If you combine European spending on defense, foreign aid, intelligence gathering, and policing—all of them vital to any sustained war against international crime—it easily matches the current American defense budget. Notwithstanding the macho preening that sometimes passes for foreign policy analysis in contemporary Washington, the United States is utterly dependent on friends and allies in order to achieve its goals.

If America is to get and keep foreign support, it is going to have to learn to wield what Nye calls "soft power." Grand talk of a new American Empire is illusory, Nye believes: another misleading historical allusion to put with "Vietnam" and "Munich" in the catalogue of abused analogies. In Washington today one hears loud boasts of unipolarity and hegemony, but the fact, Nye writes, is that

> the success of U.S. primacy will depend not just on our military or economic might but also on the soft power of our culture and values and on policies that make others feel they have been consulted and their interests have been taken into account. Talk about empire may dazzle us and mislead us into thinking we can go it alone.[11]

Soft power, in Nye's usage, sounds a lot like common sense, and would have seemed that way to every postwar American administration from Harry

Truman to George Bush Sr. If you want others to want what you want, you need to make them feel included. Soft power is about influence, example, credibility, and reputation. The Soviet Union, in Nye's account, lost it in the course of its invasions of Hungary and Czechoslovakia in 1956 and 1968. America's soft power is enhanced by the openness and energy of its society; it is diminished by needlessly crass behavior, like Bush's blunt assertion that the Kyoto agreement was "dead." Scandinavian states, and Canada, exercise influence far above their weight in international affairs because of their worldwide identification with aid and peacekeeping. This, too, is soft power.

YOU DON'T NEED TO AGREE with Nye in every instance to sympathize with his overall thesis. What he is proposing, after all, is that the government of the United States pay what Thomas Jefferson once called "a decent Respect to the Opinions of Mankind." Far from representing a frustrating impediment to the pursuit of national interest, the judicious exercise of restraint and cooperation can only enhance it, in a world where America is anyway powerless to defend its many interests unaided. Nye has little patience for those, like the present national security adviser, in whose blinkered perspective the United States should "proceed from the firm ground of national interest and not from the interest of an illusory international community."

In Nye's account, the national interest in a democracy "is simply what citizens, after proper deliberation, say it is." Given the nature of modern democracy that is a little naive, but any definition of American interest could surely accommodate a modicum of reduced sovereignty in exchange for a basket of public goods whose benefits would be shared with the world at large.

The costs of American obstinacy are well illustrated by the recent international skirmish over the International Criminal Court (ICC). The Bush administration opposes the court, claiming that Americans serving abroad would be exposed to frivolous prosecutions. Accordingly, in anticipation of the court's inauguration on July 1, 2002, the United States in late June threatened to withdraw from UN peacekeeping missions and veto all such operations in the future unless Americans are guaranteed a blanket exemption from the court's jurisdiction. Perhaps taken a little aback by the refusal of other UN Security Council members to accede to such arm-twisting, the United States agreed after lengthy and fraught discussions to a face-saving compromise: UN peacekeepers from countries that have not signed on to the ICC will have one year of immunity from prosecution, renewable every July 1.

The behavior of the United States in this affair was deeply unseemly. There are only 700 Americans currently serving overseas in UN peacekeeping missions (out of a total of 45,000 personnel), and the ICC already contained clauses, inserted explicitly to mollify Washington, that virtually exempted UN missions from prosecution. The initial American position this June had clearly been taken with the object of undermining the International Criminal Court and UN peacekeeping activities—both of them scorned and abominated by Dick Cheney, Donald Rumsfeld, and Condoleezza Rice. Washington's stance is particularly embarrassing because it makes a mockery of American insistence upon the international pursuit and prosecution of terrorists and other political criminals; and because it provides American cover for countries and politicians who have real cause to fear the new court. All of our allies on the UN Security Council voted against the United States on this matter; meanwhile Washington's opposition to the International Criminal Court is shared by Iran, Iraq, Pakistan, Indonesia, Israel, and Egypt.[12]

Nevertheless, many widely sought goals could be reached merely by the United States ceasing to oppose them: Washington has refused to sign the international Protocol on Involvement of Children in Armed Conflict, and Congress won't ratify the international Convention on Discrimination against Women: in the first case because the Pentagon wants to reserve the right to recruit a handful of seventeen-year-olds, in the second because of the anti-abortion lobby. Like racial segregation in the 1950s, such policies bring worldwide discredit to the United States: a sure impediment to the pursuit of American interest, however you define it. Even the mere appearance of taking the world seriously would enhance American influence immeasurably—from European intellectuals to Islamic fundamentalists, anti-Americanism feeds voraciously off the claim that the United States is callously indifferent to the views and needs of others.

There is a world of difference between encouraging others to want what you want and seducing them into wanting what you have. Many American commentators miss this distinction, and parochially assume that the world is divided into those who want what America has got and those who hate America for having it. Joseph Nye is careful to avoid such solipsism. But even he takes it for granted that the United States and its Western allies are basically at one and share common values and goals: all that is needed to close the rift that has opened up between Europe and the United States is a more subtle and sensitive exercise of American diplomatic clout. I am not so sure.

II.

Superficially, the Atlantic gap is a by-product of post–cold war restructuring. The purpose of NATO is now unclear and opinion is split (in Europe as in the United States) over whether and how Europeans should organize collectively for their own defense in the absence of a Soviet threat. The European Union, free to enlarge to its east, is absorbed by internal debates over how to do this and the consequences for its own governance. The "big" three members (Germany, France, Great Britain) are wary of having their actions constrained by more than twenty smaller states, while the latter cling nervously to their equal status within the Union. The world outside does not have Europe's undivided attention.

For the sake of the euro the E.U. has imposed strict spending constraints on its members, just as postwar baby boomers are retiring and placing heavy demands on national pension funds. And to this must be added the incendiary anti-immigrant rhetoric coming from the far right. For all these reasons, and because of their erstwhile dependence on the American nuclear umbrella, Europeans are reluctant to divert public resources to military spending and for the most part they don't fully appreciate America's post–September 11 appre-

hension over terrorism—the British and the Spanish have lived with murderous domestic terrorism for over thirty years.

In any case, although Europeans today feel more "European" than they
used to, the E.U. will never be a "superpower," for all its economic heft.[13]
"Europe" does not think strategically, and even its largest members are in
no position to do so in isolation. Even when they all agree—as in their anx-
ious frustration at Bush's failed Middle East policy—European leaders cannot line up as one to say so. Europeans are right to criticize the propensity
of America to march out, dispose of its enemies, and then retreat to its for-
tress. As Chris Patten, the E.U. commissioner for external affairs, put it after
the "axis of evil" speech, "True friends are not sycophants," and the United
States needs its friends.[14] But it is not as if they have an alternative strategy to
propose.

But there is more to the breach within the West than squabbles over defense. The cold war and the Atlantic alliance concealed for half a century deep
differences between two sharply contrasting sorts of society. The Europeans
"underspend" on defense not just because the American guarantee allowed
them to enter a garden of Perpetual Peace,[15] but also because in the third quarter of this century they chose to devote a lot of money to expensive (and very
popular) public services. The result is that in many crucial respects Europe
and the United States are actually less alike than they were fifty years ago.

This observation flies in the face of claims about "globalization" and
"Americanization" advanced not just by enthusiastic proponents of the process, but also by its angry critics. Yet there is less to the promise of a new
American century than meets the eye. In the first place, we have been here
before. It is a cardinal tenet of the prophets of globalization that the logic of
economic efficiency must sweep all before it (a characteristically nineteenth-
century fallacy they share with Marxists). But that was also how it seemed at
the peak of the last great era of globalization, on the eve of World War I, when
many observers likewise foresaw the decline of the nation-state and a coming
age of international economic integration.

What happened, of course, was something rather different, and 1913 levels of international trade, communication, and mobility would not be reached again until the mid-1970s. The contingencies of domestic politics trumped the "laws" of international economic behavior, and they may do so again. Capitalism is indeed global in its reach, but its local forms have always been richly variable and they still are. This is because economic practices shape national institutions and legal norms and are shaped by them in their turn; they are deeply embedded in very different national and moral cultures.

PARTLY FOR THIS REASON, the American model is not obviously more appealing to people elsewhere and its triumph is far from sure. Europeans and Americans live quite different sorts of lives. More than one in five Americans are poor, whereas the figures for continental Western Europe hover around 8 percent. Sixty percent more babies die in their first year of life in the United States than in France or Germany. The disparity between rich and poor is vastly greater in the United States than anywhere in continental Europe (or than it was in the United States twenty years ago); but whereas fewer than one American in three supports significant redistribution of wealth, 63 percent of Britons favor it and the figures are higher still on the European continent.

Even before modern European welfare states were established, most employed Europeans had compulsory health insurance (since 1883 in the German case), and all Western Europeans now take for granted the interlocking mesh of guarantees, protections, and supports whose reduction or abolition they have consistently opposed at the polls. The social and occupational insecurity familiar to tens of millions of Americans has long been politically intolerable anywhere in the European Union. If Fascism and Communism were the European reactions to the last great wave of laissez-faire globalization (as Joseph Nye and others have proposed), then "welfare capitalism" is Europe's insurance against a rerun. On prudential grounds if for no other reason, the rest of the West is not about to take the American path.

But what of the claim that Europeans, like everyone else in the world, will have little choice? Much is said about the coming ineluctable triumph of

American economic practice at the expense of the lumbering, unproductive, inflexible European variant. Yet handicapped as they are by all the supposed impedimenta of their statist past, the economies of Belgium, France, and the Netherlands last year were actually *more* productive for each hour worked than that of the United States, while the Irish, the Austrians, the Danes, and the Germans were very close behind.[16]

Between 1991 and 1998 productivity on average actually *grew faster* in Europe than in the United States. The United States nonetheless outpaces Europe in gross terms. This is because more Americans work; the state takes less from their wages (and provides less in return); they work longer hours—28 percent more than Germans, 43 percent more than the French; and they take shorter vacations or none at all.

Whether Europe (or anywhere else) would look more like America if the American economic model were adopted there is a moot point. The modern American economy is not replicable elsewhere. The "war on terror" is not the only matter in which the United States is critically dependent upon foreigners. The American economic "miracle" of the past decade has been fueled by the $1.2 billion per day in foreign capital inflow that is needed to cover the country's foreign trade deficit, currently running at $450 billion per year. It is these huge inward investment flows that have kept share prices up, inflation and interest rates down, and domestic consumption booming.

If a European, Asian, or Latin American country ran comparable trade deficits, it would long since be in the hands of the International Monetary Fund. The United States is uniquely placed to indulge such crippling dependence on foreign investors because the dollar has been the world's reserve currency since World War II. How long the American economy can operate thus before it is brought painfully to earth by a loss of overseas confidence is a much-debated topic; as is the related claim that it was these rivers of foreign cash, rather than the unprecedented productivity of the new high-tech sectors, that drove the prosperity of the 1990s.[17] What is clear is that for all its recent allure, the American model is unique and not for export.

Far from universalizing its appeal, globalization has if anything diminished foreign enthusiasm for the American model: the reduction in public ownership of goods and services in Europe over the past twenty years has not been accompanied by any reduction in the state's social obligations—except in Britain where, tellingly, governments have had to backtrack in the face of public opposition. And it is because they inhabit such very different societies that Europeans and Americans see the world so differently and value sharply contrasting international processes and outcomes.

Just as modern American leaders typically believe that in domestic public life citizens are best left to their own devices, with limited government intervention, so they project this view onto international affairs as well. Seen from Washington, the world is a series of discrete challenges or threats, calibrated according to their implications for America. Since the United States is a global power, almost anything that happens in the world is of concern to it; but the American instinct is to address and resolve any given problem in isolation.

There is also a refreshingly American confidence that problems may indeed *be* resolved—at which point the United States can return home. This emphasis upon an "exit strategy," upon being in the world but not quite of it, always at liberty to retire from the fray, has its domestic analogue in modern American life. Like many of its citizens, especially since September 11, the United States feels most comfortable when retreating to its "gated community."

This is not an option for Europeans and others, for whom today's world is a spiderweb of interlocking legal regimes and agencies, regulating and overseeing almost every aspect of life. The problems facing Europe today—crime, immigration, refugees, environmental hazards, institutional integration—are inherently chronic and they all transcend borders. Governments habitually work in concert or through multilateral institutions. Just as the public sector has displaced individual initiative in many parts of national life, so the habit of collaboration shapes European approaches to international affairs. In these respects it is Europe that has successfully "globalized" and the United States that lags far behind.

For all these reasons, and because so much of American foreign policy is driven by insular considerations that will not soon change, it is hard to share Joseph Nye's optimistic conclusions about the future of American "soft power." The United States is quite literally its own worst enemy: it is when pandering to domestic constituencies that American presidents most often alienate foreign opinion. Bombastic rhetoric and unilateralist posturing go down well at home and may even intimidate foreign foes (though this seems uncertain). But they surely terrify and estrange a third constituency, America's many friends and admirers abroad.

And yet America is still esteemed and even revered overseas, not because of globalization but in spite of it. America is not epitomized by MTV and McDonald's, or by Enron or by Bernie Ebbers of WorldCom. America is not even particularly admired abroad for its awesome military establishment, any more than it is respected for its unparalleled wealth. American power and influence are actually very fragile, because they rest upon an idea, a unique and irreplaceable myth: that the United States really does stand for a better world and is still the best hope of all who seek it.

The real threat to America, which the Bush administration has not even begun to comprehend, is that in the face of American neglect and indifference this myth will fade and "large proportions of key societies [will] turn against the U.S. and the global values of free trade and free society."[18] This would spell the end of "the West" as we have understood it for half a century. The postwar North Atlantic community of interest and mutual friendship was unprecedented and invaluable: its loss would be a disaster for everyone.[19]

What gives America its formidable international influence is not its unequaled capacity for war but the trust of others in its good intentions. That is why Washington's opposition to the International Criminal Court does so much damage. It suggests that the United States does not trust the rest of the world to treat Americans fairly. But if America displays a lack of trust in others, the time may come when they will return the compliment.

IN THE SPRING OF 2001 the tiny south Balkan state of Macedonia was on the verge of civil war. Its Macedonian Slav majority confronted a rebellion by the frustrated, disadvantaged Albanian minority; the government, led by un-reconstructed National-Communists, was itching to unleash a brutal and bloody "police action." With great difficulty, intermediaries from Britain and elsewhere negotiated a fragile agreement: the insurgents would disarm and, in return, parliament would pass laws to protect and enfranchise the country's Albanian citizens. For a few weeks everyone held their breath—if Macedonia "blew," the South Balkans might explode, sucking Greece, Turkey, and NATO into the cauldron.

But Macedonia did not "blow" and the agreement held and still holds. At the crest of the emergency I asked an Albanian friend what was stopping the Macedonian government, demonstrably unhappy with the accords, from tear-ing them up and doing its worst. "Colin Powell's fax machine," he replied. The moral authority of America's secretary of state (and it was only moral—the United States had no intention of dispatching soldiers); the fact that Mace-donia mattered enough to America for Powell to place his weight on the scales—these considerations sufficed to defuse a significant regional crisis.

So long as such obscure, faraway countries continue to matter to America, America will matter to them and to everyone else, and its power for good will continue. But if America stops caring, it will also cease to count. If Washing-ton stops trusting, it will lose the trust of others. The fax machine will fall si-lent and we shall all be a lot lonelier and infinitely more vulnerable; the United States above all.

This essay, a review of *The Paradox of American Power: Why the World's Only Superpower Can't Go It Alone* by Joseph S. Nye Jr., first appeared in *The New York Review of Books* in August 2002.

Notes to Chapter XV

[1] The attack of September 11 produced a small avalanche of books on anti-Americanism and its implications. See, for example, *The Age of Terror: America and the World after September 11*, Strobe Talbott and Nayan Chanda, eds. (New York: Basic Books, 2001); *How Did This Happen? Terrorism and the New War*, James F. Hoge Jr. and Gideon Rose, eds. (New York: Public Affairs, 2001); and *Granta: What We Think of America*, Ian Jack, ed. (New York: Grove, 2002).

[2] Charles Krauthammer, "The New Unilateralism," *Washington Post*, June 8, 2001.

[3] In the course of his speech Bush mentioned Europe just once. NATO and the EU he passed over in silence.

[4] Charles Krauthammer, "The Axis of Petulance," *Washington Post*, March 1, 2002. Variations on this theme can be found in the writings of William Kristol and Robert Kagan, the Bush administration's house intellectuals. See, for example, Robert Kagan and William Kristol, "The Bush Era," *The Weekly Standard*, February 11, 2002.

[5] *The Economist*, June 1–7, 2002, p. 27.

[6] On the Bush administration's move toward developing nuclear weapons for actual use, see Steven Weinberg, "The Growing Nuclear Danger," *New York Review of Books*, July 18, 2002.

[7] *Bound to Lead: The Changing Nature of American Power* (New York: Basic Books, 1990).

[8] For a lucid account of realist thinking in the history of international relations, see the new book by Jonathan Haslam, *No Virtue Like Necessity: Realist Thought in International Relations since Machiavelli* (New Haven: Yale University Press, 2002).

[9] Gary Hart and Warren Rudman, *New World Coming: American Security in the Twenty-First Century, Phase I Report* (U.S. Commission on National Security/21st Century, 1999), p. 4, quoted in Joseph S. Nye, *The Paradox of American Power: Why the World's Only Superpower Can't Go It Alone* (New York: Oxford University Press, 2003), p. x.

[10] Before September 11, the chief impediment to the international regulation of money-laundering and tax havens, the sinews of terrorism, was the U.S. Treasury Department.

[11] Joseph Nye, "Lessons in Imperialism," *Financial Times*, June 17, 2002.

[12] In recent months the United States has more than once found itself in questionable company. Last November, when America vetoed a protocol designed to put teeth into the thirty-year-old Biological Weapons Convention and effectively destroyed a generation of efforts to halt the spread of these deadly arms, only a handful of the 145 signatories to the convention took Washington's side: among these were China, Russia, India, Pakistan, Cuba, and Iran. As a united force for good in international affairs, "the West" hardly exists. All too often Washington's position now pits it against the Western Europeans, Canadians, Australians, and a majority of Latin American states, while American "unilateralism" is supported (for their own reasons) by an unseemly rogues' gallery of dictatorships and regional troublemakers.

[13] The latest of many books on Europe's collective destiny is David P. Calleo, *Rethinking Europe's Future* (Princeton, NJ: Princeton University Press, 2001), a learned and thoughtful exposition of the European Union, its history and prospects.

[14] See *Financial Times*, February 15, 2002.

[15] See Robert Kagan, "Power and Weakness," *Policy Review*, no. 113, June/July, 2002, where

Europe's self-indulgent, "Kantian" paradise is unflatteringly contrasted with the Promethean tasks faced by America back in the real world of international anarchy.

[16] See *Financial Times*, February 20, 2002.

[17] For a relentlessly negative account of the deficiencies of the American model, see Will Hutton, *The World We're In* (New York: Little, Brown, 2002), to which I am indebted for some of the figures cited above. Hutton's critique would be more convincing if he did not paint quite such a rosy picture of the European alternative.

[18] Michael J. Mazarr, "Saved from Ourselves?" in *What Does the World Want from America?*, Alexander T. J. Lennon, ed. (forthcoming from MIT Press, November 2002), p. 167; first published in *The Washington Quarterly*, vol. 25, no. 2 (Spring 2002).

[19] See William Wallace, "US Unilateralism: A European Perspective," in *Multilateralism and US Foreign Policy: Ambivalent Engagement*, Stewart Patrick and Shepard Forman, eds. (Boulder, CO: Lynne Rienner, 2002), pp. 141–166.

CHAPTER XVI

The Way We Live Now

I.

We are witnessing the dissolution of an international system. The core of that system, and its spiritual heart, was the North Atlantic alliance: not just the 1949 defense treaty but a penumbra of understandings and agreements beginning with the Atlantic Charter of 1941 and spreading through the United Nations and its agencies; the Bretton Woods accords and the institutions they spawned; conventions on refugees, human rights, genocide, arms control, war crimes, and much more besides. The merits of this interlocking web of transnational cooperation and engagement went well beyond the goal of containing and ultimately defeating Communism. Behind the new ordering of the world lay the memory of thirty calamitous years of war, depression, domestic tyranny, and international anarchy, as those who were present at its creation fully understood.[1]

Thus the end of the cold war did not make the postwar order redundant. Quite the contrary. In a post-Communist world the fortunate lands of Western Europe and North America were uniquely well placed to urge upon the rest of the world the lessons of their own achievement: markets and democracy, yes, but also the benefits of good-faith participation in the institutions and practices of an integrated international community. That such a community must retain the means and the will to punish its enemies was effectively if belatedly illustrated in Bosnia and Kosovo (and, in the breach, in Rwanda). As these episodes suggested, and September 11, 2001, confirmed, only the United States has the resources and the determination to defend the interdependent world that it did so much to foster; and it is America that will always be the prime target of those who wish to see that world die.

It is thus a tragedy of historical proportions that America's own leaders are today corroding and dissolving the links that bind the United States to its closest allies in the international community. The United States is about to make war on Iraq for reasons that remain obscure even to many of its own citizens. The war that they *do* understand, the war on terrorism, has been unconvincingly rolled into the charge sheet against one Arab tyrant. Washington is abuzz with big projects to redraw the map of the Middle East; meanwhile the true Middle Eastern crisis, in Israel and the Occupied Territories, has been subcontracted to Ariel Sharon. After the war, in Iraq as in Afghanistan, Palestine, and beyond, the United States is going to need the help and cooperation (not to mention the checkbooks) of its major European allies; and there will be no lasting victory against Osama bin Laden or anyone else without sustained international collaboration. This is not, you might conclude, the moment for our leaders enthusiastically to set about the destruction of the Western alliance; yet that is what they are now doing. (The enthusiasm is well represented in *The War over Iraq* by Lawrence Kaplan and William Kristol, which I shall discuss below.)

The Europeans are not innocent in the matter. Decades of American nuclear reassurance induced unprecedented military dystrophy. The Franco-German condominium of domination was sooner or later bound to provoke a backlash among Europe's smaller nations. The inability of the European Union to build a consensus on foreign policy, much less a force with which to implement it, has handed Washington a monopoly in the definition and resolution of international crises. No one should be surprised if America's present leaders have chosen to exercise it. What began some years ago as American frustration at the Europeans' failure to organize and spend in their own defense has now become a source of satisfaction for U.S. hawks. The Europeans don't agree with us? So what! We don't need them, and anyway what can they do? They're feeling hurt and resentful in Brussels, or Paris, or Berlin? Well, they've only themselves to blame. Remember Bosnia.[2]

YET TODAY it is the Bush administration that is resentful and frustrated: it turns out that the French, at least, can actually do quite a lot. Together with the Belgians and Germans in NATO, and the Russians and Chinese at the UN, they can thwart, foil, delay, hinder, check, confound, embarrass, and above all irritate the Americans. In the run-up to war in Iraq the United States is now paying the price for two years of contemptuous disdain for international opinion. The *lèse-majesté* of the French in particular has driven America's present leadership into unprecedented public expressions of anger at its own allies for breaking ranks: in President Bush's deathless words, "Either you are with us or you are with the terrorists." Worse, it has led to paroxysms of sneering Europhobia in the U.S. media, shamelessly promoted by politicians and commentators who should know better.

Two myths dominate public discussion of Europe in America today. The first, which would be funny but for the harm it is causing, is the notion of an "Old" and a "New" Europe. When Defense Secretary Donald Rumsfeld proposed this distinction in January it was taken up with malicious alacrity on the Pentagon cheerleading bench. In the *Washington Post* Anne Applebaum enthusiastically seconded Rumsfeld: Britain, Italy, Spain, Denmark, Poland, Hungary, and the Czech Republic (the signatories to a letter in the *Wall Street Journal* supporting President Bush) have all "undergone liberalization and privatization" of their economies, she wrote, bringing them closer to the American model. They, not the "Old Europe" of France and Germany, can be counted on in the future to speak for "Europe."[3]

The idea that Italy has embarked on "economic liberalization" will come as news to Italians, but let that pass. The more egregious error is to suppose that "pro-American" Europeans can be so conveniently distinguished from their "anti-American" neighbors. In a recent poll by the Pew Research Center, Europeans were asked whether they thought "the world would be more dangerous if another country matched America militarily." The "Old European" French and Germans—like the British—tended to agree. The "New European" Czechs and Poles were less worried at the prospect. The same poll asked respondents whether they thought that "when differences occur with America, it is because of [my country's] different values" (a key indicator of cultural anti-Americanism): only 33 percent of French respondents and 37 percent of Germans answered "yes." But the figures for Britain were 41 percent; for Italy 44 percent; and for the Czech Republic 62 percent (almost as high as the 66 percent of Indonesians who feel the same way).[4]

In Britain, the *Daily Mirror*, a mass-market tabloid daily that has hitherto supported Tony Blair's New Labour Party, ran a full-page front cover on January 6 mocking Blair's position; in case you haven't noticed, it informed him, Bush's drive to war with Iraq is about oil for America. Half the British electorate opposes war with Saddam Hussein under any circumstances. In the Czech Republic just 13 percent of the population would endorse an American attack on Iraq without a UN mandate; the figure in Spain is identical. In traditionally pro-American Poland there is even less enthusiasm: just 4 percent of Poles would back a unilateralist war. In Spain, voters from José María Aznar's own Popular Party overwhelmingly reject his support for the war; his allies in Catalonia have joined Spain's opposition parties in condemning "an unprovoked unilateral attack" by the United States on Iraq; and most Spaniards are adamantly opposed to a war with Iraq even with a second UN resolution. As for American policy toward Israel, opinion in "New European" Spain is distinctly less supportive than opinion in the "Old" Europe of Germany or France.[5]

IF AMERICA IS TO DEPEND on its "New" European friends, then, it had better lower its expectations. Among the pro-U.S. signatories singled out for praise by Mr. Rumsfeld, Denmark spends just 1.6 percent of GNP on defense; Italy 1.5 percent; Spain a mere 1.4 percent—less than half the defense commitment of "Old European" France. The embattled Italian prime minister Silvio Berlusconi has many motives for getting photographed next to a smiling George Bush; but one of them is to ensure that Italy can hold on to its American security umbrella and avoid paying for its own defense.

As for the East Europeans: yes, they like America and will do its bidding if they can. The United States will always be able to bully a vulnerable country like Romania into backing America against the International Criminal Court. But in the words of one Central European foreign minister opposed to U.S. intervention at the time of the 1999 Kosovo action: "We didn't join NATO to fight wars." In a recent survey, 69 percent of Poles (and 63 percent of Italians) oppose any increased expenditure on defense to enhance Europe's standing as a power in the world. If the *New York Times* is right and George Bush now regards Poland, Britain, and Italy as his chief European allies, then—Tony Blair apart—America is leaning on a rubber crutch.[6]

And what of Germany? American commentators have been so offended at Germany's willingness to "appease" Saddam, so infuriated by Gerhard Schröder's lack of bellicose fervor and his "ingratitude" toward America that few have stopped to ask why so many Germans share Günter Grass's view that "the President of the United States embodies the danger that faces us all." Germany today is different. It *does* have a distinctively pacifist culture (quite unlike, say, France). If there is to be war, many Germans feel, let it be *ohne mich* (without me). This transformation is one of the historic achievements of the men of "Old" Europe. When American spokesmen express frustration at it, they might take a moment to reflect on what it is they are asking—though at a time when Saddam Hussein is casually compared to Adolf Hitler, and the U.S. defense secretary can call Germany a "pariah state" along with Cuba and Libya, this may be too much to expect. But should we really be so quick to demand martial enthusiasm of Germany?

A SECOND EUROPHOBIC MYTH now widely disseminated in the United States is more pernicious. It is the claim that Europe is awash in anti-Semitism,

that the ghosts of Europe's judeophobic past are risen again, and that this atavistic prejudice, Europe's original sin, explains widespread European criticism
of Israel, sympathy for the Arab world, and even support for Iraq. The main
source for these claims is a spate of attacks on Jews and Jewish property in the
spring of 2002, and some widely publicized opinion polls purporting to demonstrate the return of anti-Jewish prejudice across the European continent.
American commentary on these data has in turn emphasized the "anti-Israel"
character of European media reports from the Middle East.[7]

To begin with the facts: according to the American Anti-Defamation
League (ADL), which has worked harder than anyone to propagate the image
of rampant European anti-Semitism, there were twenty-two significant anti-
Semitic incidents in France in April 2002, and a further seven in Belgium; for
the whole year 2002 the ADL catalogued forty-five such incidents in France,
varying from anti-Semitic graffiti on Jewish-owned shops in Marseilles to
Molotov cocktails thrown into synagogues in Paris, Lyon, and elsewhere. But
the same ADL reported sixty anti-Semitic incidents on U.S. college campuses
alone in 1999. Measured by everything from graffiti to violent assaults, anti-
Semitism has indeed been on the increase in some European countries in recent years; but then so it has in America. The ADL recorded 1,606 anti-Semitic
incidents in the United States in the year 2000, up from 900 in 1986. Even if
anti-Semitic aggression in France, Belgium, and elsewhere in Europe has
been grievously underreported, there is no evidence to suggest it is more widespread in Europe than in the United States.[8]

But what of attitudes? Evidence from the European Union's Eurobarom-
eter polls, the leading French polling service SOFRES, and the ADL's own
surveys all point in the same direction. There is in many European countries,
as in the United States, a greater tolerance for mild verbal anti-Semitism than
in the past, and a continuing propensity to believe long-standing stereotypes
about Jews: e.g., that they have a disproportionate influence in economic life.
But the same polls confirm that young people all over Europe are much less
tolerant of prejudice than their parents were. Among French youth especially,
anti-Semitic sentiment has steadily declined and is now negligible. An over-

whelming majority of young people questioned in France in January 2002 believe that we should speak more, not less, of the Holocaust; and nearly nine out of ten of them agreed that attacks on synagogues were "scandalous." These figures are broadly comparable to results from similar surveys taken in the United States.[9]

Most of the recent attacks on Jews in Western Europe were the work of young Arabs or other Muslims, as local commentators acknowledge.[10] Assaults on Jews in Europe are driven by anger at the government of Israel, for whom European Jews are a convenient local surrogate. The rhetorical armory of traditional European anti-Semitism—the "Protocols of the Elders of Zion," Jews' purported economic power and conspiratorial networks, even blood libels—has been pressed into service by the press and television in Cairo and elsewhere, with ugly effects all across the youthful Arab diaspora.

THE ADL ASSERTS that all this "confirms a new form of anti-Semitism taking hold in Europe. This new anti-Semitism is fueled by anti-Israel sentiment and questions the loyalty of Jewish citizens." That is nonsense. Gangs of unemployed Arab youths in Paris suburbs like Garges-lès-Gonesse surely regard French Jews as representatives of Israel, but they are not much worried about their patriotic shortcomings. As to Jewish loyalties: one leading question in the ADL surveys—"Do you believe Jews are more likely to be loyal to Israel than to [your country]"—elicits a consistently higher positive response in the United States than in Europe. It is *Americans*, not Europeans, who are readier to assume that a Jew's first loyalty might be to Israel.

The ADL and most American commentators conclude from this that there is no longer any difference between being "against" Israel and "against" Jews. But this is palpably false. The highest level of pro-Palestinian sympathy in Europe today is recorded in Denmark, a country which also registers as one of the least anti-Semitic *by the ADL's own criteria*. Another country with a high and increasing level of sympathy for the Palestinians is the Netherlands; yet the Dutch have the lowest anti-Semitic "quotient" in Europe and nearly half of them are "worried" about the possible rise of anti-Semitism. Furthermore, it is the self-described "left" in Europe that is most uncompromisingly pro-Palestinian, while the "right" displays both anti-Arab and anti-Jewish (but often pro-Israel) bias. Indeed, this is one of the few areas of public life in which these labels still carry weight.[11]

Overall, Europeans are more likely to blame Israel than Palestinians for the present morass in the Middle East, but only by a ratio of 27:20. Americans, by contrast, blame Palestinians rather than Israel in the proportion of 42:17. This suggests that Europeans' responses are considerably more balanced, which is what one would expect: the European press, radio, and television provide a fuller and fairer coverage of events in the Middle East than is available to most Americans. As a consequence, Europeans are better than Americans at distinguishing criticism of Israel from dislike of Jews.

One reason may be that some of Europe's oldest and most fully accredited anti-Semites are publicly sympathetic to Israel. Jean-Marie Le Pen, in an interview in the Israeli daily *Haaretz* in April 2002, expressed his "understanding" of Ariel Sharon's policies ("A war on terror is a brutal thing")—comparable in his opinion to France's no less justified antiterrorist practices in Algeria forty years earlier.[12] The gap separating Europeans from Americans on the question of Israel and the Palestinians is the biggest impediment to transatlantic understanding today. Seventy-two percent of Europeans favor a Palestinian state against just 40 percent of Americans. On a "warmth" scale of 1–100, American feelings toward Israel rate 55, whereas the European average is just 38—and somewhat cooler among the "New Europeans": revealingly, the British and French give Israel the same score. It is the *Poles* who exhibit by far the coolest feelings toward Israel (Donald Rumsfeld please note).[13]

II.

In recent weeks both these American fables about Europe have been folded into an older prejudice now given an ominous new twist: intense suspicion of

France and the French. France's procrastination at the UN has brought forth in the United States an unprecedented burst of rhetorical venom. This is something new. When De Gaulle broke with the unified NATO command in 1966, Washington—along with France's other allies—was annoyed and said so. But it would not have occurred to American statesmen, diplomats, politicians, newspaper editors, or television pundits that France had somehow "betrayed" America, or that De Gaulle was a "coward" and the French were ungrateful for the sacrifices Americans had made on their behalf and should be punished accordingly. Eisenhower, Kennedy, Johnson, and Nixon all respected De Gaulle in spite of his foibles, and he returned the compliment.[14]

Today, respectable columnists demand that France be kicked off the Security Council for obstructing the will of the United States, and they remind their readers that if it had been left to France "most Europeans today would be speaking either German or Russian." Their colleagues in less-restrained publications "want to kick the collective butts of France" for forgetting D-Day. Where are the French when "American kids" come to rescue them, they ask: first from Hitler, now from Saddam Hussein ("an equally vile tyrant")? "Hiding. Chickening out. Proclaiming *Vive les wimps!*" Part of a "European chorus of cowards." As a new bumper sticker has it: "First Iraq, then France."[15]

American vilification of the French—openly encouraged in the U.S. Congress, where tasteless anti-French jokes were publicly exchanged with Colin Powell during a recent appearance there—degrades us, not them. I hold no brief for the Élysée, which has a long history of cynical dealing with dictators, from Jean-Bedel Bokassa to Robert Mugabe, including Saddam Hussein along the way. And the Vichy years will be a stain on France until the end of time. But talk of French "surrender monkeys" comes a touch too glibly to American pundits, marinated in self-congratulatory war movies from John Wayne to Mel Gibson.

In World War I, which the French fought from start to finish, France lost three times as many fighting men as America has lost in all its wars combined. In World War II, the French armies holding off the Germans in May–June 1940 suffered 124,000 dead and 200,000 wounded in six weeks, more than America did in Korea and Vietnam combined. Until Hitler brought the United States into the war against him in December 1941, Washington maintained correct diplomatic relations with the Nazi regime. Meanwhile the *Einsatzgruppen* had been at work for six months slaughtering Jews on the Eastern Front, and the Resistance was active in occupied France.

Fortunately we shall never know how middle America would have responded if instructed by an occupying power to persecute racial minorities in its midst. But even in the absence of such mitigating circumstances the precedents are not comforting—remember the Tulsa pogrom of May 1921, when at least 350 blacks were killed by whites. Perhaps, too, Americans should hesitate before passing overhasty judgments about "age-old" French anti-Semitism[16]: by the end of the nineteenth century France's elite École Normale Supérieure was admitting (by open competition) brilliant young Jews—Léon Blum, Émile Durkheim, Henri Bergson, Daniel Halévy, and dozens of others—who would never have been allowed near some of America's Ivy League colleges, then and for decades to come.

IT IS DEEPLY SADDENING to have to restate these things. Perhaps they are of no consequence. Why should it matter that Americans today think so ill of France and Europe that America's leaders sneer ignorantly at "Old" Europe and demagogic pundits urge their readers to put out the ungrateful Eurotrash? After all, French anti-Americanism is an old and silly story, too; but it has never seriously impeded transatlantic relations and grand strategy.[17] Are we not just seeing the compliment returned, albeit at an unusually high volume?

I don't believe so. The Americans who laid the framework for the only world most of us have ever known—George Marshall, Dean Acheson, George Kennan, Charles Bohlen, and the presidents they served—knew what they wished to achieve and why the European-American relationship was so crucial to them. Their successors today have their own very different conviction. In their view Europeans, and the various alliances and unions in which they are entwined, are an irritating impediment to the pursuit of American interests. The United States has nothing to lose by offending or alienating these disposable allies of convenience, and much to gain by tearing up the entangling web of controls that the French and their ilk would weave around our freedom of movement.

This position is unambiguously stated in a new short book by Lawrence Kaplan and William Kristol, *The War over Iraq: Saddam's Tyranny and America's Mission.*[*] Both men are Washington-based journalists. But Kristol, who once gloried in the title of chief of staff to Vice President Dan Quayle and is now a political analyst for Fox TV, is also the editor of *The Weekly Standard* and one of the "brains" behind the neoconservative turn in U.S. foreign policy. Kristol's views are shared by Richard Perle, Paul Wolfowitz, and others in the power elite of the Bush administration, and he articulates in only slightly restrained form the prejudices and impatience of the White House leadership itself.

The War over Iraq is refreshingly direct. Saddam is a bad man, he ought to be removed, and only the United States can do the job. But that is just the beginning. There will be many more such tasks, indeed an infinity of them in coming years. If the United States is to perform them satisfactorily—"to secure its safety and to advance the cause of liberty"—then it must cut loose from the "world community" (always in scare quotes). People will hate us for our "arrogance" and our power in any event, and a more "restrained" American foreign policy won't appease them, so why waste time talking about it? The foreign strategy of the United States must be "unapologetic, idealistic, assertive and well funded. America must not only be the world's policeman or its sheriff, it must be its beacon and guide."

WHAT IS WRONG WITH THIS? In the first place, it displays breathtaking ignorance of the real world, as ultra-"realist" scenarios frequently do. Because

---

[*]Lawrence F. Kaplan and William Kristol, *The War Over Iraq: Saddam's Tyranny and America's Mission* (San Francisco: Encounter, 2003).

it confidently equates American interest with that of every right-thinking person on the planet, it is doomed to arouse the very antagonism and enmity that provoke American intervention in the first place (only a hardened European cynic would suggest that this calculation has been silently incorporated into the equation). The authors, like their political masters, unhesitatingly suppose *both* that America can do as it wishes without listening to others, *and* that in so doing it will unerringly echo the true interests and unspoken desires of friend and foe alike. The first claim is broadly true. The second bespeaks a callow provinciality.[18]

Second, the Kristol/Wolfowitz/Rumsfeld approach is morbidly self-defeating. Old-fashioned isolationism, at least, is consistent: if we stay out of world affairs we won't have to depend on anyone. So is genuine Wilsonian internationalism: we plan to be at work *in* the world so we had better work *with* the world. A similar consistency informs conventional Kissinger-style realpolitik: we have interests and we want certain things, other countries are just like us and they want certain things, too—so let's make deals. But the new "unilateralist internationalism" of the present administration tries to square the circle: we do what we want in the world, but on our own terms, indifferent to the desires of others when they don't share our objectives.

Yet the more the United States pursues its "mission" in the world, the more it is going to need help, in peacekeeping, nation building, and facilitating cooperation among our growing community of newfound friends. These are projects at which modern America is not markedly adept and for which it depends heavily on allies. Already, in Afghanistan and the Balkans, the German "pariah" state alone provides 10,000 peacekeeping soldiers to secure the ground won by American arms. U.S. voters are famously allergic to tax increases. They are unlikely to raise the sort of money needed to police and reconstruct much of Western Asia, not to mention other zones of instability where Kristol's "mission" may lead us. So who will pay? Japan? The EU? The UN? Let us hope that their leaders don't look too closely at Kaplan and Kristol's sneeringly unflattering remarks in their regard.

Some of what the authors have to say about past failings is on target. The

UN, like Western Europe, vacillated shamefully over Bosnia and Kosovo. The Clinton administration, like Bush senior before it, turned away from humanitarian crises in the Balkans and Central Africa. If the United States under Bush junior is now resolved to fight brutal tyrants and armed political psychopaths, so much the better for us all. But that certainly wasn't the case before September 11. Back then American conservatives were disengaging from the international sphere at dizzying speed—who now remembers Condoleezza Rice's contemptuous dismissal of "nation building"? Why should America's friends place their trust in this newfound commitment and expose themselves to violent reprisals on its behalf?

No reasonable person could object to the hot pursuit of Osama bin Laden. And there is a case, too, for military action against an Iraq that refuses to disarm. But to extend these into a mission statement for open-ended and unimpeded American actions to transform the condition of half of humanity, at will and in the teeth of international dissent; indeed, gleefully to anticipate, as Kristol and Kaplan and others do, the prospect of such international opposition—this sounds too much like a practice in search of its theory. It is also vitiated by one uncomfortably hard nugget of bad faith.

"Israel" has one of the longest index entries in this little book. "Palestine" has none, though there is one lonely reference to the PLO, listed as an Iraqi-supported terrorist group. Kristol and Kaplan go to considerable lengths to emphasize the importance of Israel as an American strategic partner in the new Middle East they envisage, and they offer as one justification of a full-scale war on Iraq that this would improve Baghdad's relations with Israel. But nowhere do they evince any concern for the Israel-Palestine imbroglio itself: a rapidly burgeoning humanitarian crisis, the single greatest source of instability and terrorism in the region, and a festering object of disagreement and distrust between the two sides of the Atlantic. The omission is glaring and revealing.

Unless Kristol and his political mentors can explain why an ambitious new American international mission to put the globe to rights is silent on Israel; why the newly empowered American "hegemon" is curiously unable and unwilling to bring any pressure to bear on one small client state in the world's most unstable region, then few outside their own circle are going to take their "mission statements" seriously. Why should the U.S. administration and its outriders care? For a reason that the men who constructed the postwar international system would immediately have appreciated. If America is not taken seriously; if it is obeyed rather than believed; if it buys its friends and browbeats its allies; if its motives are suspect and its standards double—then all the overwhelming military power of which Kristol and Kaplan so vaingloriously boast will afford it nothing. The United States can go out and win not just the Mother of All Battles but a whole matriarchal dynasty of Desert Storms; it will inherit the wind—and worse besides.

So please, let us stop venting our anxieties and insecurities in vituperative macho digs at Europe. Whatever his motives, French president Jacques Chirac has been voicing opinions shared by the overwhelming majority of Europeans and a sizable minority of Americans, not to speak of most of the rest of the world. To claim that he, and they, are either "with us or with the terrorists"— that disagreement is betrayal, dissent is treason—is, to say the least, willfully imprudent. Whether we need the Europeans more than they need us is an interesting question and one I shall take up in a subsequent essay, but the United States has everything to lose if Europeans fall to squabbling among themselves for American favors; our leaders should be ashamed of themselves for gleefully encouraging this.[19] As Aznar, Blair, and their collaborators wrote in their controversial open letter of January 30, 2003, "Today more than ever, the transatlantic bond is a guarantee of our freedom." This is as true today as it was in 1947—and it cuts both ways.

This essay, a review of *The War Over Iraq: Saddam's Tyranny and America's Mission* by Lawrence F. Kaplan and William Kristol, first appeared in *The New York Review of Books* in March 2003.

NOTES TO CHAPTER XVI

[1] See, classically, Dean Acheson, *Present at the Creation: My Years in the State Department* (New York: Norton, 1969).

[2] In the course of the 1990s the British steadfastly blocked efforts at the UN to implement military intervention against Milošević, while French generals on the ground simply ignored orders, with the covert backing of their government.

[3] Anne Applebaum, "Here Comes the New Europe," *Washington Post*, January 29, 2003. See also Amity Schlaes, "Rumsfeld Is Right About Fearful Europe," *Financial Times*, January 28, 2003, in which the author castigates Germans for lacking "vision": what the Americans did for ungrateful Germans in Berlin in 1990 they are now set to repeat in Baghdad.

[4] See *The Economist*, January 4, 2003.

[5] For Czech and Polish attitudes to war with Iraq, see *The Economist*, February 1, 2003. For Spanish opposition to Aznar, see *El País*, February 3, 2003. Spanish commentators are especially sensitive to the need for European unity, and Aznar is deeply resented for what is seen by many in Spain as his feckless action in signing the *WSJ* statement. Many of Aznar's own supporters regard it as insultingly insufficient for him to repeat, as he has taken to doing, that "between Bush and Saddam Hussein I will always side with Bush." But then Aznar has career ambitions: he is angling for future appointment to a senior international position, and he needs American and British support.

[6] See the survey of transatlantic attitudes in a poll conducted by the Chicago Council on Foreign Relations and the German Marshall Fund of the United States at www.worldviews .org. For NATO member state defense expenditures see *La Repubblica*, February 11, 2003. See also the *New York Times*, January 24, 2003. The antiwar views of a Central European diplomat were expressed in a private communication. Like many other politicians from former Communist Europe, he was reluctant to air his criticisms of American policy in public: partly from a genuine affection and gratitude toward America, partly out of apprehension concerning the consequences for his country.

[7] See Christopher Caldwell, "Liberté, Egalité, Judéophobie," *The Weekly Standard*, May 6, 2002. Some American commentators take their cue from a recent spate of books published in Paris, purporting to demonstrate that France's 500,000 Jews face a second Holocaust at the hands of "anti-racist" anti-Semites. The most hysterical of these pamphlets is *La Nouvelle Judéophobie* by Pierre-André Taguieff (Paris: Fayard, 2002), in which the author (who has written sixteen other books on the same topic in the past thirteen years) writes of a "planetary Judeophobia." Taguieff's mischievous scaremongering was the subject of an admiring puff by Martin Peretz in *The New Republic*, February 3, 2003. In a similar key see also Gilles William Goldnadel, *Le Nouveau Bréviaire de la haine: Antisémitisme et antisionisme* (Paris: Ramsay, 2001), and Raphaël Draï, *Sous le signe de Sion: L'antisémitisme nouveau est arrivé* (Paris: Michalon, 2001). Draï's first chapter is titled "Israel en danger de paix? D'Oslo à Camp David II."

[8] See "Global Anti-Semitism" at www.adl.org/anti_semitism/anti-semitism*global*incidents.asp, and "ADL Audit: Anti-Semitic Incidents Rise Slightly in US in 2000" at www.adl.org/ presrele/asus_12/3776_12.asp.

[9] See "L'image des juifs en France" at www.sofres.com/etudes/pol/130600_imagejuifs.htm; "Les jeunes et l'image des juifs en France" at www.sofres.com /etudes/pol/120302_juifs_r

.htm; "Anti-Semitism and Prejudice in America: Highlights from an ADL Survey, November 1998" at www.adl.org/antisemitism_survey/survey_main.asp.

[10] "C'est un fait, ces actes [antisémites] sont commis, pour l'essentiel, par des musulmans," in Denis Jeambar, "Silence coupable," *L'Express*, December 6, 2001.

[11] For an illuminating graph of the prejudices and allegiances of the far left and far right in contemporary Germany, see "Politik," *Die Zeit*, January 9, 2003, p. 5.

[12] Adar Primor, "Le Pen Ultimate," *Haaretz.com*, April 18, 2002.

[13] See Craig Kennedy and Marshall M. Bouton, "The Real Transatlantic Gap," *Foreign Policy*, November–December 2002, based on the recent survey by the Chicago Council on Foreign Relations and the German Marshall Fund. For fuller details see "Differences over the Arab-Israeli Conflict," www.worldviews.org/detailreports/compreport/html/ch3s3.html.

[14] At the time of the Cuban missile crisis, De Gaulle made unambiguously clear to JFK that whatever actions it chose to take, the United States had France's unwavering support and trust.

[15] See Thomas L. Friedman, "Vote France off the Island," *New York Times*, February 9, 2003; Steve Dunleavy, "How Dare the French Forget," *New York Post*, February 10, 2003. What the French may truly have forgotten is how the United States financed France's "dirty war" in Vietnam, from 1947 to 1954. But then since this is something American commentators also prefer to overlook, it tends not to figure on the "France owes us" charge sheet.

[16] Rejecting what he termed "[President Jacques] Chirac's . . . accusation" that the American Jewish Congress works in collaboration with the political leadership in Jerusalem, American Jewish Congress President Jack Rosen in July 2002 termed French attitudes "reminiscent of ancient anti-Semitic stereotypes of worldwide Jewish conspiracies." See www.ajcongress.org/pages/ RELS2002/JUL_2002 /jul02_04.htm.

[17] In a forthcoming article I shall discuss some recent books on French and European anti-Americanism.

[18] And corresponds to a widespread assumption in the United States, that everyone else in the world really desires nothing more than to be American and come to America. This is especially inaccurate in the case of Europeans, who understand very well the differences between American and European society and institutions. Most people in the non-Western world would indeed like to experience in their own country the independence and prosperity that Americans enjoy in the United States; but that is another matter and one that carries somewhat different implications for American foreign policy.

[19] It is entirely appropriate that when asked what he thought of Donald Rumsfeld's latest destructive efforts in this vein at the recent Munich conference of defense ministers, William Kristol expressed his unbounded admiration for the U.S. defense secretary's performance. Fox Television News, February 12, 2003.

CHAPTER XVII

Anti-Americans Abroad

I.

If you want to understand how America appears to the world today, consider the sport-utility vehicle. Oversized and overweight, the SUV disdains negotiated agreements to restrict atmospheric pollution. It consumes inordinate quantities of scarce resources to furnish its privileged inhabitants with supererogatory services. It exposes outsiders to deadly risk in order to provide for the illusory security of its occupants. In a crowded world, the SUV appears as a dangerous anachronism. Like U.S. foreign policy, the sport-utility vehicle comes packaged in sonorous mission statements; but underneath it is just an oversized pickup truck with too much power.

The simile may be modern, but the idea behind it is not. "America" has been an object of foreign suspicion for even longer than it has been a beacon and haven for the world's poor and downtrodden. Eighteenth-century commentators—on the basis of very little direct observation—believed America's flora and fauna to be stunted, and of limited interest or use. The country could never be civilized, they insisted, and much the same was true of its unsophisticated new citizens. As the French diplomat (and bishop) Talleyrand observed, anticipating two centuries of European commentary: *"Trente-deux réligions et un seul plat"* (["thirty-two religions and just one dish"]—which

Americans typically and understandably tended to eat in a hurry). From the perspective of a cosmopolitan European conservative like Joseph de Maistre, writing in the early years of the nineteenth century, the United States was a regrettable aberration—and too crude to endure for long.

Charles Dickens, like Alexis de Tocqueville, was struck by the conformism of American public life. Stendhal commented upon the country's "egoism"; Baudelaire sniffily compared it to Belgium (!) in its bourgeois mediocrity; everyone remarked upon the jejune patriotic pomp of the United States. But in the course of the next century, European commentary shifted perceptibly from the dismissive to the resentful. By the 1930s, the United States' economic power was giving a threatening twist to its crude immaturity. For a new generation of anti-democratic critics, the destabilizing symptoms of modern life—mass production, mass society, and mass politics—could all be traced to America.

LIKE ANTI-SEMITISM, to which it was often linked, anti-Americanism was a convenient shorthand for expressing cultural insecurity. In the words of the Frenchman Robert Aron, writing in 1935, Henry Ford, F. W. Taylor (the prophet of work rhythms and manufacturing efficiency), and Adolf Hitler were, like it or not, the "guides of our age." America was "industrialism." It threatened the survival of individuality, quality, and national specificity. "America is multiplying its territory, where the values of the West risk finding their grave," wrote Emmanuel Berl in 1929. Europeans owed it to their heritage to resist their own Americanization at every turn, urged George Duhamel in 1930: "We Westerners must each firmly denounce whatever is American in his house, his clothes, his soul."[1]

World War II did not alleviate this irritation. Radical anti-Americanism in the early cold war years echoed the sentiments of conservative anti-Americanism twenty years earlier. When Simone de Beauvoir charged that America was "becoming Fascist," Jean-Paul Sartre claimed that McCarthy-ite America "had gone mad," the novelist Roger Vailland asserted that the fridge was an American plot to destroy French domestic culture, and *Le Monde* declared that "Coca-Cola is the Danzig of European Culture," they were denouncing the same American "enemy" that had so alarmed their political opponents a generation before.[2] American behavior at home and abroad fed this prejudice but did not create it. In their anger at the United States, European intellectuals had for many decades been expressing their anxieties about changes closer to home.

The examples I have quoted are from France, but English ambivalence toward America is also an old story; the German generation of the 1960s blamed America above all for the crass consumerism and political amnesia of their parents' postwar Federal Republic; and even in Donald Rumsfeld's "new" Europe the United States, representing "Western" technology and progress, has on occasion been blamed for the ethical vacuum and cultural impoverishment that global capitalism brings in its train.[3] Nevertheless, anti-Americanism in Europe at least has always had a distinctively French tinge. It is in Paris that European ambivalence about America takes polemical form.

PHILIPPE ROGER HAS WRITTEN a superb history of French anti-Americanism, elegant, learned, witty.[*] This enjoyable exercise, in the very best traditions of French scholarship, richly deserves to be published in English translation, unabridged. The book's argument is far too subtle and intricate to summarize briefly, but the word "genealogy" in the title should be taken seriously. This is not strictly a history, since Roger treats his material as a "semiotic bloc"; and he doesn't pay much attention to the record of French "pro-Americanism" that would need to be discussed to present a balanced account.

Instead, in nearly six hundred pages of close textual exegesis, Roger demonstrates not only that the core of French anti-Americanism is very old in-

---

[*]Philippe Roger, *L'Ennemi américain: Généalogie de l'antiaméricanisme* français (Paris: Seuil, 2002).

deed, but also that it was always fanciful, only loosely attached to American reality. Anti-Americanism is a *récit*, a tale (or fable), with certain recurring themes, fears, and hopes. Starting out as an aesthetic distaste for the New World, French anti-Americanism has since moved through the cultural to the political; but the sedimentary evidence of earlier versions is never quite lost to sight.

Roger's book is strongest on the eighteenth and nineteenth centuries. His coverage of the twentieth century stops with the generation of Sartre—the moment, as he reminds us, when it became conventional for French anti-American texts to begin by denying that they were. That seems reasonable—there are a number of satisfactory accounts of the anti-Americanism of our own times, and Roger is interested in tracing origins, not outcomes.[4] And by ending short of the present he can permit himself a sardonic, upbeat conclusion:

> What if anti-Americanism today were no more than a mental slavery that the French impose on themselves, a masochist lethargy, a humdrum resentment, a passionless Pavlovian reaction? That would offer grounds for hope. There are few vices, even intellectual ones, that can long withstand the boredom they elicit.

Unfortunately, there is a fresh twist in the story. Anti-Americanism today is fueled by a new consideration, and it is no longer confined to intellectuals. Most Europeans and other foreigners today are untroubled by American products, many of which are in any case manufactured and marketed overseas. They are familiar with the American "way of life," which they often envy and dislike in equal parts. Most of them don't despise America, and they certainly don't hate Americans. What upsets them is U.S. foreign policy; and they don't trust America's current president. This is new. Even during the cold war, many of America's political foes actually quite liked and trusted its leaders. Today, even America's friends don't like President Bush: in part for the policy he pursues, in part for the manner in which he pursues it.

THIS IS THE BACKGROUND to a recent burst of anti-American publications from Paris. The most bizarre of these was a book by one Thierry Meyssan, purporting to show that the September 11 attack on the Pentagon never happened.* No airliner ever crashed into the building, he writes: the whole thing is a hoax perpetrated by the American defense establishment to advance its own interests. Meyssan's approach echoes that of Holocaust deniers. He begins by assuming the nonexistence of a well-accredited event, then reminds us that no amount of evidence—*especially* from firsthand witnesses—can prove the contrary. The method is well summarized in his dismissal of the substantial body of eyewitness testimony running counter to his claim: "Far from warranting their evidence, the quality of these witnesses just shows how far the U.S. Army will go to distort the truth."[5]

The most depressing thing about Meyssan's book is that it was a best seller. There is an audience in France for the farther reaches of paranoid suspicion of America, and September 11 seems to have aroused it. More typical, though, is the shopping list of complaints in books with titles like *Pourquoi le monde déteste-t-il l'Amérique?*, *Le livre noir des États-Unis*, and *Dangereuse Amérique.*[†] The first two are by British and Canadian authors respectively, though they have sold best in their French editions; the third is coauthored by a prominent French Green politician and former presidential candidate.

Characteristically presented with real or feigned regret ("We are not anti-American, but . . ."), these works are an inventory of commonly cited American shortcomings. The United States is a selfish, individualistic society devoted to commerce, profit, and the despoliation of the planet. It is as uncaring of its own poor and sick as it is indifferent to the rest of humankind. The United States rides roughshod over international laws and treaties and threatens the

---

* Thierry Meyssan, *11 September 2001: L'Effroyable Imposture* (Chatou: Carnot, 2003).
† Ziauddin Sardar and Merryl Wyn Davies, *Pourquoi le monde déteste-t-il l'Amérique?* (Paris: Fayard, 2002); Peter Scowen, *Le livre noir des États-Unis* (Paris: Mango, 2003); Noël Mamère and Patrick Farbiaz, *Dangereuse Amérique: chronique d'une guerre annoncée* (Paris: Ramsay, 2003).

moral, environmental, and physical future of humanity. It is inconsistent and hypocritical in its foreign dealings and it wields unparalleled military clout. It is, in short, a bull in the global china shop, wreaking havoc.[6]

Much of this is recycled from earlier criticisms of America. Peter Scowen's complaints (his chapter headings include "Les atrocités de Hiroshima et de Nagasaki" and "Une culture vide"), like those of Ziauddin Sardar and Merryl Wyn Davies ("American Hamburgers and Other Viruses") or Noël Mamère and Patrick Farbiaz ("L'américanisation du monde," "Une croisade qui sent le pétrole" [A crusade smelling of oil]), blend traditional themes with new accusations. They are a mixture of conservative cultural distaste (America is ugly, rootless, and crass), anti-globalization rhetoric (America is polluting the world), and neo-Marxist reductionism (America is run by and for the oil companies). Domestic American critics add race into the mix—not content with trampling over everyone else, the United States rides roughshod across its own history.[7]

Some of the criticisms of American policy and practice are well founded. Others are drivel. In their catalogue of claims against America, Sardar and Davies blame the United States for the cold war, imposed on a reluctant Western Europe: "Both France and Italy had major Communist Parties—and still do [*sic*]—but with their own very specific histories that owed little to Russia." "International Communism," in other words, was an American invention. This revisionist myth died many years ago. Its posthumous revival suggests that an older, political anti-Americanism is gaining new traction from the Bush administration's foreign ambitions.[8] Once a rogue state, always a rogue state.

ACCORDING TO EMMANUEL TODD, however, there is no need to worry. In his recent book, *Après l'empire* (also a best seller), he argues that the sun is setting on imperial America.* We are entering a post-American age. America

---

*Emmanuel Todd, *Après l'empire: essai sur la décomposition du système américain* (Paris: Gallimard, 2002).

will continue to jeopardize international stability. But Europeans (and Asians) can take some comfort from the knowledge that the future is theirs. American military power is real, but redundant; meanwhile its tottering economy is vulnerably dependent upon the rest of the world, and its social model holds no appeal. Between 1950 and 1990 the United States was a benevolent and necessary presence in the world, but not anymore. The challenge today is to manage America's growing irrelevance.

Todd is not at all a conventional "anti-American," and some of what he has to say is of interest—though English readers seeking to understand the case for American decline would do better to read Charles Kupchan.[9] Todd is right to say that asymmetric globalization—in which the United States consumes what others produce, and economic inequalities grow apace—is bringing about a world unsympathetic to American ambition. Post-Communist Russia, post-Saddam Iraq, and other modernizing societies may adopt capitalism ("the only reasonable economic organization") and even become democratic, but they won't mimic American "hyperindividualism" and they will share European preferences on many things. The United States, in Todd's view, will cling desperately to the vestiges of its ambition and power; to maintain its waning influence it will seek to sustain "a certain level of international tension, a condition of limited but endemic war." This process has already begun, and September 11 was its trigger.

The problem with Emmanuel Todd, and it will be immediately familiar to anyone who has read any of his previous books, is less his conclusions than his reasoning. There is something of the Ancient Mariner about this writer. He has a maniacal tale to tell and he recounts it in book after book, gripping the reader relentlessly as though to say "Don't you get it? It's all about fertility!" Todd is an anthropological demographer by training. In 1976 he published *La Chute finale: Essai sur la décomposition de la sphère soviétique*, in which he prophesied the end of the USSR: "A slight increase in Russian infant mortality between 1970 and 1974 made me understand the rotting away of the Soviet Union back in 1976 and allowed me to predict the system's collapse." On his account, the decline in the Soviet birthrate revealed to him "the likely emergence of normal Russians, perfectly capable of overthrowing communism."

Emmanuel Todd was not the only person back in the 1970s predicting an unhealthy future for Communism. Nevertheless, the link he claims to have uncovered between fertility and regime collapse has gone to his head. In his new book, world history is reduced to a series of unidirectional, monocausal correlations linking birthrates, literacy rates, timeless family structures, and global politics. The Yugoslav wars were the result of "fertility gaps" between Slavs and Muslims. The American Civil War can be traced to the low birthrates of the Anglo-Saxon settler class. And if "individualistic" America faces grim prospects today, this is because the "family structures" of the rest of the world favor very different political systems.

In Emmanuel Todd's parallel universe, politics—like economic behavior—is inscribed in a society's "genetic code." The egalitarian family systems of Central Asia reveal an "anthropology of community" that made Communism more acceptable there (elsewhere he has attributed regional variations in French, Italian, and Finnish voting patterns to similar differences in family life[10]). Today, the "universalist Russian temperament" based on the extended Russian family offers a nonindividualistic socioeconomic model that may be the democracy of the future. "A priori, there is no reason not to imagine a liberal and democratic Russia protecting the planet against American efforts to shore up their global imperial posture." Hence the unchained fury of the "differentialist" tendencies—American, Israeli, and others.

Todd goes further. He absurdly exaggerates America's current woes, real as they are. Extrapolating from the Enron example, he concludes that all American economic data are as unreliable as that of the Soviets: the truly parlous state of the U.S. economy has been kept hidden. And he offers his own variant on the "clash of civilizations." The coming conflict between Islam and the United States brings into opposition the "effectively feminist," women-based civilization of America and the masculinized ethic of Central Asian and Arab warrior societies. Here, too, America will be isolated, for Europeans will feel just as threatened by the United States as their Arab neighbors do. Once again, it all comes down to family life, with a distinctive modern twist: "The status of the American woman, threatening and castrating (*castratrice et menaçante*), [is] as disturbing for European men as the all-powerful Arab male is for European women." The Atlantic gap begins in the bedroom. You couldn't invent it.

To leave Emmanuel Todd for Jean-François Revel is to abandon the mad scientist for the self-confident patrician. Revel is an august Immortal of the Académie Française. He is the author of many books (thirty-one to date), as the reader of his latest essay is firmly reminded.* Revel's style suggests a man unfamiliar with self-doubt and unused to contradiction. He tends to sweeping, unsupported generalizations—by his account, most of Europe's political and cultural elite "never understood anything about communism"—and his version of French anti-Americanism at times approaches caricature. This is a pity, because some of what he writes makes good sense.

Thus Revel is right to draw attention to the contradiction at the heart of much French criticism of America. If the United States is such a social disaster, a cultural pygmy, a political innocent, and an economic meltdown waiting to happen, why worry? Why devote so much resentful attention to it? Alternatively, if it is as powerful and successful as many fear, might it not be doing something right? Revel is correct for the most part to charge certain French intellectuals with bad faith when they assert that they had nothing against America's anti-Communist policies in earlier decades and object only to the excesses of the present. The record suggests otherwise.

As a Frenchman, Revel is well placed to remind his fellow citizens that France, too, has social problems—the much-vaunted French education system

---

*Jean-François Revel, *L'Obsession anti-américaine: son fonctionnement, ses causes, ses conséquences* (Paris: Plon, 2002).

neither assimilates cultural and religious minorities nor does it support and nourish cultural difference. France, too, has slums, violence, and delinquency. And Jean-Marie Le Pen's success in last year's presidential elections is a standing rebuke to all of France's political class for its failure to address the problems of immigration and race.[11] Revel makes legitimate fun of France's cultural administrators, who can vandalize their own national heritage at least as recklessly as the barbaric Americans. No American booster could ever match Culture Minister Jack Lang's 1984 "Projet Culturel Extérieur de la France," in which France's cultural ambitions are described by Lang himself as "probably unequaled in any other country." And what does it say about the sophistication of the French press and television that they devoted so much credulous space to the elucubrations of M. Meyssan?

ONE COULD GO ON. Mocking the French for their pretensions (and their memory holes) is almost as easy as picking apart the hypocrisies of U.S. foreign policy. And Revel is right to describe modern anti-globalization activists with their anti-market rhetoric as a "divine surprise" for the European left, a heaven-sent cause at a post-ideological moment when Europe's radicals were adrift. But Revel's astute observations of what is wrong in France risk being discredited by his inability to find *anything* wrong with America. His entire book is a paean of blinkered praise for a country that, regrettably, does not exist. Like the anti-Americans he disdains, he has conjured up his American subject out of thin air.

In Revel's America the melting pot works "*fort bien*" and there is no mention of ghettos. According to him, Europeans misread and exaggerate U.S. crime statistics, whereas in reality crime in America is not a problem. Health coverage in America works well: most Americans are insured at work, the rest benefit from publicly funded Medicare and Medicaid. Anyway, the system's shortcomings are no worse than those of France's own provisions for health care. The American poor have the same *per capita* income as the *average* citizen of Portugal, so they can't be called poor (Revel has apparently never heard of cost-of-living indices). There is no "underclass." Meanwhile the United States has had social democracy longer than Europe, and American television and news coverage is much better than you think.

As for American foreign policy: in Revel-land the United States has stayed fully engaged in the Israel-Palestine conflict, is resolutely nonpartisan, and its policy has been a success. The American missile defense program worries M. Revel a lot less than it does some American generals. Unlike 50 percent of the U.S. electorate, Académicien Revel saw nothing amiss in the conduct of the 2000 presidential election. As for evidence of growing American anti-French sentiment, stuff, and nonsense: *"pour ma part, je ne l'ai jamais constaté"* ("as for me, I've never seen it"). In short, whatever French critics and others say about the United States, Jean-François Revel maintains the opposite. Voltaire could not have done a better job satirizing traditional French prejudices: Pangloss in Wonderland.

II.

Somewhere between Emmanuel Todd and Jean-François Revel there is an interesting European perspective on George Bush's America. The two sides of the Atlantic really are different today. First, America is a credulous and religious society: since the midfifties, Europeans have abandoned their churches in droves; but in the United States there has been virtually no decline in churchgoing and synagogue attendance. In 1998 a Harris poll found that 66 percent of even non-Christian Americans believed in miracles and 47 percent of them accredited the Virgin Birth; the figures for all Americans are 86 percent and 83 percent, respectively. Some 45 percent of Americans believe there is a Devil. In a recent *Newsweek* poll 79 percent of American respondents accepted that biblical miracles really happened. According to a 1999 *Newsweek* poll, 40 percent of all Americans (71 percent of Evangelical Protestants) believe that the world will end in a battle at Armageddon between Jesus and the

Antichrist. An American president who conducts Bible study in the White House and begins cabinet sessions with a prayer may seem a curious anachronism to his European allies, but he is in tune with his constituents.[12]

Second, the inequalities and insecurities of American life are still unthinkable across the Atlantic. Europeans remain wary of excessive disparities of income, and their institutions and political choices reflect this sentiment. Moreover it is prudence, rather than the residue of "Socialism," that explains European hesitation over unregulated markets and the dismantling of the public sector and local resistance to the American "model." This makes sense—for most people in Europe, as elsewhere in the world, unrestricted competition is at least as much a threat as an opportunity.

Europeans want a more interventionist state at home than Americans do, and they expect to pay for it. Even in post-Thatcher Britain, 62 percent of adults polled in December 2002 would favor higher taxes in return for improved public services. The figure for the United States was under 1 percent. This is less surprising when one considers that in America (where the disparities between rich and poor are greater than anywhere else in the developed world) fully 19 percent of the adult population claims to be in the richest 1 percent of the nation—and a further 20 percent believe they will enter that 1 percent in their lifetime![13]

What Europeans find perturbing about America, then, is precisely what most Americans believe to be their nation's strongest suit: its unique mix of moralistic religiosity, minimal provision for public welfare, and maximal market freedom—the "American way of life"—coupled with a missionary foreign policy ostensibly directed at exporting that same cluster of values and practices. Here the United States is ill served by globalization, which highlights for the world's poorer countries the costs of exposure to economic competition and reminds West Europeans, after the long sleep of the cold war, of the true fault lines bisecting the hitherto undifferentiated "West."

These transatlantic distinctions will matter more, not less, in years to come: long-standing social and cultural contrasts are being highlighted and reinforced by irresolvable policy disagreements. Already the schism over the U.S. war on Iraq has revealed something new. In the early years of the cold war anti-American demonstrations in Europe took their cue from Soviet-financed "peace movements," but the political and economic elites were firmly in the American camp. Today, no one is manipulating mass anti-war protests and West European leaders are breaking with America on a major international issue. The United States has been forced to bribe and threaten in unprecedented public ways, with embarassingly limited success (even in Turkey as I write, thanks to the unpredictable workings of democracy).

THE IRAQ CRISIS HAS EXPOSED three kinds of weakness in the modern international system. We have been reminded once again of how fragile the United Nations is, how seemingly inadequate to the hopes vested in it. Yet the recent American attitude toward the UN—give us what we want or we shall take it anyway—has paradoxically strengthened practically everyone else's appreciation of the institution's importance. The UN may lack an army, but it has acquired, over the past fifty years, a distinctive legitimacy; and legitimacy is a kind of power. In any case, the UN is all we have. Those who abuse it for their own ends do so at serious risk to their credibility as international citizens.

The second ostensible victim of the crisis has been the European Union. On the face of things Europe is now bitterly divided, thanks in equal measure to American mischief and European leaders' own incompetence. But crises can be salutary. Once the Iraq war is over the British are going to be asking hard questions about the American commitment they made in the wake of a previous Middle Eastern miscalculation, at Suez in 1956. The East Europeans will pray for short memories in Brussels, Berlin, and Paris when it comes to preparing the Union's budget. Turkish politicians are already questioning their country's once sacrosanct relationship with America. And Jacques Chirac may have his country's last, best chance to shape a Europe independent of America and its equal in international affairs. The "hour of Europe" may not have struck, but Washington's utter indifference to European opinion has rung a fire bell in the night.

The third kind of weakness concerns the United States itself: not in spite of its overwhelming military might, but because of it. Unbelievably, President Bush and his advisers have managed to make America seem the greatest threat to international stability; a mere eighteen months after September 11, the United States may have gambled away the confidence of the world. By staking a monopoly claim on Western values and their defense, the United States has prompted other Westerners to reflect on what divides them from America. By enthusiastically asserting its right to reconfigure the Muslim world, Washington has reminded Europeans in particular of the growing Muslim presence in their own cultures and its political implications.[14] In short, the United States has given a lot of people occasion to rethink their relationship with it.

You don't have to be a French intellectual to believe that an overmuscled America, in a hostile international environment, is weaker, not stronger, than it was before. It is also more likely to be belligerent. What it won't be, however, is irrelevant. International politics is sometimes about good and evil, but it is always about power. The United States has considerable power and the nations of the world need the United States on their side. A United States that oscillated unpredictably between unilateral preemptive wars and narcissistic indifference would be a global disaster, which is why so many countries at the UN tried desperately to accommodate Washington's wishes, whatever their leaders' private misgivings.

Meanwhile, "moderates" in Washington insist that all these concerns will be laid to rest if the war against Saddam turns out to have been quick, victorious, and relatively "clean." But a military campaign is not retroactively justified by its success alone, and anyway much collateral harm is already done. The precedent of preemptive and preventive war against a hypothetical threat; the incautious, intermittent acknowledgment that this war has objectives far beyond disarming Baghdad; the alienation of foreign sentiment: these constitute war damage however successfully America handles the peace. Has the world's "indispensable nation" (Madeleine Albright) miscalculated and over-reached? Almost certainly. When the earthquake abates, the tectonic plates of international politics will have shifted forever.

This essay first appeared in *The New York Review of Books* in May 2003 as a review of *L'Ennemi américain: Généalogie de l'antiaméricanisme français* by Philippe Roger, *11 septembre 2001: L'Effroyable Imposture* by Thierry Meyssan, *Pourquoi le monde déteste-t-il l'Amérique?* by Ziauddin Sardar and Merryl Wyn Davies, *Le Livre noir des États-Unis* by Peter Scowen, *Dangereuse Amérique: Chronique d'une guerre annoncée* by Noël Mamère and Patrick Farbiaz, *Après l'empire: Essai sur la décomposition du système américain* by Emmanuel Todd, and *L'Obsession anti-américaine: Son fonctionnement, ses causes, ses inconséquences* by Jean-François Revel.

Notes to Chapter XVII

[1] Emmanuel Berl, *Mort de la pensée bourgeoise* (Paris: Bernard Grasset, 1929, reprinted 1970), pp. 76–77; André Siegfried, *Les États-Unis d'aujourd'hui* (Paris: Colin, 1930), quoted in Michel Winock, *Nationalisme, antisémitisme et fascisme en France* (Paris: Seuil, 1982), p. 56. See also Georges Duhamel, *Scènes de la Vie future* (Paris: Mercure de France, 1930); Robert Aron and Arnaud Dandieu, *Le Cancer américain* (Paris: Rieder, 1931); and my own *Past Imperfect: French Intellectuals, 1944–1956* (Berkeley: University of California Press, 1992), Chapter 10: "America Has Gone Mad: Anti-Americanism in Historical Perspective," pp. 187–204.

[2] For Simone de Beauvoir, see her *L'Amérique au jour le jour* (Paris: Morihien, 1948), pp. 99–100. Sartre was commenting on the trial and execution of the Rosenbergs. Vailland's thoughts on refrigeration, from his article "Le Ménage n'est pas un art de salon" (*La Tribune des nations*, March 14, 1952), are discussed by Philippe Roger in *L'Ennemi américain*, pp. 483–484. And see the editorial "Mourir pour le Coca-Cola," *Le Monde*, March 29, 1950.

[3] For German representations of the price of Americanization see Rainer Werner Fassbinder's *Marriage of Maria Braun* (1979); or Edgar Reitz's *Heimat: Eine deutsche Chronik* (1984), where the American impact on "deep Germany" is depicted as far more corrosive of values than the passage through Nazism. And it was Václav Havel, no less, who reminded his

fellow dissidents back in 1984 that rationalism, scientism, our fascination with technology and change were all the "ambiguous exports" of the West, the perverse fruits of the dream of modernity. See Václav Havel, "Svedomí a politika," *Svedectví*, vol. 18, no. 72 (1984), pp. 621–635 (quote from page 627).

[4] See Philippe Mathy, *Extrême Occident: French Intellectuals and America* (Chicago: University of Chicago Press, 1993), and *L'Amérique dans les têtes: Un Siècle de fascinations et d'aversions*, Denis Lacorne, Jacques Rupnik, and Marie-France Toinet, eds. (Paris: Hachette, 1986).

[5] *"Loin de créditer leurs dépositions, la qualité de ces témoins ne fait que souligner l'importance des moyens déployés par l'armée des États-Unis pour travestir la vérité"*; see *11 septembre 2001*, p. 23.

[6] See also Clyde V. Prestowitz, *Rogue Nation: American Unilateralism and the Failure of Good Intentions* (New York: Basic Books, April 2003).

[7] According to Mark Hertsgaard, in *The Eagle's Shadow: Why America Fascinates and Infuriates the World* (New York: Farrar, Straus and Giroux, 2002), Americans have long been in denial about their constitution's origins in the practices of the Iroquois League, to which we apparently owe an unacknowledged debt for the concepts of states' rights and the separation of powers. So much for Locke, Montesquieu, English Common Law, and the Continental Enlightenment.

[8] We are back in May 1944, when Hubert Beuve-Méry, future founder and editor of *Le Monde*, could write that "the Americans constitute a real threat to France. . . . [They] can prevent us accomplishing the necessary revolution, and their materialism lacks even the tragic grandeur of the materialism of the totalitarians." Quoted by Jean-François Revel in *L'Obsession anti-américaine*, p. 98.

[9] Charles Kupchan, *The End of the American Era* (New York: Knopf, 2002). See my discussion of Kupchan in *The New York Review*, April 10, 2003.

[10] Emmanuel Todd, *La Troisième Planète: Structures familiales et systèmes idéologiques* (Paris: Seuil, 1983). "Communism's success is principally explained by the existence . . . of egalitarian and authoritarian family structures predisposing people to see Communist ideology as natural and good"; See *Après l'empire*, p. 178.

[11] On this see also Philippe Manière, *La Vengeance du peuple: Les Élites, Le Pen et les français* (Paris: Plon, 2002).

[12] See www.pollingreport.com/religion.htm and www.pollingreport.com/religion2.htm.

[13] "A Tale of Two Legacies," *The Economist*, December 21, 2002; *Financial Times*, January 25–26, 2003.

[14] One French resident in twelve is now a Muslim. In Russia the figure is nearly one in six.

CHAPTER XVIII

The New World Order

I.

Those of us who opposed America's invasion of Iraq from the outset can take no comfort from its catastrophic consequences. On the contrary: we should now be asking ourselves some decidedly uncomfortable questions. The first concerns the propriety of "preventive" military intervention. If the Iraq war is wrong—"the wrong war at the wrong time"[1]—why, then, was the 1999 U.S.-led war on Serbia right? That war, after all, also lacked the imprimatur of UN Security Council approval. It too was an unauthorized and uninvited attack on a sovereign state—undertaken on "preventive" grounds—that caused many civilian casualties and aroused bitter resentment against the Americans who carried it out.

The apparent difference—and the reason so many of us cheered when the United States and its allies went into Kosovo—was that Slobodan Milošević had begun a campaign against the Albanian majority of Serbia's Kosovo province that had all the hallmarks of a prelude to genocide. So not only was the United States on the right side but it was intervening in real time—its actions might actually prevent a major crime. With the shameful memory of Bosnia and Rwanda in the very recent past, the likely consequences of inaction seemed obvious and far outweighed the risks of intervention. Today the Bush administration—lacking "weapons of mass destruction" to justify its rush to arms—offers "bringing freedom to Iraq" almost as an afterthought. But saving the Kosovar Albanians was what the 1999 war was all about from the start.

And yet it isn't so simple. Saddam Hussein (like Milošević) was a standing threat to many of his subjects: not just in the days when he was massacring Kurds and Shiites while we stood by and watched, but to the very end. Those of us who favor humanitarian interventions in principle—not because they flatter our good intentions but because they do good or prevent ill—could not coherently be sorry to see Saddam overthrown. Those of us who object to the unilateral exercise of raw power should recall that ten years ago we would have been delighted to see someone—anyone—intervene unilaterally to save the Rwandan Tutsis. And those of us who, correctly in my view, point to the perverse consequences of even the best-intentioned meddling in other countries' affairs have not always applied that insight in cases where we longed to see the meddling begin.

DAVID RIEFF HAS NOTHING to offer by way of a solution to these quandaries—the dominant tone of his latest book is one of disabused despair.* But the new collection of his recent essays and reports performs the salutary function of reminding us just how troubling such dilemmas can be. For many years Rieff was a prominent advocate of wholesale humanitarian intervention—not merely as a Band-Aid on the world's wounds but because, like Paul Wolfowitz among others, he earnestly believed in the desirability and possibility of bringing democratic change to places where it was needed. He includes in this collection some earlier essays that movingly pressed the case for Western intervention: in Africa, the Balkans, and elsewhere. Now, as Rieff concedes in afterthoughts appended to those same essays, he's not so sure.

Things go wrong, and not just in Iraq. International law—like the UN

---

*David Rieff, *At the Point of a Gun: Democratic Dreams and Armed Intervention* (New York: Simon & Schuster, 2005).

itself—was conceived in a world of sovereign states, a world where wars broke out between countries, peace was duly brokered among states, and a major concern of the post–World War II settlement was to guarantee the inviolability of borders and sovereignty. Today's wars typically happen *within* states. The distinctions between peacemaking and peacekeeping—between intervention, assistance, and coercion—are unclear, as are the rights of the conflicting parties and the circumstances under which foreign agencies may resort to force. In this confusing new world, well-meaning Western diplomats and observers have sometimes proven unable to distinguish between warring states—operating under conventional diplomatic norms—and locally powerful criminal tyrants, such as the leaders of Sudan. Negotiation with the latter all too often amounts to collaboration and even complicity.

As for the United Nations ("that toothless old scold," in Rieff's words), not only is it helpless to prevent criminal behavior, but by its obsession with remaining "impartial" and protecting its own people it can sometimes abet and facilitate mass murder. At Srebrenica, in July 1995, four hundred Dutch UN soldiers stood politely aside to let Ratko Mladić and his Bosnian Serb irregulars massacre seven thousand Muslim men and boys conveniently gathered together under United Nations protection in a "safe" area. This may be an extreme case—but it is in just such extreme circumstances that international agencies of all kinds, however benign their intentions, can hardly avoid compromising themselves, especially when the great powers on the Security Council refuse to authorize adequate armed support. When private charities and the UN's own high commissioner for refugees help transport, settle, house, and feed forcibly displaced peoples—whether in the south Balkans or the eastern Congo or the Middle East—are they furnishing desperately needed aid or facilitating someone else's project of ethnic cleansing? All too often the answer is: both.

RIEFF GOES FURTHER. Most humanitarian agencies, public and private, are by definition geared to addressing emergencies. In a crisis their priorities are to provide immediate assistance (and protect their own people); they have little time or inclination for long-term problem solving or political calculation. As a consequence they are vulnerable to exploitation: by the victims (Rieff is particularly sour about the KLA—Kosovo Liberation Army—which he used to admire but which now seems to him always to have been disposed to violence and bent upon the forced displacement of the remaining Serbs of Kosovo—indeed, little better than their Serbian counterparts); but above all by the major powers to whom such humanitarian entities are in practice subcontracted and whose cooperation they need.

To the extent that humanitarians thus provide cover for legally ambiguous armed intervention and its inevitable shortcomings they diminish their own reputation and moral credibility without always achieving their goals. The UN in particular risks becoming, according to Rieff, a "de facto colonial office to U.S. power"; cleaning up after American invasions and "used like a piece of fancy Kleenex . . . as usual," in the disabused description of one UN official in Iraq whom Rieff quotes approvingly. This may seem a little harsh. From bitter experience, after all, welfare agencies in dangerous places know that keeping on the right side of the occupying power, or a corrupt local chieftain or policeman—at whatever short-term cost to their credibility—is the only way to stay on the spot and thus do any good at all.

Rieff's disillusioned tone can thus take on a cynical edge—"the imperial dreams of American neoconservatives like [Max] Boot or [Robert] Kagan make so much more sense than the vacillations of the humanitarian left." And his essays betray evidence of some haste, both in their original drafting and subsequent republication: in Kosovo, we learn, "the West was finally hoist on the petard of its own lip service to the categorical imperative of human rights." Moreover, little of what Rieff has to say about the perverse effects of well-intentioned involvement in other peoples' affairs will come as news to many readers. But there was a time when Rieff would have accepted such unpleasant side effects as the better part of liberal valor: "Our choice at the millennium," he wrote a few years ago, "seems to boil down to imperialism or barbarism." In the aftermath of Iraq, however, things look different and he ruefully concedes that "I did not realize the extent to which imperialism *is* or at least can always become barbarism."[2]

Rieff is not against humanitarian intervention today. But he now thinks we should pragmatically engage each case on its merits and without illusion: above all without illusion about how much genuine change we can ever hope to effect and at what price.[3] He still believes "we" should have intervened sooner in Bosnia and that "we" are collectively responsible for allowing a genocide in Rwanda. How, then, are "we" to decide in the future when to stand aside and when to act? And who is this "we" with the responsibility and capacity to avert such catastrophes? The "international community"—which in practice means the United Nations and its various relief agencies and peace-keeping forces? Rieff, a disappointed lover, is decidedly scornful of the UN— "it is only in the African context that a derelict institution like the United Nations, understood by those who know it well as a supine organization, could be viewed as a power center"—but he has nothing better to offer.

"Derelict"? "Supine"? Rieff's contempt is widely shared. One promi-nent human rights lawyer who worked with the UN in Africa blames the organization—and its present secretary-general, Kofi Annan—for "capitulat-ing to evil" there.[4] Neoconservatives have long since dismissed the UN as an irrelevance: "The United Nations is guarantor of nothing. Except in a for-mal sense, it can hardly be said to exist."[5] The Bush administration has delib-erately nominated as its next ambassador to the UN a man who holds the institution in contempt. A recent "High-level Panel" appointed by the UN's own secretary-general acknowledges the organization's mismanagement of postconflict operations and its record of poor coordination, improvident ex-penditure, and wasteful interagency competition.[*] The panel explicitly de-scribes the UN's own notorious Commission on Human Rights as suffering from what it politely terms "a legitimacy deficit."

---

[*]Report of the Secretary-General's High-level Panel on Threats, Challenges and Change, *A More Secure World: Our Shared Responsibility* (New York: United Nations, 2004).

The fundamental problem with the United Nations, however, is neither inefficiency nor corruption nor a shortage of "legitimacy." It is weakness. The UN has no power to initiate international interventions without the unanimous approval of the Security Council, whose five permanent members all hold a veto—and, in the case of the United States at least, have never hesitated to wield it. For a long time the UN was constrained by the stalemate of the cold war, confined to grand-sounding "resolutions." Since 1990, however, the UN and its agencies have acquired an enhanced role and a special sort of international legitimacy as the world's peacemakers, peace builders, and peacekeepers—to the point (unimaginable a few decades ago) that for hundreds of millions of people worldwide, the propriety of the American invasion of Iraq hinged upon Washington's success or failure in getting the support of a second Security Council resolution.[6]

As the High-level Panel points out, the "collectively authorized use of force may not be the rule today, but it is no longer an exception." But this points to a second weakness. In a world where the violation by governments of their own subjects' rights has become the leading motive for armed intervention, the UN Charter's emphasis upon the inviolability of sovereign states presents a conundrum. Offsetting the rights of individuals against the prerogatives of states is hardly a new challenge (it was a particular preoccupation of Dag Hammarskjöld, the UN's secretary-general between 1953 and 1961[7]), but the UN still has few resources, legal or logistical, with which to meet it. Above all, it has no army or armed police of its own. It has thus preferred to shy away from confrontations requiring the use of force, leading its own panel to conclude that "the biggest source of inefficiency in our collective security institutions has simply been an unwillingness to get serious about preventing deadly violence."

THAT SAME PANEL, however, is very clear about what the United Nations has nonetheless achieved. Its greatest success has been to convince democrats and tyrants alike of the need to at least appear legitimate by securing or invoking UN approval as a fig leaf for their actions. The presence today of UN peacekeepers throughout the world—from Bosnia to Abkhazia to East Timor—may have the occasional perverse and paradoxical outcome, as Rieff and others gloomily document; but their absence, or their presence in insufficient numbers or with an inadequate mandate, is almost always catastrophic. Where the writ of the UN cannot run—because a powerful illiberal state won't brook any interference in its domestic affairs (as in Chechnya, or among the Uighur people of western China)—bad things happen. All in all, the record of the UN is not so reprehensible. As the High-level Panel concludes:

> We found that the UN has been much more effective in addressing the major threats to peace and security than it is given credit for.

The sixteen UN panelists who reason thus are not a bunch of starry-eyed humanitarian lefties. They include four former prime ministers, the president of the highly respected International Crisis Group (Gareth Evans, a former Australian foreign minister), a retired British envoy to the UN, and General Brent Scowcroft, national security adviser to the first President Bush. For a UN committee their conclusions are refreshingly hardheaded and thus carry unusual weight. And what they conclude is this. There is today a "yearning for an international system governed by the rule of law." Such an international system can only work if it is backed by "deployable military resources," and only the member states of the United Nations can furnish their organization, its agencies, and their employees with those resources. If they persist in failing to do so, it will quickly become apparent, as it did in the midnineties, that the "UN had exchanged the shackles of the cold war for the straitjacket of Member State complacency and Great Power indifference."

At the same time, the international system as we now know it cannot survive if those separate member states choose instead to deploy their resources unilaterally. In practice there is only one UN member state that is in a position to do this, serially and on a worldwide scale, and the UN panelists make it clear what they think about that:

In a world full of perceived potential threats,[8] the risk to the global order and the norm of non-intervention on which it continues to be based is simply too great for the legality of unilateral preventive action, as distinct from collectively endorsed action, to be accepted.

The "we" in my question about future interventions, in other words, can only be the international community of nations. But Kofi Annan's High-level Panel is under no misapprehensions regarding the facts of international life:

> If there is to be a new security consensus, it must start with the understanding that the front-line actors in dealing with all the threats we face, new and old, continue to be individual sovereign States.

II.

And so we come full circle to my starting point. There are lots of individual sovereign states. But only one of them, the United States of America, has both the will and the means to back international armed intervention and help deliver it. This has been obvious for some time, of course. But far from being grounds for international anxiety it was for many a source of reassurance. Not only did the United States appear to share the humanitarian and democratic purposes of the various agencies and alliances it had helped set in place in 1945, but it was governed by a political class that saw the advantage of exercising a degree of self-restraint, believing with Harry Truman that

> we all have to recognize—no matter how great our strength—that we must deny ourselves the license to do always as we please.[9]

Great powers, of course, are not philanthropists. The United States never ceased to pursue the national interest as successive administrations understood it. But for ten years following the end of the cold war the United States and the "international community" appeared, however fortuitously, to share a common set of interests and objectives; indeed, American military preponderance fueled all manner of liberal dreams for global improvement. Hence the enthusiasms and hopes of the nineties—and hence, too, the angry disillusion today. For the United States of President George W. Bush most decidedly does not share the interests and objectives of the international community. Many in that community would say that this is because the United States itself has changed in unprecedented and quite frightening ways. Andrew Bacevich would agree with them.

Bacevich is a graduate of West Point, a Vietnam veteran, and a conservative Catholic who now directs the study of international relations at Boston University. He has thus earned the right to a hearing even in circles typically immune to criticism. What he writes should give them pause. His argument is complex, resting on a close account of changes in the U.S. military since Vietnam, on the militarization of strategic political thinking, and on the role of the military in American culture. But his conclusion is clear. The United States, he writes, is becoming not just a militarized state but a military society: a country where armed power is the measure of national greatness, and war, or planning for war, is the exemplary (and only) common project.[*]

Why does the U.S. Department of Defense currently maintain 725 official U.S. military bases outside the country and 969 at home (not to mention numerous secret bases)? Why does the United States spend more on "defense" than all the rest of the world put together? After all, it has no present or likely enemies of the kind who could be intimidated or defeated by "star wars" missile defense or bunker-busting "nukes." And yet this country is obsessed with war: rumors of war, images of war, "preemptive" war, "preventive" war, "surgical" war, "prophylactic" war, "permanent" war. As President Bush explained

---

[*]Andrew J. Bacevich, *The New American Militarism: How Americans Are Seduced by War* (New York: Oxford University Press, 2005).

at a news conference on April 13, 2004, "This country must go on the offense and stay on the offense."

Among democracies, only in America do soldiers and other uniformed servicemen figure ubiquitously in political photo ops and popular movies. Only in America do civilians eagerly buy expensive military service vehicles for suburban shopping runs. In a country no longer supreme in most other fields of human endeavor, war and warriors have become the last, enduring symbols of American dominance and the American way of life. "In war, it seemed," writes Bacevich, "lay America's true comparative advantage."

Bacevich is good on the intellectual roots of the cult of therapeutic aggression—citing among others the inimitable Norman Podhoretz (America has an international mission and must never "come home"). He also summarizes the realist case for war—rooted in what will become the country's increasingly desperate struggle to control the fuel supply. The United States consumes 25 percent of all the oil produced in the world every year but has proven reserves of its own amounting to less than 2 percent of the global total. This struggle Bacevich calls World War IV: the contest for supremacy in strategic, energy-rich regions like the Middle East and Central Asia.[10] It began at the end of the seventies, long before the formal conclusion of "World War III" (i.e., the cold war).

In this setting today's "Global War on Terror" is one battle, perhaps just a sideshow, among the potentially limitless number of battles that the United States will be called upon (or will call upon itself) to fight. These battles will all be won because the United States has a monopoly of the most advanced weaponry—and they may be acceptable to the American people because, in Bacevich's view, that same weaponry, air power especially, has given war "aesthetic respectability" once again. But the war itself has no foreseeable end.

As a former soldier, Bacevich is much troubled by the consequent militarization of American foreign relations, and by the debauching of his country's traditional martial values in wars of conquest and occupation. And it is clear that he has little tolerance for Washington's ideologically driven overseas adventures: the uncertain benefits for the foreign recipients are far outweighed by the moral costs to the United States itself.[11] For Bacevich's deepest concern lies closer to home. In a militarized society the range of acceptable opinion inevitably shrinks. Opposition to the "commander in chief" is swiftly characterized as lèse-majesté; criticism becomes betrayal. No nation, as Madison wrote in 1795 and Bacevich recalls approvingly, can "preserve its freedom in the midst of continual warfare."[12] "Full-spectrum dominance" begins as a Pentagon cliché and ends as an executive project.

ALTHOUGH I THINK BACEVICH is right to see war as the heart of the matter, there is more to the current U.S. political climate than just the cult of arms. The unrepublican veneration of our presidential "leader" has made it uniquely difficult for Americans to see their country's behavior as others see it. The latest report from Amnesty International—which says nothing that the rest of the world doesn't already know or believe but which has been denied and ridiculed by President Bush—is a case in point.* The United States "renders" (i.e., kidnaps and hands over) targeted suspects to third-party states for interrogation and torture beyond the reach of U.S. law and the press. The countries to whom we outsource this task include Egypt, Saudi Arabia, Jordan, Syria(!), Pakistan, and Uzbekistan. Where outsourcing is impractical, we import qualified interrogators from abroad: in September 2002 a visiting Chinese "delegation" was invited to participate in the "interrogation" of ethnic Uighur detainees held at Guantánamo.

At the United States' own interrogation centers and prisons in Iraq, Afghanistan, and Guantánamo Bay, at least twenty-seven "suspects" have been killed in custody. This number does not include extrajudicial, extraterritorial "targeted assassinations": a practice inaugurated by Benito Mussolini with the

---

* Amnesty International, *Guantánamo and Beyond: The Continuing Pursuit of Unchecked Executive Power* (2005).

murder of the Rosselli brothers in Normandy in 1937, pursued with vigor by Israel, and now adopted by the Bush administration. The Amnesty report lists sixty alleged incarceration and interrogation practices routinely employed at U.S. detention centers, Guantánamo in particular. These include immersion in cold water to simulate drowning, forced shaving of facial and body hair, electric shocks to body parts, humiliation (e.g., being urinated upon), sexual taunting, the mocking of religious belief, suspension from shackles, physical exertion to the point of exhaustion (e.g., rock carrying), and mock execution.

Any and all of these practices will be familiar to students of Eastern Europe in the fifties or Latin America in the seventies and eighties—including the reported presence of "medical personnel." But American interrogators have also innovated. One technique has been forcibly to wrap suspects—and their Korans—in Israeli flags: a generous gesture to our only unconditional ally, but calculated to ensure that a new generation of Muslims worldwide will identify the two countries as one and hate them equally.

All of these practices—and many, many others routinely employed at Guantánamo, at Kandahar and Bagram in Afghanistan, at al-Qaim, Abu Ghraib, and elsewhere in Iraq—are in breach of the Geneva Conventions and the UN Convention Against Torture, to both of which the United States is a signatory (in January 2002, even the British Secret Intelligence Service warned its personnel in Afghanistan not to take part in the "inhumane or degrading treatment" of prisoners that was practiced by their U.S. allies, lest they incur criminal liability).[13]

The same practices are also in breach of U.S. law. The "legal black hole" in which these things go on is formed by the breathtakingly cynical claim that since they are being done to foreign nationals on territory over which the United States lacks ultimate sovereignty (for these purposes we readily acknowledge Cuba's ownership of Guantánamo Bay), neither American law nor American courts have any jurisdiction. The 70,000 detainees currently held outside the United States may be kept incarcerated and incommunicado for as long as the Global War on Terror is fought—which could be decades.

PERHAPS THE MOST DEPRESSING aspect of this grim story is the undisguised contempt with which the Bush administration responds to criticism. In part this is because criticism itself has become so uncommon. With rare exceptions—notably the admirable Seymour Hersh in *The New Yorker*—the American press has signally failed to understand, much less confront, the threat posed by this administration. Bullied into acquiescence, newspapers and television in the United States have allowed the executive power to ignore the law and abuse human rights free of scrutiny or challenge. Far from defying an overmighty government, investigative journalists were actively complicit before the Iraq war in spreading reports of weapons of mass destruction. Pundits and commentators bayed for war and sneered—as they continue to sneer—at foreign critics or dissenting allies. Amnesty International and other foreign human rights groups are now doing the work of domestic media grown supine and subservient.

Small wonder, then, that the administration and its servants treat the public (including the legislature) with such disdain. At the Senate hearings in January 2005 prior to his appointment as U.S. attorney general, Alberto Gonzales painstakingly explained to the assembled senators that since the international Convention Against Torture is subordinate to U.S. law, the Fourteenth Amendment to the U.S. Constitution applies only to the states and not the federal government, and the Fifth Amendment doesn't apply to foreigners detained abroad, the United States has no legal obligations regarding "cruel, inhuman or degrading treatment with respect to aliens overseas." Lesser breeds without the Law. . . .

In March 2005 the U.S. National Defense Strategy openly stated that "our strength as a nation-state will continue to be challenged by those who employ a strategy of the weak using international fora, judicial processes, and terrorism." At least that makes clear who and what we regard as our enemies. Yet Secretary of State Condoleezza Rice could declare in the very same month, on

March 14, 2005, that "too few in the world . . . know of the value we place on international institutions and the rule of law." Indeed.

III.

Historians and pundits who leap aboard the bandwagon of American Empire have forgotten a little too quickly that for an empire to be born, a republic has first to die. In the longer run no country can expect to behave imperially— brutally, contemptuously, illegally—abroad while preserving republican values at home. For it is a mistake to suppose that institutions alone will save a republic from the abuses of power to which empire inevitably leads. It is not institutions that make or break republics, it is men. And in the United States today, the men (and women) of the country's political class have failed. Congress appears helpless to impede the concentration of power in the executive branch; indeed, with few exceptions it has contributed actively and even enthusiastically to the process.

The judiciary is little better.[14] The "loyal opposition" is altogether too loyal. Indeed there seems little to be hoped from the Democratic Party. Terrified to be accused of transgressing the consensus on "order" and "security," its leaders now strive to emulate and even outdo Republicans in their aggressive stances. Senator Hillary Clinton, the party's likely candidate for the 2008 presidential elections, was last seen ostentatiously prostrating herself before the assembled ranks of the America-Israel Political Action Committee.[15]

At the outer edges of the U.S. imperium, in Bratislava or Tiflis, the dream of republican America still lives on, like the fading light from a distant, dying star. But even there the shadows of doubt are growing. Amnesty International cites several cases of detainees who "just could not believe Americans could act this way." Those are exactly the words said to me by an Albanian friend in Macedonia—and Macedonian Albanians have good reason to count themselves among this country's best friends and unconditional admirers. In Madrid a very senior and rather conservative Spanish diplomat recently put it thus:

> We grew up under Franco with a dream of America. That dream encouraged us to imagine and later to build a different, better Spain. All dreams must fade—but not all dreams must become nightmares. We Spanish know a little about political nightmares. What is happening to America? How do you explain Guantánamo?[16]

The American people have a touching faith in the invulnerability of their republic. It would not occur to most of them even to contemplate the possibility that their country might fall into the hands of a meretricious oligarchy; that, as Andrew Bacevich puts it, their political "system is fundamentally corrupt and functions in ways inconsistent with the spirit of genuine democracy." But the twentieth century has taught most other peoples in the world to be less cocksure. And when foreigners look across the oceans at the United States today, what they see is far from reassuring.

For there is a precedent in modern Western history for a country whose leader exploits national humiliation and fear to restrict public freedoms; for a government that makes permanent war as a tool of state policy and arranges for the torture of its political enemies; for a ruling class that pursues divisive social goals under the guise of national "values"; for a culture that asserts its unique destiny and superiority and that worships military prowess; for a political system in which the dominant party manipulates procedural rules and threatens to change the law in order to get its own way; where journalists are intimidated into confessing their errors and made to do public penance. Europeans in particular have experienced such a regime in the recent past and they have a word for it. That word is not "democracy."

ONE IMPLICATION OF THE SHADOW falling across the American republic is that the brief era of consensual international intervention is already closing.

This has nothing to do with the contradictions or paradoxes of humanitarian undertakings. It is the consequence of the discrediting of the United States. Hard as it may be for Americans to grasp, much of the world no longer sees the United States as a force for good. It does the wrong things and has the wrong friends. During the cold war, to be sure, the United States also supported many unsavory regimes. But back then there was a certain logic to its choices: Washington propped up anti-Communist dictators in pursuit of an anti-Communist cold war: *raison d'état*. Today we align ourselves with the world's most brutal, terrorizing tyrants in a war ostensibly against brutal terror and tyranny. We are peddling a simulacrum of democracy from an armored truck at fifty miles per hour and calling it freedom. This is a step too far. The world is losing faith in America.

That, as David Rieff would be the first to acknowledge, is not good news. For there is a fundamental truth at the core of the neocon case: the well-being of the United States of America is of inestimable importance to the health of the whole world. If the United States hollows out and becomes a vast military shell without democratic soul or substance, no good can come of it. Only the United States can do the world's heavy humanitarian lifting (often quite literally). We have already seen what happens when Washington merely drags its feet, as it did in Rwanda and is doing over Darfur today. If the United States ceases to be credible as a force for good, the world will not come to a stop. Others will still protest and undertake good works in the hope of American support. But the world will become that much safer for tyrants and crooks—at home and abroad.

For the United States isn't credible today: its reputation and standing are at their lowest point in history and will not soon recover. And there is no substitute on the horizon: the Europeans will not rise to the challenge. The bleak outcome of the recent referendums in France and the Netherlands seems likely to have eliminated the European Union as an effective international political actor for some years to come. The cold war is indeed behind us, but so too is the post–cold war moment of hope. The international anarchy so painstakingly averted by two generations of enlightened American statesmen may soon engulf us again. President Bush sees "freedom" on the march. I wish I shared his optimism. I see a bad moon rising.

This essay first appeared in *The New York Review of Books* in July 2005 as a review of *At the Point of a Gun: Democratic Dreams and Armed Intervention* by David Rieff; *The New American Militarism: How Americans Are Seduced by War* by Andrew J. Bacevich; *A More Secure World: Our Shared Responsibility*, Report of the UN Secretary-General's High-level Panel on Threats, Challenges and Change; and *Guantánamo and Beyond: The Continuing Pursuit of Unchecked Executive Power* by Amnesty International.

Notes to Chapter XVIII

[1] Tony Judt, "The Wrong War at the Wrong Time," *New York Times*, October 20, 2002.

[2] For a recent summary of our achievements in Iraq, see, e.g., Zvi Bar'el, "Why Isn't Iraq Getting on Its Feet?," *Haaretz*, June 3, 2005. The author concludes that "the full extent of the institutionalized corruption under American rule, and now under the rule of the new Iraqi government, may never be known. Investigators are not going out into the field to scrutinize data because it would mean risking their lives, and the ministers in the new Iraqi government have been appointing cronies to ensure loyalty."

[3] That is also the message of *The Dark Sides of Virtue: Reassessing International Humanitarianism* (Princeton, NJ: Princeton University Press, 2004), by David Kennedy, an international lawyer at Harvard. Kennedy accuses international humanitarians—lawyers, doctors, relief agencies, election observers, and the like—of fetishizing their own structures and routines. They are too readily tempted, he suggests, into idealizing (and idolizing) their own work, with the result that they ignore or downplay both the frequently perverse outcomes of their efforts—furnishing cover for dictators and others with agendas of their own—and alternative, more radical solutions and policies that fall outside their remit.

[4] Kenneth Cain, "How Many More Must Die Before Kofi Quits?" *The Observer* (London), April 3, 2005. That the UN did indeed capitulate to evil in Rwanda is beyond doubt—see Roméo Dallaire, *Shake Hands with the Devil: The Failure of Humanity in Rwanda* (New York: Carroll and Graf, 2004), and the review by Guy Lawson in *The New York Review*, May 26, 2005. But Kofi Annan and his UN colleagues are by no means uniquely to blame—there is more than enough responsibility to go around, in Brussels, Paris, and Washington.

[5] Charles Krauthammer, "The Unipolar Moment," *Foreign Affairs*, vol. 70, p. 25, quoted in Andrew Bacevich, *The New American Militarism*, p. 84.

[6] Something the United States could not secure unless it accepted the UN inspectors' recommendation and allowed inspections to continue, which the Bush administration firmly refused to do.

[7] See, e.g., Kennedy, *The Dark Sides of Virtue*, p. 258.

[8] The panel lists six clusters of threats to the world community, of which "terrorism" is just one. The other five are economic and social threats (e.g., poverty and environmental degradation); interstate conflicts; internal conflicts (including genocide and other crimes); the proliferation, loss, or use of nuclear, biological, and chemical weapons; and transnational organized crime.

[9] *Public Papers of the Presidents of the United States: Harry S. Truman, 1945* (U.S. Government Printing Office, 1961), p. 141.

[10] We are in the Near East, he suggests, for much the same reason that Winston Churchill urged his colleagues to install Great Britain there a hundred years ago, when the British fleet switched from coal-burning to oil-burning ships: "mastery." Winston S. Churchill, *The World Crisis* (1923), p. 136, quoted by Bacevich, *The New American Militarism*, p. 191.

[11] Perhaps for this reason Bacevich is decidedly unfair to General Wesley Clark, blaming him for the conduct and consequences of a war (in Kosovo) over which he had very limited control. For a different perspective see David Halberstam, *War in a Time of Peace: Bush, Clinton and the Generals* (New York: Scribner, 2001).

[12] "Overgrown military establishments," as George Washington reminded the nation in his Farewell Address, "are inauspicious to liberty . . . and are to be regarded as particularly hostile to republican liberty."

[13] See *Guantánamo and Beyond: The Continuing Pursuit of Unchecked Executive Power*, p. 90.

[14] The Amnesty International report documents numerous instances where judges appointed since the year 2000 routinely adjudicate in favor of the administration's treatment of detainees held in the "war on terror."

[15] In her May 24, 2005, speech to AIPAC, Clinton took the occasion to condemn Syria, Iran, Hamas, Hezbollah, and the Palestinian "structures of terror" while enthusiastically endorsing the theme of the organization's annual conference: "Israel. An American Value."

[16] Conversation at Real Instituto Elcano, Madrid, October 14, 2004.

CHAPTER XIX

Is the UN Doomed?

The United Nations is a curiously contentious topic. Mention it in the United States (especially in Washington) and you will likely be referred to "scandal," "waste," and "failure"; to the popular image of an expensive international excrescence, a breeding ground for inertia, sinecures, and time-servers, an impediment to the efficient pursuit and prosecution of American national interest. In these circles, the UN is at best a good idea gone badly "wrong."

Elsewhere, however, you are just as likely to be reminded of the astonishing reach of the UN: through its various agencies in the fields of population, environment, agriculture, development, education, medicine, refugee care, and much else besides, the United Nations addresses humanitarian crises and challenges that most people in the West cannot begin to imagine. And then there is peacekeeping: between its blue-helmeted soldiers, its border observers, police trainers, election monitors, weapons inspectors, and the rest, the UN mounts an international peacemaking and peacekeeping force not much smaller than the entire U.S. military complement in Iraq. Seen from this angle the world would be a decidedly nastier place if the United Nations didn't exist.[1]

That the United Nations should be so controversial might have surprised its founders—especially the many Americans among them. Back in 1945 there was great enthusiasm for the project, whose justification and purposes appeared self-evident. The very scale of the catastrophe that the nation-states of the world had brought upon themselves suggested grounds for optimism: governments and peoples would surely know better than to let *that* happen again. The United Nations, its charter, and its agencies would be their chosen means of prevention. The inadequacies of the League of Nations would be addressed and powerful sovereign states would work through the United Nations rather than around or against it.

Six decades later, the UN certainly has problems. One of these was present from the start. In the aftermath of Nazism, whose surviving leaders were being tried at Nuremberg for, among other things, the crime of "planning, preparing, initiating and waging a war of aggression," the UN's founders emphasized the right of sovereign states to be secure from foreign interference—including, except in very unusual circumstances, interference from the UN itself. Article II, Part 7 reads, "Nothing contained in the present Charter shall authorize the United Nations to intervene in matters which are essentially within the domestic jurisdiction of any state."

But the UN was also intended to be far more proactive than the League when it came to preventing rulers and governments from abusing citizens and others *within* their own borders. Over time it has established demanding expectations with respect to human rights and the treatment of minorities—whose abuse might legitimately trigger international intervention. This apparent contradiction between sovereignty and internationalism has been steadily exacerbated by the expansion in member states,[2] many of whom abuse their subjects as a matter of course; but also by the rise in the number of failed states, where the nature of sovereignty itself becomes unclear.

In the 1990s in Haiti, Somalia, Bosnia, or Rwanda, and today in Iraq and Sudan, with whom should the UN in practice deal? The local criminal chieftain? The very regime responsible for the crisis in the first place? In the era of globalization, with the rise of multinational corporations and other economic agents that are not even states at all but far exceed many of them in wealth and influence, and when the worst abuses are often the work of nonstate actors, the core functions of the classic state have come quite unglued and it is unclear who should now undertake them, and how.[3] What, in such times, is the role of the United Nations, an idea and an institution rooted, as its very name suggests, in the era of nation-states?

COMPARED WITH THESE urgent dilemmas, you might suppose that the problems that the UN (like any huge bureaucracy) faces and has always faced in operating efficiently and eliminating cronyism and graft would not dominate debate about the organization's role in the world. But you would be wrong. Ever since Joe McCarthy condemned the United Nations as an agent of Communist influence there have been American commentators only too glad to smear the institution. The latest and nastiest in a long line of attacks comes from Eric Shawn, a self-styled "newsman."[4]

Shawn, like many implacable critics of the UN, purports to wish the place well: "I join countless others in profound disillusionment that a noble ideal has morphed into a bastion of arrogance and, too often, inaction."[*] But this emollient humbug is soon displaced by a breathless "investigation" of the UN's catalogue of crimes. The UN is "rife with abject incompetence." "UN ambassadors and staff enjoy luxurious and tax-free Manhattan lifestyles and other perks." There is much prurient attention to reports of "peacekeepers . . . raping and having sex with twelve-year-old girls"—summarized on the dust jacket as "how UN workers have repeatedly turned children into their sexual prey"—and a tone of dripping contempt in every reference to Kofi Annan, the "ringleader of UN World."

Behind this screed—whose tone and prejudices faithfully reproduce those of Fox News, Mr. Shawn's employer—there is, however, a serious purpose. What Shawn and his fellows despise about the United Nations is the impedi-

---

[*] Eric Shawn, *The UN Exposed: How the United Nations Sabotages America's Security and Fails the World* (New York: Sentinel, 2006).

ment it has presented to American goals, the invasion of Iraq above all. That any country or combination of countries should have had the temerity to dissent from America's drive to war infuriates Mr. Shawn. That one Security Council member in particular—France—should have vetoed Washington's efforts to railroad the international community renders him apoplectic: the refusal of France and others to send an additional 100,000 troops "to help Iraq achieve full stability" is a "continued double-cross of the Iraqi people," the most "blatant example of the moral and political irrelevance of what the UN stands for."

It isn't just the French, of course. In Shawn's account, the entire UN organization is geared to taking American money while supporting America's enemies and hurting her interests. The senior staff are viscerally anti-American. Supporting evidence offered in the case of the Englishman Mark Malloch Brown, UN deputy secretary-general, nicely illustrates the author's method. In 1983 Malloch Brown stood (unsuccessfully) as a parliamentary candidate for the Social Democratic Party (SDP). Twenty years later, in 2003, Britain's Liberal Democratic Party—successor to the now-defunct SDP—voted against Tony Blair's decision to send troops to Iraq. QED. And the place is full of Malloch Browns with comparably tainted pasts:

> The UN should not be forgiven for its role in the war simply because democratic elections have finally been held in Iraq. Americans deserve answers from the occupants of that rectangular building overlooking New York City's East River.

Shawn's tract comes with a patina of respectability: it is published by a subsidiary of Penguin Books and has a blurb from Rudolph Giuliani.[5] And the author is proud to cite his links to men like Charles Hill, a retired diplomat-in-residence at Yale and source of some of Shawn's meaner-spirited one-liners. But *The UN Exposed* is in truth just an exercise in character assassination and chauvinist bile dressed up as journalism. Had Eric Shawn been serious about investigating the problems of the United Nations, he would have employed himself rather more usefully while visiting New Haven by speaking instead to Paul Kennedy.

The Parliament of Man, Professor Kennedy's latest book, is a comprehensive and accessible introduction to the history, tasks, and dilemmas of the United Nations.* It is an appealing and serious essay by a scholar who, for all his careful cataloguing of the organization's woes, never loses sight of the larger truth encapsulated in his closing sentences: "The UN," he writes, has brought great benefits to our generation and, with civic resolution and generosity by all of us who can contribute further to its work, will bring benefits to our children's and grandchildren's generations as well.

The first impression one gets from Kennedy, as, too, from James Traub's excellent account of Kofi Annan's last years in office, is that the UN is distinctly well served by its senior staff. In recent years the caliber of high-ranking civil service and diplomatic appointees in many Western countries has declined, as salaries and opportunities in the private sector seduce young men and women away from a career in public service. The United Nations, however, has continued to draw upon unusually talented and dedicated public servants. This was true in its early days, when it was run by statesmen like Dag Hammarskjöld and Ralph Bunche and attracted idealists like Brian Urquhart (the first British officer to enter Bergen-Belsen) and René Cassin (the French jurist who drafted the 1948 Universal Declaration of Human Rights).

It is still true today. The secretary-generals themselves are international political appointees of varying caliber (neither Kurt Waldheim nor Boutros Boutros-Ghali covered himself with glory[6]). But any government that could boast the services of Lakhdar Brahimi (head of the UN mission in Afghanistan from October 2001 to January 2005), Mohamed ElBaradei (director general of the International Atomic Energy Agency since 1997), Mary Robinson

---

* Paul Kennedy, *The Parliament of Man: The Past, Present, and Future of the United Nations* (New York: Random House, 2006).

(UN high commissioner for human rights, 1997–2002), Louise Arbour (her successor and former chief prosecutor for the international criminal tribunals for the former Yugoslavia and for Rwanda), the late Sergio Vieira de Mello or Jean-Marie Guéhenno (head of UN Peacekeeping Operations since October 2000)—or indeed Kofi Annan himself, the most impressive secretary-general since Hammarskjöld—would consider itself quite extraordinarily fortunate.[7]

What has the UN achieved? In the first place, it has survived. The idea of an international conflict-resolving and problem-addressing agency is an old one, with its roots in eighteenth-century Kantian dreams of Perpetual Peace. Early and partial incarnations—the International Red Cross (founded in 1864), the Hague Peace Conferences of 1899 and 1907 and the Geneva Conventions to which they gave rise, the League of Nations itself—lacked legitimacy and above all enforcement power in a world of warring nation-states. The United Nations, by contrast, profited from the great power standoff of the cold war decades and the era of decolonization, both of which made it a natural agora and forum for debating international issues; and it was blessed, from the beginning until recently, with the backing of the United States.

The UN also benefited, if that is the word, from the steady accretion of international responsibilities that no one else wanted to take on, "foundlings dropped off at the UN's door in the middle of the night," in Kennedy's words: from the Congo in 1960, through Somalia, Cambodia, Rwanda, and Bosnia in the nineties to East Timor, Sierra Leone, Ethiopia-Eritrea, and the Congo (again) today. Many of these missions failed, and all cost lots of money. But they are a sobering reminder of why we need an international organization of some sort. And they represent just the most visible of UN undertakings.

For there are actually many UNs, of which the political and military branches (General Assembly, Security Council, Peacekeeping Operations) are only the best known. To name but a few: UNESCO (the Educational, Scientific, and Cultural Organization, founded in 1945); UNICEF (the International Children's Emergency Fund, 1946); WHO (the World Health Organization, 1948), UNRWA (the Relief and Works Agency, 1949), UNHCR (the High

Commissioner for Refugees, 1950), UNCTAD (the Conference on Trade and Development, 1963), and ICTY (the International Criminal Tribunal for the former Yugoslavia, 1993). Such transnational units don't include intergovernmental programs administered under the UN's aegis; nor do they cover the many field agencies established to address particular crises. These include UNGOMAP (the Good Offices Mission to Afghanistan and Pakistan that successfully oversaw the Soviet withdrawal there), UNAMSIL (the Mission in Sierra Leone, 1999), UNMIK (the Mission in Kosovo, 1999) and many others before and since.

Much of the work done by these units is routine. And the "soft" tasks of the UN—addressing health and environmental problems, assisting women and children in crisis, educating farmers, training teachers, providing small loans, monitoring rights abuse—are sometimes performed just as well by national or nongovernmental agencies, though in most cases only at UN prompting or in the wake of a UN-sponsored initiative. But in a world where states are losing the initiative to such nonstate actors as the EU or multinational corporations, there are many things that would not happen at all if they were not undertaken by the United Nations or its representatives—the UNICEF-sponsored Convention on the Rights of the Child is a case in point.[8] And while these organizations cost money, we should recall that UNICEF, for example, has a budget considerably smaller than that of many international businesses.

The United Nations works best when everyone acknowledges the legitimacy of its role. When monitoring or overseeing elections or truces, for example, the UN is often the only external interlocutor whose good intentions and rightful authority are acknowledged by all the contending parties. Where this is not the case—at Srebrenica in 1995, for example—disaster ensues, since the UN troops can neither use force to defend themselves nor intervene to protect others. The reputation of the UN for evenhandedness and good faith is thus its most important long-term asset. Without it the organization becomes just another tool of one or more powerful states and resented as such.

The refusal in 2003 of the Security Council to authorize the disastrous U.S. war on Iraq thus saved the UN from possibly terminal discredit in the eyes of much of the rest of the world.

THE PRACTICAL PROBLEMS the UN faces in meeting expectations are easy to enumerate. Everything it does costs money, and the UN only has money if the member states provide it. The secretary-general and his staff are, it should be recalled, always and only executing the members' wishes. The UN has no army or police force of its own. In the past the Netherlands, Scandinavia, and Canada (the "concerned North"), along with a handful of other states like Poland, Italy, Brazil, and India, have furnished the UN with trained and equipped troops for its purposes. Today, a UN contingent is more likely to be provided by poorer countries from Africa or Asia, eager for UN cash but whose soldiers are inexperienced, undisciplined, and not always well regarded by those whose peace they have come to keep.[9] And of course a fresh contingent has to be raised for each crisis.

Clearly, if the UN is to exercise its emerging "responsibility to protect"— which was not part of its original remit or design—it needs an army of its own (as Brian Urquhart, among others, has proposed).[10] As things now stand, even when the Security Council does agree to authorize a military mission the secretary-general has to begin an interminable round of negotiations and cajoling for money, soldiers, policemen, nurses, arms, trucks, and supplies. Without such additional assistance the organization is helpless: in 1993, peace-keeping expenses alone exceeded the UN's entire annual budget by over 200 percent. And therefore single-state interventions (the French in Côte d'Ivoire or Chad, the British in Sierra Leone), or a sub-UN coalition such as the NATO attack on Serbia in 1999, will continue to be faster and more effective solutions in a crisis than the UN.[11]

The Security Council, the UN's executive committee, is itself one of the most intractable problems. Most of the members rotate, but the five permanent members have not changed since 1945. The special status of the United States, China, and Russia (formerly the USSR) is resented but not really questioned. But many countries now express irritation at the continuing privileges of Great Britain and France. Why not Germany instead? Or just a single, rotating "European" slot? Shouldn't there be at least one new member: Brazil, say, or India, or Nigeria, to reflect changes in the world since 1945? The French earned themselves a reprieve thanks to their internationally popular stand against the Iraq war, but these complaints will not go away.

Because agreement on Security Council reform is hard to reach—no one wants to give up their veto and adding more veto-wielding members would make things worse—certain problems are endemic. So long as China (and sometimes Russia) chooses to protect the "sovereign" rights of criminal regimes like Sudan with whom they do business, the UN will be unable to intervene to prevent genocide in Darfur. So long as the United States exercises its veto over Security Council resolutions critical of Israel, the UN will be impotent in the Middle East. Even when the Security Council does vote unanimously—as it did last August in calling for a cease-fire in Lebanon—the refusal of just one powerful member (in this case the United States) to oblige its client to acquiesce is sufficient to blunt the will of the entire international community.

Many critics would respond that this is because there is no international community. The machinery of both the Security Council and the General Assembly (the UN parliament) is, according to the generally sympathetic James Traub, "paralytic."* Representatives of the world's states come to New York to pronounce and perform, but they hardly form a "community" with common interests and purposes; and even if they did, the UN would be unable to implement these. Hence the rising chorus of demands for "reform." But what does this mean? The UN needs many things. It needs to acquire intelligence-gathering capacities of its own, certainly, the better to anticipate and analyze crises. It needs to become more efficient at making and imple-

---

*James Traub, *The Best Intentions: Kofi Annan and the UN in the Era of American World Power* (New York: Farrar, Straus and Giroux, 2006).

menting decisions; it could slim down its overlapping committees and programs, rationalize its regulations, legislation, conferences, and spending. And
it needs to be far more aware than it has been hitherto of incompetence and
corruption. As Kofi Annan himself has acknowledged, the UN management
is "a problem . . . in need of reform."

But reforming the practices of the UN would mean reforming the behavior of the member states. Everyone from the United States to the tiniest sub-
Saharan statelet has an agenda and a vested interest, and few will sacrifice
their own advantage for the higher goals of the community at large. Thus the
long-standing emphasis on "equitable geographical distribution" (rather than
competence) when assigning committee memberships has its merits: it helps
protect small, peripheral states from being railroaded by the rich powers and
coalitions of powers. But it has also produced a Human Rights Commission
with Sudan as a voting member and the infamous 1978 UNESCO declaration calling for restraints on press freedom. Kofi Annan himself warned recently that the new Human Rights Council (whose current members include
Azerbaijan, Cuba, and Saudi Arabia) will rapidly discredit itself if it focuses
overwhelmingly on Israeli rights violations while ignoring "grave violations
committed by other states as well." But the impediments remain.[12]

SADLY, THE GREATEST IMPEDIMENT of all is the United Nations' most
powerful member state and major paymaster, the United States. Much attention in the past year has been paid to the egregiously unsympathetic personality of the American ambassador to the UN, John Bolton. And Bolton is—or
was (President Bush having reluctantly abandoned the attempt to extend his
interim appointment)—a significant obstacle to the smooth functioning of the
UN at many levels. As James Traub shows, genuine efforts at institutional and
procedural reform over the course of the past two years were serially torpe-
doed by Bolton and his staff, who demanded "massive management reform"
but blocked any compromises that might actually achieve it.

In effect, Bolton formed a de facto coalition with states like Zimbabwe,

Belarus, and others who have their own reasons for keeping the UN ineffective and out of their domestic affairs. And because the United States refused to concede an inch in recent negotiations on reform of the Human Rights Council, the establishment of peace-building commissions, or a new international disarmament regime, countries that might otherwise have been constrained to give ground (Iran and Pakistan in particular) felt no compunction in rejecting stricter rules on, for example, nonproliferation. The member states (mostly European) that sought ways to trade untrammeled national sovereignty for a more effective international legal regime or a workable set of rules for collective action found themselves in a permanent minority.

Bolton didn't merely oppose effective reform at the UN but also seized every opportunity to sneer at the institution itself, describing it variously as "incapable" and "irrelevant."[13] In so doing he placed his country in decidedly odd company. After the United States vetoed a December 2006 Security Council motion to condemn Israel for the killing of nineteen Palestinian civilians at Beit Hanoun, the UN General Assembly (where there are no vetoes) passed a text merely expressing "regret" at the deaths. But the United States opposed even this motion, joined by its usual allies—Israel, Palau, and the Marshall Islands—and, on this occasion, Australia. Earlier in the year, when proposals for a reformed Human Rights Council finally reached the floor of the General Assembly, 188 countries voted to implement them. Four votes were cast against: Israel, the Marshall Islands, the United States, and Belarus.

Bolton's personal style may have been distinctive, but his votes were cast on behalf of his bosses in Washington. For a while it was put about that Bolton's extreme dislike of the UN did not in fact represent official American opinion; that Condoleezza Rice had "parked" Bolton on New York's East River to keep him from wreaking havoc back in Washington. But even if true, this merely shows that the U.S. secretary of state and her colleagues have still less respect for the UN than was previously supposed; assigning Bolton there was widely interpreted as a calculated expression of contempt.[14]

And indeed, Bolton was not the problem, merely the symptom. His "preemptive belligerence," his description of the UN as a "twilight zone," his habit of calling treaties "political obligations" rather than legal ones, for example, may seem nothing more than the rhetorical provocations of a hired thug; but in fact they reflect a seismic shift in America's relations with the rest of the world. American presidents from Truman to Clinton generally appreciated that the United States could get an awful lot from the United Nations— political support, international acquiescence, legal cover—for a modest outlay in cash and compromises. Now we oppose every little concession. This is new. Back in the cold war it was Mr. Khrushchev who banged his shoe on the table at the UN; it was Moscow that placed restrictions on every UN initiative and vehemently opposed any constraints upon its sovereign "rights." Now Washington performs this role—a revealing indication not of strength but (as in the Soviet case) of weakness.[15]

A petulant United States, expecting the UN to sweep up after it and generally perform international miracles but resolutely opposed to furnishing it with the means to do so and intent upon undermining its credibility at every turn, is an insuperable handicap and a leading source of the very shortcomings American commentators now deplore. The grubby scandals of the UN's recent past—notably the "oil-for-food" scam—are inconsequential; certainly they caused less harm (and generated far fewer illicit gains) than any number of recent corporate scandals in the United States, Australia, and elsewhere; not to mention the as-yet-uncalculated corruption and theft attendant upon the Iraq war and its aftermath. But the greater scandals—the UN's inept handling of the Bosnian catastrophe, its incompetence in Rwanda, and its inaction over Darfur—are all directly attributable to the reticence (or worse) of the major powers, the Unites States included.[16]

Is the UN doomed, then, to go the way of the unjustly maligned League of Nations? Probably not. But the fate of the League is a reminder of the continuing reluctance of the United States to embrace the lessons of the past hundred years of history. After all, the twentieth century turned out well for the United States and the habit of supposing that what worked in the past will continue to work in the future is deeply ingrained in American thinking. Conversely it is no accident that our European allies—for whom the twentieth century was a traumatic catastrophe—are predisposed to accept that cooperation, not combat, is the necessary condition of survival—even at the expense of some formal sovereign autonomy. British military casualties at the Battle of Passchendaele in 1917 alone exceed all U.S. losses in World Wars I and II combined. The French army lost twice the total number of U.S. Vietnam casualties in the course of just six weeks' fighting in 1940. Italy, Poland, Germany, and Russia all lost more soldiers and civilians in World War I—and again in World War II—than the United States has lost in all its foreign wars put together (in the Russian case by a factor of ten on both occasions). Such contrasts make quite a difference in how you see the world.

Thus today only an American diplomat would be caught saying, or even thinking, that, as Ms. Rice puts it, the "world is a messy place and someone has to clean it up."[17] The broader international consensus has it, rather, that precisely *because* the "world is a messy place"—and thanks to horrible experiences with self-assigned "cleaners"—the more safety nets and the fewer new brooms we deploy, the better our chances of survival. This was once also the view of an American diplomatic elite—the generation of George Kennan, Dean Acheson, and Charles Bohlen—far better informed about international realities and foreign perspectives than the men and women running U.S. foreign policy today.

Kennan and his contemporaries understood something that their successors have missed. In a world where most states and peoples, most of the time, see a benefit to complying with international laws and conventions, those who scorn or break the rules may have a passing advantage—they can do things that others won't. But they suffer long-term loss: they become pariahs or else—as in the U.S. case—are intensely disliked and distrusted even if their presence is unavoidable. And thus their influence, whether inside the international institutions they affect to ignore or outside of them, can only diminish, leaving them with nothing but force with which to persuade their critics.

If the United States is to be brought around—if, as Kofi Annan put it in a valedictory speech at the Truman Library in Independence, Missouri, the United States of America is to resume its lost leadership of the world community—then it will need to begin by recognizing, in Eisenhower's words, that "with all the defects, with all the failures that we can chalk up against it, the UN still represents man's best organized hope to substitute the conference table for the battlefield." In Europe this realization only took root after Europeans had spent thirty years torturing and killing tens of millions of other Europeans; so long as they were merely torturing and killing colonial "natives," attitudes changed little.

Here in the United States, at the time of writing, the death of more than three thousand American soldiers in Iraq has registered with the public; but the killing of hundreds of thousands of Iraqis hardly at all. Indeed, the latest face-saving cliché in Washington is that the unfolding catastrophe in their country is the Iraqis' own fault: we did our best but they let us down. And while the United States continues (with full congressional approval) to "render" and torture suspects in the "war on terror," we are unlikely to change our minds about the virtues of an International Court or the primacy of international law.

ALL IN ALL, THEN, it seems unlikely that even the humiliating defeat of the Iraq war will change many Americans' minds about the virtues of international cooperation. Something else, however, just may. For there is one common twenty-first-century international experience that American citizens and politicians cannot avoid sharing with the rest of the globe, however little they know of the outside world and however barnacled and prejudiced their views about it. Within the lifetime of many readers of this essay, the world is going to slip ever faster into an environmental catastrophe.

It is no coincidence that the two countries most responsible for this prospect—China and the United States of America—are also the two Security Council members least amenable to collective action in general; nor is it surprising that the man they have chosen to succeed Kofi Annan as UN secretary-general is Ban Ki-moon of South Korea, not someone hitherto known for pressing inconvenient agendas or speaking out of turn. His initial pronouncements, notably his equivocation over the propriety of Saddam Hussein's execution, have not been reassuring. But in the coming decades we are going to face "natural" disasters, droughts, famines, floods, resource wars, population movements, economic crises, and regional pandemics on a wholly unfamiliar scale.

Individual states will have neither the means nor—thanks to globalization—the practical authority to limit the damage or make good the losses. Substate actors such as the Red Cross or Doctors Without Borders will at best be able to apply Band-Aids. "Acting with others"—the emerging post-Bush mantra—will be utterly insufficient: mere coalitions of the willing (or the subservient) will be powerless. We shall be forced to acknowledge the authority and guidance of those who know what has to be done. In short, we shall have to act *through* others: in collaboration, in cooperation, and with little reference to separate national interests or boundaries, which will in any case lose much of their meaning. Thanks to the United Nations and its various agencies, such as WHO, Paul Kennedy writes, we have already "established international early-warning, assessment, response, and coordination mechanisms for when states fray or collapse." We shall have to learn to apply these to circumstances in which it is not states but whole societies that face collapse or failure, and where even Americans will not have the reassuring option of fighting "them" over "there" in order not to have to fight them "here."

The United Nations, "unique and irreplaceable," is all that we have achieved by way of a collective capacity to respond to such a crisis, when we finally awaken to it. If we didn't already have such an organization we probably would not know how to invent it today. But we do have it and in years to come we shall consider ourselves fortunate to have inherited its founders' decisions, if not their optimism. And so the good news is that in the long run the case for a UN will be made—indeed, it will make itself, if only when the UN headquarters (to the great relief of Eric Shawn and his friends) is constrained to leave Manhattan's East River bank, as the waters around New York City inexorably rise. The bad news, of course, is that—as Keynes reminded us—in the long run we are all dead.

This essay first appeared in *The New York Review of Books* in February 2007 as a review of *The UN Exposed: How the United Nations Sabotages America's Security and Fails the World* by Eric Shawn; *The Parliament of Man: The Past, Present, and Future of the United Nations* by Paul Kennedy; and *The Best Intentions: Kofi Annan and the UN in the Era of American World Power* by James Traub.

Notes to Chapter XIX

[1] See, generally, Michael W. Doyle and Nicholas Sambanis, *Making War and Building Peace: United Nations Peace Operations* (Princeton, NJ: Princeton University Press, 2006).

[2] There were 50 founding members in 1945; there are now 191.

[3] For some implications of the modern state's loss of control of its core functions, see Arjun Appadurai, *Fear of Small Numbers: An Essay on the Geography of Anger* (Durham, NC: Duke University Press, 2006).

[4] Shawn's self-promoting Web site can be found at www.ericshawnnewsman.com.

[5] Other blurbs are from Ann Coulter, Jesse Helms, and Christopher Hitchens ("The United Nations organization has become like one of the banana republics which dominate so many of its sessions and committees").

[6] Kennedy, generous to a fault, is altogether too kind to Boutros-Ghali, who conspicuously failed to take seriously the crisis in Bosnia, and whose representative there—Yasushi Akashi—was utterly inadequate to his task.

[7] On Annan, and in addition to the book by James Traub reviewed here, see the new biography by Stanley Meisler, *Kofi Annan: A Man of Peace in a World of War* (Hoboken, NJ: Wiley, 2007). In an address to the UN Security Council on December 12, Annan pressed the case for an urgent settlement of the Israel-Palestine crisis. The dispassionate cogency of his reasoning quite puts to shame the clichés (or, worse, silence) of the rest of today's world "leaders." An excerpt from his address appears on page 48 of the February 15, 2007, issue of the *New York Review of Books*.

[8] Only two UN member states have refused to ratify this convention: Somalia . . . and the United States.

[9] The failure of the African Union troops to make any difference in Darfur is a case in point—though here it was the local Sudanese government that insisted upon a non-Western contingent in the full knowledge (and desire) that it would prove ineffective in stopping the massacres.

[10] Between 1945 and 1988 the UN initiated just thirteen peacekeeping operations. Between 1988 and 1995 it initiated a further nineteen, mostly in the Balkans, Africa, and the Middle East, with many more to come. On the emergence and implications of this unanticipated UN function, see James Dobbins et al., *The UN's Role in Nation-Building: From the Congo to Iraq* (Santa Monica, CA: Rand, 2005).

[11] The peacekeeping budget issue should be kept in proportion, however. In 2006 all of the UN's worldwide peacekeeping operations together cost $5 billion. The American adventure in Iraq is estimated by the Congressional Budget Office to cost vastly more than this—$6 billion each month.

[12] See "Annan Calls for Anti-Terror Strategy Built on Human Rights," *Financial Times*, December 9/10, 2006.

[13] Back in 2001, as U.S. undersecretary of state for arms control and international security [*sic*], Bolton successfully derailed a UN Conference on the Illicit Trade in Small Arms and Light Weapons, and was even accompanied to the meeting by members of the National Rifle Association.

[14] It remains to be seen whether the nomination of Ambassador Zalmay Khalilzad to replace Bolton denotes a change of heart or merely of tone.

[15] In its early days the Security Council's business was impeded mostly by Soviet vetoes. In recent years, however, it is the United States that has been the chief villain. Since 1972 it has vetoed more than thirty Security Council resolutions critical of Israel, and dozens more on other issues from South Africa to international law.

[16] For a decidedly unsympathetic account of the UN Secretariat's failure to stand up to its paymasters when it really mattered, see Adam LeBor, *"Complicity with Evil": The United Nations in the Age of Modern Genocide* (New Haven: Yale University Press, 2006).

[17] Condoleezza Rice, then national security adviser, in the fall of 2002. See Jeffrey Goldberg, "Breaking Ranks: What Turned Brent Scowcroft Against the Bush Administration?," *The New Yorker*, November 2, 2005.

CHAPTER XX

What Have We Learned, if Anything?

The twentieth century is hardly behind us but already its quarrels and its achievements, its ideals and its fears are slipping into the obscurity of mis-memory. In the West we have made haste to dispense whenever possible with the economic, intellectual, and institutional baggage of the twentieth century and encouraged others to do likewise. In the wake of 1989, with boundless confidence and insufficient reflection, we put the twentieth century behind us and strode boldly into its successor swaddled in self-serving half-truths: the triumph of the West, the end of History, the unipolar American moment, the ineluctable march of globalization and the free market.

The belief that that was then and this is now embraced much more than just the defunct dogmas and institutions of cold war–era Communism. During the nineties, and again in the wake of September 11, 2001, I was struck more than once by a perverse contemporary insistence on not understanding the context of our present dilemmas, at home and abroad; on not listening with greater care to some of the wiser heads of earlier decades; on seeking actively to forget rather than remember, to deny continuity and proclaim novelty on every possible occasion. We have become stridently insistent that the past has little of interest to teach us. Ours, we assert, is a new world; its risks and opportunities are without precedent.

Perhaps this is not surprising. The recent past is the hardest to know and understand. Moreover, the world really has undergone a remarkable transformation since 1989 and such transformations are always unsettling for those who remember how things were before. In the decades following the French Revolution, the *douceur de vivre* of the vanished ancien régime was much regretted by older commentators. A century later, evocations and memoirs of pre–Word War I Europe typically depicted (and still depict) a lost civilization, a world whose illusions had quite literally been blown apart: "Never such innocence again."[1]

But there is a difference. Contemporaries might have regretted the world before the French Revolution. But they had not forgotten it. For much of the nineteenth century Europeans remained obsessed with the causes and meaning of the upheavals that began in 1789. The political and philosophical debates of the Enlightenment had not been consumed in the fires of revolution. On the contrary, the Revolution and its consequences were widely attributed to that same Enlightenment which thus emerged—for friend and foe alike—as the acknowledged source of the political dogmas and social programs of the century that followed.

In a similar vein, while everyone after 1918 agreed that things would never be the same again, the particular shape that a postwar world should take was everywhere conceived and contested in the long shadow of nineteenth-century experience and thought. Neoclassical economics, liberalism, Marxism (and its Communist stepchild), "revolution," the bourgeoisie and the proletariat, imperialism, and "industrialism"—the building blocks of the twentieth-century political world—were all nineteenth-century artifacts. Even those who, along with Virginia Woolf, believed that "on or about December 1910, human character changed"—that the cultural upheaval of Europe's fin de siècle had utterly transformed the terms of intellectual exchange—nonetheless devoted a surprising amount of energy to shadowboxing with their predecessors.[2] The past hung heavy across the present.

TODAY, IN CONTRAST, WE WEAR the last century rather lightly. To be sure, we have memorialized it everywhere: shrines, inscriptions, "heritage sites," even historical theme parks are all public reminders of "the Past." But the twentieth century that we have chosen to commemorate is curiously out of focus. The overwhelming majority of places of official twentieth-century memory are either avowedly nostalgo-triumphalist—praising famous men and celebrating famous victories—or else, and increasingly, they are opportunities for the recollection of selective suffering.

The twentieth century is thus on the path to becoming a moral memory palace: a pedagogically serviceable Chamber of Historical Horrors whose way stations are labeled "Munich" or "Pearl Harbor," "Auschwitz" or "Gulag," "Armenia" or "Bosnia" or "Rwanda"; with "9/11" as a sort of supererogatory coda, a bloody postscript for those who would forget the lessons of the century or who failed to learn them. The problem with this lapidary representation of the last century as a uniquely horrible time from which we have now, thankfully, emerged is not the description—it was in many ways a truly awful era, an age of brutality and mass suffering perhaps unequaled in the historical record. The problem is the message: that all of that is now behind us, that its meaning is clear, and that we may now advance—unencumbered by past errors—into a different and better era.

But such official commemoration does not enhance our appreciation and awareness of the past. It serves as a substitute, a surrogate. Instead of teaching history we walk children through museums and memorials. Worse still, we encourage them to see the past—and its lessons—through the vector of their ancestors' suffering. Today, the "common" interpretation of the recent past is thus composed of the manifold fragments of separate pasts, each of them (Jewish, Polish, Serb, Armenian, German, Asian-American, Palestinian, Irish, homosexual . . .) marked by its own distinctive and assertive victimhood.

The resulting mosaic does not bind us to a shared past, it separates us from it. Whatever the shortcomings of the national narratives once taught in school, however selective their focus and instrumental their message, they had at least the advantage of providing a nation with past references for present experience. Traditional history, as taught to generations of schoolchildren and college students, gave the present a meaning by reference to the past: today's names, places, inscriptions, ideas, and allusions could be slotted into a memorized narrative of yesterday. In our time, however, this process has gone into reverse. The past now acquires meaning only by reference to our many and often contrasting present concerns.

This disconcertingly alien character of the past is doubtless in part the result of the sheer speed of contemporary change. "Globalization" really has churned up people's lives in ways that their parents or grandparents would be hard put to imagine. Much of what had for decades, even centuries, seemed familiar and permanent is now passing rapidly into oblivion. The past, it seems, really is another country: they did things differently there.

The expansion of communication offers a case in point. Until the last decades of the twentieth century most people in the world had limited access to information; but—thanks to national education, state-controlled radio and television, and a common print culture—within any one state or nation or community people were all likely to know many of the same things. Today, the opposite applies. Most people in the world outside of sub-Saharan Africa have access to a near infinity of data. But in the absence of any common culture beyond a small elite, and not always even there, the fragmented information and ideas that people select or encounter are determined by a multiplicity of tastes, affinities, and interests. As the years pass, each one of us has less in common with the fast-multiplying worlds of our contemporaries, not to speak of the world of our forebears.

All of this is surely true—and it has disturbing implications for the future of democratic governance. Nevertheless, disruptive change, even global transformation, is not in itself unprecedented. The economic "globalization" of the late nineteenth century was no less turbulent, except that its implications were initially felt and understood by far fewer people. What is significant about the present age of transformations is the unique insouciance with which we have abandoned not merely the practices of the past but their very memory. A world just recently lost is already half forgotten.

WHAT, THEN, IS IT THAT we have misplaced in our haste to put the twentieth century behind us? In the United States, at least, we have forgotten the meaning of war. There is a reason for this. In much of continental Europe, Asia, and Africa the twentieth century was experienced as a cycle of wars. War in the last century signified invasion, occupation, displacement, deprivation, destruction, and mass murder. Countries that lost wars often lost population, territory, resources, security, and independence. But even those countries that emerged formally victorious had comparable experiences and usually remembered war much as the losers did. Italy after World War I, China after World War II, and France after both wars might be cases in point: all were "winners" and all were devastated. And then there are those countries that won a war but "lost the peace," squandering the opportunities afforded them by their victory. The Western Allies at Versailles and Israel in the decades following its June 1967 victory remain the most telling examples.

Moreover, war in the twentieth century frequently meant civil war: often under the cover of occupation or "liberation." Civil war played a significant role in the widespread "ethnic cleansing" and forced population transfers of the twentieth century, from India and Turkey to Spain and Yugoslavia. Like foreign occupation, civil war is one of the terrible "shared" memories of the past hundred years. In many countries "putting the past behind us"—i.e., agreeing to overcome or forget (or deny) a recent memory of internecine conflict and intercommunal violence—has been a primary goal of postwar governments: sometimes achieved, sometimes overachieved.

War was not just a catastrophe in its own right; it brought other horrors in its wake. World War I led to an unprecedented militarization of society, the worship of violence, and a cult of death that long outlasted the war itself and prepared the ground for the political disasters that followed. States and societies seized during and after World War II by Hitler or Stalin (or by both, in sequence) experienced not just occupation and exploitation but degradation and corrosion of the laws and norms of civil society. The very structures of civilized life—regulations, laws, teachers, policemen, judges—disappeared or else took on sinister significance: far from guaranteeing security, the state itself became the leading source of insecurity. Reciprocity and trust, whether in neighbors, colleagues, community, or leaders, collapsed. Behavior that would be aberrant in conventional circumstances—theft, dishonesty, dissemblance, indifference to the misfortune of others, and the opportunistic exploitation of their suffering—became not just normal but sometimes the only way to save your family and yourself. Dissent or opposition was stifled by universal fear.

War, in short, prompted behavior that would have been unthinkable as well as dysfunctional in peacetime. It is war, not racism or ethnic antagonism or religious fervor, that leads to atrocity. War—total war—has been the crucial antecedent condition for mass criminality in the modern era. The first primitive concentration camps were set up by the British during the Boer War of 1899–1902. Without World War I there would have been no Armenian genocide and it is highly unlikely that either Communism or Fascism would have seized hold of modern states. Without World War II there would have been no Holocaust. Absent the forcible involvement of Cambodia in the Vietnam War, we would never have heard of Pol Pot. As for the brutalizing effect of war on ordinary soldiers themselves, this of course has been copiously documented.[3]

THE UNITED STATES AVOIDED almost all of that. Americans, perhaps alone in the world, experienced the twentieth century in a far more positive light. The United States was not invaded. It did not lose vast numbers of citizens, or huge swathes of territory, as a result of occupation or dismemberment. Although humiliated in distant neocolonial wars (in Vietnam and now in Iraq), the United States has never suffered the full consequences of defeat.[4] Despite their ambivalence toward its recent undertakings, most Americans still feel that the wars their country has fought were mostly "good wars." The

United States was greatly enriched by its role in the two world wars and by their outcome, in which respect it has nothing in common with Britain, the only other major country to emerge unambiguously victorious from those struggles but at the cost of near bankruptcy and the loss of empire. And compared with other major twentieth-century combatants, the United States lost relatively few soldiers in battle and suffered hardly any civilian casualties.

This contrast merits statistical emphasis. In World War I the United States suffered slightly fewer than 120,000 combat deaths. For the UK, France, and Germany the figures are respectively 885,000, 1.4 million, and over 2 million. In World War II, when the United States lost about 420,000 armed forces in combat, Japan lost 2.1 million, China 3.8 million, Germany 5.5 million, and the Soviet Union an estimated 10.7 million. The Vietnam Veterans Memorial in Washington, D.C., records the deaths of 58,195 Americans over the course of a war lasting fifteen years: but the French army lost double that number in six weeks of fighting in May–June 1940. In the U.S. Army's costliest engagement of the century—the Ardennes offensive of December 1944–January 1945 (the "Battle of the Bulge")—19,300 American soldiers were killed. In the first twenty-four hours of the Battle of the Somme (July 1, 1916), the British army lost more than 20,000 dead. At the Battle of Stalingrad, the Red Army lost 750,000 men and the Wehrmacht almost as many.

With the exception of the generation of men who fought in World War II, the United States thus has no modern memory of combat or loss remotely comparable to that of the armed forces of other countries. But it is civilian casualties that leave the most enduring mark on national memory and here the contrast is piquant indeed. In World War II alone the British suffered 67,000 civilian dead. In continental Europe, France lost 270,000 civilians. Yugoslavia recorded over half a million civilian deaths, Germany 1.8 million, Poland 5.5 million, and the Soviet Union an estimated 11.4 million. These aggregate figures include some 5.8 million Jewish dead. Further afield, in China, the death count exceeded 16 million. American civilian losses (excluding the merchant navy) in both world wars amounted to less than 2,000 dead.

As a consequence, the United States today is the only advanced democracy where public figures glorify and exalt the military, a sentiment familiar in Europe before 1945 but quite unknown today. Politicians in the United States surround themselves with the symbols and trappings of armed prowess; even in 2008 American commentators excoriate allies that hesitate to engage in armed conflict. I believe it is this contrasting recollection of war and its impact, rather than any structural difference between the United States and otherwise comparable countries, which accounts for their dissimilar responses to international challenges today. Indeed, the complacent neoconservative claim that war and conflict are things Americans understand—in contrast to naive Europeans with their pacifistic fantasies—seems to me exactly wrong: it is Europeans (along with Asians and Africans) who understand war all too well. Most Americans have been fortunate enough to live in blissful ignorance of its true significance.

That same contrast may account for the distinctive quality of much American writing on the cold war and its outcome. In European accounts of the fall of Communism, from both sides of the former Iron Curtain, the dominant sentiment is one of relief at the closing of a long, unhappy chapter. Here in the United States, however, the story is typically recorded in a triumphalist key.[5] And why not? For many American commentators and policymakers the message of the twentieth century is that war works. Hence the widespread enthusiasm for our war on Iraq in 2003 (despite strong opposition to it in most other countries). For Washington, war remains an option—on that occasion the first option. For the rest of the developed world it has become a last resort.[6]

IGNORANCE OF TWENTIETH-CENTURY history does not just contribute to a regrettable enthusiasm for armed conflict. It also leads to a misidentification of the enemy. We have good reason to be taken up just now with terrorism and its challenge. But before setting out on a hundred-year war to eradicate terrorists from the face of the earth, let us consider the following. Terrorists are nothing new. Even if we exclude assassinations or attempted assassinations of presidents and monarchs and confine ourselves to men and women who kill random unarmed civilians in pursuit of a political objective, terrorists have been with us for well over a century.

There have been anarchist terrorists, Russian terrorists, Indian terrorists, Arab terrorists, Basque terrorists, Malay terrorists, Tamil terrorists, and dozens of others besides. There have been and still are Christian terrorists, Jewish terrorists, and Muslim terrorists. There were Yugoslav ("partisan") terrorists settling scores in World War II; Zionist terrorists blowing up Arab marketplaces in Palestine before 1948; American-financed Irish terrorists in Margaret Thatcher's London; U.S.-armed mujahideen terrorists in 1980s Afghanistan; and so on.

No one who has lived in Spain, Italy, Germany, Turkey, Japan, the UK, or France, not to speak of more habitually violent lands, could have failed to notice the omnipresence of terrorists—using guns, bombs, chemicals, cars, trains, planes, and much else—over the course of the twentieth century and beyond. The only thing that has changed in recent years is the unleashing in September 2001 of homicidal terrorism within the United States. Even that was not wholly unprecedented: the means were new and the carnage unexampled, but terrorism on U.S. soil was far from unknown over the course of the twentieth century.

But what of the argument that terrorism today is different, a "clash of cultures" infused with a noxious brew of religion and authoritarian politics: "Islamofascism"? This, too, is an interpretation resting in large part on a misreading of twentieth-century history. There is a triple confusion here. The first consists of lumping together the widely varying national Fascisms of interwar Europe with the very different resentments, demands, and strategies of the (equally heterogeneous) Muslim movements and insurgencies of our own time—and attaching the moral credibility of the anti-Fascist struggles of the past to our own more dubiously motivated military adventures.

A second confusion comes from conflating a handful of religiously motivated stateless assassins with the threat posed in the twentieth century by wealthy, modern states in the hands of totalitarian political parties committed to foreign aggression and mass extermination. Nazism was a threat to our very existence and the Soviet Union occupied half of Europe. But al-Qaeda? The comparison insults the intelligence—not to speak of the memory of those who fought the dictators. Even those who assert these similarities don't appear to believe them. After all, if Osama bin Laden were truly comparable to Hitler or Stalin, would we really have responded to September 11 by invading . . . Baghdad?

But the most serious mistake consists of taking the form for the content: defining all the various terrorists and terrorisms of our time, with their contrasting and sometimes conflicting objectives, by their actions alone. It would be rather as though one were to lump together the Italian Red Brigades, the German Baader-Meinhof Gang, the Provisional IRA, the Basque ETA, Switzerland's Jura Separatists, and the National Front for the Liberation of Corsica; dismiss their differences as insignificant; label the resulting amalgam of ideological kneecappers, bomb throwers, and political murderers "European Extremism" (or "Christo-Fascism," perhaps?) . . . and then declare uncompromising, open-ended armed warfare against it.

This abstracting of foes and threats from their context—this ease with which we have talked ourselves into believing that we are at war with "Islamofascists," "extremists" from a strange culture, who dwell in some distant "Islamistan," who hate us for who we are and seek to destroy "our way of life"—is a sure sign that we have forgotten *the* lesson of the twentieth century: the ease with which war and fear and dogma can bring us to demonize others, deny them a common humanity or the protection of our laws, and do unspeakable things to them.

How ELSE ARE we to explain our present indulgence for the practice of torture? For indulge it we assuredly do. The twentieth century began with the Hague Conventions on the laws of war. As of 2008 the twenty-first century has to its credit the Guantánamo Bay detention camp. Here and in other (secret) prisons in the United States terrorists or suspected terrorists are routinely tortured. There is ample twentieth-century precedent for this, of course, and not only in dictatorships. The British tortured terrorists in their East African colonies as late as the 1950s. The French tortured captured Algerian terrorists in the "dirty war" to keep Algeria French.[7]

At the height of the Algerian war Raymond Aron published two powerful essays urging France to quit Algeria and concede its independence: this, he insisted, was a pointless war that France could not win. Some years later Aron was asked why, when opposing French rule in Algeria, he did not also add his voice to those who were speaking out against the use of torture in Algeria. "But what would I have achieved by proclaiming my opposition to torture?" he replied. "I have never met anyone who is in favor of torture."[8]

Well, times have changed. In the United States today there are many respectable, thinking people who favor torture—under the appropriate circumstances and when applied to those who merit it. Professor Alan Dershowitz of Harvard Law School writes that "the simple cost-benefit analysis for employing such nonlethal torture [to extract time-sensitive information from a prisoner] seems overwhelming." Professor Jean Bethke Elshtain of the University of Chicago's School of Divinity acknowledges that torture remains a horror and is "in general [sic] . . . forbidden." But when interrogating "prisoners in the context of a deadly and dangerous war against enemies who know no limits . . . there are moments when this rule may be overridden."[9]

These chilling assertions are echoed by New York's Senator Charles Schumer (a Democrat), who at a Senate hearing in 2004 claimed that "there are probably very few people in this room or in America who would say that torture should never ever be used." Certainly not Supreme Court Justice Antonin Scalia, who informed the BBC's Radio Four in February 2008 that it would be absurd to say that you couldn't torture. In Scalia's words,

Once you acknowledge that, we're into a different game. How close does the threat have to be? How severe can the infliction of pain be? I don't think these are easy questions at all. . . . But I certainly know you can't come in smugly and with great self-satisfaction and say, "Oh, it's torture, and therefore it's no good."[10]

But it was precisely that claim, that "it's torture, and therefore it's no good," which until very recently distinguished democracies from dictatorships. We pride ourselves on having defeated the "evil empire" of the Soviets. Indeed so. But perhaps we should read again the memoirs of those who suffered at the hands of that empire—the memoirs of Eugen Loebl, Artur London, Jo Langer, Lena Constante, and countless others—and then compare the degrading abuses they suffered with the treatments approved and authorized by President Bush and the U.S. Congress. Are they so very different?[11]

Torture certainly "works." As the history of twentieth-century police states suggests, under extreme torture most people will say anything (including, sometimes, the truth). But to what end? Thanks to information extracted from terrorists under torture, the French army won the 1957 Battle of Algiers. Just over four years later the war was over, Algeria was independent, and the "terrorists" had won. But France still carries the stain and the memory of the crimes committed in its name. Torture really is no good, especially for republics. And as Aron noted many decades ago, "torture—and lies—[are] the accompaniment of war. . . . What needed to be done was end the war."[12]

We are slipping down a slope. The sophistic distinctions we draw today in our war on terror—between the rule of law and "exceptional" circumstances, between citizens (who have rights and legal protections) and noncitizens to whom anything can be done, between normal people and "terrorists," between "us" and "them"—are not new. The twentieth century saw them all invoked. They are the selfsame distinctions that licensed the worst horrors of the recent past: internment camps, deportation, torture, and murder—those very crimes that prompt us to murmur "never again." So what exactly is it that we think we have learned from the past? Of what possible use is our self-righteous cult of memory and memorials if the United States can build its very own internment camp and torture people there?

Far from escaping the twentieth century, we need, I think, to go back and look a bit more carefully. We need to learn again—or perhaps for the first time—how war brutalizes and degrades winners and losers alike and what happens to us when, having heedlessly waged war for no good reason, we are encouraged to inflate and demonize our enemies in order to justify that war's indefinite continuance. And perhaps, in this protracted electoral season, we could put a question to our aspirant leaders: Daddy (or, as it might be, Mommy), what did you do to prevent the war?

This essay first appeared in *The New York Review of Books* in May 2008.

Notes to Chapter XX

[1] Never such innocence,
Never before or since,
As changed itself to past
Without a word—the men
Leaving the gardens tidy,
The thousands of marriages
Lasting a little while longer:
Never such innocence again.
—Philip Larkin, *MCMXIV*

[2] See, for example, Lytton Strachey, *Eminent Victorians*, first published in 1918.

[3] See *Vernichtungskrieg: Verbrechen der Wehrmacht 1941–1944*, Hannes Heer and Klaus Naumann, eds. (Hamburg, Germany: Hamburger Edition, 1995). Many German soldiers on the eastern front and in Yugoslavia recorded their worst crimes for the delectation of family and friends. The American prison guards in Abu Ghraib are their lineal descendants.

[4] The defeated South did indeed experience just such consequences following the Civil War, however. And its subsequent humiliation, resentment, and backwardness are the American exception that illustrates the rule.

[5] See my discussion of *The Cold War: A New History* (New York: Penguin, 2005) by John Lewis Gaddis, in *The New York Review*, March 23, 2006.

[6] It should be noted, however, that a younger generation of political leaders in the UK— starting with Tony Blair—has proven almost as indifferent to the lessons of the twentieth century as their American contemporaries.

[7] See Caroline Elkins, *Imperial Reckoning: The Untold Story of Britain's Gulag in Kenya* (New York: Henry Holt, 2005); Marnia Lazreg, *Torture and the Twilight of Empire: From Algiers to Baghdad* (Princeton, NJ: Princeton University Press, 2008); and Darius Rejali, *Torture and Democracy* (Princeton, NJ: Princeton University Press, 2007).

[8] Raymond Aron, *La Tragédie Algérienne* (Paris: Plon, 1957), *L'Algérie et la République* (Paris:

Plon, 1958), and *Le Spectateur engagé* (Paris: Julliard, 1981), p. 210. For a firsthand account of torture, see Henri Alleg, *The Question* (Lincoln, NE: Bison, 2006; originally published in 1958 as *La Question*). *La Torture dans la République*, by the late Pierre Vidal-Naquet, is a penetrating account of how torture rots the political system that authorizes it. First published in English in 1963, this book has long been out of print. It should be retranslated and made required reading for every congressman and presidential candidate in the United States.

[9] Alan M. Dershowitz, *Why Terrorism Works: Understanding the Threat, Responding to the Challenge* (New Haven: Yale University Press, 2002), p. 144; Jean Bethke Elshtain, "Reflections on the Problem of 'Dirty Hands,'" in *Torture: A Collection*, Sanford Levinson, ed. (New York: Oxford University Press, 2004), pp. 80–83.

[10] Senator Schumer is quoted in the *Wall Street Journal*, November 2, 2007. For Justice Scalia's remarks, see www.usatoday.com/news/washington/2008-02-13-scalia_N.htm.

[11] Lena Constante, *The Silent Escape: Three Thousand Days in Romanian Prisons* (Berkeley: University of California Press, 1995); Jo Langer, *Une Saison à Bratislava* (Paris: Seuil, 1981); Eugen Loebl, *My Mind on Trial* (New York: Harcourt Brace Jovanovich, 1976); Artur Gerard London, *L'Aveu, dans l'engrenage du Procès de Prague* (Paris: Gallimard, 1971).

[12] Aron, *Le Spectateur engagé*, pp. 210–211.

Part Four

The Way We Live Now

CHAPTER XXI

The Glory of the Rails

More than any other technical design or social institution, the railway stands for modernity. No competing form of transport, no subsequent technological innovation, no other industry has wrought or facilitated change on the scale that has been brought about by the invention and adoption of the railway. Peter Laslett once referred to "the world we have lost"—the unimaginably different character of things as they once were. Try to think of a world before the railway and the meaning of distance and the impediment it imposed when the time it took to travel from, for example, Paris to Rome—and the means employed to do so—had changed little for two millennia. Think of the limits placed on economic activity and human life chances by the impossibility of moving food, goods, and people in large numbers or at any speed in excess of ten miles per hour; of the enduringly *local* nature of all knowledge, whether cultural, social, or political, and the consequences of such compartmentalization.

Above all, think of how different the world looked to men and women before the coming of the railways. In part this was a function of restricted perception. Until 1830, few people knew what unfamiliar landscapes, distant towns, or foreign lands looked like because they had no opportunity or reason to visit them. But in part, too, the world before the railways appeared so very different from what came afterward and from what we know today because the railways did more than just facilitate travel and thereby change the way the world was seen and depicted. They transformed the very landscape itself.

Railways were born of the industrial revolution—the steam engine itself was already sixty years old when it acquired wheels in 1825, and without the coal that it helped pump to the surface the steam engine could not work. But it was the railways that gave life and impetus to that same industrial revolution: they were the largest consumers of the very goods whose transportation they facilitated. Moreover, most of the technical challenges of industrial modernity—long-distance telegraphic communication, the harnessing of water, gas, and electricity for domestic and industrial use, urban and rural drainage, the construction of very large buildings, the gathering and moving of human beings in large numbers—were first met and overcome by railway companies.

TRAINS—OR, RATHER, the tracks on which they ran—represented the conquest of space. Canals and roads might be considerable technical achievements; but they had almost always been the extension, through physical effort or technical improvement, of an ancient or naturally occurring resource: a river, a valley, a path, or a pass. Even Telford and McAdam did little more than pave over existing roads. Railway tracks reinvented the landscape. They cut through hills, they burrowed under roads and canals, they were carried across valleys, towns, estuaries. The permanent way might be laid over iron girders, wooden trestles, brick-clad bridges, stone-buttressed earthworks, or impacted moss; importing or removing these materials could utterly transform town or country alike. As trains got heavier, so these foundations grew ever more intrusive: thicker, stronger, deeper.

Railway tracks were purpose-built: nothing else could run on them—and trains could run on nothing else. And because they could only be routed and constructed at certain gradients, on limited curves, and unimpeded by interference from obstacles like forests, boulders, crops, and cows, railways demanded—and were everywhere accorded—powers and authority over men and nature alike: rights of way, of property, of possession, and of destruction that were (and remain) wholly unprecedented in peacetime. Communities that accommodated themselves to the railway typically prospered. Towns and villages that made a show of opposition either lost the struggle; or else, if they succeeded in preventing or postponing a line, a bridge, or a station in their midst, got left behind: expenditure, travelers, goods, and markets all bypassed them and went elsewhere.

The conquest of space led inexorably to the reorganization of time. Even the modest speeds of early trains—between twenty and thirty-five miles per hour—were beyond the wildest imaginings of all but a handful of engineers. Most travelers and observers reasonably assumed not only that the railway had revolutionized spatial relations and the possibilities of communication, but also that—moving at unprecedented velocity and with no impediments to heed their advance—trains were extraordinarily dangerous. As indeed they were. Signaling, communication, and braking systems were always one step behind the steady increase in power and speed of the engines: until well into the later twentieth century, trains were better at moving than stopping. This being so, it was vital to keep them at a safe distance from one another and to know at all times where they were. And thus—from technical considerations and for reasons of safety as much as commerce, convenience, or publicity— was born the railway timetable.

It is hard today to convey the significance and implications of the timetable, which first appeared in the early 1840s: for the organization of the railways themselves, of course, but also for the daily lives of everyone else. The pre-modern world was space-bound; its modern successor, time-bound. The transition took place in the middle decades of the nineteenth century and with remarkable speed, accompanied by the ubiquitous station clock: on prominent, specially constructed towers at all major stations, inside every station booking hall, on platforms, and (in the pocket form) in the possession of railway employees. Everything that came after—the establishment of nationally and internationally agreed time zones; factory time clocks; the ubiquity of the wristwatch; time schedules for buses, ferries, and planes, for radio and television programs; school timetables; and much else—merely followed suit. Railways were proud of the indomitable place of trains in the organization and command of time—see Gabriel Ferrer's painted ceiling (1899) in the dining room of the Gare (now Musée) d'Orsay: an "Allegory on Time" reminding diners that their trains will not wait for dessert.

UNTIL THE OPENING of the Liverpool and Manchester Railway in 1830, people did not travel together in large groups. A typical stagecoach held four inside and ten outside. But it was not much used, and certainly not by those with any choice. The wealthy and the adventurous traveled alone or *en famille*—on horseback, in a post chaise or a private carriage—and no one else traveled far or often. But rail travel was mass transit from the very outset—even the earliest trains conveyed hundreds of people—and it was thus important to establish and offer distinctions: by price, comfort, service, and above all the company a voyager was likely to keep. Otherwise the better class of traveler would not come and the poorest would be priced out.

And thus railways established "classes" of travel: typically three, but up to five in the Russian Empire and India. These classes, which gave rise to our modern use of "first class," "second class," etc., for both practical and metaphorical purposes, were reproduced not just in train wagons and their furnishings but in waiting rooms, public bathrooms, ticket offices, restaurants, and all the many facilities provided at stations. In the fullness of time the particular facilities made available to *first-class* travelers—dining cars, club cars, smoking cars, sleeping cars, Pullman cars—reproduced and came to define (in literature, in art, and in design) solid, respectable, prosperous bourgeois life. In their most ostentatious form—typically the long-distance or international train, the *20th Century Limited,* the *Golden Arrow,* or the *Orient Express*—these exclusive facilities defined modern travel as a peculiarly enviable form of cultural ostentation, high style for a privileged minority.

In time, the railways simplified their social stratification into just two classes. In this they reflected the changes after World War I in much of the

West, though not always elsewhere. In part this was also a response to competition. From the 1930s, the motorcar was starting to challenge the train as the conveyance of choice for short and even medium-length journeys. Because the car—like its defunct horse-drawn predecessors the post chaise and carriage—was par excellence a *private* vehicle it threatened not just *rail* travel but the very idea of public transportation as a respectable and desirable way to move. As before 1830, so after 1950: those who could afford to do so opted increasingly for privacy. There was no longer either the need or the desire to regulate publicly provided transport with such careful attention to socially calibrated rankings.

TRAINS ARE ABOUT MOVING PEOPLE. But their most visible incarnation, their greatest public monument, was static: the railway station. Railway stations—large terminal stations especially—have been studied for their practical uses and significance: as organizers of space, as innovative means of accumulating and dispatching unprecedented numbers of people. And indeed the huge new city stations in London, Paris, Berlin, New York, Moscow, Bombay, and elsewhere wrought a revolution in the social organization of public space. But they were also of unique importance in the history of architecture and urban design, of city planning and public life.

Bringing a railway line into a large town or city was a monumental challenge. Beyond the technical and social issues—the clearance or removal of whole districts (usually the poorest: over two hundred shops, workshops, and churches, together with thousands of tenement homes, were bulldozed to make space for Grand Central Station), the bridging and tunneling past urban and natural obstacles—there was the implication of placing at the heart of an old city a new technology, a substantial edifice, and a steady, daily flow and ebb of many tens of thousands of people. Where should stations be placed? How should they be integrated into the existing urban fabric? What should they *look* like?

The solutions to these questions created modern urban life. From the 1850s (with the building of the Gare de l'Est in Paris) to the 1930s (with the completion of Milan's gargantuan Stazione Centrale) terminal stations from Budapest to St. Louis anchored the contemporary city. Their design ranged from Gothic to "Tudorbethan," from Greek revival to baroque, from Beaux Arts to neoclassical. Some, notably in early-twentieth-century America, were carefully modeled on Rome: the dimensions of Penn Station in New York were calibrated to those of the Baths of Caracalla (AD 217), while the barrel vault ceiling in Washington's Union Station borrowed directly from the transept vaults in the Baths of Diocletian (AD 306).

These massive edifices—which sometimes offered a clue to their nether function but in later years tended to camouflage it, speaking to other urban structures rather than the rail shed behind them—were a source of immense pride for the city and often furnished an occasion to redesign, in fact if not in name, much of the rest of the town. Major European cities—Berlin, Brussels, Paris, London—were reshaped around their railway terminuses, with broad avenues leading up to them, urban subway and tram networks designed to link the incoming rail lines (typically, as in London, in a loose circle with radial spokes), and urban renewal projects keyed to the likely growth of demand for housing generated by the railway.

The railway station became a new and dominant urban space: a large city terminus employed well over 1,000 people directly; at its peak Penn Station in New York employed 3,000 people, including 355 porters or "redcaps." The hotel built above or adjacent to the station and owned by the railway company employed hundreds more. Within its halls and under the arches supporting its tracks the railway provided copious additional commercial space. From the 1860s through the 1950s, most people entered or exited a city through its railway terminuses, whose size and splendor—whether seen at close quarters or at the distant end of a new avenue built to enhance its significance (the new Boulevard de Strasbourg ending at the Gare de l'Est in Paris, for example)—spoke directly and deliberately to the commercial ambitions and civic self-image of the modern metropolis.

———

As THE DESIGN of the station made quite explicit, railways were never just functional. They were about travel as pleasure, travel as adventure, travel as the archetypical modern experience. Patrons and clients were not supposed to just buy a ticket and go; they were meant to linger and imagine and dream (which is one reason why "platform tickets" came into being and were very much used). That is why stations were designed, often quite deliberately, on the model of cathedrals, with their spaces and facilities divided into naves, apses, side chapels, and ancillary offices and rituals. As the locus classicus for such winks and nods to neo-ecclesiastical monumentalism, see St. Pancras Station (1868) in London. Stations had restaurants, shops, personal services. They were for many decades the preferred site of a city's primary postal and telegraph offices. And above all, they were the ideal space in which to advertise themselves.

The railway poster, the railway advertisement, the brochure—advertising routes, tours, excursions, exotic places and possibilities—came remarkably early in the history of train travel. It was perfectly clear even to the first generation of train managers that they would be creating needs that they alone could meet; and that the more needs they could generate, the greater their business. Within limits the railway companies handled by themselves the business of advertising their wares—most famously in the magnificently stylized art-deco and expressionist posters that dominated station walls and newspaper advertisements from circa 1910 to circa 1940. But although they often owned hotels and even steamships, railways were not equipped to manage the full vertical range of services they had opened up, and this business fell into the hands of a new breed, the tour manager or travel agent, of whom the most important by far was the family of Thomas Cook of Derbyshire.

Cook (1808–1892) exemplifies both the commercial energies released by the possibilities of rail travel and the range of experiences to which these led. Beginning with a small family firm organizing Sunday excursion trains for local temperance clubs, Cook accumulated knowledge about trains, buses, and boats, together with contacts in hotels and places of interest: first in Britain, then in continental Europe, and finally across the Americas. Cook and his successors and imitators organized travel itself; indeed, and in collaboration with the railways, Cook and his successors invented the "resorts" to which people might now travel: bookable by Cook and reachable by rail, whether in the mountains, by the sea, or in "beauty spots" freshly identified for the purpose.

But above all, tour organizers furnished information *about* travel. They made it possible for voyagers to imagine and foresee (and pay for) their journey before making it, thereby enhancing the anticipation while minimizing the risk. Cook's brochures, booklets, and advisory guides—advising travelers on where to go, what to expect, what to wear, what to say, and how to say it— were marketed above all in the new railway station outlets opened by news-agents and booksellers. By 1914 Cook had gone to the logical next step of opening branch offices in or next to railway stations and hotels, publishing railway timetables and even underwriting the train cars and facilities provided en route.

THE ILLUSTRATIONS ON railway billboards, or on the colorful literature circulated by tour guides and travel agents, capture something else about the railways: their place in modern art, their versatile serviceability as an icon of the contemporary and the new. Artists themselves were never in any doubt about this. From Turner's *Rain, Steam and Speed* (1844) through Monet's *Gare Saint-Lazare* (1877), Edward Hopper's *Station* (1908), Campbell Cooper's *Grand Central Station* (1909), and on to the classic poster designs of the inter-war London Underground (not least Harry Beck's classic map design of 1932, imitated if not emulated in every subsequent railway and subway map the world over), railway trains and stations formed either theme or backdrop to four generations of modern pictorial art.

But it was in the most modern of all the modern arts that the railway was appreciated and exploited to greatest effect. Cinema and railways peaked in tandem—from the 1920s through the 1950s—and they are historically inseparable. One of the first films ever made was about a train—*L'Arrivée d'un train à la Ciotat* (Lumière Brothers, 1895). Trains are a sensual experience: visual and (especially in the age of steam) aural. They were thus a "natural" for cinematographers. Stations are anonymous, and full of shadows and movement and space. Their attraction for filmmakers is not mysterious. But the sheer range of films that exploit stations, trains, and the prospect or memory of rail travel remains quite striking. No other form of travel has lent itself to international cinema in quite this way: the horse and the motorcar lack the versatility of the train. Westerns and road movies date quickly, and while they had an international market, they were only ever produced in the United States.

It would be otiose to itemize the films that concern or exploit the railways, from *The General* (1927) to *Murder on the Orient Express* (1974). But it is worth reflecting on perhaps the best known of them all, David Lean's *Brief Encounter* (1945), a film in which the station and the train and its destinations do more than just furnish the props and the occasion for emotions and opportunities. The very specificity of the detail (the transcendent authority of the timetable, the configuration of the station and its location in town and community, the physical experience and plot significance of steam and cinders) makes them far more than a setting. The scenes at Carnforth Station, juxtaposed with the domestic life whose tranquillity they threaten, represent risk, opportunity, uncertainty, novelty, and change: life itself.

This is the first part of an essay Tony Judt wrote in 2007 as a study for a book to be entitled *Locomotion*. Due to his illness and untimely death, the book was never written. This essay appeared posthumously in *The New York Review of Books* in December 2010.

CHAPTER XXII

Bring Back the Rails!

THE WAY WE LIVE NOW

Railways have been declining since the 1950s. There had always been competition for the traveler (and, though less marked, for freight). From the 1890s horse-drawn trams and buses, followed a generation later by the electric or diesel or petrol variant, were cheaper to make and run than trains. Lorries (trucks)—the successor to the horse and cart—were always competitive over the short haul. With diesel engines they could now cover long distances. And there were now airplanes and, above all, there were cars: the latter becoming cheaper, faster, safer, more reliable every year.

Even over the longer distances for which it was originally conceived, the railway was at a disadvantage: its start-up and maintenance costs—in surveying, tunneling, laying track, building stations and rolling stock, switching to diesel, installing electrification—were greater than those of its competitors and it never succeeded in paying them off. Mass-produced cars, in contrast, were cheap to build and the roads on which they ran were subsidized by taxpayers. To be sure, they carried a high social overhead cost, notably to the environment, but that would only be paid at a future date. Above all, cars represented the possibility of *private* travel once again. Rail travel, in what were increasingly open-plan trains whose managers had to fill them in order to break even, was decidedly *public* transport.

Facing such hurdles, the railway was met after World War II by another challenge. The modern city was born of rail travel. The very possibility of placing millions of people in close proximity with one another, or else transporting them considerable distances from home to work and back, was the achievement of the railways. But in sucking up people from the country into the town and draining the countryside of communities and villages and workers, the train had begun to destroy its own raison d'être: the movement of people between towns and from remote country districts to urban centers. The major facilitator of urbanization, it fell victim to it. Now that the overwhelming majority of nonelective journeys were either very long or very short, it made more sense for people to undertake them in planes or cars. There was still a place for the short-haul, frequently stopping suburban train and, in Europe at least, for middle-distance expresses. But that was all. Even freight transportation was threatened by cheap trucking services, underwritten by the state in the form of publicly funded freeways. Everything else was a losing proposition.

And so railways declined. Private companies, where they still existed, went bankrupt. In many cases they were taken over by newly formed public corporations at public expense. Governments treated railways as a regrettable if unavoidable burden upon the exchequer, restricting their capital investment and closing "uneconomic" lines.

JUST HOW "INEXORABLE" this process had to be varied from place to place. "Market forces" were at their most unforgiving—and railways thus most threatened—in North America, where railway companies reduced their offerings to the minimum in the years after 1960, and in Britain, where in 1964 a national commission under Dr. Richard Beeching axed an extraordinary number of rural and branch lines and services in order to maintain the economic "viability" of British Railways. In both countries the outcome was an unhappy one: America's bankrupt railways were de facto "nationalized" in the 1970s. Twenty years later, Britain's railways, in public hands since 1948, were unceremoniously sold off to such private companies as were willing to bid for the most profitable routes and services.

In continental Europe, despite some closures and reductions in services, a culture of public provision and a slower rate of automobile growth preserved most of the railway infrastructure. In most of the rest of the world, poverty and backwardness helped preserve the train as the only practicable form of mass communication. Everywhere, however, railways—the harbingers and emblems of an age of public investment and civic pride—fell victim to a dual loss of faith: in the self-justifying benefits of public services, now displaced by considerations of profitability and competition; and in the physical representation of collective endeavor through urban design, public space, and architectural confidence.

The implications of these changes could be seen, most starkly, in the fate of stations. Between 1955 and 1975 a mix of antihistoricist fashion and corporate self-interest saw the destruction of a remarkable number of terminal stations— precisely those buildings and spaces that had most ostentatiously asserted rail travel's central place in the modern world. In some cases—Euston (London), the Gare du Midi (Brussels), Penn Station (New York)—the edifice that was demolished had to be replaced in one form or another, because the station's core people-moving function remained important. In other instances—the Anhalter Bahnhof in Berlin, for example—a classical structure was simply removed and nothing planned for its replacement. In many of these changes, the actual station was moved underground and out of sight, while the visible building—no longer expected to serve any uplifting civic purpose—was demolished and replaced by an anonymous commercial center or office building or recreation center, or all three. Penn Station—or its near contemporary, the monstrously anonymous Gare Montparnasse in Paris—is perhaps the most notorious case in point.[1]

The urban vandalism of the age was not confined to railway stations, of course, but they (along with the services they used to provide, such as hotels, restaurants, or cinemas) were by far its most prominent victim. And a symbolically appropriate victim, too: an underperforming, market-insensitive relic of high modern values. It should be noted, however, that rail travel itself did not decline, at least in quantity: even as railway stations lost their charm and their symbolic public standing, the number of people actually using them continued to rise. This was of course especially the case in poor, crowded lands where there were no realistic alternatives—India being the best illustration but by no means the only one.

Indeed, despite underinvestment and a degree of intercaste social promiscuity that renders them unappealing to the country's new professionals, the railways and stations of India, like those of much of the non-Western world (e.g., China, Malaysia, or even European Russia), probably have a secure future. Countries that did not benefit from the rise of the internal combustion engine in the mid-twentieth-century age of cheap oil would find it prohibitively expensive to reproduce American or British experience in the twenty-first century.

THE FUTURE OF RAILWAYS, a morbidly grim topic until very recently, is of more than passing interest. It is also quite promising. The aesthetic insecurities of the first post–World War II decades—the "New Brutalism" that favored and helped expedite the destruction of many of the greatest achievements of nineteenth-century public architecture and town planning—have passed. We are no longer embarrassed by the rococo or neo-Gothic or Beaux Arts excesses of the great railway stations of the industrial age and can see such edifices instead as their designers and contemporaries saw them: as the cathedrals of their age, to be preserved for their sake and for ours. The Gare du Nord and the Gare d'Orsay in Paris, Grand Central Station in New York and Union Station in St. Louis, St. Pancras in London, Keleti Station in Budapest, and dozens of others have all been preserved and even enhanced: some in their original function, others in a mixed role as travel and commercial centers, others still as civic monuments and cultural mementos.

Such stations, in many cases, are livelier and more important to their communities than they have been at any time since the 1930s. True, they may never again be fully appreciated in the role they were designed to serve—as dramatic entrance portals to modern cities—if only because most people who use them connect from tube to train, from underground taxi rank to platform escalator, and never even see the building from the outside or from a distance, as it was meant to be seen. But millions do use them. The modern city is now so large, so far-flung—and so crowded and expensive—that even the better-heeled have resorted to public transport once again, if only for commuting. More than at any point since the late 1940s, our cities rely for their survival upon the train.

The cost of oil—effectively stagnant from the 1950s through the 1990s (allowing for crisis-driven fluctuations)—is now steadily rising and unlikely ever to fall back to the level at which unrestricted car travel becomes economically viable again. The logic of the suburb, incontrovertible with oil at $1 a gallon, is thus placed in question. Air travel, unavoidable for long-haul journeys, is now inconvenient and expensive over medium distances: and in Western Europe and Japan the train is both a pleasanter and a *faster* alternative. The environmental advantages of the *modern* train are now very considerable, both technically and politically. An electrically powered rail system, like its companion light-rail or tram system within cities, can run on any convertible fuel source whether conventional or innovative, from nuclear power to solar power. For the foreseeable future this gives it a unique advantage over every other form of powered transportation.

It is not by chance that *public* infrastructural investment in rail travel has been growing for the past two decades everywhere in Western Europe and through much of Asia and Latin America (exceptions include Africa, where such investment is anyway still negligible, and the United States, where the concept of public funding of any kind remains grievously underappreciated). In very recent years railway buildings are no longer buried in obscure subterranean vaults, their function and identity ingloriously hidden under a bushel of office buildings. The new, publicly funded stations at Lyon, Seville, Chur (Switzerland), Kowloon, or London Waterloo International assert and celebrate their restored prominence, both architectural and civic, and are increasingly the work of innovative major architects like Santiago Calatrava or Rem Koolhaas.

Why this unanticipated revival? The explanation can be put in the form of a counterfactual: it is possible (and in many places today actively under consideration) to imagine public policy mandating a steady *reduction* in the nonnecessary use of private cars and trucks. It is possible, however hard to visualize, that air travel could become so expensive and/or unappealing that its attraction for people undertaking nonessential journeys will steadily diminish. But it is simply not possible to envision any conceivable modern, urban-based economy shorn of its subways, its tramways, its light rail and suburban networks, its rail connections, and its intercity links.

We no longer see the modern world through the image of the train, but we continue to live in the world the trains made. For any trip under 10 miles or between 150 and 500 miles in any country with a functioning railway network, the train is the quickest way to travel as well as, taking all costs into account, the cheapest and least destructive. What we thought was late modernity—the post-railway world of cars and planes—turns out, like so much else about the decades 1950–1990, to have been a parenthesis: driven, in this case, by the illusion of perennially cheap fuel and the attendant cult of privatization. The attractions of a return to "social" calculation are becoming as clear to modern planners as they once were, for rather different reasons, to our Victorian predecessors. What was, for a while, old-fashioned has once again become very modern.

THE RAILWAY AND MODERN LIFE

Ever since the invention of trains, and because of it, travel has been the symbol and symptom of modernity: trains—along with bicycles, buses, cars, motorcycles, and airplanes—have been exploited in art and commerce as the sign and proof of a society's presence at the forefront of change and innovation. In most cases, however, the invocation of a particular form of transport as the emblem of novelty and contemporaneity was a one-time thing. Bicycles were "new" just once, in the 1890s. Motorbikes were "new" in the 1920s, for Fascists and Bright Young Things (ever since they have been evocatively "retro"). Cars (like planes) were "new" in the Edwardian decade and again, briefly, in the 1950s; since then and at other times they have indeed stood for many qualities—reliability, prosperity, conspicuous consumption, freedom—but not "modernity" per se.

Trains are different. Trains were already modern life incarnate by the 1840s—hence their appeal to "modernist" painters. They were still performing that role in the age of the great cross-country expresses of the 1890s. Nothing was more ultramodern than the new, streamlined superliners that graced the neoexpressionist posters of the 1930s. Electrified tube trains were the idols of modernist poets after 1900, in the same way that the Japanese Shinkansen and the French TGV are the very icons of technological wizardry and high comfort at 190 mph today. Trains, it would seem, are perennially modern— even if they slip from sight for a while. Much the same applies to railway stations. The petrol "station" of the early trunk road is an object of nostalgic affection when depicted or remembered today, but it has been constantly replaced by functionally updated variations and in its original form survives only in nostalgic recall. Airports typically (and irritatingly) survive well past the onset of aesthetic or functional obsolescence; but no one would wish to preserve them for their own sake, much less suppose that an airport built in 1930 or even 1960 could be of use or interest today.

But railway stations built a century or even a century and a half ago— Paris's Gare de l'Est (1852), London's Paddington Station (1854), Bombay's Victoria Station (1887), Zurich's Hauptbahnhof (1893)—not only appeal aesthetically and are increasingly objects of affection and admiration: they *work*. And more to the point, they work in ways fundamentally identical to the way they worked when they were first built. This is a testament to the quality of their design and construction, of course; but it also speaks to their perennial contemporaneity. They do not become "out of date." They are not an adjunct to modern life, or part of it, or a byproduct of it. Stations, like the railway they punctuate, are integral to the modern world itself.

We often find ourselves asserting or assuming that *the* distinctive feature of modernity is the individual: the unreducible subject, the freestanding person, the unbound self, the unbeholden citizen. This modern individual is commonly and favorably contrasted with the dependent, deferential, unfree subject of the pre-modern world. There is something in this version of things, of course; just as there is something in the accompanying idea that modernity is also a story of the modern state, with its assets, its capacities, and its ambitions. But taken all in all, it is, nevertheless, a mistake—and a dangerous mistake. The *truly* distinctive feature of modern life—the one with which we lose touch at our peril—is neither the unattached individual nor the unconstrained state. It is what comes in between them: *society*. More precisely civil—or (as the nineteenth century had it) bourgeois—society.

The railways were and remain the necessary and natural accompaniment to the emergence of civil society. They are a collective project for individual benefit. They cannot exist without common accord (and, in recent times, common expenditure), and by design they offer a practical benefit to individual and collectivity alike. This is something the market cannot accomplish—except, on its own account of itself, by happy inadvertence. Railways were not always environmentally sensitive—though in overall pollution costs it is not clear that the steam engine did more harm than its internally combusted competitor—but they were and had to be socially responsive. That is one reason why they were not very profitable.

IF WE LOSE the railways we shall not just have lost a valuable practical asset whose replacement or recovery would be intolerably expensive. We shall have acknowledged that we have forgotten how to live collectively. If we throw away the railway stations and the lines leading to them—as we began to do in the 1950s and 1960s—we shall be throwing away our memory of how to live the confident civic life. It is not by chance that Margaret Thatcher—who famously declared that "there is no such thing as Society. There are individual men and women, and there are families"—made a point of never traveling by train. If we cannot spend our collective resources on trains and travel contentedly in them it is not because we have joined gated communities and need nothing but private cars to move between them. It will be because we have become gated *individuals* who don't know how to share public space to common advantage. The implications of such a loss would far transcend the demise of one system of transport among others. It would mean we had done with modern life.

This is the second part of the essay on locomotion. It appeared posthumously in *The New York Review of Books* in January 2011.

Note to Chapter XXII

[1] Penn Central Railroad went out of business in 1972, just eight years after opting for profit over prestige and flattening Manhattan's Penn Station to make way for Madison Square Garden.

CHAPTER XXIII

The Wrecking Ball
of Innovation

S*upercapitalism* is Robert Reich's account of the way we live now.* Its story
is familiar, its diagnosis superficial. But there are two reasons for paying
attention to it. The author was President Clinton's first secretary of labor.
Reich emphasizes this connection, adding that "the Clinton administration—
of which I am proud to have been a part—was one of the most pro-business
administrations in American history." Indeed, this is a decidedly "Clinton-
esque" book, its shortcomings perhaps a foretaste of what to expect (and not
expect) from another Clinton presidency. And Reich's subject—economic life
in today's advanced capitalist economy and the price we are paying for it in the
political and civic health of democracies—is important and even urgent,
though the "fixes" that he proposes are unconvincing.

Reich's theme goes as follows: during what he calls the "Not Quite Golden
Age" of American capitalism, from the end of World War II through the
1970s, American economic life was stable and in comfortable equilibrium. A
limited number of giant firms—like General Motors—dominated their predictable and secure markets; skilled workers had steady and (relatively) safe

---

*Robert B. Reich, *Supercapitalism: The Transformation of Business, Democracy, and Everyday Life*
(New York: Knopf, 2007).

jobs. For all the lip service paid to competition and free markets, the American economy (in this respect comparable to the economies of Western Europe) depended heavily upon protection from foreign competition, as well as standardization, regulation, subsidies, price supports, and government guarantees. The natural inequities of capitalism were softened by the assurance of present well-being and future prosperity and a widespread sentiment, however illusory, of common interest. "While Europeans set up cartels and fussed with democratic socialism, America went right to the heart of the matter—creating democratic capitalism as a planned economy, run by business."[1]

But since the midseventies, and with increasing ferocity in recent years, the winds of change—"supercapitalism"—have blown all that away. Thanks to technologies initially supported by or spun off from cold war research projects—such as computers, fiber optics, satellites, and the Internet—commodities, communications, and information now travel at a vastly accelerated pace. Regulatory structures set in place over the course of a century or more were superseded or dismantled within a few years. In their place came increased competition both for global markets and for the cataract of international funds chasing lucrative investments. Wages and prices were driven down, profits up. Competition and innovation generated new opportunities for some and vast pools of wealth for a few; meanwhile they destroyed jobs, bankrupted firms, and impoverished communities.

Reflecting the priorities of the new economy, politics are dominated by firms and financiers ("Walmart and Wall Street" in Reich's summary) lobbying for sectional advantage: "Supercapitalism has spilled over into politics, and engulfed democracy." As investors—and above all as consumers—Americans in particular have benefited in ways their parents could not have imagined. But no one is looking after the broader public interest. Investment values have gone through the roof, but "the institutions that used to aggregate *citizen* values have declined." Public policy debates in the contemporary United States, as Robert Reich observes, "are, on closer inspection, matters of mundane competitive advantage in pursuit of corporate profit." The notion of the "common good" has disappeared. Americans have lost control of their democracy.

Reich has a nice eye for the instructive example. The wealth gap in the United States is now at its widest since 1929: in 2005, 21.2 percent of U.S. national income accrued to just 1 percent of earners. In 1968 the CEO of General Motors took home, in pay and benefits, about sixty-six times the amount paid to a typical GM worker; in 2005 the CEO of Walmart earned nine hundred times the pay of his average employee. Indeed, the wealth of the Walmart founders' family that year was estimated at about the same ($90 billion) as that of the bottom 40 percent of the U.S. population: 120 million people. If the overall economy has grown "exuberantly" but "median household income has gone nowhere over the last three decades, . . . where has all the wealth gone? Mostly to the very top." As for the intrepid boldness of the latest generation of "wealth creators": Reich lists the tax breaks, pension guarantees, safety nets, "superfunds," and bailouts provided in recent years to savings and loans, hedge funds, banks, and other "risk takers" before dryly concluding that arrangements "that confer all upside benefit on private investors and all downside risk on the public are bound to stimulate great feats of entrepreneurial daring."

THIS IS ALL WELL SAID. But what is to be done? Here Reich is less forthcoming. The facts he amasses *appear* to point to an incipient collapse of the core values and institutions of the republic. Congressional bills are written to private advantage; influential contributors determine the policies of presidential candidates; individual citizens and voters have been steadily edged out of the public sphere. In Reich's many examples it is the modern international corporation, its overpaid executives, and its "value-obsessed" shareholders who seem to incarnate the breakdown of civic values. These firms' narrowly construed attention to growth, profit, and the short term, the reader might conclude, has obscured and displaced the broader collective goals and common interests that once bound us together.

But this is not at all the conclusion Robert Reich would have us reach. In his version of our present dilemmas no one is to blame. "As citizens, we may feel that inequality on this scale cannot possibly be good for a democracy. . . .

But the super-rich are not at fault." "Have top executives become greedier?" No. "Have corporate boards grown less responsible?" No. "Are investors more docile?" "There's no evidence to support any of these theories." Corporations aren't behaving very socially responsibly, as Reich documents. But that isn't their job. We shouldn't expect investors or consumers or companies to serve the common good. They are just seeking the best deal. Economics isn't about ethics. As the British Prime Minister Harold Macmillan once observed, "If people want morality, let them get it from their archbishops."

In Reich's account, there are no "malefactors of great wealth."[2] Indeed, he contemptuously dismisses any explanation that rests on human choice or will or class interest or even economic ideas. All such explanations, in his words, "collapse in the face of the facts." The changes recorded in his book apparently just "happened," in a subjectless illustration of the creative destruction inherent in the capitalist dynamic: Schumpeter lite, as it were. If anything, Reich is a technological determinist. New "technologies have empowered consumers and investors to get better and better deals." These deals have "sucked . . . social values . . . out of the system. . . . The story of what transpired has no heroes or villains."

There is a familiar triangulation at work here. The author gets to display indignation at the downside of modern capitalism, without ever having to attribute responsibility ("we *may* feel," etc.) or pass a judgment of his own. Corporations just do what they do. To be sure, if we don't like what that means for us as a society, Reich would have us don our citizen's cap and change it. But this doesn't really square with the book's repeated insistence on the iron logic of technology and self-interest. And so, not surprisingly, the solutions that Reich proposes to these epochal developments and the risks they pose are curiously humdrum: a few marginal tax changes, trade pacts to contain minimum wage clauses, some legislative regulation of lobbying.

But even these small amendments to current practice are at odds with Reich's framing assumption: that our interests as "investors" and "consumers" have triumphed over our capacity to act as "citizens." If his account of the workings of modern economic life is true—if, as he puts it, "under supercapitalism, the 'long term' is the present value of future earnings"—then tinkering with campaign finance laws is either irrelevant (because it would change nothing) or else impossible, because it would be opposed by those same "competing business interests" which caused the distortion in the first place. In any case, why would we or our representatives choose suddenly, in Reich's terms, to act as disinterested "citizens" rather than the self-seeking "consumers" or "investors" we have become? What—for any individual citizen—would be the incentive? At whose behest would we suddenly opt for our "civic" identity over our "economic" one?

Reich's way of cataloguing human behavior—as though our affinities and preferences ("consumer," "investor," "citizen") can be partitioned and pigeon-holed into noncommunicating boxes—is not convincing. It generates good sound bites—"As citizens [we] are sincerely concerned about global warming; as consumers and investors [we] are actively turning up the heat." But it can't explain why *American* citizens are trapped in this paradox while citizens in some other places have begun to address it. The trouble is that Reich's categories faithfully reflect his epistemologically thin view of society: by "citizen" he means no more than economic man + enlightened self-interest. There is something missing here. Not only are there no "heroes," no "villains," and no one to "blame." There are no politics either.

WE LIVE IN AN ECONOMIC AGE. For two centuries following the French Revolution, Western political life was dominated by a struggle pitting left against right: "progressives"—whether liberal or socialist—against their conservative opponents. Until recently these ideological frames of reference were still very much alive and determined the rhetoric if not the reality of public choice. But in the course of the past generation the terms of political exchange have altered beyond recognition. Whatever remained of the reassuring fatalism of the old left narrative—the inspiring conviction that "History" was on your side—was buried after 1989 along with "real existing Socialism." The traditional political right suffered a related fate. From the 1830s through the 1970s, to be on the Right meant opposing the Left's account of inevitable change and progress: "conservatives" conserved, "reactionaries" reacted. They were "counterrevolutionary." Hitherto energized by its rejection of now-defunct progressive convictions, the political right today has also lost its bearings.

The new master narrative—the way we think of our world—has abandoned the social for the economic. It presumes an "integrated system of global capitalism," economic growth, and productivity rather than class struggles, revolutions, and progress. Like its nineteenth-century predecessors, this story combines a claim about improvement ("growth is good") with an assumption about inevitability: globalization—or, for Robert Reich, "supercapitalism"—is a *natural* process, not a product of arbitrary human decisions. Where yesterday's theorists of revolution rested their worldview upon the inevitability of radical social upheaval, today's apostles of growth invoke the analogously ineluctable dynamic of global economic competition. Common to both is the confident identification of *necessity* in the present course of events. We are immured, in Emma Rothschild's words, in an uncontested "society of universal commerce."[3] Or as Margaret Thatcher once summarized it: There Is No Alternative.

Like their political forebears, contemporary economic writers often tend to the reductive: "In the long run," three respected economists write, "only one economic statistic really matters: the *growth of productivity*."[4] And today's dogma—like other dogmas of the recent past—is indifferent to those aspects of human existence not readily subsumed into its own terms of reference: just as the emphasis of the old thinking was on behavior and opinions that could be categorized as a product of "social class," so contemporary debate foregrounds interests and preferences that can be rendered in economic terms. We are predisposed to look back upon the twentieth century as an age of extremes and delusions from which we have now, thankfully, emerged. But are we not also deluded?

In our newfound worship of productivity and the market have we not simply inverted the faith of an earlier generation? Nothing is more ideological, after all, than the proposition that all affairs and policies, private and public, must turn upon the globalizing economy, its unavoidable laws and its insatiable demands. Together with the promise of revolution and its dream of social transformation, this worship of economic necessity was also the core premise of Marxism. In transiting from the twentieth century to the twenty-first, have we not just abandoned one nineteenth-century belief system and substituted another in its place?

LIKE THE OLD MASTER NARRATIVE, the new one offers scant guidance to making hard political choices. To take a simple instance: the real reason Robert Reich's "citizen" might be confused about global warming is not because he is also a part-time investor and consumer. It is because global warming is both a consequence of economic growth and a contributor to it. In which case, if "growth" is good and global warming bad, how is one to choose? *Is* growth a self-evident good? Whether contemporary wealth creation and efficiency-induced productivity growth actually deliver the benefits they proclaim—opportunity, upward mobility, happiness, well-being, affluence, security—is perhaps more of an open question than we are disposed to acknowledge. What if growth increased social resentments rather than alleviated them?[5] We should consider the noneconomic implications of public policy choices.

Take the case of welfare reform—in which Reich himself was very active, both as Bill Clinton's labor secretary and as the author many years ago of a proposal to replace public welfare with grants to businesses that hire the unemployed.[6] In 1996 the Clinton administration effectively eliminated most federally guaranteed entitlements to public assistance. Reversing the developments of the previous half century, Congress ended universal benefits and made welfare conditional upon a demonstrated willingness to seek and accept work. This was in line with developments elsewhere: the shift from welfare to "workfare" characterized reforms in Britain, Holland, and even Scandinavia (e.g., the 1991 Norwegian Social Services Act entitling local authorities to impose work requirements upon welfare recipients). Universal rights and need-based provisions were replaced with a system of "work-enabling" incentives and rewards: the proclaimed goal of getting people "off" welfare accompanied a belief that the outcome would be both morally exemplary and economically efficient.

But what looks like sensible economic policy carries an implicit civic cost. One of the fundamental objectives of the twentieth-century welfare state was to make full citizens of everyone: not just voting citizens in Robert Reich's limited sense but rights-bearing citizens with an unconditional claim upon the attention and support of the collectivity. The outcome would be a more cohesive society, with no category of person excluded or less "deserving." But the new, "discretionary" approach makes an individual's claim upon the collectivity once again contingent on good conduct. It reintroduces a *conditionality* to social citizenship: only those with a job are full members of the community. Others may receive the help necessary for full participation, but not until they pass certain tests and demonstrate appropriate behavior.

Stripped of its rhetorical finery, modern welfare reform thus returns us to the spirit of England's New Poor Law of 1834, which introduced the principle of least eligibility, whereby relief for the unemployed and indigent was to be inferior in quality and quantity to the lowest prevailing wages and conditions of employment. And above all, welfare reform reopens a distinction between active (or "deserving") citizens and others: those who, for whatever reason, are excluded from the active workforce. To be sure, the old universal welfare systems were not market-friendly. But that was the point: welfare, in T. H. Marshall's words, was supposed "to supersede the market by taking goods and services out of it, or in some way to control and modify its operations so as to produce a result it would not have produced itself."[7]

MARKET OPTIMIZATION—displacing social or political evaluations of public policy with measures evaluated primarily for their economic efficiency—is also the proclaimed justification for the privatization frenzy of recent years. But here, as with welfare reform, what purports to represent the future has actually begun to resemble the past, breaking up the public and collective agencies of the modern era into fragmented and privately held assets reminiscent of a much earlier age. With the advent of the modern state (notably over the course of the past century), transport, hospitals, schools, mails, armies, prisons, police forces, and affordable access to culture—all of them essential services not obviously well served by the workings of the profit motive—were taken under public regulation or control. They are now being handed back to private entrepreneurs (or, in the case of many European cultural budgets, to the vagaries of individual delusion and frailty in the form of semiprivate national lotteries).

In some cases—transportation and mails, notably—these services don't promise an economic return (e.g., when they have to be provided in remote places) and taxpayers must underwrite or guarantee the private sector's profit margin in order for the state to find buyers. This is just old-fashioned subsidy under another name; and (as Robert Reich acknowledges) a perennial source of moral hazard, inviting irresponsibility and often corruption. In other cases private companies take a hitherto public responsibility—provision of prisons or railroad carriages or health care—off the hands of the state, sometimes paying a fee for the privilege and recouping their outlay by charging citizens or communities who use the facility in question. Typically, the public treasury reaps a one-time gain and is relieved of an administrative burden, but at the expense of foregone future income and a loss of control over the quality of the service contracted out. In Britain today this is designated as PPP: "Public–Private Partnership." In ancien régime France they called it tax farming.[8]

The real impact of privatization, like welfare reform, deregulation, the technological revolution, and indeed globalization itself, has been to reduce the role of the state in the affairs of its citizens: to get the state "off our backs" and "out of our lives"—a common objective of economic "reformers" everywhere—and make public policy, in Robert Reich's approving words, "business-friendly." The twentieth-century state in its "soul-engineering" guise has surely left a bad taste. It was often inefficient, sometimes repressive, occasionally genocidal. But in reducing (and implicitly discrediting) the state, in forsaking public interest for private advantage wherever possible, we have also devalued those goods and services that represent the collectivity and its shared purposes, steadily "reducing the incentive for competent and ambitious persons to join or stay in state service."[9] And this carries a very considerable risk.

The market requires norms, habits, and "sentiments" external to itself to hold it together, to ensure the very political stability that capitalism needs in order to thrive. But it also tends to corrode those same practices and sentiments. This much has long been clear.[10] The benign "invisible hand"—the unregulated free market—may have been a favorable inaugural condition for commercial societies. But it cannot reproduce the noncommercial institutions and relations—of cohesion, trust, custom, restraint, obligation, morality, authority—that it inherited and which the pursuit of individual economic self-interest tends to undermine rather than reinforce.[11] For similar reasons, the relationship between capitalism and democracy (or capitalism and political freedom) should not be taken for granted: see China, Russia, and perhaps even Singapore today. Efficiency, growth, and profit may not always be a precondition or even a consequence of democracy so much as a substitute for it.

IF MODERN DEMOCRACIES ARE TO survive the shock of Reich's "super-capitalism," they need to be bound by something more than the pursuit of private economic advantage, particularly when the latter accrues to ever fewer beneficiaries: the idea of a society held together by pecuniary interests alone is, in Mill's words, "essentially repulsive." A civilized society requires more than self-interest, whether deluded or enlightened, for its shared narrative of purpose. "The greatest asset of *public* action is its ability to satisfy vaguely felt needs for higher purpose in the lives of men and women."[12]

The danger today is that, having devalued public action, we are no longer clear just what *does* bind us together. The late Bernard Williams, after describing the "objective teleology of human nature" in Greek ethical thought—the belief that there are facts about man's place in the world which determined that he was meant to lead a cooperative life—concluded that some version of this belief has been held by most ethical outlooks subsequently; we are perhaps more conscious now of having to do without it than anyone has been since some fifth-century Sophists first doubted it.

In which case who, today, will take responsibility for what Jan Patočka called the "Soul of the City"?[13]

There are two overriding reasons to worry about the soul of the city, and to fear that it cannot be satisfactorily substituted with a story of indefinite economic growth, or even the creative destruction of the wrecking ball of capitalist innovation. The first reason is that this story is not very appealing. It leaves a lot of people out, both at home and abroad; it wreaks havoc with the natural environment; and its consequences are unattractive and uninspiring. Abundance (as Daniel Bell once observed) may be the American substitute for Socialism; but as shared social objectives go, shopping remains something of an underachievement. In the early years of the French Revolution the Marquis de Condorcet was dismayed at the prospect of commercial society that was opening before him (as it is opening before us): the idea that "liberty will be no more, in the eyes of an avid nation, than a necessary condition for the security of financial operations."[14] We ought to share his revulsion.

The second source of anxiety is that the never-ending story may not last. Even economies have histories. The last time the capitalist world passed through a period of unprecedented expansion and great wealth creation, during the "globalization" *avant le mot* of the world economy in the imperial decades preceding World War I, there was a widespread assumption in Britain—much as there is in the United States and Western Europe today—that this was the threshold of an unprecedented age of indefinite peace and prosperity. Anyone seeking an account of this confidence—and what became of it—can do no better than read Keynes's *Economic Consequences of the Peace*, a summary of the illusions of a world on the edge of catastrophe, written in the aftermath of the war that was to put an end to all such irenic fancies for the next fifty years.[15]

It was Keynes, too, who anticipated and helped prepare for the "craving for security" that Europeans would feel after the three decades of war and economic collapse that followed the end of the Gilded Age. Thanks in large measure to the state-provided public services and safety nets incorporated into their postwar systems of governance, the citizens of the advanced countries lost the gnawing sense of insecurity and fear that had dominated and polarized political life from 1914 through the early fifties and which was largely responsible for the appeal of both Fascism and Communism in those years.

BUT WE HAVE good reason to believe that this may be about to change. Fear is reemerging as an active ingredient of political life in Western democracies. Fear of terrorism, of course; but also, and perhaps more insidiously, fear of the uncontrollable speed of change, fear of the loss of employment, fear of losing ground to others in an increasingly unequal distribution of resources, fear of losing control of the circumstances and routines of one's daily life. And, perhaps above all, fear that it is not just we who can no longer shape our lives but that those in authority have lost control as well, to forces beyond their reach.

Half a century of security and prosperity has largely erased the memory of the last time an "economic age" collapsed into an era of fear. We have become stridently insistent—in our economic calculations, our political practices, our international strategies, even our educational priorities—that the past has little of relevance to teach us. Ours, we insist, is a new world; its risks and opportunities are without precedent. Our parents and grandparents, however, who lived the consequences of the unraveling of an earlier economic age, had a far sharper sense of what can happen to a society when private and sectional interests trump public goals and obscure the common good.

We need to recover some of that sense. We are likely, in any event, to rediscover the state thanks to globalization itself. Populations experiencing increased economic and physical insecurity will retreat to the political symbols, legal resources, and physical barriers that only a territorial state can provide.

This is already happening in many countries: note the rising attraction of protectionism in American politics, the appeal of "anti-immigrant" parties across Western Europe, the call for "walls," "barriers," and "tests" everywhere. "Flat worlders" may be in for a surprise. Moreover, while it may be true that globalization and "supercapitalism" reduce differences *between* countries, they typically amplify inequality *within* them—in China, for instance, or the United States—with disruptive political implications.

If we are indeed going to experience a return of the state, an enhanced need for the security and resources that only a state can provide, then we should be paying more attention to the things states can do. Today we speak contemptuously of the state: not as the natural benefactor of first resort but as a source of economic inefficiency and social intrusion best excluded from citizens' affairs wherever possible. The very success of the mixed-economy welfare states—in providing the social stability and ideological demobilization which made possible the prosperity of the past half century—has led a younger generation to take that same stability and ideological quiescence for granted and demand the elimination of the "impediment" of the taxing, regulating, and generally interfering state. This discounting of the public sector has become the default condition of policy discourse in much of the developed world.

But if I am right and our present circumstances will not endure indefinitely, we might do well to take a second glance at the way our twentieth-century predecessors responded to the political challenges of economic uncertainty. We may discover, as they did, that the universal provision of social services and some restriction upon inequalities of income and wealth are important economic variables in themselves, furnishing the necessary public cohesion and political confidence for a sustained prosperity—and that only the state has the resources and the authority to provide those services and enforce those restrictions in our collective name.

We may find that a healthy democracy, far from being threatened by the regulatory state, actually depends upon it: that in a world increasingly polarized between insecure individuals and unregulated global forces, the legitimate authority of the democratic state may be the best kind of intermediate institution we can devise. What, after all, is the alternative? Our contemporary cult of untrammeled economic freedom, combined with a heightened sense of fear and insecurity, is leading to reduced social provision and minimal economic regulation; but these are accompanied by ever-extending governmental oversight of communication, movement, and opinion. "Chinese" capitalism, as it were, Western-style. Is this what we want?

This essay, a review of *Supercapitalism: The Transformation of Business, Democracy, and Everyday Life* by Robert B. Reich, first appeared in *The New York Review of Books* in December 2007.

NOTES TO CHAPTER XXIII

[1] This is hardly an original claim, of course. As the Nobel-winning economist James Tobin observed some years ago, "It was a bunch of planners—Truman, Churchill, Keynes, Marshall, Acheson, Monnet, Schuman, MacArthur in Japan—whose vision made possible the prosperous postwar world." *World Finance and Economic Stability: Selected Essays of James Tobin* (Northampton, MA: Edward Elgar, 2003), p. 210.

[2] Nor is there any talk of the "unacceptable face of capitalism," as Edward Heath described an earlier generation of super-rich international businessmen. It is telling that both a Republican president, Theodore Roosevelt, and a Conservative prime minister were more willing to condemn capitalist excess than President Clinton's former secretary of labor.

[3] Emma Rothschild, *Economic Sentiments: Adam Smith, Condorcet and the Enlightenment* (Cambridge, MA: Harvard University Press, 2002), p. 250. As Rothschild observes, the "rhetoric of the endlessness of commerce is more unquestioned [today] . . . than at any time in the nineteenth or twentieth centuries" (p. 6).

[4] William J. Baumol, Robert E. Litan, and Carl J. Schramm, *Good Capitalism, Bad Capitalism, and the Economics of Growth and Prosperity* (New Haven, CT: Yale University Press, 2007), p. 230.

[5] Among recent contributions to this long-standing discussion see in particular Avner Offer, *The Challenge of Affluence* (New York: Oxford University Press, 2006), reviewed in *The New York Review*, October 11, 2007, and Benjamin Friedman, *The Moral Consequences of Economic Growth* (New York: Knopf, 2005), reviewed in *The New York Review*, January 12, 2006; also Fred Hirsch, *Social Limits to Growth* (Cambridge, MA: Harvard University Press, 1976), and, classically, John Kenneth Galbraith, *The Affluent Society* (Boston: Houghton Mifflin, 1958). As Hirsch observes (p. 66, note 19), the question, for example, of whether

redistribution "destroys wealth" can't be answered by economic criteria alone. It depends on what constitutes "wealth," i.e., what we value.

6 See Robert Reich, *The Next American Frontier: A Provocative Program for Economic Renewal* (New York: Viking, 1984).

7 T. H. Marshall, "Value Problems of Welfare Capitalism," *Journal of Social Policy*, vol. 1, no. 1 (1972), pp. 19–20, quoted in Neil Gilbert, *Transformation of the Welfare State: The Silent Surrender of Public Responsibility* (New York: Oxford University Press, 2002), p. 135. As Gilbert concludes, "Policies devoted entirely to cultivating independence and private responsibility leave little ground for a life of honorable dependence for those who may be unable to work."

8 For privatization at work, in the country which has been most exposed to its depredations, see Christian Wolmar, *On the Wrong Line: How Ideology and Incompetence Wrecked Britain's Railways* (London: Aurum, 2005), and Allyson Pollock, *NHS plc: The Privatisation of Our Health Care* (Brooklyn, NY: Verso, 2004). Gordon Brown, Britain's new prime minister, recently invited some of America's more notorious for-profit health companies—Aetna and United Healthcare among them—to bid for the management of Britain's hospital operations. Even the ultra-free-market *Economist* acknowledges the fallacy of "privatisation": commenting on the bankruptcy of Metronet, one of the firms now running London's Underground, it noted that since the government has "awarded Metronet 'hundreds of millions of pounds' to carry on its work . . . it is taxpayers who will have to foot the bill." See *The Economist*, July 21, 2007.

9 See Victor Perez-Diaz, "Political Symbolisms in Liberal Democracies" (unpublished paper, January 2007), p. 16.

10 See, for example, Adam Smith, *The Theory of Moral Sentiments* (1759). Also Daniel Bell, *The Cultural Contradictions of Capitalism* (New York: Basic Books, 1976).

11 "If we cannot moderate the extremes of fortune generated by the market and perpetuated by inheritance, the consensual basis of the market economy may not survive." Tobin, *World Finance and Economic Stability*, p. 209. For "favorable inaugural condition" see Hirsch, *Social Limits to Growth*, p. 11. The crucial role of public coordinating institutions in furnishing the preconditions for stable markets and economic growth is also brought out in Barry Eichengreen's recent study of postwar European capitalism, *The European Economy Since 1945: Coordinated Capitalism and Beyond* (Princeton, NJ: Princeton University Press, 2006).

12 Albert O. Hirschman, *Shifting Involvements: Private Interest and Public Action* (Princeton, NJ: Princeton University Press, 1982, 2002), p. 126 (emphasis added).

13 Bernard Williams, *The Sense of the Past: Essays in the History of Philosophy* (Princeton, NJ: Princeton University Press, 2006), pp. 44–45. Concerning Patocka's question I am grateful to Dr. Jacques Rupnik for his unpublished paper "The Legacy of Charter 77 and the Emergence of a European Public Space."

14 "Esquisse d'un tableau historique des progrès de l'esprit humain" (*Oeuvres de Condorcet*, VI, 191), quoted in Rothschild, *Economic Sentiments*, p. 201.

15 John Maynard Keynes, *The Economic Consequences of the Peace* (New York: Harcourt Brace Jovanovich, 1920), Chapter 2: "Europe Before the War." Economic mirages are not confined to imperial capitals. Here is how Ivo Andric described the optimistic delusions of his fellow

Bosnians in those same halcyon times: "Such were those three decades of relative prosperity and apparent peace . . . when many . . . thought there was some infallible formula for the realization of a centuries-old dream of full and happy development of individuality in freedom and progress, when the . . . century spread out before the eyes of millions of men its many-sided and deceptive prosperity and created its *fata morgana* of comfort, security and happiness for all and everyone at reasonable prices and even on credit terms." Ivo Andric, *The Bridge on the Drina* (Chicago: University of Chicago Press, 1977), p. 173.

CHAPTER XXIV

What Is Living and What Is Dead in Social Democracy?

Americans would like things to be better. According to public opinion surveys in recent years, everyone would like their child to have improved life chances at birth. They would prefer it if their wife or daughter had the same odds of surviving maternity as women in other advanced countries. They would appreciate full medical coverage at lower cost, longer life expectancy, better public services, and less crime.

When told that these things are available in Austria, Scandinavia, or the Netherlands, but that they come with higher taxes and an "interventionary" state, many of those same Americans respond: "But that is Socialism! We do not want the state interfering in our affairs. And above all, we do not wish to pay more taxes."

This curious cognitive dissonance is an old story. A century ago, the German sociologist Werner Sombart famously asked: *Why is there no Socialism in America?* There are many answers to this question. Some have to do with the sheer size of the country: shared purposes are difficult to organize and sustain on an imperial scale. There are also, of course, cultural factors, including the distinctively American suspicion of central government.

And indeed, it is not by chance that social democracy and welfare states have worked best in small, homogeneous countries, where issues of mistrust and mutual suspicion do not arise so acutely. A willingness to pay for other people's services and benefits rests upon the understanding that they in turn will do likewise for you and your children: because they are like you and see the world as you do.

Conversely, where immigration and visible minorities have altered the demography of a country, we typically find increased suspicion of others and a loss of enthusiasm for the institutions of the welfare state. Finally, it is incontrovertible that social democracy and the welfare states face serious practical challenges today. Their survival is not in question, but they are no longer as self-confident as they once appeared.

But my concern tonight is the following: Why is it that here in the United States we have such difficulty even *imagining* a different sort of society from the one whose dysfunctions and inequalities trouble us so? We appear to have lost the capacity to question the present, much less offer alternatives to it. Why is it so beyond us to conceive of a different set of arrangements to our common advantage?

Our shortcoming—forgive the academic jargon—is *discursive*. We simply do not know how to talk about these things. To understand why this should be the case, some history is in order: as Keynes once observed, "A study of the history of opinion is a necessary preliminary to the emancipation of the mind." For the purposes of mental emancipation this evening, I propose that we take a minute to study the history of a prejudice: the universal contemporary resort to "economism," the invocation of economics in all discussions of public affairs.

For the last thirty years, in much of the English-speaking world (though less so in continental Europe and elsewhere), when asking ourselves whether we support a proposal or initiative, we have not asked, is it good or bad? Instead we inquire: Is it efficient? Is it productive? Would it benefit gross domestic product? Will it contribute to growth? This propensity to avoid moral considerations, to restrict ourselves to issues of profit and loss—economic questions in the narrowest sense—is not an instinctive human condition. It is an acquired taste.

We have been here before. In 1905 the young William Beveridge—whose 1942 report would lay the foundations of the British welfare state—delivered a lecture at Oxford in which he asked why it was that political philosophy had been obscured in public debates by classical economics. Beveridge's question applies with equal force today. Note, however, that this eclipse of political thought bears no relation to the writings of the great classical economists themselves. In the eighteenth century, what Adam Smith called "moral sentiments" were uppermost in economic conversations.

Indeed, the thought that we might restrict public policy considerations to a mere economic calculus was already a source of concern. The Marquis de Condorcet, one of the most perceptive writers on commercial capitalism in its early years, anticipated with distaste the prospect that "liberty will be no more, in the eyes of an avid nation, than the necessary condition for the security of financial operations." The revolutions of the age risked fostering a confusion between the freedom to make money . . . and freedom itself. But how did we, in our own time, come to think in exclusively economic terms? The fascination with an etiolated economic vocabulary did not come out of nowhere.

ON THE CONTRARY, we live in the long shadow of a debate with which most people are altogether unfamiliar. If we ask who exercised the greatest influence over contemporary Anglophone economic thought, five foreign-born thinkers spring to mind: Ludwig von Mises, Friedrich Hayek, Joseph Schumpeter, Karl Popper, and Peter Drucker. The first two were the outstanding "grandfathers" of the Chicago School of free-market macroeconomics. Schumpeter is best known for his enthusiastic description of the "creative, destructive" powers of capitalism, Popper for his defense of the "open society" and his theory of totalitarianism. As for Drucker, his writings on management exercised enormous influence over the theory and practice of business in the prosperous decades of the postwar boom.

Three of these men were born in Vienna, a fourth (von Mises) in Austrian Lemberg (now Lvov), the fifth (Schumpeter) in Moravia, a few dozen miles north of the imperial capital. All were profoundly shaken by the interwar catastrophe that struck their native Austria. Following the cataclysm of World War I and a brief Socialist municipal experiment in Vienna, the country fell to a reactionary coup in 1934 and then, four years later, to the Nazi invasion and occupation.

All were forced into exile by these events and all—Hayek in particular—were to cast their writings and teachings in the shadow of the central question of their lifetime: Why had liberal society collapsed and given way—at least in the Austrian case—to Fascism? Their answer: the unsuccessful attempts of the (Marxist) left to introduce into post-1918 Austria state-directed planning, municipally owned services, and collectivized economic activity had not only proven delusionary, but had led directly to a counterreaction.

The European tragedy had thus been brought about by the failure of the *Left*: first to achieve its objectives and then to defend itself and its liberal heritage. Each, albeit in contrasting keys, drew the same conclusion: the best way to defend liberalism, the best defense of an open society and its attendant freedoms, was to keep government far away from economic life. If the state was held at a safe distance, if politicians—however well-intentioned—were barred from planning, manipulating, or directing the affairs of their fellow citizens, then extremists of Right and Left alike would be kept at bay.

The same challenge—how to understand what had happened between the wars and prevent its recurrence—was confronted by John Maynard Keynes. The great English economist, born in 1883 (the same year as Schumpeter), grew up in a stable, confident, prosperous, and powerful Britain. And then, from his privileged perch at the treasury and as a participant in the Versailles peace negotiations, he watched his world collapse, taking with it all the reassuring certainties of his culture and class. Keynes, too, would ask himself the question that Hayek and his Austrian colleagues had posed. But he offered a very different answer.

Yes, Keynes acknowledged, the disintegration of late Victorian Europe was the defining experience of his lifetime. Indeed, the essence of his contributions to economic theory was his insistence upon *uncertainty*: in contrast to the confident nostrums of classical and neoclassical economics, Keynes would insist upon the essential unpredictability of human affairs. If there was a lesson to be drawn from depression, Fascism, and war, it was this: uncertainty—elevated to the level of insecurity and collective fear—was the corrosive force that had threatened and might again threaten the liberal world.

Thus Keynes sought an increased role for the social security state, including but not confined to countercyclical economic intervention. Hayek proposed the opposite. In his 1944 classic, *The Road to Serfdom*, he wrote:

> No description in general terms can give an adequate idea of the similarity of much of current English political literature to the works which destroyed the belief in Western civilization in Germany, and created the state of mind in which naziism could become successful.

In other words, Hayek explicitly projected a Fascist outcome should Labour win power in England. And indeed, Labour did win. But it went on to implement policies many of which were directly identified with Keynes. For the next three decades, Great Britain (like much of the Western world) was governed in the light of Keynes's concerns.

SINCE THEN, as we know, the Austrians have had their revenge. Quite why this should have happened—and happened where it did—is an interesting question for another occasion. But for whatever reason, we are today living out the dim echo—like light from a fading star—of a debate conducted seventy years ago by men born for the most part in the late nineteenth century. To be sure, the economic terms in which we are encouraged to think are not conventionally associated with these far-off political disagreements. And yet without an understanding of the latter, it is as though we speak a language we do not fully comprehend.

The welfare state had remarkable achievements to its credit. In some countries it was Social Democratic, grounded in an ambitious program of socialist legislation; in others—Great Britain, for example—it amounted to a series of pragmatic policies aimed at alleviating disadvantage and reducing extremes of wealth and indigence. The common theme and universal accomplishment of the neo-Keynesian governments of the postwar era was their remarkable success in curbing inequality. If you compare the gap separating rich and poor, whether by income or assets, in all continental European countries along with Great Britain and the United States, you will see that it shrinks dramatically in the generation following 1945.

With greater equality there came other benefits. Over time, the fear of a return to extremist politics—the politics of desperation, the politics of envy, the politics of insecurity—abated. The Western industrialized world entered a halcyon era of prosperous security: a bubble, perhaps, but a comforting bubble in which most people did far better than they could ever have hoped in the past and had good reason to anticipate the future with confidence.

The paradox of the welfare state, and indeed of all the Social Democratic (and Christian Democratic) states of Europe, was quite simply that their success would over time undermine their appeal. The generation that remembered the 1930s was understandably the most committed to preserving institutions and systems of taxation, social service, and public provision that they saw as bulwarks against a return to the horrors of the past. But their successors—even in Sweden—began to forget why they had sought such security in the first place.

It was social democracy that bound the middle classes to liberal institutions in the wake of World War II (I use "middle class" here in the European sense). They received in many cases the same welfare assistance and services as the poor: free education, cheap or free medical treatment, public pensions, and the like. In consequence, the European middle class found itself by the 1960s with far greater disposable incomes than ever before, with so many of life's necessities prepaid in tax. And thus the very class that had been so exposed to fear and insecurity in the interwar years was now tightly woven into the postwar democratic consensus.

By the late 1970s, however, such considerations were increasingly neglected.

Starting with the tax and employment reforms of the Thatcher-Reagan years, and followed in short order by deregulation of the financial sector, inequality has once again become an issue in Western society. After notably diminishing from the 1910s through the 1960s, the inequality index has steadily grown over the course of the past three decades.

In the United States today, the "Gini coefficient"—a measure of the distance separating rich and poor—is comparable to that of China.[1] When we consider that China is a developing country where huge gaps will inevitably open up between the wealthy few and the impoverished many, the fact that here in the United States we have a similar inequality coefficient says much about how far we have fallen behind our earlier aspirations.

Consider the 1996 Personal Responsibility and Work Opportunity Act (a more Orwellian title would be hard to conceive), the Clinton-era legislation that sought to gut welfare provision here in the United States. The terms of this act should put us in mind of another act, passed in England nearly two centuries ago: the New Poor Law of 1834. The provisions of the New Poor Law are familiar to us, thanks to Charles Dickens's depiction of its workings in *Oliver Twist*. When Noah Claypole famously sneers at little Oliver, calling him "Work'us" ("Workhouse"), he is implying, for 1838, precisely what we convey today when we speak disparagingly of "welfare queens."

The New Poor Law was an outrage, forcing the indigent and the unemployed to choose between work at any wage, however low, and the humiliation of the workhouse. Here and in most other forms of nineteenth-century public assistance (still thought of and described as "charity"), the level of aid and support was calibrated so as to be less appealing than the worst available alternative. This system drew on classical economic theories that denied the very possibility of unemployment in an efficient market: if wages fell low enough and there was no attractive alternative to work, everyone would find a job.

For the next 150 years, reformers strove to replace such demeaning practices. In due course, the New Poor Law and its foreign analogues were succeeded by the public provision of assistance as a matter of right. Workless citizens were no longer deemed any the less deserving for that; they were not penalized for their condition nor were implicit aspersions cast upon their good standing as members of society. More than anything else, the welfare states of the mid-twentieth century established the profound impropriety of defining civic status as a function of economic participation.

In the contemporary United States, at a time of growing unemployment, a jobless man or woman is not a full member of the community. In order to receive even the exiguous welfare payments available, they must first have sought and, where applicable, accepted employment at whatever wage is on offer, however low the pay and distasteful the work. Only then are they entitled to the consideration and assistance of their fellow citizens.

Why do so few of us condemn such "reforms"—enacted under a Democratic president? Why are we so unmoved by the stigma attaching to their victims? Far from questioning this reversion to the practices of early industrial capitalism, we have adapted all too well and in consensual silence—in revealing contrast to an earlier generation. But then, as Tolstoy reminds us, there are "no conditions of life to which a man cannot get accustomed, especially if he sees them accepted by *everyone* around him."

This "disposition to admire, and almost to worship, the rich and the powerful, and to despise, or, at least, to neglect persons of poor and mean condition . . . is . . . the great and most universal cause of the corruption of our moral sentiments." Those are not my words. They were written by Adam Smith, who regarded the likelihood that we would come to admire wealth and despise poverty, admire success and scorn failure, as the greatest risk facing us in the commercial society whose advent he predicted. It is now upon us.

THE MOST REVEALING INSTANCE of the kind of problem we face comes in a form that may strike many of you as a mere technicality: the process of privatization. In the last thirty years, a cult of privatization has mesmerized Western (and many non-Western) governments. Why? The shortest response is that, in an age of budgetary constraints, privatization appears to save money. If the state owns an inefficient public program or an expensive public service—a waterworks, a car factory, a railway—it seeks to offload it onto private buyers.

The sale duly earns money for the state. Meanwhile, by entering the private sector, the service or operation in question becomes more efficient thanks to the working of the profit motive. Everyone benefits: the service improves, the state rids itself of an inappropriate and poorly managed responsibility, investors profit, and the public sector makes a one-time gain from the sale.

So much for the theory. The practice is very different. What we have been watching these past decades is the steady shifting of public responsibility onto the private sector to no discernible collective advantage. In the first place, privatization is inefficient. Most of the things that governments have seen fit to pass into the private sector were operating at a loss: whether they were railway companies, coal mines, postal services, or energy utilities, they cost more to provide and maintain than they could ever hope to attract in revenue.

For just this reason, such public goods were inherently unattractive to private buyers unless offered at a steep discount. But when the state sells cheap, the public takes a loss. It has been calculated that, in the course of the Thatcher-era UK privatizations, the deliberately low price at which long-standing public assets were marketed to the private sector resulted in a net transfer of £14 billion from the taxpaying public to stockholders and other investors.

To this loss should be added a further £3 billion in fees to the banks that transacted the privatizations. Thus the state in effect paid the private sector some £17 billion ($30 billion) to facilitate the sale of assets for which there would otherwise have been no takers. These are significant sums of money—approximating the endowment of Harvard University, for example, or the annual gross domestic product of Paraguay or Bosnia-Herzegovina.[2] This can hardly be construed as an efficient use of public resources.

In the second place, there arises the question of moral hazard. The only reason that private investors are willing to purchase apparently inefficient public goods is because the state eliminates or reduces their exposure to risk. In the case of the London Underground, for example, the purchasing companies were assured that whatever happened they would be protected against serious loss—thereby undermining the classic economic case for privatization: that the profit motive encourages efficiency. The "hazard" in question is that the private sector, under such privileged conditions, will prove at least as inefficient as its public counterpart—while creaming off such profits as are to be made and charging losses to the state.

The third and perhaps most telling case against privatization is this. There can be no doubt that many of the goods and services that the state seeks to divest have been badly run: incompetently managed, underinvested, etc. Nevertheless, however badly run, postal services, railway networks, retirement homes, prisons, and other provisions targeted for privatization remain the responsibility of the public authorities. Even after they are sold, they cannot be left entirely to the vagaries of the market. They are inherently the sort of activity that *someone* has to regulate.

THIS SEMIPRIVATE, SEMIPUBLIC DISPOSITION of essentially collective responsibilities returns us to a very old story indeed. If your tax returns are audited in the United States today, although it is the government that has decided to investigate you, the investigation itself will very likely be conducted by a private company. The latter has contracted to perform the service on the state's behalf, in much the same way that private agents have contracted with Washington to provide security, transportation, and technical know-how (at a profit) in Iraq and elsewhere. In a similar way, the British government today contracts with private entrepreneurs to provide residential care services for the elderly—a responsibility once controlled by the state.

Governments, in short, farm out their responsibilities to private firms that claim to administer them more cheaply and better than the state can itself. In the eighteenth century this was called tax farming. Early modern governments often lacked the means to collect taxes and thus invited bids from private individuals to undertake the task. The highest bidder would get the job, and was free—once he had paid the agreed sum—to collect whatever he could and retain the proceeds. The government thus took a discount on its anticipated tax revenue, in return for cash up front.

After the fall of the monarchy in France, it was widely conceded that tax farming was grotesquely inefficient. In the first place, it discredits the state, represented in the popular mind by a grasping private profiteer. Second, it generates considerably less revenue than an efficiently administered system of government collection, if only because of the profit margin accruing to the private collector. And third, you get disgruntled taxpayers.

In the United States today, we have a discredited state and inadequate public resources. Interestingly, we do not have disgruntled taxpayers—or, at least, they are usually disgruntled for the wrong reasons. Nevertheless, the problem we have created for ourselves is essentially comparable to that which faced the ancien régime.

As in the eighteenth century, so today: by eviscerating the state's responsibilities and capacities, we have diminished its public standing. The outcome is "gated communities," in every sense of the word: subsections of society that fondly suppose themselves functionally independent of the collectivity and its public servants. If we deal uniquely or overwhelmingly with private agencies, then over time we dilute our relationship with a public sector for which we have no apparent use. It doesn't much matter whether the private sector does the same things better or worse, at higher or lower cost. In either event, we have diminished our allegiance to the state and lost something vital that we ought to share—and in many cases used to share—with our fellow citizens.

This process was well described by one of its greatest modern practitioners: Margaret Thatcher reportedly asserted that "there is no such thing as society. There are only individual men and women and families." But if there is no such thing as society, merely individuals and the "night watchman" state— overseeing from afar activities in which it plays no part—then what will bind us together? We already accept the existence of private police forces, private mail services, private agencies provisioning the state in war, and much else besides. We have "privatized" precisely those responsibilities that the modern state laboriously took upon itself in the course of the nineteenth and early twentieth centuries.

What, then, will serve as a buffer between citizens and the state? Surely not "society," hard pressed to survive the evisceration of the public domain. For the state is not about to wither away. Even if we strip it of all its service attributes, it will still be with us—if only as a force for control and repression. Between state and individuals there would then be no intermediate institutions or allegiances: nothing would remain of the spider's web of reciprocal services and obligations that bind citizens to one another via the public space they collectively occupy. All that would be left is private persons and corporations seeking competitively to hijack the state for their own advantage.

The consequences are no more attractive today than they were before the modern state arose. Indeed, the impetus to state building as we have known it derived quite explicitly from the understanding that no collection of individuals can survive long without shared purposes and common institutions. The very notion that private advantage could be multiplied to public benefit was already palpably absurd to the liberal critics of nascent industrial capitalism. In the words of John Stuart Mill, "the idea is essentially repulsive of a society only held together by the relations and feelings arising out of pecuniary interests."

WHAT, THEN, is to be done? We have to begin with the state: as the incarnation of collective interests, collective purposes, and collective goods. If we cannot learn to "think the state" once again, we shall not get very far. But what precisely should the state do? Minimally, it should not duplicate unnecessarily: as Keynes wrote, "The important thing for Government is not to do things which individuals are doing already, and to do them a little better or a little worse; but to do those things which at present are not done at all." And we know from the bitter experience of the past century that there are some things that states should most certainly *not* be doing.

The twentieth-century narrative of the progressive state rested precariously upon the conceit that "we"—reformers, Socialists, radicals—had History on our side: that our projects, in the words of the late Bernard Williams, were "being cheered on by the universe."[3] Today, we have no such reassuring story to tell. We have just survived a century of doctrines purporting with alarming confidence to say what the state should do and to remind individuals—forcibly if necessary—that the state knows what is good for them. We cannot return to all that. So if we are to "think the state" once more, we had better begin with a sense of its limits.

For similar reasons, it would be futile to resurrect the rhetoric of early-twentieth-century social democracy. In those years, the democratic left emerged as an alternative to the more uncompromising varieties of Marxist revolutionary Socialism and—in later years—to their Communist successor. Inherent in social democracy there was thus a curious schizophrenia. While marching confidently forward into a better future, it was constantly glancing nervously over its left shoulder. *We*, it seems to say, are not authoritarian. *We* are for freedom, not repression. *We* are democrats who also believe in social justice, regulated markets, and so forth.

So long as the primary objective of Social Democrats was to convince voters that they were a respectable radical choice within the liberal polity, this defensive stance made sense. But today such rhetoric is incoherent. It is not by chance that a Christian Democrat like Angela Merkel can win an election in Germany against her social democratic opponents—even at the height of a financial crisis—with a set of policies that in all its important essentials resembles their own program.

Social democracy, in one form or another, is the prose of contemporary European politics. There are very few European politicians, and certainly fewer still in positions of influence, who would dissent from core social democratic assumptions about the duties of the state, however much they might differ as to their scope. Consequently, Social Democrats in today's Europe have nothing distinctive to offer: in France, for example, even their unreflective disposition to favor state ownership hardly distinguishes them from the Colbertian instincts of the Gaullist right. Social democracy needs to rethink its purposes.

The problem lies not in social democratic policies, but in the language in which they are couched. Since the authoritarian challenge from the Left has lapsed, the emphasis upon "democracy" is largely redundant. We are all democrats today. But "social" still means something—arguably more now than some decades back when a role for the public sector was uncontentiously conceded by all sides. What, then, is distinctive about the "social" in the social democratic approach to politics?

IMAGINE, IF YOU WILL, a railway station. A real railway station, not New York's Pennsylvania Station: a failed 1960s-era shopping mall stacked above a coal cellar. I mean something like Waterloo Station in London, the Gare de l'Est in Paris, Mumbai's dramatic Victoria Terminus, or Berlin's magnificent new Hauptbahnhof. In these remarkable cathedrals of modern life, the private sector functions perfectly well in its place: there is no reason, after all, why newsstands or coffee bars should be run by the state. Anyone who can recall the desiccated, plastic-wrapped sandwiches of British Railway's cafés will concede that competition in this arena is to be encouraged.

But you cannot run trains competitively. Railways—like agriculture or the mails—are at one and the same time an economic activity and an essential public good. Moreover, you cannot render a railway system more efficient by placing two trains on a track and waiting to see which performs better: railways are a natural monopoly. Implausibly, the English have actually instituted such competition among bus services. But the paradox of public transport, of course, is that the better it does its job, the less "efficient" it may be.

A bus that provides an express service for those who can afford it and avoids remote villages where it would be boarded only by the occasional pensioner will make more money for its owner. But someone—the state or the

local municipality—must still provide the unprofitable, inefficient local service. In its absence, the short-term economic benefits of cutting the provision
will be offset by long-term damage to the community at large. Predictably,
therefore, the consequences of "competitive" buses—except in London where
there is enough demand to go around—have been an increase in costs assigned to the public sector, a sharp rise in fares to the level that the market can
bear, and attractive profits for the express bus companies.

Trains, like buses, are above all a *social* service. Anyone could run a profitable rail line if all they had to do was shunt expresses back and forth from
London to Edinburgh, Paris to Marseilles, Boston to Washington. But what of
rail links to and from places where people take the train only occasionally? No
single person is going to set aside sufficient funds to pay the economic cost of
supporting such a service for the infrequent occasions when he uses it. Only
the collectivity—the state, the government, the local authorities—can do this.
The subsidy required will always appear inefficient in the eyes of a certain sort
of economist: surely it would be cheaper to rip up the tracks and let everyone
use their car?

In 1996, the last year before Britain's railways were privatized, British Rail
boasted the lowest public subsidy for a railway in Europe. In that year the
French were planning for their railways an investment rate of £21 per head of
population; the Italians £33; the British just £9.[4] These contrasts were accurately reflected in the quality of the service provided by the respective national
systems. They also explain why the British rail network could be privatized
only at great loss, so inadequate was its infrastructure.

But the investment contrast illustrates my point. The French and the Italians have long treated their railways as a social provision. Running a train to a
remote region, however cost-ineffective, sustains local communities. It reduces
environmental damage by providing an alternative to road transport. The railway station and the service it provides are thus a symptom and symbol of society as a shared aspiration.

I suggested above that the provision of train service to remote districts makes social sense even if it is economically "inefficient." But this, of course, begs an important question. Social Democrats will not get very far by proposing laudable social objectives that they themselves concede to cost more than the alternatives. We would end up acknowledging the virtues of social services, decrying their expense . . . and doing nothing. We need to rethink the devices we employ to assess all costs: social and economic alike.

Let me offer an example. It is cheaper to provide benevolent handouts to the poor than to guarantee them a full range of social services as of right. By "benevolent" I mean faith-based charity, private or independent initiative, income-dependent assistance in the form of food stamps, housing grants, clothing subsidies, and so on. But it is notoriously humiliating to be on the receiving end of that kind of assistance. The "means test" applied by the British authorities to victims of the 1930s depression is still recalled with distaste and even anger by an older generation.[5]

Conversely, it is not humiliating to be on the receiving end of a right. If you are entitled to unemployment payments, pension, disability, municipal housing, or any other publicly furnished assistance as of right—without anyone investigating to determine whether you have sunk low enough to "deserve" help—then you will not be embarrassed to accept it. However, such universal rights and entitlements are expensive.

But what if we treated humiliation itself as a cost, a charge to society? What if we decided to "quantify" the harm done when people are shamed by their fellow citizens before receiving the mere necessities of life? In other words, what if we factored into our estimates of productivity, efficiency, or well-being the difference between a humiliating handout and a benefit as of right? We might conclude that the provision of universal social services, public health insurance, or subsidized public transportation was actually a cost-effective way to achieve our common objectives. Such an exercise is inherently contentious: How do we quantify "humiliation"? What is the measurable cost of depriving isolated citizens of access to metropolitan resources? How much are we willing to pay for a good society? Unclear. But unless we ask such questions, how can we hope to devise answers?[6]

—————

WHAT DO WE MEAN when we speak of a "good society"? From a normative perspective we might begin with a moral "narrative" in which to situate our collective choices. Such a narrative would then substitute for the narrowly economic terms that constrain our present conversations. But defining our general purposes in that way is no simple matter.

In the past, social democracy unquestionably concerned itself with issues of right and wrong: all the more so because it inherited a pre-Marxist ethical vocabulary infused with Christian distaste for extremes of wealth and the worship of materialism. But such considerations were frequently trumped by ideological interrogations. Was capitalism doomed? If so, did a given policy advance its anticipated demise or risk postponing it? If capitalism was not doomed, then policy choices would have to be conceived from a different perspective. In either case the relevant question typically addressed the prospects of "the system" rather than the inherent virtues or defects of a given initiative. Such questions no longer preoccupy us. We are thus more directly confronted with the ethical implications of our choices.

What precisely is it that we find abhorrent in financial capitalism, or "commercial society" as the eighteenth century had it? What do we find instinctively amiss in our present arrangements and what can we do about them? What do we find unfair? What is it that offends our sense of propriety when faced with unrestrained lobbying by the wealthy at the expense of everyone else? What have we lost?

The answers to such questions should take the form of a moral critique of the inadequacies of the unrestricted market or the feckless state. We need to understand *why* they offend our sense of justice or equity. We need, in short, to return to the kingdom of ends. Here social democracy is of limited assistance, for its own response to the dilemmas of capitalism was merely a belated expression of Enlightenment moral discourse applied to "the social question." Our problems are rather different.

We are entering, I believe, a new age of insecurity. The last such era, memorably analyzed by Keynes in *The Economic Consequences of the Peace* (1919), followed decades of prosperity and progress and a dramatic increase in the internationalization of life: "globalization" in all but name. As Keynes describes it, the commercial economy had spread around the world. Trade and communication were accelerating at an unprecedented rate. Before 1914, it was widely asserted that the logic of peaceful economic exchange would triumph over national self-interest. No one expected all this to come to an abrupt end. But it did.

We, too, have lived through an era of stability, certainty, and the illusion of indefinite economic improvement. But all that is now behind us. For the foreseeable future we shall be as economically insecure as we are culturally uncertain. We are assuredly less confident of our collective purposes, our environmental well-being, or our personal safety than at any time since World War II. We have no idea what sort of world our children will inherit, but we can no longer delude ourselves into supposing that it must resemble our own in reassuring ways.

We must revisit the ways in which our grandparents' generation responded to comparable challenges and threats. Social democracy in Europe, the New Deal, and the Great Society here in the United States were explicit responses to the insecurities and inequities of the age. Few in the West are old enough to know just what it means to watch our world collapse.[7] We find it hard to conceive of a complete breakdown of liberal institutions, an utter disintegration of the democratic consensus. But it was just such a breakdown that elicited the Keynes–Hayek debate and from which the Keynesian consensus and the social democratic compromise were born: the consensus and the compromise in which we grew up and whose appeal has been obscured by its very success.

If social democracy has a future, it will be as a social democracy of fear.[8] Rather than seeking to restore a language of optimistic progress, we should begin by reacquainting ourselves with the recent past. The first task of radical dissenters today is to remind their audience of the achievements of the twentieth century, along with the likely consequences of our heedless rush to dismantle them.

The Left, to be quite blunt about it, has something to conserve. It is the *Right* that has inherited the ambitious modernist urge to destroy and innovate in the name of a universal project. Social Democrats, characteristically modest in style and ambition, need to speak more assertively of past gains. The rise of the social service state, the century-long construction of a public sector whose goods and services illustrate and promote our collective identity and common purposes, the institution of welfare as a matter of right and its provision as a social duty: these were no mean accomplishments.

That these accomplishments were no more than partial should not trouble us. If we have learned nothing else from the twentieth century, we should at least have grasped that the more perfect the answer, the more terrifying its consequences. Imperfect improvements upon unsatisfactory circumstances are the best that we can hope for, and probably all we should seek. Others have spent the last three decades methodically unraveling and destabilizing those same improvements: this should make us much angrier than we are. It ought also to worry us, if only on prudential grounds: Why have we been in such a hurry to tear down the dikes laboriously set in place by our predecessors? Are we so sure that there are no floods to come?

A social democracy of fear is something to fight for. To abandon the labors of a century is to betray those who came before us as well as generations yet to come. It would be pleasing—but misleading—to report that social democracy, or something like it, represents the future that we would paint for ourselves in an ideal world. It does not even represent the ideal past. But among the options available to us in the present, it is better than anything else to hand. In Orwell's words, reflecting in *Homage to Catalonia* upon his recent experiences in revolutionary Barcelona:

> There was much in it that I did not understand, in some ways I did not even like it, but I recognized it immediately as a state of affairs worth fighting for.

I believe this to be no less true of whatever we can retrieve from the twentieth-century memory of social democracy.

This essay was adapted from Tony Judt's last public lecture, given at New York University on October 19, 2009. A video of the lecture can be found on the Web site of the Remarque Institute: remarque.as.nyu.edu/object/io_1256242927496.html.

NOTES TO CHAPTER XXIV

[1] See "High Gini Is Loosed Upon Asia," *The Economist*, August 11, 2007.

[2] See Massimo Florio, *The Great Divestiture: Evaluating the Welfare Impact of the British Privatizations, 1979–1997* (Cambridge, MA: MIT Press, 2004), p. 163. For Harvard, see "Harvard Endowment Posts Solid Positive Return," *Harvard Gazette*, September 12, 2008. For the GDP of Paraguay or Bosnia-Herzegovina, see www.cia.gov/library/publications/the-world-factbook/geos/xx.html.

[3] Bernard Williams, *Philosophy as a Humanistic Discipline* (Princeton, NJ: Princeton University Press, 2006), p. 144.

[4] For these figures see my "'Twas a Famous Victory," *The New York Review*, July 19, 2001.

[5] For comparable recollections of humiliating handouts, see *The Autobiography of Malcolm X* (New York: Ballantine, 1987). I am grateful to Casey Selwyn for pointing this out to me.

[6] The international Commission on Measurement of Economic Performance and Social Progress, chaired by Joseph Stiglitz and advised by Amartya Sen, recently recommended a different approach to measuring collective well-being. But despite the admirable originality of their proposals, neither Stiglitz nor Sen went much beyond suggesting better ways to assess economic performance; noneconomic concerns did not figure prominently in their report. See www.stiglitz-sen-fitoussi.fr/en/index.htm.

[7] The exception, of course, is Bosnia, whose citizens are all too well aware of just what such a collapse entails.

[8] By analogy with "The Liberalism of Fear," Judith Shklar's penetrating essay on political inequality and power.

CHAPTER XXV

Generations in the Balance

With Daniel Judt

DANIEL: Had I been eighteen in November 2008, I would have voted for Barack Obama. However, being fourteen, I settled for voicing my support for him and expressing joy at his election. I believed, innocently, that his administration would put its foot down, stamping out the environmental crisis that his predecessors had allowed to fester unnoticed. I felt Mr. Obama knew how to do the right thing morally, even if it meant going against the "right thing" politically.

Less than two years later, I have become hugely pessimistic about the moral resolve of ourgovernment and corporate world. Deepwater Horizon has been the tipping point. I was already skeptical: an increase in offshore drilling, our government's passive stance at Copenhagen, and the absence of any environmental legislation saw to that.

But BP made me realize that the generation in office just doesn't get it. They see the environmental crisis in the same light as they see political debacles and economic woes. Politics pass and economies rebound, but the environment doesn't. It's that sense of "We'll get that done right after we have dealt with everything else" that makes me so angry. The world is not an expendable resource; fixing the damage you have inflicted will be the issue for my generation. It is that simple.

TONY: Well, I am sixty-two and I did vote for Barack Obama. I held out no great hopes. It was clear from the outset that this was someone who would concede rather than confront—and that's a shortcoming in a politician, if not in a man. We have seen the consequences: not in the Middle East, nor in economic regulation, nor over detainees, nor in immigration reform has Mr. Obama followed through. *The audacity of hope?*

As for the corporations, we baby boomers were right to be cynical. Like Goldman Sachs, oil companies are not benign economic agents, serving a need and taking a cut. They are, in Theodore Roosevelt's words, "malefactors of great wealth." But our cynicism dulled our response to truly criminal behavior: "They would do that, wouldn't they?" It is one thing to watch while Goldman Sachs pillages the economy, quite another to be invited to stand aside while BP violates the Gulf Coast. Yes, we should be a lot angrier than we are.

We are staring into our future and it does not work. The gush of filth is a reminder that we have surrendered our independence to a technology we cannot master. Our energies are misdirected to expensive foreign wars whose purposes grow ever more obscure. We rail at one another in "cultural" clashes irrelevant to our real problems.

Meanwhile, the clockwork precision of our classical constitution has ground to a halt—depending as it does on a consensus that no longer exists. Taking the long view, this is how republics die. "Someone" clearly has to do "something." What do you propose?

DANIEL: Just as you are too forgiving of unacceptable corporate behavior, maybe you are too resigned politically. To actually effect change, you need to come in thinking that real change is possible. My generation saw things that way; that is why so many young people supported Mr. Obama. Perhaps more than any other constituency in the United States, we believed that engagement would make things happen. But the more we are told that crises are to be expected and cannot be prevented by those in power—that we must put our faith in God, as the president advised on Tuesday—the more our faith in government slips away.

Politicians depend on the public: given a strong enough consensus, they will act. That's what I would have had you do—and that's what we have to do now: build a consensus and act. Your generation talked a lot about engagement. So engage. Use the lever of public opinion to force strong environmental legislation.

In reconciling ourselves after BP to "getting back to normal," we will have missed a vital opportunity. We need a new "normal." And we need to ask ourselves new questions: not whether we can afford to invest in a different way of life—solar energy, mass transportation, the phasing out of our dependency on oil—but how long we can afford not to. You owe us this.

TONY: I am a little queasy about all this generation talk. After all, I am the same age as Bill Clinton and George W. Bush, but I take no responsibility for them. Actually, while I agree that we need to build a national consensus, I don't think the challenge is to convince Americans about pollution or even climate change. Nor is it just a matter of getting them to make sacrifices for the future. The challenge is to convince them once again of how much they could do if they came together.

But that requires leadership—and I can't help noticing that you rather let the president off the hook. After all, if you and your contemporaries have lost faith in the man and "the system," that's partly his fault. But you, too, have a responsibility.

Coming together to elect someone is not enough, if you then go back to texting and Twittering. You have to stay together, know what you want and fight for it. It won't work the first time and it won't work perfectly, but you can't give up. That, too, is politics.

You are wrong to think that I have lost faith in government. Big government built this country. Without it there would have been no transcontinental railroad. Land-grant colleges—the glory of American public education—

were the work of the Morrill Acts of 1862 and 1890. The nation invested substantial sums of money for the public good: remember the Marshall Plan, the G.I. Bill and the interstate highways, without which our postwar economy could never have boomed as it did. And don't forget the Civil Rights Act: a hugely controversial moral revolution that took great political courage.

I have not lost faith in government—but I worry about whether today's politicians are up to the challenge.

DANIEL: You're right—I do let the president off a little. But to have so many young people help elect a government after years of skepticism is no small feat. He almost single-handedly instilled political vigor in those of us who knew only shame over the previous administration. Without that surge of hope and thirst for action it is very possible that most members of my generation would have abandoned politics in disgust before they even began. For that mobilization, we have Mr. Obama to thank.

Of course he deserves criticism. But what we must not do—both as a generation and as a nation—is to let our disillusion devolve into pessimism and laziness. What we now face is a moral challenge from which we cannot back down.

I was afraid that in your skepticism you had lost faith and given up—you have to admit that the radicalism of your generation never quite lived up to its potential. You always say that politics is "the art of the possible": but if we could turn our anger into positive action, then surely the possible becomes a whole lot more probable. Is anger a wise guide to action? Admittedly, if used for the wrong causes or taken the wrong way, it can be disastrous. But isn't it better than sitting back and complaining while we are led over the edge?

TONY: Yes, it is not beyond us to sacrifice in the present for long-term advantage, to set aside the pursuit of quarterly economic growth as the supreme goal of public policy. We offer ourselves easy choices—high taxation or free markets—and are then surprised to learn that they do not speak to our needs.

Technological fixes are the hubris of our time. But as the folks at BP have helpfully demonstrated, there is a limit to how many caps you can put on a leak; sometimes you need to start afresh.

The challenge goes beyond oil slicks and moral revulsion. In the bigger picture, big oil has no long-term future: sooner or later the contemptible little sheikdoms that have arisen upon a pool of liquid greed will sink back into the desert. But why should BP and the emirs script the endgame? Nothing man-made is inevitable: Chinese capitalism—unregulated profit accompanied by serial environmental catastrophe—is not the only possible future.

The president spoke on Tuesday of pressing forward with congressional legislation. But at the moment that amounts to little more than "cap and trade": a shell game for corporations that has been tried in Europe and already been found wanting.

What we need is a Marshall Plan for the fifty states. Federal money raised from defense savings and, yes, taxes—a loan to our successors—should be made available on condition it is spent on public infrastructure, mass transit, renewable energy, and education. Anything less is unworthy of the crisis that a 60,000-barrel-a-day leak has unleashed. Are you up to it? If you want to change the world, you had better be willing to fight for a long time. And there will be sacrifices. Do you really care enough or are you just offended at disturbing pictures?

DANIEL: We have no choice but to care enough. The sacrifices you foresee are nothing compared to the ones we will be forced to make if we sit back and wait. Most important, we don't have the luxury of fighting for a long time.

Look, we are powerless and will be for a while to come. In fact, we are in the worst possible position: we are old enough to understand better than you what has to be done, but far too young to do it. All we can do is say it.

This exchange first appeared in *The New York Times* in June 2010.

Part Five

In the Long Run
We Are All Dead

CHAPTER XXVI

François Furet
(1927–1997)

François Furet, who died on July 12 this year at the age of seventy, was one of the most influential men in contemporary France. This may seem a strange observation to make of someone who spent much of his life teaching in universities and whose writings consisted for the most part of a series of scholarly studies of the French Revolution. It is a tribute to Furet, and an illustration of the enduring place of the intellectual in modern French culture, that his influence was so very great.

But François Furet was no ordinary intellectual, and no ordinary historian. In his younger days, like so many other French historians and writers of his generation, he was a member of the French Communist Party. He left the Party in 1956, resigning in protest at the Soviet invasion of Hungary; as he would later acknowledge, "It was the most intelligent thing I have ever done." Furet's experience in the French Communist Party shaped his personal and scholarly concerns for the rest of his life. After graduating from the Sorbonne, Furet devoted his academic work to the study of the Revolution of 1789, publishing in 1965 *The French Revolution*, a widely reviewed two-volume general study of the era, written with the late Denis Richet. In this book, Furet approached the history of revolutionary France from the then-fashionable perspective of the Annales School, emphasizing continuities with the French past, especially long-term social and economic processes.

This new study of the revolutionary era was already a radical departure from the accepted contemporary interpretation. In the tradition of Marc Bloch, Lucien Febvre, and Fernand Braudel, the Annales approach, addressing long-lasting underlying structures and paying scant attention to political upheavals, was having a marked impact on the historiography of medieval and early modern France. Interpretation of the events of 1789–1799, however, was heavily influenced by the Marxists who dominated the study of the national revolutionary past after World War II. But in the following two decades, Furet was to go on to publish a series of utterly original essays, quite unlike anything he or others had written before, that have transformed our understanding of France's revolutionary past. In a remarkable series of books, beginning with *Penser la Révolution française* (1978) and culminating in *La Révolution 1770–1880* (1988), Furet destroyed what he himself called the "revolutionary cate-chism": the Marxist and neo-Marxist account of France's revolution as the model and forerunner of bourgeois revolutions everywhere, based on an interpretation of the years 1789–1794 as the classic instance of class conflict.[1]

FURET'S SIGNAL CONTRIBUTION to the interpretation of the French Revolution was this: he removed from the center of our historical concerns the old insistence upon social categories and conflicts, and replaced it with an emphasis upon the political and intellectual debates and outcomes of France's revolutionary past, reminding his readers that the Revolution was above all a radical shift in the balance of philosophical and political power, not of economic class interests. Like Alexis de Tocqueville, Furet appreciated that the men of that era, especially the theorists and spokesmen of the first revolution, from 1789 to 1791—Antoine Barnave, Emmanuel Joseph Sieyès, Jean-Joseph Mounier—were engaged in something dramatically new. Because they needed to justify and make legitimate not only the overthrow of an established authority but also their own claim to replace it, they were obliged to imagine and exploit a new version of the French past, the French state, and the French people, infusing each of these with characteristics appropriate to the ambitions of the new political class that had taken power in France. In short, they had to invent modern politics.

In Furet's hands, then, the French Revolution became once again what it had been in the writings of Mignet, Thiers, Guizot, and the other great liberal historians of the early nineteenth century: a struggle between competing and often incompatible philosophical assertions and political arguments. In this struggle, the French failure by 1792 to secure and agree on a new form of institutional legitimacy gave birth not only to the unstable and self-consuming radicalism of the Jacobin years, but also to the cycle of dictatorship, counter-revolution, authoritarianism, restoration, revolution, and reaction that would characterize French history in the nineteenth century and divide the nation for almost two centuries.

Furet, like Marx, Tocqueville, and the other students of the French past whom he so much admired, stood in some awe of the French revolutionaries, whom they all saw as the founding fathers of modern politics; he refused to believe, however, that they or their followers were merely engaged in the local version of a conflict of classes, or interests, or sexes, whose broader story and meaning was somehow inscribed in History. As he noted in one of his last published essays:

> The grandeur of their adventure, and the secret of its lasting reverberations, comes from their struggle—on the stage of history itself—with the classical philosophical question of their century: how to institute and secure the social contract.[2]

That is a remark that would have seemed obvious to François Guizot and other liberal historians of the Revolution whose reputation Furet did so much to rescue from unjustified neglect; it is a telling commentary on the historiography of a later age that Furet's assertion, and his concerns, seemed so subversive.

IN FRANCE, the appearance of Furet's work coincided with the decline of Marxism as a dominant tendency in French intellectual and scholarly circles, and helped to complete that process. Moreover, by dismantling long-accepted clichés about the social-revolutionary origins of modern France, Furet helped his contemporaries learn to think about politics itself, and the ways in which France is governed now and might be governed in years to come. It was not inscribed in the genetic code of French history, he argued, that the nation must be indefinitely divided between an ideologically myopic Left and an intransigently aggrieved Right. This division no longer described anything real about France: the French Revolution was over. Furet's recasting of our understanding of the French Revolution was itself a significant factor in helping to displace the hitherto omnipresent revolutionary heritage in French political debates. As a result, it is once again possible in France to discuss politics, political philosophy, and the place of the state in society without constant recourse to the old categories: the bourgeoisie, the proletariat, class conflict, the "historical process," revolution versus reform, and so forth.

It should not be inferred from these remarks that François Furet was some kind of political reactionary, exacting revenge upon France's revolutionary inheritance and its scholarly avatars. Unlike the politics of many former Communists, his became and remained resolutely liberal in the classical sense. Like the men of 1791, he thought that a limited state, well-secured rights to property and liberty, and agreement among citizens on the proper nature and place of the institutions of government were not just desirable ends but the best that could prudently be hoped for. And unlike many Frenchmen of later generations, he understood the damage that had been done to his country and its public affairs by the absence of such agreements and such institutions. For Furet, the "revolutionary catechism" was sustained by the dream of an ultimate revolution, a revolution that had been left unfinished by the unhappy events of 1794, the Terror and the Thermidorian reaction. This conception, he thought, was not just a scholarly mistake but a civic handicap, and one he strove to help overcome.

WHATEVER NOW HAPPENS in our understanding of the French past, or in the French present itself, François Furet's achievement is incontrovertible. Nothing will ever be as it was before he came along. If he had just stopped there, Furet would already have made a huge contribution to the study of the European past and to the political culture of his own country.[3] But he did not stop there. For eight years, from 1977 to 1985, Furet was the president of L'École des Hautes Études en Sciences Sociales. Under his presidency the school was intellectually renewed, with many imaginative younger scholars and writers taking their place at the center of French academic and cultural life. Furet also played the leading part in establishing the Institut Raymond Aron. This institute, dedicated to the memory of the country's greatest contemporary social theorist, a man who was much neglected by his French peers during his lifetime, has become the focal point for the rebirth of French liberal thought today.

In recent years Furet's interests had moved further still into the present, and in 1995 he published *Le Passé d'une illusion*, a book-length essay on the twentieth century in the form of a history of the myth of Communism.[4] This polemical tour de force took France by storm. As an account of the Communist mirage in our century Furet's book was not particularly original: he himself acknowledged that Boris Souvarine, Hannah Arendt, and a school of brilliant German refugee scholars such as Franz Borkenau and Franz Neumann before him had said many of the same things. But Furet's genius lay in combining a scholarly survey of contested pasts with a polemical, reasoned argument directed toward the present. Leninism, he argued, transferred to our century the fable of revolutionary renewal and transcendence that the myth of the Great Revolution had bequeathed to France. It was a pathological distortion of Western universalist aspirations; and the voluntary intellectual servitude of its admirers in the West wrought deep and lasting harm to their own societies no less than to those further east where it flourished for so long.

Furet was an effective and economical stylist, and part of the appeal of his book lay in its skillful demolition of the shibboleths of progressive thought in our time. Of postwar intellectual enthusiasm for Tito's Yugoslavia (given a free ride in most histories of Communism), Furet noted: "Here was the exotic land indispensable for imaginative indulgence—after the Russia of the October revolution, now it was the turn of the unfortunate Balkans to be rebaptized as the avant-garde of European society." Of early cold war propaganda that tried to mobilize anti-Fascist sentiment against De Gaulle, Adenauer, and successive U.S. presidents by hinting at their "proto-Fascist" leanings, Furet remarked ruefully that "never has a dishonored regime been accorded so many posthumous incarnations in the imagination of its conquerors."

The book was a great success. A best seller in France and widely read throughout Europe, it is seen by many commentators as having driven the final nail into the coffin of Leninism (in a political culture where the corpse was still warm) by eviscerating a utopian illusion intimately dependent upon the more broadly disseminated idea of revolution in the West of the past two centuries. Furet's reiterated insistence upon the relationship between the myth of the French Revolution and the credit misguidedly accorded its Russian successor offended some of his critics, who thought he had exaggerated his case. But he hadn't. It was the impeccably French and unimpeachably republican Ligue des Droits de l'Homme that in 1936 established a commission to investigate the great Moscow trials of that year. The conclusion to its report perfectly illustrates Furet's argument in *Le Passé d'une illusion* as well as the broader case he had argued for two decades: "It would be a *denial* [my italics] of the French Revolution . . . to refuse [the Russian] people the right to strike down the fomenters of civil war, or conspirators in liaison with foreigners."

FRANÇOIS FURET'S SAD DEATH comes shortly after his election to the Académie Française, establishing him as one of the "immortal" glories of his country. Many of the Academy's members, past and present, have contributed rather less to the country's glory than it has suited that august institution to acknowledge, and Furet was the first to be amused at the irony of his elevation.[5] But to the extent that it recognized the distinction of his achievement and its lasting impact upon his country, it was an honor richly deserved. All the same nothing about François Furet bespoke the conventional image of the pompous, vainglorious academician. He remained, at the age of seventy, what he had been throughout his career: an accessible, engaged, and utterly driven scholar, as much at home in a graduate seminar at the University of Chicago as he was explaining his views to a mass public on French national television.

Furet had little tolerance for mediocrity or pretension and he abhorred time-wasting; the difficulties of his early life had made him "melancholic," as his colleague Mona Ozouf described him in her funeral eulogy, and he had a world-weary sense of the passing of time and the evil that might lie ahead. If he took thought for the future, it was in order to work harder today. He had an awesome capacity for work and was a remarkably quick study, as his books attest. But he found time to be a courageous and outspoken advocate, and gave unstinting support to students, colleagues, and causes, from Algerian independence to civil liberties, even when (as on the occasion of the bicentennial celebrations of the French Revolution) this made him enemies among scholars and others nostalgic for the simplistic past of which he had deprived them.[6]

François Furet left behind no theory of revolution, no textbook of historical method, no school of French historiography.[7] His interests were too disparate for that. In any case, he was himself an enthusiastic member of an older school of social and historical investigation, that of Alexis de Tocqueville. Some have thought that Furet privately aspired to do for our time what Tocqueville did for his, and the two men certainly shared the intuition that past history and present politics were intimately connected and could only be understood, explained (and exorcised) in relation to one another. But as André Maurois once remarked of Raymond Aron's half-acknowledged ambition to be the Montesquieu of his time, he might have come a lot closer to his goal had he taken a little more distance from the course of events. Furet, like Aron and to his credit, was incapable of remaining detached from contemporary politics, and the unity of his *oeuvre* perhaps suffered accordingly. But as he once wrote in these pages about Tocqueville, his "achievement . . . does not lie in any single doctrine but in the acute and sometimes ambivalent ways he confronted the questions of equality, democracy, and tyranny that arose in his time and that continue unresolved in our own."[8]

This essay first appeared in *The New York Review of Books* in November 1997.

NOTES TO CHAPTER XXVI

[1] *Penser la Révolution française* (Paris: Gallimard, 1978), translated as *Interpreting the French Revolution* (New York: Cambridge University Press, 1981); *Marx et la Révolution française* (Paris: Flammarion, 1986), translated as *Marx and the French Revolution* (Chicago: University of Chicago Press, 1988); *La Gauche et la révolution française au milieu du XIXe siècle* (Paris: Hachette, 1986); *Dictionnaire Critique de la Révolution Française* (Paris: Flammarion, 1988), edited with Mona Ozouf and translated as *A Critical History of the French Revolution* (Cambridge, MA: Belknap Press/Harvard University Press, 1989); *La Révolution: de Turgot à Jules Ferry, 1770–1880* (Paris: Hachette, 1988), translated as *Revolutionary France 1770–1880* (Oxford, UK: Blackwell, 1992).

[2] "*L'idée française de la révolution*," published posthumously in *Le Débat*, 96 (September–October 1996), pp. 13–33.

[3] Furet's impact on the American scholarly community, in contrast, was rather muted. Indeed, he was and is resented by many specialists on the French Revolution. In part this is for the same reason that he was initially suspect among some in France: his rejection of the *marxisant* version of the French past, with its emphasis on social forces and processes, deprived conventional practitioners of the "old" social history of their primary interpretive crutch. But in recent years many partisans of the "new" cultural history have also held against him his attention to political argument and to ideas—and they were aggrieved by his caustic dismissal of their efforts to "deconstruct" the Revolution into a series of "representations." Sometimes it is indeed in his own country that a prophet is honored.

[4] *Le Passé d'une illusion: Essai sur l'idée communiste au XXe siècle* (Paris: Robert Laffont; Calmann-Lévy, 1995).

[5] His election to the Académie was energetically opposed by its surviving Vichyite members, as well as by Gaullists and others who still remembered Furet's engagement on the side of Algerian independence in the late fifties.

[6] It was on the occasion of the 1989 bicentennial that certain U.S. historians of early modern France, peeved at his extraordinary influence on France's collective understanding of its past, distinguished themselves by ad hominem attacks on Furet.

[7] Having once been described by a French newspaper as an American member of the "school of Furet," I suppose I should declare an interest. But however flattering, the description is misleading; the school does not exist.

[8] "The Passions of Tocqueville," *New York Review of Books,* June 27, 1985.

CHAPTER XXVII

Amos Elon

(1926–2009)

I first met Amos Elon in Germany in the 1990s. We were participants in one of a series of meetings generously hosted by the Bertelsmann Foundation, where Germans, Israelis, and Jews gathered to exchange platitudes. Most of those present sought either to proselytize and grandstand (in the case of Israelis and Jews) or else to avoid giving offense (in the case of the Germans). Amos, uniquely, did neither. There, as on every occasion when I heard him speak, he succeeded in being both outspoken and yet somehow effortlessly sensible—he dominated conversation by force of reason. He had a mordant wit and a dismissive eye; he was contemptuous of fools and pedants; he smiled only rarely but when he did so it was real. He made a lasting impression upon me.

The German setting was altogether fitting. Amos, who was born in Vienna and was the author of an influential biography of Theodor Herzl, never lost his attachment to German culture and history, a subject on which he wrote frequently and with empathetic insight. *The Pity of It All*, his 2002 study of the Jewish presence in Germany from the Enlightenment to Hitler, displayed a fine sensitivity to the tragedy of Germany's Jews. For good and ill they remained profoundly attached to their cultural homeland, long after they were forced to leave it for Israel or America or elsewhere: more than the Jews of any other European land, they would feel their loss.[1]

But it is for his writings on Zionism and Israel, and his lifelong engagement with the country and its dilemmas, that Amos Elon will be best remembered. In *The Israelis: Founders and Sons* (1971) he offered a critical history of Zionism, its practitioners, and its heirs; an account that directly confronts the shortcomings of the Zionist project and its outcome. Today such critical accounts are common currency in debates in Israel; in those days they were rare indeed. Amos Elon's commitment to Israel, the country where he lived and worked for most of his life, was never in question. But for just this reason his awkward stance, relentlessly engaging with the country's failings, set him apart. His courageous refusal to endorse the clichés with which Israel's defenders parry every criticism contrasts not only with the defensiveness of contemporary left-wing Israeli commentators but also and especially with the pusillanimous apologetics of Israel's American claque.

Thus Amos, unlike so many of the land-fixated commentators among his fellow countrymen, was one of the first to recognize that the settlements in the territories Israel has occupied since 1967 were a self-imposed catastrophe: "The settlements . . . have tied Israel's hands in any negotiation to achieve lasting peace. . . . [They] have only made it less secure."[2] That a country with the strongest military in its region, and with an unbroken string of armed victories behind it, should be so obsessed with the security risks of relinquishing a few square miles of land may seem odd indeed. But it speaks to the changes that have overtaken Elon's homeland in recent decades.

As he foresaw in 2003, Israeli insistence upon ruling over an Arab population that will eventually become a majority within the country's borders can only lead to a single authoritarian state encompassing two mutually hostile nations: one dominant, the other subservient. With what outcome? "If Israel persists in its current settlement policy, . . . the end result is more likely to resemble Zimbabwe than post-apartheid South Africa."[3] Many have since come to this depressing conclusion; I believe Amos was the first to make the point.

AMOS WROTE more in sorrow than anger. Many years ago, when few nonspecialists were even paying attention, he wrote despairingly of "the human

energies wasted for more than a generation on short-sighted settlement programs. . . . Think of what might have been achieved had the billions poured
into the shifting sands of Sinai, the Golan Heights, and the West Bank, been
spent on more useful causes."[4] Such misplaced efforts he attributed to what he
called "the astonishing mediocrity of Israeli politicians." That was written in
2002. The incompetence and political cowardice of a generation of Israeli
Labor statesmen, from the sainted Golda Meir to the egregious Shimon Peres,
were already manifest. But there was worse to come: Amos Elon would live to
see the resurrection of Benjamin Netanyahu and the obscene elevation to foreign minister of Avigdor Lieberman, sad confirmation of his assessment.

Amos was perfectly well aware that the present Middle Eastern imbroglio
was the achievement of all sides. His sympathy for the "stateless, dispossessed,
and dispersed Palestinians" did not blind him to the ineptness of their leaders.[5] He had met enough Arab and Palestinian politicians to know just how
inadequate they were to the tragedy of their peoples and the tasks facing them.
In all his writings, notably an influential 1996 *New York Review of Books* essay
entitled "Israel and the End of Zionism," he was distinctly evenhanded in acknowledging the errors of both sides. But the historic mistakes of the Palestinians had come primarily before 1948, whereas Israel was overwhelmingly
responsible for the disastrous missteps that followed its great victory in 1967.

Zionism, as Amos came to realize, had outlived its usefulness. "As a measure of . . . 'affirmative action,' Zionism was useful during the formative years.
Today it has become redundant."[6] What had once been the nationalist ideology of a stateless people has undergone a tragic transition. It has, for a growing
number of Israelis, been corrupted into an uncompromising ethno-religious
real estate pact with a partisan God, a pact that justifies any and all actions
against real or imagined threats, critics, and enemies. The Zionist project, a
doctrine dating to the state-building nationalisms of the late nineteenth century, has long since lost its way. It can mean little—though it can do much
harm—in an established democratic state with aspirations to normality. In
any case it has been hijacked by ultras. Herzl's dream of a "normal" Jewish
country has become an exclusivist sectarian nightmare, a development that

Amos illustrated by slightly misquoting Keats: "Fanatics have a dream by which they weave a paradise for a sect."[7]

FOR MUCH OF HIS WORKING LIFE Amos Elon was a journalist, employed by the liberal daily *Haaretz*. During the 1950s and 1960s he worked frequently as a foreign correspondent ranging from Communist Eastern Europe to Washington, D.C. He seems to have interviewed just about everyone, from John F. Kennedy (with whom he attended wild parties at the height of the Camelot years) to Yasser Arafat. He used to tell a revealing story. In an interview he conducted in the early 1960s in Washington, with a senior Israeli diplomat who was about to leave his post and return home, he questioned his fellow Israeli closely. "What do you think you achieved during your posting here in the U.S.?" Elon asked him. "Oh, that's easy," the diplomat replied. "I believe I have succeeded in convincing Americans that anti-Zionism is anti-Semitism." Back in those years, Amos told me, he found the diplomat's assertion simply bizarre; he could hardly then have imagined that this cynical political equation would become received opinion among his countrymen and their supporters.

This growing inability—in America above all, but in Israel, too—to distinguish between Jews and Israel, Israel and Zionism, Zionism and fanatical theological exclusivism, helps explain why an Israeli like Amos Elon would in his later years find himself living in Tuscany (where he died on May 25). Many Israelis, especially younger and better-educated men and women, today live outside their country, attracted by the cosmopolitan cities of Europe and the United States. A few of them have chosen exile rather than serve in an army of occupation. But for a man of Elon's generation, already adult when his country came into being and utterly committed to the necessity and success of Zionism, the decision to sell his home in Jerusalem and settle permanently abroad was far more wrenching and carries profound implications. A moral exile in his own land, Amos—the consummate Israeli in so many ways—was once again rootless; or at any rate rooted only in his defiant cosmopolitanism.

A regrettable consequence of this self-exile of one of their country's great-est journalists is that many Israelis today are unfamiliar with his writings. To be sure, his books are available in Hebrew. And his frequent essays in *The New York Review of Books* and elsewhere were read with close attention by his admirers. But the audience in Israel for Elon's sort of writing has steadily declined over the decades. This in no way diminishes the significance of his passing. Quite the contrary. The fact that most Israelis today will not be mourning him merely illustrates and compounds their loss—and ours.

This essay first appeared in *The New York Review of Books* in July 2009.

NOTES TO CHAPTER XXVII

[1] *The Pity of It All: A History of the Jews in Germany, 1743–1933* (New York: Metropolitan Books, 2002). Amos Elon's other books include *The Israelis: Founders and Sons* (New York: Holt, Rinehart and Winston, 1971); *Herzl* (New York: Holt, Rinehart and Winston, 1975); *Journey Through a Haunted Land: The New Germany* (New York: Holt, Rinehart and Winston, 1967); and *A Blood-Dimmed Tide: Dispatches from the Middle East* (New York: Columbia University Press, 1997).

[2] Amos Elon, "No Exit," *New York Review of Books*, May 23, 2002.

[3] Omer Bartov, Amos Elon, and others, "An Alternative Future: An Exchange," *New York Review of Books*, December 4, 2003.

[4] Amos Elon, "Israel and the End of Zionism," *New York Review of Books*, December 19, 1996.

[5] Amos Elon, " 'Exile's Return': A Response to Justus Reid Wiener," *New York Review of Books*, Febuary 24, 2000.

[6] Elon, "Israel and the End of Zionism."

[7] Elon, " 'Exile's Return.' " The original excerpt from Keats's poem *The Fall of Hyperion* reads "Fanatics have their dreams, wherewith they weave/A paradise for a sect."

CHAPTER XXVIII

Leszek Kołakowski

(1927–2009)

I heard Leszek Kołakowski lecture only once. It was at Harvard in 1987 and he was a guest at the seminar on political theory taught by the late Judith Shklar. *Main Currents of Marxism* had recently been published in English and Kołakowski was at the height of his renown. So many students wanted to hear him speak that the lecture had been moved to a large public auditorium and guests were permitted to attend. I happened to be in Cambridge for a meeting and went along with some friends.

The seductively suggestive title of Kołakowski's talk was "The Devil in History." For a while there was silence as students, faculty, and visitors listened intently. Kołakowski's writings were well known to many of those present and his penchant for irony and close reasoning was familiar. But even so, the audience was clearly having trouble following his argument. Try as they would, they could not decode the metaphor. An air of bewildered mystification started to fall across the auditorium. And then, about a third of the way through, my neighbor—Timothy Garton Ash—leaned across. "I've got it," he whispered. "He really *is* talking about the Devil." And so he was.

It was a defining feature of Leszek Kołakowski's intellectual trajectory that he took evil extremely seriously. Among Marx's false premises, in his view, was the idea that all human shortcomings are rooted in social circumstances. Marx had "entirely overlooked the possibility that some sources of conflict and aggression may be inherent in the permanent characteristics of the species."[1] Or, as he expressed it in his Harvard lecture: "Evil . . . is not contingent . . . but a stubborn and unredeemable fact." For Leszek Kołakowski, who lived through the Nazi occupation of Poland and the Soviet takeover that followed, "the Devil is part of our experience. Our generation has seen enough of it for the message to be taken extremely seriously."[2]

Most of the obituaries that followed Kołakowski's recent death at the age of eighty-one altogether missed this side of the man. That is hardly surprising. Despite the fact that much of the world still believes in a God and practices religion, Western intellectuals and public commentators today are ill at ease with the idea of revealed faith. Public discussion of the subject lurches uncomfortably between overconfident denial ("God" certainly does not exist, and anyway it's all His fault) and blind allegiance. That an intellectual and scholar of Kołakowski's caliber should have taken seriously not just religion and religious ideas but the very Devil himself is a mystery to many of his otherwise admiring readers and something they have preferred to ignore.

Kołakowski's perspective is further complicated by the skeptical distance that he maintained from the uncritical nostrums of official religion (not least his own, Catholicism) and by his unique standing as the only internationally renowned scholar of Marxism to claim equal preeminence as a student of the history of religious thought.[3] Kołakowski's expertise in the study of Christian sects and sectarian writings adds depth and piquancy to his influential account of Marxism as a religious canon, with major and minor scriptures, hierarchical structures of textual authority, and heretical dissenters. Leszek Kołakowski shared with his Oxford colleague and fellow Central European Isaiah Berlin a disabused suspicion of all dogmatic certainties and a rueful insistence upon acknowledging the price of any significant political or ethical choice: There are good reasons why freedom of economic activity should be limited for the sake of security, and why money should not automatically produce more money. But the limitation of freedom should be called precisely that, and should not be called a higher form of freedom.[4]

He had little patience for those who supposed, in the teeth of twentieth-century history, that radical political improvement could be secured at little moral or human cost—or that the costs, if significant, could be discounted against future benefits. On the one hand he was consistently resistant to all simplified theorems purporting to capture timeless human verities. On the other, he regarded certain self-evident features of the human condition as too obvious to be ignored, however inconvenient:

> There is nothing surprising in the fact that we strongly resist the implications of many banal truths; this happens in all fields of knowledge simply because most truisms about human life are unpleasant.[5]

But the above considerations need not—and for Kołakowski did not—suggest a reactionary or quietist response. Marxism might be a world-historical category error. But it did not follow that Socialism had been an unmitigated disaster; nor need we conclude that we cannot or should not work to improve the condition of humanity:

> Whatever has been done in Western Europe to bring about more justice, more security, more educational opportunities, more welfare and more state responsibility for the poor and helpless, could never have been achieved without the pressure of socialist ideologies and socialist movements, for all their naïveties and delusions. . . . Past experience speaks in part for the socialist idea and in part against it.

This carefully balanced appreciation of the complexities of social reality—the idea that "human fraternity is disastrous as a political program but indispensable as a guiding sign"—already places Kołakowski at a tangent to most intellectuals in his generation. In East and West alike, the more common tendency was to oscillate between excessive confidence in the infinite possibilities for human improvement and callow dismissal of the very notion of progress. Kołakowski sat athwart this characteristic twentieth-century chasm. Human fraternity, in his thinking, remained "a regulative, rather than a constitutive, idea."[6]

The implication here is the sort of practical compromise we associate today with social democracy—or, in continental Western Europe, with its Christian Democratic confrère. Except, of course, that social democracy today—uncomfortably burdened with the connotations of "Socialism" and its twentieth-century past—is all too often the love that dare not speak its name. Leszek Kołakowski was no Social Democrat. But he was critically active in the real political history of his time, and more than once. In the early years of the Communist state, Kołakowski (though still not yet thirty) was the leading Marxist philosopher in Poland. After 1956, he shaped and articulated dissenting thought in a region where all critical opinion was doomed sooner or later to exclusion. As professor of the history of philosophy at Warsaw University he delivered a famous public lecture in 1966 excoriating the Communist Party for betraying the people—an act of political courage that cost him his Party card. Two years later he was duly exiled to the West. Thereafter, Kołakowski served as a reference and beacon for the youthful domestic dissenters who were to form the core of Poland's political opposition from the mid-1970s, who provided the intellectual energy behind the Solidarity movement and who took effective power in 1989. Leszek Kołakowski was thus an entirely engaged intellectual, notwithstanding his contempt for the pretensions and vanities of "engagement." Intellectual engagement and "responsibility," much debated and idolized in continental European thought in the generation following World War II, struck Kołakowski as fundamentally vacant concepts:

> Why should intellectuals be specifically responsible, and differently responsible than other people, and for what? . . . A mere feeling of responsibility is a formal virtue that by itself does not result in a specific obligation: it is possible to feel responsible for a good cause as well as for an evil one.

This simple observation seems rarely to have occurred to a generation of French existentialists and their Anglo-American admirers. It may be that one needed to have experienced firsthand the attraction of utterly evil goals (of Left and Right alike) to otherwise responsible intellectuals in order to understand to the full the costs as well as the benefits of ideological commitment and moral unilateralism.

As the above suggests, Leszek Kołakowski was no conventional "continental philosopher" in the sense usually ascribed to the phrase in contemporary academic usage and with particular reference to Heidegger, Sartre, and their epigones. But then nor did he have much in common with Anglo-American thought in the form that came to dominate English-speaking universities after World War II—which no doubt accounts for his isolation and neglect during his decades in Oxford.[7] The sources of Kołakowski's particular perspective, beyond his lifelong interrogation of Catholic theology, are probably better sought in experience than in epistemology. As he himself observed in his magnum opus, "All kinds of circumstances contribute to the formation of a worldview, and . . . all phenomena are due to an inexhaustible multiplicity of causes."[8]

In Kołakowski's own case, the multiplicity of causes includes not just a traumatic childhood during World War II and the catastrophic history of Communism in the years that followed, but the very distinctive setting of Poland as it passed through these cataclysmic decades. For while it is not always clear exactly where Kołakowski's particular thinking is leading, it is perfectly evident that it never came from "nowhere."

The most cosmopolitan of Europe's modern philosophers—at home in five major languages and their accompanying cultures—and in exile for over twenty years, Kołakowski was never "rootless." In contrast with, for example, Edward Said, he questioned whether it was even possible in good faith to disclaim all forms of communal loyalty. Neither in place nor ever completely out of place, Kołakowski was a lifelong critic of nativist sentiment; yet he was adulated in his native Poland and rightly so. A European in his bones, Kołakowski never ceased to interrogate with detached skepticism the naive illusions of pan-Europeanists, whose homogenizing aspirations reminded him of the dreary utopian dogmas of another age. Diversity, so long as it was not idolized as an objective in its own right, seemed to him a more prudent aspiration and

one that could only be assured by the preservation of distinctive national iden-
tities.[9] It would be easy to conclude that Leszek Kołakowski was unique. His
distinctive mix of irony and moral seriousness, religious sensibility and episte-
mological skepticism, social engagement and political doubt was truly rare (it
should also be said that he was strikingly charismatic—exercising much the
same magnetism at any gathering as the late Bernard Williams, and for some
of the same reasons[10]). But it does not seem unreasonable to recall that for just
these reasons—charisma included—he also stood firmly in a very particular
line of descent. His sheer range of cultivation and reference; the allusive, disabused wit; the uncomplaining acceptance of academic provincialism in the
fortunate Western lands where he found refuge; the experience and memory
of Poland's twentieth century imprinted, as it were, on his mischievously ex-
pressive features: all of these identify the late Leszek Kołakowski as a true
Central European intellectual—perhaps the last. For two generations of men
and women, born between 1880 and 1930, the characteristically Central European experience of the twentieth century consisted of a multilingual education
in the sophisticated urban heartland of European civilization, honed, capped,
and side-shadowed by the experience of dictatorship, war, occupation, devastation, and genocide in that selfsame heartland.

No sane person could want to repeat such an experience merely in order to
replicate the quality of thought and thinkers that such a sentimental education
produced. There is something more than a little distasteful about expressions
of nostalgia for the lost intellectual world of Communist Eastern Europe,
shading uncomfortably close to regret for the loss of other people's repression.
But as Leszek Kołakowski would have been the first to point out, the relationship between Central Europe's twentieth-century history and its astonishing
intellectual riches nevertheless existed; it cannot simply be dismissed.

What it produced was what Judith Shklar, in another context, once described as a "liberalism of fear": the uncompromising defense of reason and
moderation born of firsthand experience of the consequences of ideological
excess; the ever-present awareness of the possibility of catastrophe, at its worst
when misunderstood as opportunity or renewal, of the temptations of total-

izing thought in all its protean variety. In the wake of twentieth-century history, *this* was the Central European lesson. If we are very fortunate, we shall not have to relearn it again for some time to come; when we do, we had better hope that there will be someone around to teach it. Until then, we would do well to reread Kołakowski.

This essay first appeared in *The New York Review of Books* in September 2009.

Notes to Chapter XXVIII

[1] "The Myth of Human Self-Identity," in *The Socialist Idea: A Reappraisal*, Leszek Kołakowski and Stuart Hampshire, eds. (New York: Basic Books, 1974), p. 32.

[2] Leszek Kołakowski, "The Devil in History," in *My Correct Views on Everything* (South Bend, IN: St. Augustine's Press, 2005), p. 133.

[3] For a representative instance of Kołakowski's approach to the history of religious thought, see, for example, *God Owes Us Nothing: A Brief Remark on Pascal's Religion and on the Spirit of Jansenism* (Chicago: University of Chicago Press, 1995). It would not be too much to say that Kołakowski was a twentieth-century Pascalian, cautiously placing his bet on reason in place of faith.

[4] Leszek Kołakowski, *Modernity on Endless Trial* (Chicago: University of Chicago Press, 1990), pp. 226–227.

[5] Kołakowski and Hampshire, *The Socialist Idea*, p. 17.

[6] Kołakowski, *Modernity on Endless Trial*, p. 144.

[7] Elsewhere, his achievements were copiously acknowledged. In 1983 he was awarded the Erasmus Prize. In 2004 he was the first recipient of the Kluge Prize of the Library of Congress, where he had been the Jefferson Lecturer twenty years previously. Three years later he was awarded the Jerusalem Prize.

[8] Leszek Kołakowski, *Main Currents of Marxism, Volume III: The Breakdown* (New York: Clarendon Press/Oxford University Press, 1978), p. 339. I am grateful to Leon Wieseltier for reminding me of this reference.

[9] Kołakowski, *Modernity on Endless Trial,* p. 59. For Edward Said, see *Out of Place: A Memoir* (New York: Vintage, 2000).

[10] At a party in his honor following the Cambridge lecture, I recall watching with bemused admiration and no little envy as virtually every young woman in the room migrated to the corner where a sixty-year-old philosopher, already wizened and supported by a cane, held court before their adoring eyes. One should never underestimate the magnetic attraction of sheer intelligence.

Chronological List of Tony Judt's Published Essays and Criticism

"The Development of Socialism in France: The Example of the Var," *Historical Journal* 18, no. 1 (1975).

"The Origins of Rural Socialism in Europe: Economic Change and the Provençal Peasantry," *Social History* 1, no. 1 (1976).

"Introduction to 'Socialists and Socialism in the Twentieth Century,'" *Journal of Contemporary History* 11, nos. 2–3 (1976).

"The French Socialists and the Cartel des Gauches of 1924," *Journal of Contemporary History* 11, nos. 2–3 (1976).

"Minerva's Owl and Other Birds of Prey: Reflections on the Condition of Labor History in Europe," *International Labor and Working Class History* (Fall 1979).

"A Clown in Regal Purple: Social History and the Historians," *History Workshop Journal* 7 (1979).

"On the Syntax of the History of Socialism," *Historical Journal* 22, no. 3 (1979).

"The Rules of the Game," *Historical Journal* 23, no. 3 (1980).

"Une historiographie pas comme les autres: The French Communists and Their History," *European Studies Review* (October 1982).

"Class Composition and Social Structure of Socialist Parties After the First World War, the Case of France," Annali della Fondazione Giangiocomo Feltrinelli (1983/84).

"The Spreading Notion of the Town: Some Recent Writings on French and Italian Communism," *Historical Journal* 28, no. 4 (1985).

"Revolutionary Ends," *Times Literary Supplement*, September 26, 1986.

"Wojna sie skonczyla? O wojne hiszpanskiej po 50 latach" (La Guerre est finie? The Spanish Civil War After 50 Years), *Zeszyty Literackie* 19 (1987).

"The Dilemmas of Dissidence: The Politics of Opposition in East-Central Europe," *Eastern European Politics and Societies* 2, no. 2 (Spring 1988).

"Moving Pictures: Reflections on Shoah, Heimat, and Le Changrin et la Pitié," *Radical History Review* 41 (Spring 1988).

"The Mitterrand Transition," *Dissent* (Fall 1988).

"The Rediscovery of Central Europe," *Daedelus* (January 1990).

"A Nation-Builder and His Successors: Tomas Masaryk and Czechoslovak History," *Times Literary Supplement*, January 26–February 1, 1990.

"The Unmastered Future: Notes on the Present Condition of Central Europe," *Tikkun* (March 1990).

"Whose Common Culture?," *Times Literary Supplement*, September 14–20, 1990.

"The War Between the French," *Times Literary Supplement*, September 28–October 5, 1990.

"La Rivoluzione francese e l'idea socialist" in *La Rivoluzione francese e l'Europa*, François Furet, ed. (Bari: Laterza, 1989 [New York: Hachette, 1990]).

"Radical Politics in a New Key" in *Critique and Construction: A Symposium on Robert Unger's Politics,* Robin Lovin and Michael Perry, eds. (New York: Cambridge University Press, 1990).

"Justice as Theatre," *Times Literary Supplement,* January 18–24, 1991.

"A Stepson to the Republic," *New York Times*, February 24, 1991.

"The Judgements of Paris: French Intellectuals Since the Dreyfus Affair," *Times Literary Supplement*, June 28, 1991.

"To Live in Truth: Václav Havel and the Privatizing of the Intellectuals," *Times Literary Supplement,* October 11, 1991.

"Chronicle of a Death Foretold: Modern European History and the 'Death of Marxism,'" *History Today* (October 1991).

"Bewitched, Bothered, and Bewildered," *Washington Post*, November 17, 1991.

"Here Be Monsters: The Training Ground of Vichy's National Elite," *Times Literary Supplement*, April 17, 1992.

"Die Linke links liegen lassen?," *Transit* (Spring 1992).

Misjudgement of Paris: French Illusions and the Eastern Europe That Never Was," *Times Literary Supplement*, May 15, 1992.

"One Bloody Family Feud," *New York Times*, June 26, 1992.

"A bal sorsa," *2000 Irodalmi és társadalmi havi lap* (Budapest, October 1992).

"Intellectual Follies," *Washington Post*, November 8, 1992.

"Unvollendete Demontage: Die versäumte Selbstaufklärung der Linken," *Frankfurter Allgemeine Zeitung,* November 10, 1992.

"The Past Is Another Country: Myth and Memory in Post-War Europe," *Daedelus* 121, no. 4 (Fall 1992).

"We Have Discovered History: Defeat, Resistance, and Intellectuals in France," *Journal of Modern History* 64 (December 1992).

"*Ex Oriente Lux?* Post-Celebratory Speculations on the 'Lessons' of '89" in *Towards Greater Europe,* Colin Crouch and David Marquand, eds. (Oxford, UK: Blackwell, 1992).

"Metamorphosis: The Democratic Revolution in Czechoslovakia" in *Eastern Europe in Revolution*, Ivo Banac, ed. (Ithaca, NY: Cornell University Press, 1992).

"His Mother Done It," *New York Times*, May 23, 1993.

"Rights in France: Reflections on the Etiolation of a Political Language," *Tocqueville Review* (Spring 1993).

"Chauvin and His Heirs: The Problems of Adjusting to a Multiracial France," *Times Literary Supplement,* July 9, 1993.

"Betrayal in France: The Holocaust, the French and the Jews," *New York Review of Books*, August 12, 1993.

"Their Favorite Thief," *New York Review of Books*, October 21, 1993.

"How the East Was Won," *New York Review of Books*, December 16, 1993.

"Politische Mythen im Nachkriegseuropa," *Transit* 6 (1993).

"Die unvollendete Demontage: Zur gegenwärtigen Krise der Linken" in *What's Left? Prognosen zer Linken* (Hamburg, Germany: Rotbuch Verlag, 1993).

"The Inheritors: The New Europe's New Right," *Times Literary Supplement*, February 11, 1994.

"The Paris Strangler," *New Republic*, March 7, 1994.

"The New Old Nationalism," *New York Review of Books*, May 26, 1994.

"1989: The End of *Which* European Era?," *Daedelus* (Summer 1994).

"Vichy: entre le tabou et l'obsession," *Le Monde*, September 21, 1994.

"How Much Is Really Left of the Left?," *Times Literary Supplement*, September 23, 1994.

"The Lost World of Albert Camus," *New York Review of Books*, October 6, 1994.

"Truth and Consequences," *New York Review of Books*, November 3, 1994.

"Low Marx," *New Republic*, April 3, 1995.

"At Home in This Century," *New York Review of Books*, April 6, 1995.

"Downhill All the Way," *New York Review of Books*, May 25, 1995.

"French War Stories," *New York Times*, July 19, 1995.

"What Are American Interests?," *New York Review of Books*, October 5, 1995.

"Two Dissenters," *Times Literary Supplement*, January 1996.

"Das Ende er Illusionen," *Focus Magazin*, January 8, 1996.

"Austria and the Ghost of the New Empire," *New York Review of Books*, February 15, 1996.

"A Hero of His Times: The Twentieth-Century Saga of Manés Sperber," *New Republic*, April 1, 1996.

"France Without Glory," *New York Review of Books*, May 23, 1996.

"Europe: The Grand Illusion," *New York Review of Books*, July 11, 1996.

"Holy Warrior," *New York Review of Books*, October 31, 1996.

"The First Casualties of Capitalism," *Times Literary Supplement*, November 8, 1996.

"The Dualist," *New Republic*, April 14, 1997.

"New Germany, Old NATO," *New York Review of Books*, May 29, 1997.

"Continental Rift," *New York Times*, June 5, 1997.

"Crimes and Misdemeanors," *New Republic*, September 22, 1997.

"The Social Question Redivivus," *Foreign Affairs,* September/October 1997.

"Why the Cold War Worked," *New York Review of Books*, October 9, 1997.

"Françoise Furet," *New York Review of Books*, November 6, 1997.

"The Longest Road to Hell," *New York Times,* December 22, 1997.

"On the Brink," *New York Review of Books*, January 15, 1998.

"The Stranger," *New Republic*, February 16, 1998.

"On European Identity," *Time*, April 1, 1998.

"Counsels on Foreign Relations," *New York Review of Books*, August 13, 1998.

"Freedom and Freedonia," *New Republic*, September 7, 1998.

"The 'Third Way' Is No Route to Paradise," *New York Times*, September 27, 1998.

"À la Recherche du Temps Perdu," *New York Review of Books*, December 3, 1998.

"Tyrannized by Weaklings," *New York Times*, April 5, 1999.

"A New World Disorder," *Los Angeles Times*, April 11, 1999.

"The Reason Why," *New York Review of Books*, May 20, 1999.

"The Courage of the Elementary," *New York Review of Books*, May 20, 1999.

"Europe, Without America to Lean On," *New York Times*, June 20, 1999.

"To the End of the World," *New York Times*, June 27, 1999.

"A Superpower Flaunts Its Ignorance," *New York Times*, October 17, 1999.

"Is There a Belgium?," *New York Review of Books*, December 2, 1999.

"The Deadliest Century Is Done," *Newsweek*, December 27, 1999.

"Extremism, Without the Virtue," *New York Times*, January 30, 2000.

"Arthur Koestler: The Homeless Mind," *New Republic*, February 2000.

"Austrian Conundrums," *London Evening Standard*, February 5, 2000.

"The Farce Version of History," *Newsweek,* February 14, 2000.

"Austrian Politics and the Far Right in Europe," *Newsweek,* February 28, 2000.

"Tale from the Vienna Woods," *New York Review of Books*, March 1, 2000.

"Writing History, Facts Optional," *New York Times*, April 13, 2000.

"The Story of Everything," *New York Review of Books*, September 1, 2000.

"The New Old Foreign Policy," *New York Review of Books*, November 1, 2000.

"Alice in Euro-land," *Die Zeit*, November 7, 2000.

"The White House and the World," *New York Review of Books*, December 21, 2000.

"Europe Is One, Until Disaster Strikes," *New York Times*, February 6, 2001.

"Could the French Have Won?," *New York Review of Books*, February 22, 2001.

"The French Difference," *New York Review of Books*, April 12, 2001.

"The End of History," *New Republic*, May 14, 2001.

"'Twas a Famous Victory," *New York Review of Books*, July 19, 2001.

"On September 11th," *Evening Standard*, October 1, 2001.

"Romania: Bottom of the Heap," *New York Review of Books*, November 1, 2001.

"America and the War," *New York Review of Books*, November 15, 2001.

"On *The Plague*," *New York Review of Books*, November 29, 2001.

"The War on Terror," *New York Review of Books*, December 20, 2001.

Introduction to *The Marshall Plan: Fifty Years After* by Martin A. Schain (New York: Palgrave Macmillan, 2001).

Introduction to *Selected Writings* by Raymond Aron (New York: Basic Books, 2001).

Introduction to *The Plague* by Albert Camus (New York: Penguin, 2001).

"America's Restive Partners," *New York Times*, April 28, 2002.

"The Road to Nowhere," *New York Review of Books*, May 9, 2002.

"After Victory," *New Republic*, July 29, 2002.

"Its Own Worst Enemy," *New York Review of Books*, August 15, 2002.

"The Wrong War at the Wrong Time, *New York Times*, October 20, 2002.

"We'll Always Have Paris," *New York Times*, December 1, 2002.

"The Way We Live Now," *New York Review of Books*, March 27, 2003.

"America and the World," *New York Review of Books*, April 10, 2003.

"The Nation: Fortunes of War, Europe Finds No Counterweight to US Power," *New York Times*, April 20, 2003.

"Anti-Americans Abroad," *New York Review of Books*, May 1, 2003.

"Two Visions," *Newsweek International*, October 6, 2003.

"Jewish State Has Become an Anachronism," *Los Angeles Times*, October 10, 2003.

"Israel: The Alternative," *New York Review of Books*, October 20, 2003.

"The Last Romantic," *New York Review of Books*, November 20, 2003.

"Taking Another Look at Spain," *Newsweek*, March 29, 2004.

"The Artlessness of the Apology," *Washington Post*, May 9, 2004.

"The World We Have Lost," *Newsweek*, May 31, 2004.

"The Rootless Cosmopolitan," *The Nation*, July 19, 2004.

"A Matter of Public Trust," *Newsweek International*, July 26, 2004.

"On Tony Blair," *Newsweek*, October 31, 2004.

"Dreams of Empire," *New York Review of Books*, November 4, 2004.

"The Eastern Front, 2004," *New York Times*, December 5, 2004.

"Goodbye to All That?," *The Nation*, January 3, 2005.

"Europe vs. America," *New York Review of Books*, February 10, 2005.

"The New World Order," *New York Review of Books*, July 14, 2005.

"From the House of the Dead: On Modern European Memory," *New York Review of Books*, October 6, 2005.

Introduction to *From Oslo to Iraq* by Edward Said (New York: Pantheon, 2005).

"Marxisme" in *Dictionnaire Historique de la vie politique française au Xxe siècle*, Jean-Françoise Sirinielli, ed. (Paris: Presses Universitaires de France, 2005).

"A Story Still to Be Told," *New York Review of Books*, March 23, 2006.

"A Lobby, Not a Conspiracy," *New York Times*, April 19, 2006.

"The Country That Wouldn't Grow Up," *Haaretz*, May 2, 2006.

"Goodbye to All That?," *New York Review of Books*, September 21, 2006.

"Bush's Useful Idiots: The Strange Death of Liberal America," *London Review of Books*, September 21, 2006.

"Is the UN Doomed?," *New York Review of Books*, February 15, 2007.

"Defender of the Faith," *New York Times*, March 11, 2007.

"France Looks Ahead and It Doesn't Look Good," *New York Times*, April 22, 2007.

"From Military Disaster to Moral High Ground," *New York Times*, October 7, 2007.

"The Wrecking Ball of Innovation," *New York Review of Books*, December 6, 2007.

"The 'Problem of Evil' in Postwar Europe," *New York Review of Books*, February 14, 2008.

"What Have We Learned, if Anything?," *New York Review of Books*, May 1, 2008.

"Fictions on the Ground," *New York Times*, June 22, 2009.

"Amos Elon (1926–2009)," *New York Review of Books*, July 2, 2009.

"Leszek Kołakowski (1927–2009)," *New York Review of Books*, September 24, 2009.

"Food," *New York Review of Books* (blog), November 25, 2009.

"Israel Must Unpick Its Ethnic Myth," *Financial Times*, December 7, 2009.

"What Is Living and What Is Dead in Social Democracy?," *New York Review of Books*, December 17, 2009.

"Night," *New York Review of Books*, January 14, 2010.

"Kibbutz," *New York Review of Books* (blog), January 18, 2010.

"Revolutionaries," *New York Review of Books* (blog), February 10, 2010.

"Bedder," *New York Review of Books*, February 11, 2010.

"Joe," *New York Review of Books*, February 11, 2010.

"Edge People," *New York Review of Books* (blog), February 23, 2010.

"The Green Line," *New York Review of Books*, February 25, 2010.

"Girls! Girls! Girls!," *New York Review of Books* (blog), March 11, 2010.

"In Love with Trains," *New York Review of Books*, March 11, 2010.

"Paris Was Yesterday," *New York Review of Books*, March 11, 2010.

"Saved by Czech," *New York Review of Books*, March 11, 2010.

"Interview," *London Review of Books*, March 25, 2010.

"Lord Warden," *New York Review of Books*, March 25, 2010.

"Work," *New York Review of Books*, April 8, 2010.

"The Diary," *Financial Times*, April 10, 2010.

"Toni," *New York Review of Books* (blog), April 19, 2010.

"Austerity," *New York Review of Books*, May 13, 2010.

"America: My New-Found Land," *New York Review of Books*, May 27, 2010.

"Magic Mountains," *New York Review of Books*, May 27, 2010.

"Israel Without Clichés," *New York Times*, June 10, 2010.

"Generations in the Balance," *New York Times*, June 20, 2010.

"Captive Minds," *New York Review of Books* (blog), July 13, 2010.

"Words," *New York Review of Books*, July 15, 2010.

"My London," *The Guardian*, August 13, 2010.

"Meritocrats," *New York Review of Books*, August 19, 2010.

"The Glory of the Rails," *New York Review of Books*, December 23, 2010.

"Bring Back the Rails!," *New York Review of Books*, January 13, 2011.

INDEX

Aaronovitch, David, 126
Abbas, Mahmoud, 115, 158
Académie Française, 352, 354*n*5
Acheson, Dean, 76, 211, 264
Adams, Gerry, 112, 164, 165
Adenauer, Konrad, 31, 44, 66, 80, 352
Afghanistan, 155, 186, 203, 213, 244, 245
"Afterlife, The" (Judt), 10
Age of Capital, 1848–1875, The (Hobsbawm), 14
Age of Empire, 1875–1914, The (Hobsbawm), 14
Age of Extremes, The: A History of the World, 1914–1991 (Hobsbawm), 14–28
Age of Revolution, 1789–1848, The (Hobsbawm), 14
airports, 300
air travel, 298, 299
Akashi, Yasushi, 267*n*6
al-Aqsa Brigade, 117
Albright, Madeleine, 232
Algeria, 107–9, 113, 114, 153, 163, 174, 209, 279, 280
Algérie et la République, L' (Aron), 107–8, 114
al-Qaeda, 118, 278
American Anti-Defamation League (ADL), 207, 208
American Israel Public Affairs Committee, 125
Amir, Yigal, 145
Amnesty International, 244–46, 247
"Amos Elon (1926–2009)" (Judt), 9, 355–59
Anderson, Benedict, 86, 87
Andric, Ivo, 317*n*15
Anna Karenina (Tolstoy), 132
Annales School, 347–48

Annan, Kofi, 238, 241, 250*n*4, 254, 256, 257, 261, 265, 266
anti-Americanism, 184, 192–93, 200*n*1, 205, 218–33
  in France, 219–28
"Anti-Americans Abroad" (Judt), 218–33
anti-Semitism, 119, 121, 125–27, 135–37, 167, 219, 358
  criticism of Israel linked to, 126–27, 137–38, 154–55, 209
  in Europe, 206–9
  in France, 207–8, 211
  Mearsheimer-Walt essay and, 124
  in United States, 207
apartheid, 163
Applebaum, Anne, 63, 204
Après l'empire (Todd), 223–26
Arafat, Yasser, 110, 111, 115, 118–19, 158, 358
Arbour, Louise, 257
Arendt, Hannah, 129–30, 133, 135–37, 139, 140, 180, 181, 351
Armenia, 165
Arms and the Man (Shaw), 88, 92
Aron, Raymond, 10, 107–8, 114, 172, 279, 280, 351, 353
Aron, Robert, 219
Ascherson, Neal, 62, 63
assassinations, 111, 244–45, 276
Atias, Ariel, 158
At the Point of a Gun: Democratic Dreams and Armed Intervention (Rieff), 235–38, 240, 249
Austria, 36
automobiles, 289, 294, 295, 296, 298, 299, 300
Aznar, José María, 205, 215, 216*n*5

Bacevich, Andrew, 242–44, 248
Bacque, James, 60
Balkan Ghosts (Kaplan), 94
Balkans, 100, 102–4, 199, 213, 214, 352
  Goldsworthy on, 88–94, 102, 103, 104
Ban Ki-moon, 266
Bar'el, Zvi, 250*n*1
Bar-Ilan University, 145
Barnave, Antoine, 348
Barthes, Roland, 179
Bartosek, Karel, 83*n*3
Baudelaire, Charles, 219
Beauvoir, Simone de, 172, 179, 219
Beck, Harry, 292
Beeching, Richard, 295–96
Begin, Menachem, 117, 120, 123*n*3, 157
Belgium, 33, 39, 162, 204, 207, 219
Bell, Daniel, 313
Beneš, Edvard, 99
Ben-Gurion, David, 120, 148
Bergson, Henri, 211
Berl, Emmanuel, 219
Berlin, 160
Berlin, Isaiah, 10, 53–54, 361
Berlin Wall, 74, 122
Berlusconi, Silvio, 206
Bertelsmann Foundation, 41, 355
Bertram, Christoph, 126
Beuve-Méry, Hubert, 233*n*8
Beveridge, William, 321
Bevin, Ernest, 75
bin Laden, Osama, 203, 214, 278
Biological Weapons Convention, 200*n*12
Bismarck, Otto von, 66
Blair, Tony, 119, 164, 205, 206, 215, 255, 281*n*6
Blanning, Timothy, 62
Bloch, Marc, 348
Blum, Léon, 61, 80, 211
Bohemia, 94–96
Bohlen, Charles, 211, 264
Bokassa, Jean-Bedel, 210
Bolshevik Revolution, 21, 24, 54, 80, 352
Bolton, John, 261–63
Boot, Max, 237
Borkenau, Franz, 351
Bosnia, 45, 46, 185, 190, 203, 204, 214, 234, 238, 263, 267*n*6, 318*n*15, 338*n*7
  Srebrenica, 236, 258
Bound to Lead (Nye), 188
Boutros-Ghali, Boutros, 256, 267*n*6
BP oil spill, 339–41, 343
Bradbury, Malcolm, 92
Brahimi, Lakhdar, 256

Braudel, Fernand, 348
Brezhnev, Leonid, 78
Brief Encounter, 293
"Bring Back the Rails!" (Judt), 294–302
Britain, 33, 45, 46, 80, 81, 193, 204–6, 209, 275, 279
  New Poor Law in, 26, 310, 325
  railways in, 333
Brown, Gordon, 317*n*8
Bunche, Ralph, 256
Burg, Avraham, 118, 123*n*1
Burleigh, Michael, 62
buses, 332–33
Bush, George H. W., 191, 214, 240
Bush, George W., 183, 186–88, 194, 198, 204, 206, 212, 214, 216*n*5, 221, 223, 228, 231, 234–35, 238, 242–43, 250, 261, 341
  criticism and, 246
  Middle East and, 110, 111, 119, 194
  religious faith of, 229
  targeted suspects and, 244–45
Buss, Robin, 171

Cambodia, 274
Camus, Albert, ix, 10, 171–82
capitalism, 25, 195, 224, 303–4, 306, 308, 312, 313, 335
  democracy and, 312
  supercapitalism, 304, 306–8, 312, 313
Captain Swing (Hobsbawm and Rude), 13
Carlyle, Thomas, 55
Carr, Raymond, 62
cars, 289, 294, 295, 296, 298, 299, 300
Cassin, René, 256
Castro, Fidel, 19
Catherine the Great, 40
Central Europe, 85–87, 100–102, 365–66
Chamberlain, Neville, 85
Chambon-sur-Lignon, 182*n*5
Cheney, Dick, 192
China, 204, 260, 265–66, 273, 275, 312, 325, 343
Chirac, Jacques, 36, 215, 230
Christianity, 51, 228–29, 335, 361
Churchill, Winston, 66, 80, 156
cities, 295, 298
citizens, 307, 309, 311
  welfare reform and, 310
Civil Rights Act, 342
civil society, 301
civil war, 273
Clark, Wesley, 251*n*11
Clinton, Bill, 103, 110, 119, 164, 165, 188, 214, 263, 303, 309, 325, 341
Clinton, Hillary, 247

Coasts of Bohemia, The: A Czech History (Sayer), 94–100, 103
Cobb, Richard, 61
Cobbett, William, 89
cold war, 22–23, 65–84, 132, 186, 193, 194, 202, 219, 221, 223, 229, 230, 241, 249, 257, 263, 269
   American vs. European accounts of, 276
   beginning of, 79
   complications in, 81–82
   intelligence community and, 76
   nuclear weapons and, 82
   revisionism and, 75–76
Cole, G.D.H., 29n7
Combat, 172
Commission of Measurement of Economic Performance and Social Progress, 338n6
Common Agricultural Policy, 185
communication, 272, 296
Communism, 21–25, 27, 36, 47, 103, 134, 195, 223, 274, 314, 331, 352, 364
   cold war and, *see* cold war
   in Czechoslovakia, 99–100
   in France, 70–72, 223, 347
   Furet and, 347, 351
   Hobsbawm on, 18–27
   in Italy, 70–72, 223
   Todd on, 225
Condorcet, Marquis de, 313, 321
Constante, Lena, 280
Constitution, U.S., 233n7, 246
constructionalism, 87, 90
Convention on Children's Rights, 184
Convention on Discrimination Against Women, 192
Cook, Thomas, 291–92
corruption, 263, 311
"Crimes and Misdemeanors" (Judt), 47–64
Croatia, 165
Cuba, 79, 206, 245
Cumings, Bruce, 76, 84n12
Cyprus, 165
Czechoslovakia, 23, 68, 96–97, 100–101, 103, 191
   Communists in, 99–100
   Sayer on, 94–100, 103
Czech Question, The (Masaryk), 97
Czech Republic, 204, 205

Daily Mirror, 205
Daily Telegraph, 58, 63
Darfur, 249, 260, 263, 268n9
Davies, Merryl Wyn, 222n, 223
Davies, Norman, 47–64
Dayton Accords, 102

Deepwater Horizon oil spill, 339–41, 343
de Gasperi, Alcide, 66
de Gaulle, Charles, 42, 84n15, 108, 131, 158, 173, 210, 217n14, 352
de Klerk, F. W., 163
democracy, 156, 224, 248, 249, 304, 315–16
   capitalism and, 312
   Israel as, 116–18, 152
   social, *see* social democracy
Democratic Party, 247
Denmark, 204, 205, 208
Department of Defense, U.S., 242
Dershowitz, Alan, 279
De Sica, Vittorio, 10
Deutscher, Isaac, 7
Devil, 360–61
diasporas, 165–66
Dickens, Charles, 219, 325
Djilas, Milovan, 69–70
"Downhill All the Way" (Judt), 13–29
Dracula, 92
Dracula (Stoker), 88, 90
Drieu La Rochelle, Pierre, 130
Drucker, Peter, 321–22
Dubček, Alexander, 71
Duck Soup, 92
Duclos, Jacques, 84n9
Duhamel, George, 219
Dulles, John Foster, 75
Durham, Edith, 88, 93
Durkheim, Émile, 211
Durrell, Lawrence, 88, 91, 92

Eastern Europe, 85–87, 100–101, 104, 133–34, 152, 206, 365
   European Union and, 40–43
Eban, Abba, 153
École des Hautes Études en Sciences Sociales, L', 351
economic age, 307–9
Economic Consequences of the Peace, The (Keynes), 313, 336
economism, 320–21
Edelman, Marek, 57
Egypt, 244
Eichmann, Adolf, 148
Eichmann in Jerusalem: A Report on the Banality of Evil (Arendt), 129
Eisenhower, Dwight D., 77, 210, 265
ElBaradei, Mohamed, 256
Elon, Amos, 9, 355–59
Elshtain, Jean Bethke, 279
employment, 33–34, 196, 314, 326

England, *see* Britain
Enlightenment, 10, 22, 184, 270, 335
entitlements, 334
ethnic cleansing, 117, 130, 236, 273
Étranger, L' (Camus), 172, 175
Europe, 30–46, 47, 203–4, 249, 265
    aging populations in, 34–35
    anti-Semitism in, 206–9
    Eastern, *see* Eastern Europe
    Central, 85–87, 100–102, 365–66
    collaboration in, 197–98
    economies and, 32–34, 195–96, 304
    immigration in, 35–37
    myths about, 204–9
    oil and, 32
    Old and New, 204–6, 211, 220
    super-regions in, 38–39
    U.S. compared with, 195–97, 217n18, 227–29
Europe: A History (Davies), 47–64
"Europe: The Grand Illusion" (Judt), 30–46
European Union (EU), 30, 33, 34, 37–40, 46, 102,
    155, 183, 185, 189, 190, 193–94, 203, 230, 249,
    258
    Eastern Europe and, 40–43
    Israel and, 166
    workings of, 42–43
Evans, Gareth, 240
evil, 129–30, 132, 133, 135–36, 138–40, 141n4, 361,
    364
    banality of, 140, 180
    Camus's view of, 171, 180, 181
    concept of, 135
    gray zone and, 179–80

Fabians, 25
Farbiaz, Patrick, 222n
Fascism, 21, 22, 25, 36, 117, 195, 219, 274, 277, 314,
    322, 323, 352
    Camus on, 179
    Hobsbawm on, 19–22
fear, 314
    liberalism of, 365–66
    social democracy of, 336, 337
Febvre, Lucien, 348
Feith, Douglas, 126
Fernandez-Armesto, Felipe, 62
Ferrer, Gabriel, 288
Ferro, Marc, 63
"Fictions on the Ground" (Judt), 142–46
films, 292–93
Footman, David, 92
Ford, Henry, 219
Forster, E.M., 90

Fourth Geneva Convention, 143
France, 30–33, 37–39, 45, 46, 81, 187, 193, 195,
    204–6, 209, 210, 249, 331–32
    Algeria and, 107–9, 113, 114, 153, 163, 209, 279,
        280
    anti-Americanism in, 219–28
    anti-Semitism in, 207–8, 211
    Camus's *The Plague* and, 172, 173, 177, 179, 180
    Cobb and, 61
    Communists in, 70–72, 223, 347
    Furet and, 347–54
    Germany and, 112, 113, 187, 203
    railways in, 333
    Revel on, 226–27
    Revolution in, 50, 54, 67, 270, 307, 347–53, 354n3
    Russia and, 80
    suspicion of, 209–11
    United Nations and, 210, 255, 260
    voters in, 36
    in World War I, 210, 273, 275
France, in World War II, 132, 210–11, 264, 273,
    275
    German occupation, 173, 174, 177
    Resistance and, 172, 173, 178, 211
    Vichy government in, 25, 49, 132, 158, 177, 179,
        210
Franco, Francisco, 248
"François Furet (1927–1997)" (Judt), 347–54
Frederick the Great, 40
"Freedom and Freedonia" (Judt), 85–104
French Revolution, The (Furet), 347–48
Furet, François, 347–54

Gaddis, John, 65–68, 73–79
Gare Montparnasse, 296
Garton Ash, Timothy, 360
gated communities, 329
Gaza, 151–53, 155, 157, 159
General Motors (GM), 305
"Generations in the Balance" (Judt and Judt),
    339–43
Geneva Conventions, 143, 245, 257
genocide, 130, 139, 274
    Davies on, 50–52
Germany, 30–41, 43–46, 70, 79, 98–99, 104, 133,
    193, 195, 204–6, 213, 331
    casualties in world wars, 275
    Davies on, 60
    France and, 112, 113, 187, 203
    France occupied by, 173, 174, 177
    Nazism and, *see* Nazism
    Soviet Union and, 73–75, 80, 131
G.I. Bill, 342

Gibbon, Edward, 48, 55
Gide, André, 25
Gilbert, Neil, 317*n*7
Gini coefficient, 325
Giscard d'Estaing, Valéry, 120
Giuliani, Rudolph, 255
globalization, 185, 194–98, 224, 229, 253, 266, 269,
    272, 309, 311, 314–15, 336
global warming, 307, 309
"Glory of the Rails, The" (Judt), 285–93
God, 361
God's Playground (Davies), 53, 55, 57
Goldman Sachs, 340
Goldsworthy, Vesna, *Inventing Ruritania,* 88–94,
    102, 103, 104
Gonzales, Alberto, 246
good society, 335
Gorbachev, Mikhail, 77, 78
Grand Central Station, 289, 297
Grass, Günter, 206
gray zone, 179–80
Great Britain, *see* Britain
Greece, 93
Greene, Graham, 88, 92
Guantánamo Bay, 244, 245, 248, 278
Guéhenno, Jean-Marie, 257
Guizot, François, 349

Haaretz, 126, 127, 209, 358
Habsburg empire, 115–16
Haganah, 142
Hague Peace Conferences, 257
Haider, Jörg, 36
Hakuk, 142
Halévy, Daniel, 211
Hamas, 108, 109, 117, 152, 153, 157, 158, 161, 163,
    164
Hammarskjöld, Dag, 239, 256, 257
Hart, Gary, 189
Havel, Václav, 103, 179, 232*n*3
Hayek, Friedrich, 321–23, 336
health care, 195, 227, 317*n*8
Heath, Edward, 316*n*2
Hegel, Chuck, 164
Heidegger, Martin, 364
Hersh, Seymour, 246
Hertsgaard, Mark, 233*n*7
Herut Party, 117, 157
Herzl, Theodor, 355, 357
Hezbollah, 109, 118, 157
High Albania (Durham), 88, 93
highways, 342
Hill, Charles, 255

Hill, Christopher, 15
Hilton, Rodney, 15
history, 271–72, 307, 331
History of Europe, A (Roberts), 64
History Today, 63
Hitchens, Christopher, 124, 267*n*5
Hitchins, Keith, 61
Hitler, Adolf, 15, 17, 22, 61, 76, 80–81, 85, 94, 99,
    101, 111, 130, 131, 135, 187, 206, 210, 211, 219,
    273–74, 278
Hobsbawm, Eric, 13–29, 86–87
Hobsbawm generation, 13, 26–27
Holbrooke, Richard, 103
Holocaust (*Shoah*), 8, 121, 130–35, 138–40, 155,
    208, 274
    contemporary preoccupation with, 133–38
    Davies on, 51, 53–54, 57–58, 60
    Israel and, 127, 137–39, 162
    Israel-Palestine conflict and, 108–9
    universal resonance of, 139
Homage to Catalonia (Orwell), 337
Hope, Anthony, 88, 89, 90
"How I Conquered Europe" (Davies), 56
Hugo, Victor, 110
humanitarian intervention, 235–38, 241, 248–49
Hungary, 23, 98, 99, 103, 191, 204
Hus, Jan, 96
Husak, Gustav, 103

immigration, 35–37
India, 162
    railways in, 297
Indonesia, 205
innovation, 304, 313
Institut Raymond Aron, 351
intelligence community, 76
International Criminal Court (ICC), 184–85,
    191–92, 198, 206
International Protocol on Involvement of
    Children in Armed Conflict, 192
International Red Cross, 257
interrogation, 244–45, 279
Inventing Eastern Europe (Wolff), 87
*Inventing Ruritania: The Imperialism of the
    Imagination* (Goldsworthy), 88–94, 102, 103,
    104
Invention of the Jewish People, The (Sand), 148, 149
invisible hand, 312
Iran, 155, 186, 262
Iraq, 207, 224, 244
    war on, 118, 125, 127, 188, 203–5, 214, 230,
    234–35, 238, 239, 246, 255, 259, 260, 263, 265,
    274, 276

Ireland, 112, 113, 150, 163, 164–65
Irgun, 120
Irish Republican Army, 112
    Provisional, 150, 153, 164, 165
Irving, David, 60
Islam, Muslims, 231, 245
    radical, 118, 167, 277, 278
isolationism, 213
Israel, 8–9, 109, 115–23, 203, 207, 208, 214, 245,
        261, 273
    anti-Semitism linked to criticism of, 126–27,
        137–38, 154–55, 209
    blame attributed to, 152–53, 209
    choices faced by, 116–17
    clichés about, 151–55
    delegitimization of, 151–52
    as democracy, 116–18, 152
    diaspora and, 165–66
    elections in, 144
    Elon and, 355–59
    Holocaust and, 127, 137–39, 162
    and Jews and Jewishness, 121–22, 149, 150, 156,
        358
    kibbutzim in, 142
    Palestinians and, *see* Israel-Palestine conflict
    recognition of, 157, 161, 166
    settlements in, 116, 142–46, 167, 356–57
    single-state solution for, 157
    two-state solution for, 9, 120, 149, 156, 157, 167
    U.S. relations with, 124–27, 144, 146, 149–50,
        155, 165, 166, 205, 214, 228
    weapons of, 118
    Zionism and, *see* Zionism
"Israel: The Alternative" (Judt), 8–9, 115–23,
        156
"Israel and the End of Zionism" (Elon), 357
Israelis, The: Founders and Sons (Elon), 356
Israel lobby, 124–25, 127, 165
    blame attributed to, 154
"Israel Lobby, The" (Walt and Mearsheimer),
        124–27
"Israel Must Unpick Its Ethnic Myth" (Judt),
        147–50
Israel-Palestine conflict, 108–14, 116–20, 122, 123,
        137, 149, 156–67, 214, 228
    Israeli settlements and, 143, 145
    Jerusalem and, 108, 160–61, 166
    land issue in, 159
    "peace process" in, 115, 156–58, 164, 165
    "road map" in, 115, 119, 120, 145, 159, 165
    security concerns in, 159–60, 166
    trust and, 157, 158, 163
    uniqueness of, 162

    Ulster analogy and, 164–65
    United States and, 110–13, 114*n*3, 118–19
"Israel Without Clichés" (Judt), 151–55
"Is the UN Doomed?" (Judt), 252–68
Italy, 34, 38–39, 204–6, 273
    Communists in, 70–72, 223
"Its Own Worst Enemy" (Judt), 183–201

Jabotinsky, Vladimir, 117, 157
Japan, 275
Jefferson, Thomas, 191
Jerusalem, 108, 160–61, 166
Jerusalem Post, 126
Jews, 98–99, 138–39, 149, 355
    anti-Semitism and, *see* anti-Semitism
    attacks on, 122, 207, 208
    Davies on, 51–54, 57, 58, 60
    ethnic view of, 147–50
    Holocaust and, *see* Holocaust
    Israel and, 121–22, 149, 150, 156, 358; *see also*
        Israel
    Zionism and, *see* Zionism
Johnson, Lyndon B., 210
Jordan, 244
Joseph II, 40
Jospin, Lionel, 36
Jowitt, Kenneth, 23
Judt, Daniel, 1, 4, 7–8
    "Generations in the Balance," 339–43
Judt, Joe, 7
Judt, Nicholas, 2, 7–8
Jünger, Ernst, 130

Kagan, Robert, 237
Kant, Immanuel, 257
Kaplan, Lawrence, 203, 212–15
Kaplan, Robert, 94
Kardelj, Edvard, 69–70
Kassebaum, Nancy, 164
Keats, John, 358
Keen, Maurice, 55
Kennan, George, 68, 77, 211, 264
Kennedy, David, 250*n*3
Kennedy, John F., 77, 210, 217*n*14, 358
Kennedy, Paul, 256, 257, 266
Keynes, John Maynard, ix, 4, 9, 10, 29*n*9, 267,
        313–14, 320, 322–24, 330, 336
Khrushchev, Nikita, 69, 78, 79, 263
Kibbutz Hakuk, 142
Kim Il Sung, 68, 75
Kissinger, Henry, 110, 213
Koestler, Arthur, 154
Kohl, Helmut, 31, 42

Kołakowski, Leszek, 9, 360–66
Korea, 75
Kosovo, 190, 203, 206, 214, 234–35, 237
Kosovo Liberation Army (KLA), 237
Korean War, 75, 76, 211
Krauthammer, Charles, 186, 187
Kristol, William, 203, 212–15, 217n19
Kundera, Milan, 100
Kupchan, Charles, 224

Labouring Men, Industry and Empire
    (Hobsbawm), 13
land-grant colleges, 341–42
Lang, Jack, 227
Langer, Jo, 280
Larkin, Philip, 10
Laslett, Peter, 285
League of Nations, 43, 253, 257, 263
Lean, David, 293
Lebanon, 109, 110, 153, 260
Le Chambon-sur-Lignon, 182n5
Left, 307–8, 322, 332, 337, 350, 364
Lenin, V.I., 21, 47
Leninism, 351–52
Le Pen, Jean-Marie, 36, 209, 227
"Leszek Kołakowski (1927–2009)" (Judt), 9,
    360–66
Levi, Primo, 132, 179
Levy, Daniel, 127
Lewitter, L. R., 55
liberalism of fear, 365–66
Libya, 206
Lieberman, Avigdor, 143
Ligue des Droits de l'Homme, 352
Likud, 117, 157
Livni, Tzipi, 157
"Lobby, Not a Conspiracy, A" (Judt), 124–28
Loebl, Eugen, 280
London, 65
London, Artur, 83n3, 280
London Review of Books, 63, 124
London Sunday Telegraph, 62–63
London Times, 20, 62, 126
London Underground, 327–28
Lukacs, John, 79
Luther, Martin, 96
Luxembourg, 37–38

Maale Adumim, 143
Macedonia, 199, 247
Macmillan, Harold, 306
Madison, James, 244
Main Currents of Marxism (Kołakowski), 360

Maistre, Joseph de, 219
Malcolm, Noel, 62–63
Malloch Brown, Mark, 255
Mamère, Noël, 222n
Mandela, Nelson, 163
Mao Tse-tung, 17, 75
Maria Theresa, 40
market optimization, 310–11
Marshall, George, 211
Marshall, T.H., 310
Marshall Plan, 70, 342, 343
Marx, Karl, 10, 14, 20, 24, 349, 360–61
    Marxism, 16, 20, 77–78, 91–92, 103, 194, 270,
        309, 322, 331, 348, 350, 361–63
Marx Brothers, 10
    Duck Soup, 92
Masaryk, Tomáš, 58, 97
Maurois, André, 353
McCarthy, Joseph, 254
McGinnis, Martin, 112, 164
Mearsheimer, John, 124–27
Melville, Herman, 176–77
Merkel, Angela, 331
Merriman, John, 63
Metronet, 317n8
Meyssan, Thierry, 222, 227
Michnik, Adam, 103
Middle East, 118, 127, 155, 194, 203, 230, 260
    Iraq War, 118, 125, 127, 188, 203–5, 214, 230,
        234–35, 238, 239, 246, 255, 259, 260, 263, 265,
        274, 276

    Israel, see Israel; Israel-Palestine conflict
Mignet, François, 349
Mikolajczyk, Stanislaw, 24
militarization of society, 242–44, 249, 273
military bases, 242
Mill, John Stuart, 312, 330
Milošević, Slobodan, 103, 185, 234, 235
Mises, Ludwig von, 321–22
Mitchell, George, 159, 161, 164, 165
Mitterrand, François, 42
Mladic, Ratko, 236
Moby-Dick (Melville), 176–77
modernity, 299–301
Molotov, Vyacheslav, 73, 78, 79
Monde, 186, 220
Montesquieu, Charles-Louis de Secondat,
    Baron de, 353
moral hazard, 311, 327–28
Morrill Acts, 342
Morris, William, 89
Mounier, Jean-Joseph, 348
Mucha, Alphonse, 95, 97

Mugabe, Robert, 210
Munro, H.H., 88
Museum of Modern Art, 95
Mussolini, Benito, 244–45

Naimark, Norman, 70, 73
Nantes, drownings at, 51–52
Naqba, 167*n*2
national identity, 100–101
nationalism, 25, 40, 46, 86
National Front, 36
NATO, 74, 75, 186, 187, 193, 199, 204, 206, 210
Nausée, La (Sartre), 182*n*7
Nazism, 44, 50, 52, 53, 60, 132, 133, 211, 253,
    277–78, 322, 361
    Holocaust and, *see* Holocaust
    non-Jewish victims of, 134
Netanyahu, Benjamin, 145–46, 157–59, 161
Netherlands, 208–9, 249
Neumann, Franz, 351
*New American Militarism, The: How Americans
    Are Seduced by War* (Bacevich), 242–44, 248
New Criterion, 63
New Poor Law, 26, 310, 325
New Statesman, 56
Newsweek, 228
"New World Order, The" (Judt), 234–51
New Yorker, 246
New York Review of Books, 156, 357, 359
New York Times, 9, 111, 206
New York Times Book Review, 58
Nixon, Richard M., 210
North Atlantic alliance, 202
North Atlantic Treaty Organization (NATO), 74,
    75, 186, 187, 193, 199, 204, 206, 210
Novotny, Antonin, 71
nuclear weapons, 82, 188
Nuremberg trials, 130, 253
Nusseibeh, Sari, 158
Nye, Joseph S., Jr., 183, 188–91, 193, 195, 198

Obama, Barack, 339–43
    Israel and, 145–46, 161, 164
Obsession anti-américaine, L' (Revel), 226–28
oil, 32, 243, 297, 298, 340, 343
    BP spill, 339–41, 343
Oliver Twist (Dickens), 325
Olmert, Ehud, 117
Oradour, 112
Oran, 171, 172, 174, 175, 177
Orientalism, 87, 104
Origins of the Second World War, The (Taylor), 61
Orlev, Zebulun, 158

Orwell, George, 10, 89, 337
Oxford History of Romania (Hitchins), 61
Oxford University, 55–56, 63, 364
Ozouf, Mona, 353

País, 188
Paisley, Ian, 164
Pakistan, 244, 262
Palacký, František, 101
Palestine Liberation Organization (PLO), 157,
    158, 214
Palestinian Authority, 109, 110, 112, 115, 117, 152,
    158, 167
Palestinians, 109, 126, 137, 138, 145, 203, 209
    blame attributed to, 153–54, 209
    right of return and recognition of sufferings of,
        161–62, 166
    sympathy for, 208–9, 357
    see also Israel-Palestine conflict
Paradox of American Power, The: Why the
    World's Only Superpower Can't Go It Alone
    (Nye), 183, 188–91, 193, 195, 198
Parliament of Man, The: The Past, Present, and
    Future of the United Nations (Kennedy), 256
Passé d'une illusion, Le (Furet), 351–52
past, 269–82, 314
    and meaning of war, 273
Patočka, Jan, 313
Patten, Chris, 194
Paulhan, Jean, 181*n*2
Pelican History of Medieval Europe, The (Keen), 55
Pemberton (Footman), 92
Penn Station, 290, 296, 302n1
Penser la Révolution française (Furet), 348
Perle, Richard, 126, 212
Personal Responsibility and Work Opportunity
    Act, 325
Pétain, Philippe, 36, 158, 173, 174
Petkov, Nikola, 23
Pity of It All, The (Elon), 355
Plague, The (Camus), ix, 171–82
Podhoretz, Norman, 243
Poland, 23–24, 68, 80, 103, 112–13, 162, 204–6,
    209, 275, 361, 363–65
    Davies and, 52–53, 55, 57–60
Polin, 53
Polonsky, Antony, 55
Pol Pot, 274
Pope, Alexander, 10
Popper, Karl, 321–22
Postwar (Judt), 3, 8
poverty, 195, 229, 326
    inequality and, 325

Powell, Colin, 111, 187, 199, 210
Primitive Rebels (Hobsbawm), 13
Prisoner of Zenda, The (film), 92
Prisoner of Zenda, The (Hope), 88, 89, 90
privatization, 310–11, 317n8, 326–30
  of railways, 333
"'Problem of Evil' in Postwar Europe, The"
  (Judt), 129–41
productivity, 308, 309, 334
progressives, 307–8
Provisional IRA, 150, 153, 164, 165
public action, 312
Public–Private Partnership (PPP), 311
public transportation, 289, 295, 298, 311, 332–34
Putin, Vladimir, 187

Quayle, Dan, 212
Quebec, 162–63

Rabb, Theodore, 58
Rabin, Yitzhak, 145
railways, 285–93, 294–302, 311, 332–34
  advertisements for, 291, 292
  art and, 291, 292, 300
  cities and, 295, 298
  classes of travel on, 288–89
  Cook and, 291–92
  decline of, 295–96
  film and, 292–93
  future of, 297–99
  in India, 297
  modern life and, 299–301
  privatization of, 333
  safety and, 287–88
  time and, 287–88
railway stations, 289–91, 297–99, 300–301, 332
  destruction of, 296–97
Ranger, Terence, 86–87
Rates of Exchange (Bradbury), 92
Reagan, Ronald, 325
Reale, Eugenio, 70, 71
Rebel, The (Camus), 172
Reich, Robert B., 303–12
religion, 147, 228–29, 361
Remarque Institute, 3
Renoir, Jean, 10
resorts, 292
Revel, Jean-François, 226–28
Révolution 1770–1880, La (Furet), 348
Rice, Condoleezza, 192, 214, 246–47, 262, 264
Richet, Denis, 347
Rieff, David, 235–38, 240, 249
Right, 307–8, 322, 337, 350, 364

rights, 334
"Road to Nowhere, The" (Judt), 107–14
Road to Serfdom, The (Hayek), 323
Roberts, Adam, 62
Roberts, John, 63, 64
Robinson, Mary, 256–57
Roger, Philippe, 220–21
rogue state, 111
Romania, 206
Romanov empire, 115–16
Rome Treaty, 184–85
Roosevelt, Theodore, 316n2, 340
Rosen, Jack, 217n16
Rothschild, Emma, 308, 316n3
Rude, George, 13
Rudman, Warren, 189
Rumsfeld, Donald, 192, 204, 205, 209, 213, 217n19,
  220
Russia, 77, 79–80, 166, 204, 260, 312
  Davies on, 69–60
  France and, 80
  Todd on, 224–25
Russian Revolution, 21, 24, 54, 80, 352
Rwanda, 185, 203, 234, 235, 238, 249, 263

Sadat, Anwar, 123n3
Saddam Hussein, 186, 205, 206, 210, 212, 216n5,
  224, 231, 235, 266
Said, Edward, 364
Sand, Shlomo, 148, 149
Sardar, Ziauddin, 222n, 223
Sartre, Jean-Paul, 172, 182n7, 219, 221, 364
Saudi Arabia, 244
Sayer, Derek, *Coasts of Bohemia,* 94–100, 103
Scalia, Antonin, 279–80
scandals, 263
Schama, Simon, 51
Schröder, Gerhard, 206
Schumer, Charles, 279
Schumpeter, Joseph, 306, 321–22
Scowcroft, Brent, 240
Scowen, Peter, 222n, 223
Segev, Tom, 126–27
Sen, Amartya, 338n6
September 11 attacks, 111, 183, 186, 188, 189,
  193–94, 197, 200n1, 203, 214, 224, 231, 269,
  277, 278
  Meyssan on, 222
Se questo è un uomo (Levi), 132
Serbia, 234
Shakespeare, William, 85
Sharon, Ariel, 110–13, 114n2, 115, 120, 123n3, 159,
  203, 209

Shaw, George Bernard, 88, 92
Shawn, Eric, 254–56, 267
Shklar, Judith, 360, 365
Shoah, see Holocaust
Sieyès, Emmanuel Joseph, 348
Singapore, 312
Sinn Fein, 112, 165
Slánsky, Rudolf, 71
Slovaks, 96, 98–99
Slovanska epopej (Mucha), 97
Smith, Adam, 321, 326
Soboul, Albert, 28n1
social democracy, 319–38, 363
   of fear, 336, 337
   right and wrong in, 335
   "social" in, 332
Socialism, 22, 36, 307, 313, 319, 322, 331, 362, 363
society, 301, 302, 329, 330
soft power, 190–91, 198
Sombart, Werner, 319
soul of the city, 313
South Africa, 108, 153, 163–64, 356
Souvarine, Boris, 351
Soviet Union, 39, 85, 131, 134, 191
   cold war and, *see* cold war
   Cominform in, 69–73, 78
   Davies on, 59–60
   Five Year Plans in, 25
   Germany and, 73–75, 80, 131
   Hobsbawm on, 21, 22, 24–27
   ideology of leaders of, 77–79
   Todd on, 224–25
   in World War II, 131, 275
   Yugoslavia and, 69–72
Spain, 34, 39, 204, 205, 216n5, 248
Spanish Civil War, 20–21
spies, 76
Srebrenica, 236, 258
Stalin, Josef, 21–23, 26, 59, 66, 68–81, 84n15, 101, 102, 111, 273–74, 278
   Kim and, 68, 75
   non-Jewish victims of, 134
Stanford University, 55, 57
states, 148–49, 315, 330
Stendhal, 219
Stiglitz, Joseph, 338n6
Stoker, Bram, 88, 90
subsidy, 311
suburbs, 298
Sudan, 261
   Darfur, 249, 260, 263, 268n9
supercapitalism, 304, 306–8, 312, 313

Supercapitalism: The Transformation of Business, Democracy, and Everyday Life (Reich), 303–9, 312
Switzerland, 38, 162
Syria, 109, 118, 244

Taguieff, Pierre-André, 216n7
Talleyrand-Périgord, Charles Maurice de, 218–19
tax farming, 328–29
Taylor, A.J.P., 10, 61
Taylor, F.W., 219
Teige, Karel, 95
terrorism, 111, 113, 136–37, 153, 157, 163, 189, 192, 194, 196, 203, 204, 209, 215, 243, 245, 249, 276–78, 280, 314
   September 11 attacks, *see* September 11 attacks
Thatcher, Margaret, 229, 277, 302, 308, 325, 327, 329
They Dare to Speak Out (Findley), 58
Thiers, Adolphe, 349
Third Man, The (film), 10
Third Man, The (Greene), 92
Thompson, Edward, 15
Thorez, Maurice, 71
time, railways and, 287–88
Times (London), 20, 62, 126
Tito (Josip Broz), 70, 72, 102, 352
Titoism, 69, 72–73
Tobin, James, 316n1
Tocqueville, Alexis de, 219, 348, 349, 353
Todd, Emmanuel, 223–26, 228
Togliatti, Palmiro, 71
Tolstoy, Leo, 132, 326
torture, 244–45, 248, 278–80
totalitarianism, 137, 139
trains, *see* railways
transportation, 300, 302
   air, 298, 299
   buses, 332–33
   cars, 289, 294, 295, 296, 298, 299, 300
   public, 289, 295, 298, 311, 332–34
   rail, *see* railways
Traub, James, 256, 260, 261
Truman, Harry, 74–75, 77, 78, 82, 190–91, 241, 263
Truman Doctrine, 78
Tudjman, Franjo, 103–4
Tulsa pogrom, 211
Turing, Alan, 19
Turkey, 155, 166, 230

Ukrainians, 112–13
Unconditional Surrender (Waugh), 89

unemployment, 33–34, 314, 326
*UN Exposed, The: How the United Nations
    Sabotages America's Security and Fails the
    World* (Shawn), 254–56
unilateralist internationalism, 213
United Kingdom, *see* Britain
United Nations (UN), 43, 103, 111, 185, 191–92,
    204, 205, 213–14, 230, 231, 234–40, 250n4,
    252–68
  achievements of, 257
  branches and units of, 257–58
  charter of, 143, 239, 253
  controversy over, 252–53
  Convention Against Torture, 245, 246
  France and, 210, 255, 260
  General Assembly, 257, 260, 262
  High-level Panel and, 238–41
  Human Rights Council, 261, 262
  Israel and, 118–19
  Kennedy on, 256
  legitimacy of, 258
  military missions of, 259
  reform of, 260–62
  reputation of, 258–59
  scandals of, 263
  Security Council, 118, 192, 234, 236, 239, 257,
    259–60, 265–66, 268n15
  Shawn on, 254–56
  "soft" tasks of, 258
  UNESCO, 257, 261
  UNICEF, 257, 258
  United States and, 261–63, 265–66
United States, 183–201
  anti-Americanism and, *see* Anti-Americanism
  anti-Semitism in, 207
  Constitution of, 233n7, 246
  detainees and, 244–45, 247–48
  economy of, 185, 196, 304
  Europe compared with, 195–97, 217n18, 227–29
  foreign policy of, 186–92, 198, 212–15, 218, 221,
    228, 229, 231, 243
  international community and, 184–86, 190,
    203–6, 212, 263, 265
  International Criminal Court and, 184–85,
    191–92, 198, 206
  Israel and, 124–27, 144, 146, 149–50, 155, 165,
    166, 205, 214, 228
  as military society, 242–44, 249, 273, 275–76
  oil and, 243
  reputation of, 249
  soft power and, 190–91, 198
  torture and, 244–45, 278–80
  trust and, 198, 199

twentieth century as experienced by, 274–75
  United Nations and, 261–63, 265–66
  in world wars, 275
*Unresolved Past, The: A Debate in German
    History* (Berlin), 54
urbanization, 295
Urquhart, Brian, 256, 259
USSR, see Soviet Union
Uzbekistan, 244

Vailland, Roger, 219–20
Vidal-Naquet, Pierre, 281n8
Vieira de Mello, Sergio, 257
Vienna Convention on Law of Treaties, 185
Vietnam War, 75, 211, 242, 264, 274, 275
Volker, Paul, 164
Voltaire, 228
Vyshinsky, Andrei, 23

Waldheim, Kurt, 256
Wall Street Journal, 204, 216n5
Walmart, 305
Walt, Stephen, 124–27
war, 273–76, 280–81
  civil, 273
  meaning of, 273
*War over Iraq, The: Saddam's Tyranny and
    America's Mission* (Kaplan and Kristol), 203,
    212–15
Washington Post, 204
Wat, Alexander, 29n11
Waugh, Evelyn, 89
"Way We Live Now, The" (Judt), 202–17
wealth, 195, 229, 305–6, 326
  creation of, 309, 313
  inequality and, 325
Weekly Standard, 212
welfare reform, 309–11, 326
welfare state, 34–35, 195, 315, 319–20, 323–26
Welles, Orson, 10
We Now Know: Rethinking Cold War History
    (Gaddis), 65–68, 73–79
West, Rebecca, 88, 91, 93
"What Have We Learned, if Anything?" (Judt),
    269–82
"What Is Living and What Is Dead in Social
    Democracy?" (Judt), 319–38
"What Is to Be Done?" (Judt), 9, 156–67
"Why the Cold War Worked" (Judt), 65–84
Wilsonian internationalism, 213
Wolff, Larry, 87
Wolfowitz, Paul, 126, 212, 213, 235
Williams, Bernard, 10, 312–13, 331, 365

Woolf, Virginia, 270
World War I, 15, 17, 19, 115, 129–30, 165, 194, 264,
         270, 273–75, 313, 322
    casualty statistics, 275
    France in, 210, 273, 275
World War II, 15–16, 22, 46, 47, 98–99, 112–13,
         130–33, 219, 264, 273–75, 324
    casualty statistics, 275
    France in, *see* France, in World War II
    Holocaust in, *see* Holocaust
    Soviet Union in, 131, 275
"Wrecking Ball of Innovation, The" (Judt),
         303–18

Yugoslavia, 45–46, 102, 103, 162, 165, 185, 275,
         352
    Soviet Union and, 69–72

Zeit, 126
Zhdanov, Andrei, 69–72, 78, 84n9
Zimbabwe, 356
Zionism, 116, 137, 147, 155
    anti-Zionism and, 57, 58, 126, 154–55, 358
    Davies on, 57–60
    Elon and, 355–58
    religion and, 147
    Revisionist, 117, 157